Rotman
On Design

Rotman-UTP Publishing
University of Toronto Press
Toronto Buffalo London
www.utppublishing.com
Printed in Canada

ISBN 978-1-4426-1620-2

Publication cataloguing information is available
from Library and Archives Canada.

University of Toronto Press acknowledges the financial assistance
to its publishing program of the Canada Council for the Arts and the
Ontario Arts Council.

University of Toronto Press acknowledges the financial support of
the Government of Canada through the Canada Book Fund for its
publishing activities.

Interior Chalk Art: Ben Weeks
Slipcase and Interior Chalkboard Background:
Stefanie Schram (MBA '10)
Design: Underline Studio Inc.
Printing: Andora Graphics

Rotman On Design

The Best on Design Thinking from *Rotman* Magazine

Introduced by Paola Antonelli
and Roger Martin

Edited by Roger Martin and
Karen Christensen

UNIVERSITY OF TORONTO PRESS
Toronto Buffalo London

Contents

**The Foundation:
Why Design?
Why Now?**

**How Design
Fits Into the Modern
Organization**

A Skill Set Emerges

"In our world, *'prove it'* is the absolute enemy of innovation. Leaders seeking innovation must be open to *what might be*, not just to *what is*."

– Roger Martin

Introduction
Roger Martin

IN JANUARY OF 2004, I made a rather bold statement on the pages of *Rotman* Magazine when I wrote:

We are on the cusp of a design revolution in business. Competing is no longer about creating dominance in scale-intensive industries, it's about producing elegant, refined products and services in imagination-intensive industries. **As a result, business people don't just need to understand designers better – they need to *become* designers**.

Little did I know at the time how eager the business community was to learn a new approach to innovation. From banks to non-profits to healthcare organizations, people accepted the fact that the mindsets and methods behind great design are also essential to successful organizations. Within six months of that initial article, *Fast Company* published its first (now annual) 'Masters of Design' issue, and *BusinessWeek* soon jumped on board with design content in its magazine and Web site. Even *Time* magazine published a dedicated design issue.

Rotman Magazine soon became a leading purveyor of the very latest on design thinking for a management audience, and our devotion to the topic remains today. We have been honoured to partner with the world's leading design organization, IDEO, from the very start. Since Tim Brown first visited our School in 2004, 18 IDEO design thinkers have written articles for our magazine. We are pleased to feature many of these in this volume, alongside several articles from our good friend Jeanne Liedtka of the University of Virginia's Darden School of Business and input from a range of other design leaders worldwide.

Why has design had such resonance with a business audience? I believe it's because people recognize that *everything that surrounds us is subject to innovation* – not just physical objects, but political systems, economic policy, the ways in which medical research is conducted, and complete user experiences. Organizations can no longer count on quality, performance or price alone to sustain leadership in the global marketplace: design has emerged as a new competitive weapon and a key driver of innovation.

Our aim with this volume is to contribute to demystifying design, so that organizations of all types can ensure that it receives proper consideration. As you will see from the varied articles within, design is a process that is available to individuals at every level of an organization, and across industries.

In the end, design is about *shaping* a particular context for the better, rather than *taking* it as it is. Success today arises not from emulating others, but by evolving unique models, products and experiences – in short, creative solutions. That's an end result we can all get behind, and design has already proven its value in achieving it.

Roger Martin
Dean, Rotman School of Management

"Only by deeply understanding the needs of different audiences, markets and nations can designers do their job – which is to serve as the interface between *humanity* and *progress*."

– Paola Antonelli

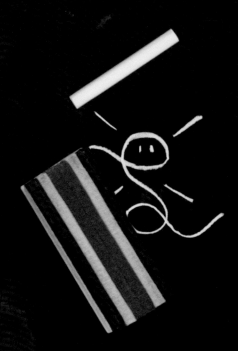

Introduction
Paola Antonelli

BACK IN UNIVERSITY, I started out as a student of Economics. I studied hard and paid close attention in class, but it didn't take long for me to become frustrated with my subject matter. This was before Behavioural Economics emerged, and it seemed to me that my rationality-obsessed subject matter was missing out on some key aspects of human behaviour. After two years, I switched my focus to Architecture, where the complete human condition – with all of its rational *and* irrational aspects – appeared to be dealt with in a more truthful manner. The realm of design quickly captured my imagination, and in my mind, it was just a matter of time before all of the economical entities caught on to it.

Today, I am pleased to see widespread recognition that design is an intellectual and creative process that can be used to great effect on different scales and in different fields. Sure, there are still plenty of people who believe design is about 'making pretty things'– and design can still result in beautiful, elegant products. But it is about *so much more* than that. Design has spread to almost every facet of human activity, from science and education to politics and policymaking, along the way introducing us to concepts such as interface design, nano design, interaction design and bio-design, to name just a few of its contributions.

Through all of this, one of the keenest audiences for design has been the realm of business. Leaders in this arena have made plenty of well-documented missteps in recent years, leading to widespread frustration amongst stakeholders and a frantic search for new models. The good news is that leaders who understand the power of design are embracing its methodologies and are learning how to use it as a bridge to creative solutions.

Whether your task is to design a product or an interaction, a delivery system or a business model, design is about rethinking what you are doing. Make no mistake: it is not a route to easy answers. Rather than solving problems, design *finds* problems, and rather than providing answers, it *asks questions*. And in our increasingly complex world, this is the stance we need to adopt.

A while back, *The Economist* asked me to think about what the world might look like in 25 years. My vision included designers and design being present at all levels of corporations and institutions, and design as an entity evolving in much the same way that Physics has – so that there is *Applied* Design and *Theoretical* Design. I see theoretical designers as the 'philosophers' of the future; whenever there is an important decision to be made, people will turn to them for input. Meanwhile, applied designers will visualize complex infrastructures and systems so that scientists, policymakers and the general public can manage and influence them.

This grand new era has already begun. Design is moving centre-stage in the eternal human quest to make beauty out of necessity. And as many educators, including those at the Rotman School of Management, are showing, Design Thinking – which harnesses design methodologies to achieve creative solutions – can be taught. As designers and design thinkers alike obtain roles that are more and more integral to the evolution of society, they will find themselves at the centre of an extraordinary wave of cross-pollination.

Going forward, I feel optimistic that a sense of responsibility and collective interest will become paramount, and that we will see a renaissance of positive efforts in the world. From beautiful chairs to clean water systems to conceptual scenarios on the impact of nanotechnology – design takes into account people's needs and concerns, helping them to live better lives. Only by deeply understanding the needs of different audiences, markets and nations can designers do their job – which is to serve as the interface between *humanity* and *progress*.

Paola Antonelli is the Senior Curator of Architecture and Design and Director of Research and Development at The Museum of Modern Art in New York City. She received her MA in Architecture from Milan Polytechnic in 1990, and worked at the design magazines *Domus* and *Abitare* before coming to MoMA in 1994. She is a Senior Fellow with The Royal College of Art in London and in 2006, she received the Smithsonian Institution's National Design Award, 'Design Mind'.

1

The Foundation: Why Design? Why Now?

IN RECENT YEARS, organizations of all shapes and sizes have begun to embrace design methodologies. People sometimes ask me if this surprises me; and the truth is, not really.

Over the years I've had a front-row seat to watch as technology got better and better. In my days at the MIT Media Lab, again and again, *Moore's Law* played out before my eyes, as computational systems and networks got faster and faster, cheaper and cheaper. As this continued, we were all told that products and services were going to keep getting better and better; but I just didn't see that happening. At some point, it became clear to me that technology alone was not going to make products and services any better.

This is when design began to emerge as 'the way to make a difference'. Not just in products and services, but in addressing questions of how to solve the world's problems and how to run your organization better as well – to figure out how to combat complexity and to create new value.

The march of technology is definitely tied to the emergence of design. One of the reasons organizations are so chaotic today is because of social media, itself a new technology. A significant side effect of the digital communications revolution is that nowadays, everyone can have a voice. Just a few years ago, front-line workers would never see the CEO or expect to talk to them; but nowadays you can e-mail your CEO – and you sort of expect him or her to write you back! You can even friend him on Facebook.

What this has done is to transform organizations from hierarchies into more of a 'heterarchy', where everyone gets to have a say. Make no mistake about it: this represents a major shift for leaders, who are going to have to evolve – and fast! And this is where the radical aspect of design – the ability to rethink things – comes into play. On the one hand, design can still help us create differently-shaped products featuring imaginative solutions; but on the other – and more importantly – design can enable organizations to run better and adapt to changing conditions.

Part of my own function now is to sit on different boards – to function as 'the person who understands design' at that level. This makes me optimistic that one day in the not-too-distant future, design will be as much a part of every organization as marketing, accounting or finance. That being said, the fact is, some things don't need design. There are things that just kind of work already – that have evolved over centuries.

My hope is not that design will be everywhere, but that design will be *where it is most needed*, which is in creating new kinds of experiences and products, and addressing the challenges organizations are facing as they move from hierarchichal to heterarchichal entities. And from what I have seen, design is up to the task.

John Maeda is president of the Rhode Island School of Design and author of *Redesigning Leadership (Design, Technology, Business, Life)* (MIT Press, 2011) and *The Laws of Simplicity (Design, Technology, Business, Life)* (MIT Press, 2006).

The Design
of Business

We are on the cusp of a design revolution
in business, and as a result, business people
don't just need to understand designers
better – they need to *become* designers.

By **Roger Martin**

THESE ARE TURBULENT TIMES FOR BUSINESS, as companies struggle to adjust to the globalization of markets and competition, the expansion of the service-based economy, the impact of deregulation and privatization, and the explosion of the knowledge revolution. All of these forces are driving firms to fundamentally rethink their business models and radically transform their capabilities – but an equally important (though less obvious) business transformation is taking place with respect to design.

As we leave behind one economic age and enter another, many of our philosophical assumptions about what constituted competitive success grew out of a different world. Value creation in the 20th century was largely defined by the conversion of *heuristics* to *algorithms*. It was about taking a fundamental understanding of a 'mystery' – a heuristic – and driving it to a formula, an algorithm – so that it could be driven to huge scale and scope. As a result, many 20th-century organizations succeeded

To be successful in the future, business people will have to become more like designers – more 'masters of heuristics' than 'managers of algorithms'.

by instituting fairly linear improvements, such as reengineering, supply chain management, enhanced customer responsiveness, and cost controls. These ideas were consistent with the traditional Taylorist view of the company as a centrally-driven entity that creates wealth by getting better and better at doing the same thing.

Competition is no longer in global scale-intensive industries; rather, it's in non-traditional, imagination-intensive industries. Today's businesses are sensing an increased demand for speed in product development, design cycles, inventory turns, and competitive response, and there are major implications for the individuals within those organizations. I would argue that in the 21st century, value creation will be defined more by the conversion of *mysteries* to *heuristics* – and that as a result, we are on the cusp of a design revolution in business.

The Progression from Mysteries to Binary Code
Over the course of time, phenomena enter our collective consciousness as *mysteries* – things that we observe, but don't really understand. For instance, the mystery of gravity once confounded our forefathers: when they looked around the world, they saw that many things, like rocks, seemed to fall to the ground almost immediately; but others didn't – like birds, and some seemed to take forever, like leaves. In art, there was the long battle to understand how to represent on a two-dimensional page what we saw in front of us in three dimensions. Music continues to be a mystery that confounds: what patterns of notes and sounds are enjoyable and make listeners feel happy and contented?

We start out with these *mysteries*, and at some point, we put enough thought into them to produce a first-level understanding of the question at hand. We develop *heuristics* – ways of understanding the general principles of heretofore mysteries. Heuristics are rules of thumb or sets of guidelines for solving a mystery by organized exploration of the possibilities.

So why do things fall down? We develop a notion of a universal force called 'gravity' that tends to pull things down. In art,

we develop a notion called 'perspective' that guides our efforts to create renderings that appear to the eye to have three-dimensions rather than two. What kind of music do people like to listen to? We learn about chords, and then create song types like ballads, or folk songs, or the blues. If one follows a set of guidelines, one will likely create something that people enjoy listening to.

Heuristics don't guarantee success – they simply increase the probability of getting to a successful outcome. They represent an incomplete understanding of a heretofore mystery. In any given field, some people barely understand heuristics, while others master them. The difference between them is the difference between one-hit-wonder **Don McLean**, author of "American Pie", and **Bruce Springsteen**, author of scores of hit songs. For McLean, the mystery remained just that: he came up with a single inspiration that created one random event – one of the biggest pop song hits of all time. Yet he failed to produce another hit of any consequence in his entire musical career. In contrast, Springsteen developed a heuristic – a way of understanding the world and the people in it – that enables him to write songs that have great meaning to people and are immensely popular. His mastery of heuristics has allowed him to generate a steady stream of hit albums/CDs over a 30-year period.

In due course, increasing understanding can (though in many cases it never does) produce an *algorithm*: a logical, arithmetic or computational procedure that, if correctly applied, ensures the solution of the problem. With gravity, great scientists like **Sir Isaac Newton** studied and experimented long and hard enough to create precise rules for determining how fast an object will fall under any circumstance. In the late 1970s, musical innovators like British techno-music guru **Brian Eno** experimented with the human heartbeat and determined that songs with a synthesized heartbeat as their rhythm track are instinctively enjoyed by listeners, no matter what you added on top of them. The end result of such algorithms is not always positive, of course: this discovery led to electro-pop and eventually to sham bands like **Milli Vanilli**, who lip-synched recorded music onstage until caught in the act by an unsuspecting audience. And in art, we eventually got paint by numbers.

In the modern era, a fourth important step has been added to the sequence of *mystery* to *heuristic* to *algorithm*. Eventually, some algorithms now get coded into software. This means reducing the algorithm – the strict set of rules – into a series of 0's and 1's – *binary code* – that enables a computer to produce a result. For example, with gravity, the fact that we had an algorithm for how things fall meant that we could program aircraft with autopilot, enabling a plane to 'fall' from the sky in the organized fashion that we want it to, so that it lands in exactly the right spot. At the coding level, there is no longer any judgment involved: the plane lands on the basis of computer instructions that are nothing but a series of 1's and 0's, because our understanding of gravity has moved from a mystery to a *heuristic* to an *algorithm* to *binary code*.

Implications for the Design of Business

The progression of the 'march of understanding' described herein has important practical implications for today's business people. Broadly speaking, value creation in the 20th century was about taking a fundamental understanding of a mystery – a heuristic – and reducing it to a formula, an algorithm – so that it could be driven to huge scale and scope.

Take **McDonalds**, for instance. In 1955, the McDonald brothers took a mystery – 'how and what do Californians want to eat'? And they created a format for answering that – a heuristic – which was the quick-service restaurant. Is this heuristic what created enormous value? No, because there were many restaurants in California doing similar things at the time, and all of them were discovering that Californians wanted faster, more convenient food. What made McDonalds different is that **Ray Kroc** came along and saw that he could drive the McDonald brothers' heuristic to an algorithm. He bought the store and figured out *exactly* how to cook a hamburger, *exactly* how to hire people, *exactly* how to set up stores, *exactly* how to manage stores, and *exactly* how to franchise stores. Under Kroc, nothing was left to chance in the McDonald's kitchen: every hamburger came out of a stamping machine weighing exactly 1.6 ounces, its thickness measured to the thousandth of an inch, and the cooking process stopped automatically after 38 seconds, when the burgers reached an internal temperature of exactly 155 degrees. By creating an algorithm out of a heuristic, Kroc was able to drive McDonalds to huge size and scope, and to its place today as a global icon.

This move from heuristic to algorithm was repeated over and over throughout the 20th century. Early in the century, **Ford** developed the algorithm for assembling cars – the assembly line – and with it grew to immense size. Late in the 20th century, **Electronic Data Services** (EDS) developed algorithms for routinizing systems integration and training COBOL programmers, and with it grew to previously unimagined size in the systems integration business. In between, **Procter & Gamble** created the algorithm for brand management, **Anheuser Busch** for making and selling beer, **Frito Lay** for making and distributing snack chips, and so on. For these companies, as well as **Dell** and **Walmart**, success depended not so much on a superior product, but on a superior process, and each is an example of the relentless 'algorithm-ization' that paved the way for massive value creation in the 20th century.

This dynamic accelerated in the latter part of the 20th century (1985-2000), when many algorithms were driven to code. Like most things in life, this final step of reducing something to binary code has good and not-so-good aspects to it. While coding enables an incredible increase in efficiency, it is also true that with coding comes the end of judgment: patterns of 0's and 1's have no judgment or artistry – they just automatically apply an algorithm. In many respects, the extreme achievement of the 20th century is soulless numbers. Neither all bad or all good, this is simply the result of the combination of the relentless march of understanding (from mystery to heuristic to algorithm) with the relentless march of *Moore's Law* (**Intel** co-founder **Gordon**

Moore's prediction that data density would double approximately every 18 months, and the resultant diminishing costs of information technology) – all of which lead to binary code.

So where do we go from here? Will there be more relentless algorithm-ization? I don't think so. I believe that we will look back on the 20th century as a *tour de force* of producing 'stuff' – lots of it, as efficiently as possible. I believe we are transitioning into a 21st century world in which value creation is moving back to the world of taking *mysteries* and turning them into *heuristics*. I see the beginnings of a fundamental backlash against algorithmization and the codification of the world around us – a realization that reaching to grab the benefits of economies of scale often involves accepting standardization and soullessness in exchange.

I believe the 21st century will go down in history as the century of producing elegant, refined products and services – products and services that delight users with the gracefulness of their utility and output; 'goods' that are produced elegantly – for example, that have the most minimal environmental footprint possible, or that produce the fewest worker injuries, whether it be broken limbs or repetitive stress syndrome.

The 21st century presents us with an opportunity to delve into mysteries and come up with new heuristics. As a society we are faced with major mysteries like, 'how can big cities actually work'? There are more of them than ever before, and while Toronto works pretty well, many cities around the world don't, and fixing that is a major mystery. Another big mystery involves how to make health care work, when there's an infinite demand and a constrained supply. These are the kind of modern mysteries that are being presented to us, and there is no algorithm for them, no coding to magically solve the problems they engender.

Implications for Business People

There are three major implications of this shift for today's business people. The first is that design skills and business skills are converging. The skill of design, at its core, is the ability to reach into the mystery of some seemingly intractable problem – whether it's a problem of product design, architectural design, or systems design – and apply the creativity, innovation and mastery necessary to convert the mystery to a heuristic – a way of knowing and understanding.

But unlike in the 20th century, this time the goal won't be to develop mass formulas or algorithms. Firms today are desperately trying to find out what each individual customer wants. **Kellogg's** cereal and **Hershey's** chocolate bars have 1-800 phone numbers printed on them encouraging consumers to call them with feedback. **Pepsi** has its Web site printed on each can.

Information is being gathered and used to cater to and customize solutions to your every need.

I would argue that to be successful in the future, business people will have to become more like designers – more 'masters of heuristics' than 'managers of algorithms'. For much of the 20th century, they moved ahead by demonstrating the latter capability. This shift creates a huge challenge, as it will require entirely new kinds of education and training, since until now, design skills have not been explicitly valued in business. The truth is, highly-skilled designers are currently leading many of the world's top organizations – they just don't know they are designers, because they were never trained as such.

The second implication is that we need a new kind of business enterprise. This new world into which we are delving will require us to tackle mysteries and develop heuristics – and that will require a substantial change in some of the fundamental ways we work. Traditional firms will have to start looking much more like design shops on a number of important dimensions, as shown in **Figure One**.

MODERN FIRMS MUST BECOME MORE LIKE DESIGN SHOPS		Figure One
Feature	**From 'Traditional Firm'**	**To 'Design Shop'**
Flow of Work Life	• Ongoing tasks • Permanent assignments	• Projects • Defined terms
Source of Status	Managing big budgets and large staffs	• Solving 'wicked problems'
Style of Work	• Defined roles • Wait until it is "right"	• Collaborative • Iterative
Mode of Thinking	• Deductive • Inductive	• Deductive • Inductive • Abductive
Dominant Attitude	• We can only do what we have budget to do • Constraints are the enemy	• Nothing can't be done • Constraints increase the challenge and excitement

The philosophy in design shops is,
'let's try it, prototype it, and improve it'.
Designers learn by doing.

Whereas traditional firms organize around ongoing tasks and permanent assignments, in design shops, work flows around projects with defined terms. The source of status in traditional firms is 'managing big budgets and large staffs', but in design shops, it derives from building a track record of finding solutions to 'wicked problems' – solving tough mysteries with elegant solutions. Whereas the style of work in traditional firms involves defined roles and waiting for the perfect answer, design firms feature extensive collaboration, focused brainstorming sessions, and constant dialogue with clients.

When it comes to innovation, businesses have much to learn from designers. The philosophy in design shops is, 'let's try it, prototype it, and improve it'. Designers learn by doing. The style of thinking in traditional firms is largely inductive – *proving that something actually operates* – and deductive – *proving that something must be*. Design shops add abductive reasoning to the fray – which involves *suggesting that something may be*, and reaching out to it. Designers may not be able to prove that something is or must be, but they nevertheless reason that it may be, and this style of thinking is critical to the creative process. Whereas the dominant attitude in traditional firms is to see constraints as the enemy and budgets as the drivers of decisions, in design firms, the mindset is "nothing can't be done for sure," and constraints only increase the excitement level.

The third implication is that we must change the focus of our thinking on design and business. The trends discussed herein have generated increased interest in design by the business world, but it is largely focused on 'the business of design': the traditional business world is trying to figure out what designers do, how they do it, and how best to manage them. This misses the point fundamentally, and it won't save the traditional firm. The focus should actually be placed on 'the design of business': We need to think much more about designing our businesses to provide elegant products and services in the most graceful manner possible.

In closing

Business people don't need to understand designers better: they need to *be* designers. They need to think and work like designers, have attitudes like designers, and learn to evaluate each other as designers do. Most companies' top managers will tell you that they have spent the bulk of their time over the last decade on improvement. But it's no longer enough to get better; you have to 'get different'.

I believe that we are on the cusp of a design revolution in business – a revolution in the purpose of business, the work of business, and the skills required of business people. The challenge of making the transformation to the Design of Business should not be underestimated. The initial goal is to help modern managers understand this new business agenda and become shapers of contexts, to increase the likelihood that their organizations will thrive in the era of design. *R*

Roger Martin is Dean, Premier's Research Chair in Productivity & Competitiveness and Professor of Strategic Management at the Rotman School of Management. He is the author of eight books, most recently, *Playing to Win: How Strategy Really Works* (Harvard Business Review Press, 2013), co-authored with A.G. Lafley. In 2011, he placed sixth on the Thinkers50 list, a bi-annual ranking of the most influential global management thinkers.

STRATEGY AS DESIGN

Today's leaders can apply many of the lessons learned in the world of design to strategy-making in the workplace.

By **Jeanne Liedtka**

AS WE STAND AT THE FRONTIER OF A BUSINESS WORLD in the midst of fundamental change, the field of business strategy is in need of new metaphors. Much of the traditional thinking about strategy formulation and implementation seems ill-suited to escalating imperatives for speed and flexibility. We need metaphors that better capture the challenges of making strategies both *real* and *realizable*, metaphors that bring life to the human dimension of creating new futures for institutions, that move us beyond the sterility of traditional approaches to strategic planning. In that spirit, I propose that we resuscitate an old metaphor that I believe offers new possibilities: the metaphor of strategy as a process of design.

The centrality of design skills to the practice of management has long been recognized. In 1969, Nobel Laureate **Herbert Simon** noted:

"Engineering, medicine, business, architecture, and painting are concerned not with the necessary but with the contingent – not with how things are, but with how they might be – in short, with design. Everyone designs who devises courses of action aimed at changing existing situations into preferred ones. Design, so construed, is the core of all professional training."

Early models of the design process describe it as consisting of two phases: analysis and synthesis. In the analytical phase, the problem is decomposed into a hierarchy of problem subsets, which in turn produce a set of requirements. In the ensuing stage of synthesis, these individual requirements are grouped and realized in a complete design. Parallels with the design of business planning processes come to mind here. Unlike in business, however, these early models – with their emphasis on systematic

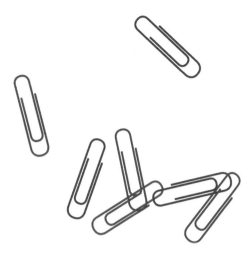

procedures – met with immediate criticism for their lack of appreciation for the complexity of design problems.

Design theorist **Horst Rittel** first called attention to what he described as the 'wicked' nature of design problems. Such problems have a unique set of properties, he argued, the most important of which is that they have no definitive formulation or solution. The definition of the problem itself is open to multiple interpretations, dependent upon the worldview of the observer, and potential solutions are many, with none of them able to be proven to be correct. Writers in the field of business have argued that many issues in strategy formulation are 'wicked' as well, and that traditional approaches to dealing with them are similarly incapable of producing intelligent solutions.

The 'first generation models', as Rittel referred to them, were ill-suited for dealing with 'wicked problems'. Rittel saw design as a process of argumentation, rather than merely analysis and synthesis. Through argumentation – whether as part of a group or solely within the designer's own mind – the designer gained insights, broadened his or her worldview, and continually refined the definition of the problem and its attendant solution. Thus, the design process came to be seen as one of negotiation rather than optimization, fundamentally concerned with learning and the search for emergent opportunities. Rittel's arguments are consistent with recent calls in the strategy literature for more attention to 'strategic conversations', in which a broad group of organizational stakeholders engage in dialogue-based planning processes out of which shared understanding and ultimately, shared choices, emerge.

Studies of the design process frequently suggest a hypothesis-driven approach similar to the traditional scientific method. After studying architects in action, philosopher and academic **Donald Schon** described design as "a shaping process," in which the situation "talks back" continually, and "each move is a local experiment which contributes to the global experiment of reframing the problem." Schon's designer begins by generating a series of creative "what if" hypotheses, selecting the most promising one for further inquiry. This inquiry takes the form of a more evaluative "if then" sequence, in which the logical implications of that particular hypothesis are more fully explored and tested. The scientific method then, with its emphasis on cycles of hypothesis-generating and testing and the acquisition of new information to continually open up new possibilities, remains central to design thinking.

Yet the nature of 'wicked problems' makes such trial and error learning problematic. Rittel makes this point from the perspective of architecture: a building, once constructed, cannot be easily changed, and so learning through experimentation in practice is undesirable. This is the ultimate source of 'wickedness' in such problems: their indeterminacy places a premium on experimentation, while the high cost of change makes such experimentation problematic.

As in business, we know that we might be able or be forced to change our strategies as we go along – but we'd rather not. This apparent paradox is what gives the design process – with its use of constructive forethought – its utility. The designer substitutes mental experiments for physical ones. In this view, design becomes a process of hypothesis-generating and testing, whose aim is to provide the builder with a plan that tries to anticipate the general nature of impending changes.

A concern of the design process is the risk of 'entrapment', in which a designer's investment in early hypotheses make them difficult to give up as the design progresses, despite the presence of disconfirming data. Design is most successful, then, when it creates a virtual world, a 'learning laboratory', where mental experiments can be conducted risk-free and where investments in early choices can be minimized.

This, I argue, offers a very different perspective from which to think about the creation of business strategies. Traditional approaches have shared the perspective of early design theorists and assumed that planning creates value primarily through a

Everyone designs who devises courses of action aimed at changing existing situations into preferred ones. Design, so construed, is the core of all professional training.

process of controlling, integrating, and coordinating – that the power of planning is in the creation of a systematic approach to problem-solving – decomposing a complex problem into sub-problems to be solved and later integrated back into a whole. While integration, coordination, and control are all potentially important tasks, a focus on these dramatically underestimates the value of planning in a time of change. The metaphor of design calls attention to planning's ability to create a virtual world in which hypotheses can be generated and tested in low-cost ways.

Invention vs. Discovery

Contemporary design theorists have been attentive to the areas in which design and science diverge, as well as converge. The most fundamental difference between the two, they argue, is that design thinking deals primarily with what *does not yet exist*; while scientists deal with explaining what *is*. That scientists *discover* the laws that govern today's reality, while designers invent a different future, is a common theme. Thus, while both methods of thinking are hypothesis-driven, the design hypothesis differs from the scientific hypothesis.

Rather than using traditional reasoning modes of induction or deduction, Stanford's **James March** argues that design thinking is *abductive*: "Science investigates extant forms. Design initiates novel forms. A scientific hypothesis is not the same thing as a design hypothesis...A speculative design cannot be determined logically, because the mode of reasoning involved is essentially abductive."

Underlying this emphasis on conjectural thinking and visualization is an ongoing inquiry into the relationship between verbal and non-verbal mediums. Design theorists accord a major role to the use of graphic and spatial modeling media – not merely for the purpose of communicating design ideas, but for the *generation* of ideas as well. "Designers think with their pencils" is a common refrain. Gestalt psychologist **Rudolf Arnheim** asserts that the image "unfolds" in the mind of the designer as the

design process progresses. And that it is, in fact, the unfolding nature of the image that makes creative design possible. The designer begins with what Arnheim calls "a centre, an axis, a direction," from which the design takes on increasing levels of detail as it unfolds.

The General vs. the Particular

In addition to the prominent role played by conjecture and experimentation in design thinking, there is also a fundamental divergence between the concern of science for generalizable laws and design's interest in the particulars of individual cases.

This quality of indeterminacy has profound implications for the design process. First, the tendency to project determinacy onto past choices – 'prediction after the fact' – is ever-present and must be avoided, or it undermines and distorts the true nature of the design process.

Secondly, creative designs do not passively await discovery; designers must actively seek them out. Third, the indeterminacy of the process suggests the possibility for both exceptional diversity and continual evolution in the outcomes produced (even within similar processes). And finally, because design solutions are always matters of *invented choice*, rather than *discovered truth*, the judgement of designers is always open to question by the broader public.

Each of these implications resonates with business experiences. The need to seek out the future is one of the most common prescriptions in today's writings on strategy. The risks that the search for the ideal of 'the one right strategy' can stifle creativity, cause myopia, and paralyze organizational decision processes have all been recognized.

Yet, the final implication – this notion of the inevitable need to justify to others the 'rightness' of the design choices made – is perhaps the most significant implication for the design of strategy processes in business organizations. Because strategic choices can never be proven to be 'right', they remain always contestable and must be made compelling to others in order to be realized. This calls into play Rittel's role of argumentation and focuses attention on others, and the role of rhetoric in bringing them into the design conversation. Participation becomes key to producing a collective learning that both educates individuals and shapes the evolving choices simultaneously. Thus, design becomes a shared process – no longer the province of a single designer.

Participation is critical, in part, because of the role that values, both individual and institutional, play in the design process. Values drive both the creation of the design and its acceptance. Successful designs must embody both existing and new values simultaneously. The ability to work with competing interests and values is inevitable in the process of designing.

The 'charette' plays a fundamental role in making design processes participative and making collective learning possible. Charettes are intensive brainstorming/planning sessions in which groups of stakeholders come together. Their intention is to share, critique, and invent in a way that accelerates the development of large-scale projects. One well-known user of charettes is the architectural firm **Duany**, **Plater-Zyberk**, who specialize in the design of new 'traditional towns' like Seaside, Florida, or **Disney**'s Celebration. In their charette for the design of a new town outside of Washington, D.C., they brought together architects, builders, engineers, local officials, traffic consultants, utility company representatives, computer experts, architecture professors, shopping mall developers, and townspeople for a discussion that lasted seven days. The more complex the design process, the more critical role the charette plays – and I believe it offers a new model for planning processes in business.

Implied Characteristics of Design Thinking

Despite the avowed plurality that design theorists describe in their attempts to define the field, a set of commonalties does emerge from their work about the attributes of design thinking.

First, design thinking is *synthetic*. Out of the often-disparate demands presented by sub-units' requirements, a coherent overall design must emerge. The process through which and the order in which the overall design and its sub-unit designs unfold remains a source of debate. What is clear is that the order in which they are given attention matters, as it determines the 'givens' of subsequent designs, but ultimately successful designs can be expected to exhibit considerable diversity in their specifics.

Secondly, design thinking is *abductive* in nature. It is primarily concerned with the process of visualizing what might be, some desired future state, and creating a blueprint for realizing that intention.

Third, design thinking is *hypothesis-driven*. Primary is the design hypothesis, which is conjectural and, as such, cannot be tested directly. Embedded in the selection of a particular promising design hypotheses, however, are a series of assumptions about a set of cause-effect relationships in today's environment that will support a set of actions aimed at transforming a situation from its current reality to its desired future state. These explanatory hypotheses must be identified and tested directly. Cycles of hypothesis generation and testing are iterative. As successive loops of "what if" and "if then" questions are explored, the hypotheses become more sophisticated and the design unfolds.

Fourth, design thinking is *opportunistic*. As the above cycles iterate, the designer seeks new and emergent possibilities. It is in the translation from the abstract/global to the particular/local that unforeseen opportunities are most likely to emerge. Sketching and modeling are important tools in the unfolding process.

Fifth, design thinking is *dialectical*. The designer lives at the intersection of often-conflicting demands – recognizing the constraints of today's materials and the uncertainties that cannot be defined away, while envisioning tomorrow's possibilities.

Finally, design thinking is *inquiring* and *value-driven* – open to scrutiny, willing to make its reasoning explicit to a broader audience, and cognizant of the values embedded within the conversation. It recognizes the primacy of the *Weltanschauung* of its audience. While the architect imbues the design with his or her own values, successful designs educate and persuade by connecting with the values of the audience, as well.

Implications for Strategy as Design

Having developed a clearer sense of the process of design itself, we can now see the possibilities that such a metaphor might hold for thinking about business strategy, in general, and the design of strategy-making processes, in particular.

1. Like design, strategic thinking is *synthetic*. It seeks internal alignment and understands interdependencies. It is systemic in its focus. It requires the ability to understand and integrate across levels, both horizontal and vertical, and to align strategies across those levels. A strategic thinker has a mental model of the complete end-to-end system of value creation, and understands the interdependencies within it. The synthesizing process creates value not only in aligning the components, but also in creatively re-arranging them. The creative solutions produced by many of today's entrepreneurs often rest more with the redesign of aspects of traditional strategies in ways that create added value for customers, rather than with dramatic breakthroughs.

2. Strategic thinking is *abductive*. It is future-focussed and inventive, providing the focus that allows individuals within an organization to leverage their energy, to focus attention, and to concentrate for as long as it takes to achieve a goal. The creation of a compelling intent relies heavily on the skill of alternative generation. Alternative generation has received far less attention in the strategic decision making literature than has alternative evaluation, but it is far more important in an environment of change.

3. Strategic thinking is *hypothesis-driven*. In an environment of ever-increasing information availability and decreasing time to think, the ability to develop good hypotheses and test them effectively is critical. Strategic thinking is both creative *and* critical in nature, and figuring out how to accomplish both types of thinking simultaneously has long troubled cognitive psychologists, since it is necessary to *suspend* critical judgment in order to think more creatively. Strategic thinking accommodates both creative and analytical thinking sequentially in its use of iterative cycles of hypothesis generating and testing. Hypothesis generation asks the question "what if...?", while hypothesis testing follows with the critical question "if..., then...?" and brings relevant data to bear on the analysis. Taken together, and repeated over time, this sequence allows us to generate ever-improving hypotheses, without forfeiting the ability to explore new ideas. Such experimentation allows an organization to move beyond simplistic notions of cause and effect to provides ongoing learning.

4. Strategic thinking is *opportunistic*. Within this intent-driven focus, there must be room for opportunism that not only furthers intended strategy but that also leaves open the possibility of new strategies emerging. This requires that an organization be capable of practicing 'intelligent opportunism' at lower levels.

5. Strategic thinking is *dialectical*. In the process of inventing the image of the future, the strategist must mediate the tension between constraint, contingency, and possibility. The underlying emphasis of strategic intent is *stretch* – to reach explicitly for potentially unattainable goals. At the same time, all elements of the firm's environment are not shapeable, and those constraints that are real must be acknowledged in designing strategy.

6. Strategic thinking is *inquiring* and, inevitably, *value-driven*. Because any particular strategy is invented, rather than discovered, it is contestable and reflective of the values of those making the choice. Its acceptance requires both connection with and movement beyond the existing mindset and value system of the rest of the organization, which relies on inviting the broader community into the strategic conversation. It is through participation in this dialogue that the strategy itself unfolds, both in the mind of the strategist and in that of the larger community that must come together to make the strategy happen.

Leveraging the Design Metaphor

What would we do differently in organizations today, if we took the design metaphor seriously? A lot, I believe.

The problems with traditional approaches to planning have long been recognized. They include the attempt to make a 'science' of planning, with its subsequent loss of creativity; the excessive emphasis on numbers; the drive for administrative efficiency at the expense of substance; and the dominance of single techniques, inappropriately applied. Yet, decades later, strategists continue to struggle to propose clear alternatives to traditional processes.

Design offers a different approach and suggests processes that are more widely participative, more dialogue-based, issue-rather-than-calendar-driven, conflict *using* rather than conflict avoiding, all aimed at invention and learning, rather than control.

If we were to take design's lead, we would involve more members of the organization in two-way strategic conversations. We would view the process as one of iteration and experimentation, and pay sequential attention to idea generation and evaluation in a way that attends first to *possibilities* before moving onto *constraints*. Finally, and perhaps most importantly, we would recognize that good designs succeed by persuading, and great designs by inspiring. *R*

Jeanne Liedtka is the United Technologies Corporation Professor of Business Administration at the University of Virginia's Darden School of Business and the former chief learning officer at United Technologies. She is the author of three books, most recently *Solving Problems with Design Thinking: Ten Stories of What Works* (Columbia University Press, 2013). This article was originally published in *California Management Review*.

IF MANAGERS THOUGHT LIKE DESIGNERS

1.
Jorn Utzon
Sydney Opera House

2.
Frank Gehry
Guggenheim Museum

3.
Coco Chanel
LBD

4.
Golden Gate
Bridge

5.
Pablo Picasso
Guernica

6.
Ingvar Kamprad
IKEA

Design has been proclaimed the 'secret weapon' for competition in the 21ˢᵗ century. Here's how today's managers can start thinking more like designers.

by **Jeanne Liedtka**

9.
Thomas Jefferson
University of Virginia

7.
New Urbanism
Seaside Community

8.
New Urbanism
Seaside Community

10.
Antoni Gaudi
Sagrada Familia

THE PROBLEMS WITH TRADITIONAL APPROACHES to planning have long been recognized. They include the attempt to make a 'science' of planning, with its subsequent loss of creativity; the excessive emphasis on numbers; the drive for administrative efficiency at the expense of substance; and the dominance of single techniques, inappropriately applied. Yet, decades later, strategists continue to struggle to propose clear alternatives to traditional processes.

Design offers a different approach and suggests processes that are more widely participative, more dialogue-based, issue-rather than calendar-driven, and conflict-*using* rather than conflict-avoiding, all aimed at invention and learning, rather than control.

But beneath all the hyperbole, we have to question what it would actually mean for business strategy if managers took the idea of design seriously. What if we tried to think the way designers do? Having studied how various kinds of designers work and create for the past decade, I offer the following ten suggestions as a starting point in the conversation.

If We Took the Design Metaphor Seriously

1. We would realize that designing business strategy is about invention. For all their talk about the art and science of management, strategists, in the analytic search for 'the one right strategy', have mostly paid attention to the science. Taking the design metaphor seriously means acknowledging the

If strategy is indeed an invention –
just one story about the future among
many – then it is always contestable.

difference between what scientists do and what designers do. Whereas scientists investigate *today* to discover explanations for what already is, designers invent *tomorrow* to create something that isn't.

We all care about strategy because we want the future to be different from the present. But powerful futures are rarely discovered primarily through analytics. They are, as **Walt Disney** said, "created first in the mind and next in the activity." This doesn't deny analysis an important role, but it does subordinate analysis to the process of invention.

As an example of the tension between invention and analysis, take the Sydney Opera House, whose designer, **Jørn Utzon**, was awarded architecture's highest honor, the Pritzker Prize, in 2003. It's hard now to imagine Australia without the Sydney Opera House, but it's quite possible that it would never have been built if initial estimates for the project had been accurate. In 1957, when Utzon's proposal was selected, accountants estimated that the project would take five years to complete and cost $7 million. In reality, it took 14 years and cost more than $100 million. **John Lowe**, who chronicled the story of the opera house, quotes **Ove Arup**, an engineer who collaborated with Utzon on the project: "If the magnitude of the task had been fully appreciated... the Opera House would never have been built. And the fact that it wasn't known...was one of the unusual circumstances that made the miracle possible." Thank goodness the accountants got the analysis wrong.

2. We'd recognize the primacy of persuasion. If strategy is indeed an invention – just one story about the future among many – then it is always contestable. Leaders must therefore persuade others of the compelling wisdom and superiority of the story they have chosen. They must, in fact, make the story seductive; in selling their strategy, they must, to put it bluntly, treat employees like lovers instead of prostitutes.

It's not easy to entice people into sharing an image of the future. After all, strategies in most industries today call on people to commit to something new and different, to step away from the security of what has worked in the past. This is never an easy sell, even for the most seasoned leaders. Like venturing into a new relationship, persuading others to share your vision works best when you issue an invitation instead of a command.

Designers understand this. Successful architects, for instance, know that to get their great buildings built, they must persuade clients to pay for them, and that requires helping clients visualize the end result. In fact, the more inventive the architect, the more critical the ability to conjure the image for the client and for what may be a very skeptical public. When **Frank Gehry** began sketching what would become the Guggenheim Museum in Bilbao, Spain, he already had a profound feel for what would draw a very traditional Basque audience to his stunningly inventive creation. Gehry explains his approach: "You bring to the table certain things...the Basques, their desire to use culture, to bring the city to the river. And the industrial feeling."

Writing in *The Los Angeles Times*, architecture critic **Nicolai Ouroussoff** describes the result: "Gehry has achieved what not so long ago seemed impossible for most architects: the invention of radically new architectural forms that nonetheless speak to the man on the street. Bilbao has become a pilgrimage point for those who, until now, had little interest in architecture. Working-class Basque couples arrive toting children on weekends. The cultural elite veer off their regular flight paths so they can tell friends that they, too, have seen the building in the flesh." Gehry's Guggenheim persuades and seduces by connecting to the Basque's past and pointing toward a new future. That is how strategies become compelling and persuasive: they show an organization its future without discounting its past. They tell us what we get to keep as well as what we must lose.

3. We'd value simplicity. Think of an object you love. Chances are that it is complex enough to perform its function well, but no more complex than it needs to be. In other words, it's an elegant solution. No design is a better exemplar of simplicity and elegance than the little black dress, or 'LBD'. The most striking aspect of the LBD, designed by **Coco Chanel** in the 1920s, is its simplicity. The LBD does not overprescribe or adorn, but instead offers a black canvas, which its wearer tailors to the function at hand: add pearls and heels to dress up; a bright scarf and flats to dress down. The possibilities are endless, making the LBD one of the most functional items in a woman's wardrobe. But the LBD goes beyond mere functionality to achieve elegance: it lacks nothing essential and contains nothing extraneous.

What if we used the LBD as a model for business strategy? We would end up with strategies that would be neither incomprehensible to all save their creators, nor banal and self-evident. They would eschew the faddish and focus on enduring elements, incorporating a versatility and openness that invited their 'wearers' to add adornments to fit the occasion at hand. Perhaps most importantly, they would emphasize our positives while acknowledging our flaws – all in the service of offering us hope for a better (thinner) tomorrow.

4. We'd aim to inspire. One of the saddest facts about the state of business design is the extent to which we settle for mediocrity. We don't even attempt to engage our audience at an emotional level, let alone to inspire. Yet the difference between great designs and those that are only 'okay' is the way the former call us to something greater.

Consider the differences between the San Francisco Bay Bridge and the Golden Gate Bridge. The Bay Bridge offers a route across the water. The Golden Gate Bridge does that, too, but it also sweeps, symbolizes, and enthralls. It has, like the Sydney Opera House, become an icon of the land it occupies. How many of our business strategies are like the Golden Gate Bridge? Too few.

5. We'd master the core skills first. Each of the designs we've looked at so far is inventive, persuasive, elegant, and inspiring. Yet all of them succeed because they also work well, and they do this because of the mastery of technical elements. The Sydney Opera House's sail-shaped roof vaults required expert engineering. The Guggenheim Bilbao's undulating titanium-clad exterior was possible only with the help of sophisticated computer modeling. And the little black dress worked because Chanel pioneered a synthetic fabric – jersey – that flowed instead of clinging.

If you examine the 1895 painting *First Communion*, you'll see evidence of extraordinary technique; the layers of white in the young girl's dress, in particular, are astonishing. Who was the artist? **Pablo Picasso**, who, at age 14, had clearly mastered conventional art. Now consider *Guernica*, which Picasso painted in 1937 to memorialize the Nazi bombing of the Basque village. There is little that is conventional about this painting, considered one of modern art's most powerful antiwar statements. Picasso, who by this time was recognized as one of the most influential artists of the twentieth century, had moved beyond conventional technique, using his mastery to push the frontiers of art.

6. We'd learn to experiment. How does one move from mastery to brilliance? From technical competence to true innovation? By experimenting. Some design experiments take place in the mind; think of the strategic planning process, in which strategists imagine and test new futures – and some find their expression in physical prototypes. Some experiments are even conducted in the real world, and here I offer my only design story from the business world: **IKEA**. When the company's visionary founder, **Ingvar Kamprad**, started out, he had only a general sense of what would become IKEA's revolutionary approach to the furniture business. Nearly every element of its now-legendary business model – showrooms and catalogs in tandem, knockdown furniture in flat parcels, and customer pickup and assembly – emerged over time from experimental responses to urgent problems. Customer pickup, for instance, became a central element of IKEA's strategy almost by chance, when frustrated customers rushed into the warehouse because there weren't enough employees to help them. The store manager realized the advantages of the customers' initiative and suggested that the idea become permanent.

7. We'd be more inclusive in our strategic conversations. The image of the solitary genius at work in his atelier is as much a myth in art, architecture, and science as it is in business. Design teaches us about the value of including multiple perspectives in the design process – turning the process into a conversation. The more complex the design challenge, the greater the benefits of multiple voices and perspectives.

Consider, for instance, the complex and political process of urban planning – in particular, the New Urbanism movement, which emerged from the experiences of the developers and architects of the innovative **Seaside Community** in Florida. What distinguishes New Urbanism from other architectural movements is its emphasis on wide participation. This participation takes the form of a *charrette*, an interactive design conversation with a long tradition in art and architecture. Derived from the French word meaning 'little cart', charrettes were used at the first formal school of architecture, the Ecole des Beaux Arts in

Paris, in the 19th century. As students progressed from one level to the next, their projects were placed on small carts, onto which students would leap to make their frantic finishing touches.

The charrette process used in New Urbanism projects is based on four principles: involve everyone from the start who might build, use, sell, approve, or block the project; work concurrently and cross-functionally (architects, planners, engineers, economists, market experts, citizens, public officials); work in short feedback loops; and work in detail. The charrette, I believe, offers a powerful alternative to the traditional strategic planning process by inviting the whole system to participate and by including local knowledge in the conversation.

8. We'd learn to talk differently. Of course, simply putting a variety of people in a room together is not enough. To produce superior designs, we must change the way we talk to one another. Most of us have learned to talk in business settings as if we are in a debate, advocating a position. But within a diverse group, debate is more likely to lead to stalemate than to breakthroughs: breakthroughs come from asking new questions, not debating existing solutions; they come from re-examining what we take as given.

As a case in point, consider the design of New York's Central Park. In 1857, the country's first public landscape design competition was held to select the plan for this park. Of all the submissions, only one – prepared by **Frederick Law Olmsted** and **Calvert Vaux** – fulfilled all of the design requirements. The most challenging requirement – that cross-town traffic be permitted without marring the pastoral feel of the park – had been considered impossible to meet by all the other designers. Olmsted and Vaux succeeded by eliminating the assumption that the park was a two-dimensional space. Instead, they imagined it in three dimensions, and sank four roads eight feet below its surface.

9. We'd work backwards. Most managers are taught a straightforward problem-solving methodology: define a problem, identify various solutions, analyze each, and choose one. Designers begin at the end of this process, as **Stephen Covey** has famously admonished, by achieving clarity about the desired outcomes of the design and then working backwards.

I'd like to illustrate this approach with a story that is close to home. **Thomas Jefferson**, who included education among his many passions and interests, devoted the last decade of his life to founding the University of Virginia. For Jefferson, the link between democracy and education was clear: without an educated populace, there was no hope of protecting the fledgling democracy that he and the other founding fathers had worked so hard to create. Jefferson's university would produce free-minded graduates, and therefore it would need to differ from prevailing educational institutions in many ways: it would be a community

where faculty and students work as partners to create a dialogue that produces the kind of learning that democracy requires. The typical large central building would be replaced with a collection of smaller buildings. This garden-encircled 'academic village' would be a *community* of learning where students would have unprecedented freedom in both the choice of curriculum and in governing their own behaviours.

To the modern observer, Jefferson's genius may appear to lie in the beauty of the architecture he created. In reality, he took much of his architectural inspiration rather directly from the sixteenth-century Italian architect **Palladio**. Jefferson's true genius lies in the power of the space that he created and its ability to evoke so vividly the purpose for which it was designed.

10. We'd start the conversation with possibilities. Great design, it has been said, occurs at the intersection of constraint, contingency, and possibility – elements that are central to creating innovative, elegant, and functional designs. But it matters greatly where you start. In business, we have tended to start strategic conversation with constraints: the constraints of budgets, of ease of implementation, of the quarterly earnings focus that Wall Street dictates. As a result, we get designs for tomorrow that merely tweak today's. Great design inevitably starts with the question "What if *anything* were possible?" After all, if strategy is an invention, a product of our imaginations, and our assumptions are bound only by what we can imagine, then removing the assumptions that arise from the belief in constraints is job number one.

For my final example, we will turn to one of my favorite cities, Barcelona, and examine the story of its great unfinished cathedral, Sagrada Familia, designed by Antoni Gaudi. Gaudi was just 32 years in 1884, when he was named principal architect of the church known as the 'Cathedral of the Poor', which would be built entirely through donations. From the outset, Gaudi envisioned the cathedral he wanted to create – a 'Bible in stone', a soaring interior that evoked a forest and an exterior with towers that reached for the heavens. He resolved to design his cathedral as though anything were possible, even though the constraints he faced were seemingly insurmountable. Gaudi chose to disregard the usual constraints of time and money. "My client is in no hurry," was his response to skeptics who doubted that the church would ever be completed. When funds became too scarce to continue construction, he went back to designing, building increasingly detailed plaster models and stepping out of his architect-builder role to raise funds personally.

The very real constraints imposed by the construction materials and techniques available at the time were impossible for Gaudi to ignore. Because the natural world served as one of the primary sources of inspiration in all of his designs, he aspired

Great design, it has been said,
occurs at the intersection of constraint,
contingency, and possibility

to create soaring spaces with natural light and found himself profoundly encumbered by the need for straight internal load-bearing walls and beams. Without the mathematical knowledge and modeling techniques available today, the physics of the cathedral's construction were also a challenge as Gaudi sought to avoid the massive arches and buttresses common to the great medieval cathedrals.

In order to work around these constraints, Gaudi sought out new tools and techniques. He found two tools, little-used in Barcelona at the time, that would become the foundation of his work. The first was the 'catenary arch', a simple arch whose shape could be simulated by suspending a chain upside down. Gaudi was able to calculate the load-bearing demands placed on the massive cathedral towers by suspending small bags of sand from the inverted chain to mimic the weight that the towers would need to bear. This created a perfect model (albeit upside down!) of the possible shapes and dimensions that a real tower could take on. Computer models run on Gaudi's towers demonstrate the surprising accuracy of his method.

The second tool that he discovered was a new material: cement. Combined with iron beams, brick or stone pillars, and a new roofing approach, cement allowed the exterior walls to bear most of the roof's weight, giving Gaudi the freedom of interior design that he craved. Gaudi died at the age of 74 (ironically, run over by a streetcar on his way to church) with his cathedral only partially completed. Ten years later, the Spanish civil war came to the city, bringing construction to a halt. Rioters burned his

workshop, destroying all of his plans and archives. Fortunately, the plaster models survived the fire and are being used today to guide the final phase of the cathedral's construction. Completion is expected within the next 20 years.

All of the design stories told here are about possibilities made real, some of them against great odds. In order to achieve such designs, we must first *aspire* to achieve them, challenging the mediocrity of much of today's design. We must also learn new skills, including the mastery of core technologies and the ability to persuade, to talk differently, to experiment. Finally, we must embrace new processes – processes that invite a more diverse set of perspectives into the strategic conversation, that work backwards from a clear sense of the outcomes that we want to create. And we must start our conversations with possibilities. The kind of exemplary designs discussed here are rarely achieved even in design – let alone in business. But as we all know, it is that which is hard to do that is most worth doing. *R*

Jeanne Liedtka is the United Technologies Corporation Professor of Business Administration at the University of Virginia's Darden School of Business and the former chief learning officer at United Technologies. She is the author of three books, most recently *Solving Problems with Design Thinking: Ten Stories of What Works* (Columbia University Press, 2013).

TIME FOR DESIGN

Cities, buildings, products, services, systems, and strategies
all face the same need to combine expertise, insight, engagement
and adaptation. It's time to confront the tensions of design.

by **Jeanne Liedtka** and **Henry Mintzberg**

NEARLY 40 YEARS AGO, Nobel Laureate in Economic Sciences **Herbert Simon** argued that, "everyone designs who devises courses of action aimed at changing existing situations into preferred ones. Design, so construed, is the core of all professional training: architecture, business, education, law, and medicine are all centrally concerned with the process of design."

Given the widespread attention given to design in the business press in recent years, it appears the time has finally come when the business world is taking this message seriously. Yet design is hardly the core of any current management training – or its practice. In fact, it's not clear that we even agree on what design means. As two business academics long interested in this topic, our purpose here is to show the robustness of the notion of design; to examine the various forms 'designing' takes; and to explore its potential for helping people manage more effectively.

The Terminology of Design

Design is both a noun and a verb. As a noun, it refers to an outcome, and some are superior to others: there are great designs, and there are mediocre designs. To appreciate the difference between great and mediocre design, consider a comparison of the Golden Gate and San Francisco Bay bridges. Both offer reliable transport across the water separating San Francisco and its neighbours – but the similarity ends there. The Golden Gate enthralls, sweeps, and symbolizes, inspiring art, music, and myth. The San Francisco Bay Bridge, meanwhile, merely gets the job done. Does this difference matter? We believe that it does – and that business has much to learn from this 'tale of two bridges'.

Functionality is an insufficient pre-condition for a great design. The personal objects that people cherish do more than just work, they share a number of other characteristics: they seem simple but complete to their users; they contain nothing extraneous,

Designers who persuade others offer *novelty* and *familiarity* in tandem because they understand how users see the world.

yet lack nothing important; they *engage* at an emotional level; beyond their ability to serve function without fanfare, they hook their users in an almost sensual way; and finally, great designs manage to be simultaneously *enduring* and *innovative*. They connect to the past with a reassuring familiarity, while surprising users with their inventiveness.

The important lessons of 'design as a noun' turn out to be reassuringly straightforward: if you want great designs, seek simplicity, emotional engagement, and that sweet spot between the familiar and the new. And, of course, do the job well. And yet, if it's all that obvious, why are we surrounded by so many mediocre designs?

That brings us to the tricky part: design as a verb. Like most things that are hard to do, this is where the competitive advantage lies. Better designing – of products, organizations, strategies – holds the key to unlocking the real potential of design for business. The basic attributes of successful designing are well-recognized: the process is synthetic, future-focused, hypothesis-driven, and opportunistic. It involves observation, the use of frameworks and prototyping. But peel back from these high-altitude accounts, and you will find that the particulars of designing involve varying approaches.

Consider the revolutionary architectural and social experiment of **Brasilia**, the most completely- planned city of the modernist movement. Rising from the largely uninhabited central plateau of Brazil in the 1950s and designed in exacting detail to be 'the model city of the future', it anchors a position at one extreme of design approaches, whereby the designer is evident, declaring his or her intentions, resisting compromise, and imposing his or her will on users.

At the other extreme are the lovely *villages perchés* (perched villages) of Provence. Evolving over time and through the participation of many, the hand of any single designer seems hardly visible. Yet these villages retain a sense of symmetry and coherence that suggests intention and conscious forethought – no less so than Brasilia.

Exploring the design continuum from the stark, fixed, and imposed, to the adapted, fluid, and evolving allows us to develop a deeper understanding of what constitutes 'design as a verb', and sets up an examination of the challenges of designing for business. To explore their range, we describe four disparate approaches to design.

The Formulaic Approach: Brasilia

First, we return to Brasilia, where the design tensions were resolved by coming down heavily in favour of the designer's global knowledge and expertise, a controlled process, and a fixed design. Architect **Oskar Niemeyer** used established techniques and official principles to reach what he considered to be an optimal answer. We use the term 'formulaic' to describe this approach.

For modernist architects, the crises of the highly-industrialized cities of the world were reflected in their traffic, congestion, and poor standards of living. Only 'total planning', they believed, could resolve these problems. By creating a new kind of city, Brasilia's designers set out to create a new kind of society, using architecture as an instrument of change. The modernist principles driving design included the organization of the city into separate zones for work, living, and recreation; the replacement of traditional streets with high-speed one-way avenues radiating out from the center; and the creation of *superquandra* – large apartment complexes containing standardized family units intended to break down traditional socioeconomic barriers. The resulting design is specified by a set of pre-existing principles, rather than emerging from a more open-ended process of experimentation. Brasilia's design consciously resists attempts at adaptation, rather than encouraging them. It is meant to stay true to what it is – a 'model' city.

The Visionary Approach: IKEA

Consider the pronounced similarities and differences between the above process and the story of **Ingvar Kamprad** and his creation, **IKEA**. Kamprad's personal ethic of thrift and simplicity

Opportunities exist in the white spaces
between divisions, regions, and functions
of every company.

provided the underlying values behind IKEA's defining intention: "To create a better everyday life for the many by offering a wide range of well-designed, functional home furnishing products at prices so low that as many people as possible will be able to afford them."

In the IKEA story, we observe a more organic design process at work. Kamprad was more the visionary than the expert, more attuned to learning and adapting than to knowing and controlling. In a sense, he had no choice – he started without the power of bulldozers or a body of principles. He had, at best, the equivalent of a small number of people with shovels and only a general notion of what they were setting out to build. And so he adapted to the constraints he could not eliminate. Nearly every element of IKEA's now legendary business model – showrooms and catalogs in tandem, knockdown furniture in flat parcels, massive stores readily accessibly by automobile, and customer pick-up and assembly – emerged over time as responses to urgent problems that the struggling furniture company faced. "Regard every problem as a possibility," was Kamprad's mantra.

Interestingly, the IKEA story also shares some characteristics of Brasilia. Both are intensely possibility-driven, with the designer's hand evident and dramatic. Yet Kamprad's visionary design process parts company with formulaic design by relying upon personal creativity, rather than formulaic technique, affording less control but more responsiveness to opportunity. The resulting design is never really fixed; it is meant to be flexible and adaptive. The fallible person – the visionary – takes over from the ostensibly infallible technique, enhancing the potential to experiment and learn.

The Conversational Approach: Seaside

This approach opens up the design process – making it a conversation among many people, all of whom should be recognized as designers. Two of today's leading proponents of involvement in the design process are **Andrea Duaney** and **Elizabeth Plater-Zyberk**, founders of New Urbanism. Their first and best-recog-

nized project, designed more than 20 years ago, was **Seaside Florida**, an 80-acre beachfront town on the Gulf of Mexico. *Architecture Week* called it "one of the most influential design paradigms of its era"; and *Newsweek*, "the most influential resort community since Versailles."

What distinguishes New Urbanism from other architectural approaches is not only a different set of principles, but also its insistence on wide participation in designing, through the use of a process called a *charrette*. In the words of Duaney and Plater-Zyberk, "The charrette brings together all interested parties who are invited to offer direction and feedback while the plan is being created. It provides a forum for ideas and offers the unique advantage of giving immediate feedback to the designers while giving mutual authorship to the plan by all those who participate." By convening a conversation that puts the entire system in the room, the architects control the boundaries, but not the conversation itself. Those involved are not merely consulted; they are engaged, and they become members of the design team. Put differently, all kinds of 'quiet designers' enter the process – bringing with them their local knowledge.

With the Seaside charrette, the architects created a *context* in which experts and users learned together, and out of which the design appeared. This process can be admittedly chaotic, which must be tolerated if creativity and consensus are to emerge. Like Brasilia, however, the design itself is eventually fixed. The charrette ends, and our quiet designers go home. Designing stops and construction starts.

The Evolving Approach: Linux

In this approach, designing in the traditional sense – as practiced by identified designers at specific points in time and resulting in fixed designs – disappears. We now enter the world of evolving, or never-ending design, not by experts, but by communities in the course of living their collective lives.

This evolutionary design is found in the **Linux** operating system and the open source software process it pioneered.

Successful leaders in both management and the physical fields of design have an acute sense of the particular, the potential, and the possible.

Linux is being designed with almost continuous adaptation in mind. In recounting the story of its origins, software designer **Eric Raymond** opens with a question: "Who would have thought that a world-class operating system could coalesce as if by magic out of part-time hacking by several thousand developers scattered all over the planet, connected only by the tenuous strands of the Internet?"

Linux's success challenged many of the basic premises of traditional software design – foremost among them, that large projects need to be built like Gothic cathedrals, carefully controlled by a small band of experts who specify every detail and release their design to users only upon completion. **Linus Torvalds**, the originator of Linux, created this revolution by starting with a basic scaffolding offered by another programmer, sharing the source code, and inviting anyone interested to participate. He released revisions early and often, and above all, treated users as co-developers, building a "self-correcting system of selfish agents" whose pace of ongoing improvement was unprecedented. "The closed-source world cannot win an evolutionary arms race with open-source communities that can put orders of magnitude more skill time into a problem," Raymond observed, because "given enough eyeballs, all bugs are shallow."

Like Duaney and Plater-Zyberg, Torvalds leads the conversation rather than writes the code. The 'community' does the designing, and designers and users become almost indistinguishable.

Lessons for Business
The four approaches outlined above reveal some of the core tensions of design and the various trade-offs that each approach makes. Following are four core tensions that hold valuable lessons for business.

1. Who drives the design?
Who should drive the design? The expert who knows better, who has the global, explicit knowledge, or the user who understands better, who has the local, tacit understanding? The paradox around deciding who designs involves the apparent trade-off between a reliance on experts and visionaries capable of radically innovative – but potentially difficult to implement – solutions versus a reliance on users with a tendency to produce 'me-too' designs that they enthusiastically execute.

Designer-dominated processes can have a clear advantage when it comes to producing designs characterized by radical change. The creation of Brasilia, for instance, was an audacious feat – it is unlikely that engaging a community of potential users would have produced such a futuristic model city. As users, most of us crave familiarity, not novelty; radical designs alienate us.

But at what cost do we exclude user involvement? The extent to which Brasilia actually achieved its designers' ambitions is mixed. The standardization intended to produce equality produced, for many, a feeling of anonymity instead. In place of gaining an enriched community, many residents felt a loss of privacy. Instead of appreciating the orderliness of the space, they missed the messiness of street life. Despite the homogeneity of the superquandra, the old class distinctions remain. The risks of a design process that relies too heavily on experts are evident here.

If this is reminiscent of strategic planning in business, that is because formulaic design has been the corporate world's preferred approach. This approach, with its emphasis on the designer's worldview and its disconnection from local knowledge, represents the 'yang' of designing. It is ambitious, aggressive, and intrusive. It relies on techniques and information that, if inaccurate, can be fatal. Its detachment from users – the people who must live with the design – is a potentially fatal flaw. Yet it is capable of great change if the bulldozers are powerful enough and the terrain is reasonably predictable.

To succeed at significant change, either the formulaic or visionary designer must persuade users to accept a radical design, or conversational and evolving designing must engage users in ways that generate more-innovative designs. Designers who persuade others offer novelty and familiarity in tandem because they understand how users see the world.

2. How does the designing happen?

This involves the tension between controlling a design process to achieve coherence and order versus opening up the conversation and risking some 'messiness' to achieve creativity and broader involvement. The inclusion of non-experts brings valuable ownership and local knowledge, but may also bring chaos and mediocre solutions. Getting more-innovative thinking from users themselves involves how this tension is resolved.

Successful leaders in both management and the physical fields of design seem to have an innate sense of when to allow flexibility into the conversation, when to tap the group's potential for creating better solutions, as well as when to abandon the search for consensus to interject order from above. They have no formulas – just an acute sense of the particular, the potential, and the possible. These leaders/designers seem able to give up enough control to find creativity without losing coherence. Kamprad's vision seems exemplary in its capacity to hold tight and let loose at the same time, in order to engage the collective creativity of the company's employees and customers. There are enormous opportunities to bring this kind of conversational design into business.

Business leaders seeking better design thinking should pay careful attention to the challenges of preventing premature consensus emerging in the face of fear of chaos, and of maintaining the fluidity that is a prerequisite for breakthrough designs. Architect **Frank Gehry** notes that clients are rarely comfortable with the indeterminacy of an iterative process; they almost always push hard to fix the design and 'end the uncertainty'. Conversational design challenges leaders in ways that formulaic and visionary design do not. Business cultures that centre on hierarchy, expediency, and authoritarian leadership get in the way of good conversations. We all know about opportunities that exist in the white spaces between divisions, regions, and functions of every company; what we do not know is how to tap these opportunities. Recognizing the role of conversations in exploring new possibilities can produce dramatic innovation.

3. When is the designing 'finished'?

The world does not stand still, but designs must – at least for a time: buildings have to be built, products brought to market, strategies implemented, and structures established. The dilemma in each case is how designs can be built to adapt, yet preserve their integrity. In other words, how can designing deal with change and continuity concurrently?

Former **Intel** chief **Andy Grove** has said that his firm's strategy process evolved in alternating cycles of chaos and single-minded focus – sometimes adapting, sometimes closing. Companies that do nothing but change – constantly reorganizing, always envisioning some new strategy or other, bringing in yet another team of change consultants – never reach closure, and so are no better off than companies that never change. Even the most evolving designs have to be fixed for a time.

The key, we believe, is to get the basics right so that the specifics can easily be changed. As Raymond observed about software design, "You often don't really understand the problem until after the first time you implement a solution. If you want to get it right, be ready to start over at least once."

In closing

Design is not just a metaphor for management, but, as Simon said, the very essence of it. Cities, products, services, systems, structures and strategies all face the same need to combine expertise, insight, engagement and adaptation. To design, and to manage in general, is not to resolve the tensions among different needs so much as to function within them. To appreciate this will be to get more of those great designs that so enhance our daily lives. **R**

Jeanne Liedtka is the United Technologies Corporation Professor of Business Administration at the University of Virginia's Darden School of Business and the former chief learning officer at United Technologies. She is the author of three books, most recently *Solving Problems with Design Thinking: Ten Stories of What Works* (Columbia University Press, 2013).
Henry Mintzberg is the Cleghorn Professor of Management Studies at McGill University. This is an excerpt of an article that appeared recently in the *Design Management Review*, a publication of the Design Management Institute.

By **Tony Golsby-Smith**

THE SECO ROAD OF THOUGH

A FRIEND OF MINE WITH A BACKGROUND IN MEDIA recently found himself in the role of CEO of a major government department. One of the first things he noticed is how abused the word 'strategy' is: everything has to be a strategy in order to get noticed. He was sure someone would have a strategy for visiting the restrooms. But the second thing he noticed was that no-one was actually thinking strategically: the more the word was used, the less meaningful it became.

It should not be like this. Strategy should be the process that enables organizations to create new futures and engage their people in exciting tasks. Instead, it mostly weighs an organization down with more data and inputs.

Arguably the strategy process is one of the weakest processes in most organizations. They are far better equipped with the tools for operational management and 'defending the status quo' than they are for inventing and shaping new futures, and there is a

OND

How Design Offers Strategy a New Tool Kit

good reason for this: modern organizations exist at the 'delivery end' of the thinking life cycle, not at the discovery end.

Once an organization becomes mature and viable, it stabilizes ideas into structures, and 'efficiency' becomes its overriding goal. But strategy is not about delivery and efficiency: it is about discovering alternative possibilities. Inherently, this will challenge the hypotheses on which the organization is built. Seen in this light, strategy will threaten the organization's stability, so the

organization will immunize itself against it. The budget process is a practical example of how this 'immune system' works: it hard-wires yesterday's assumptions about inputs and outputs into plans and commitments, and so habituates organizations into preserving the status quo.

We need a new approach to strategy that can unlock fresh energy and make it more innovative and less data driven. This is what design thinking can offer.

The heart of the Two Roads story is that the western world bought the wrong thinking system from **Aristotle**. This ranks as one of the worst investment decisions our civilization has made, and it has led us into using the wrong toolkits for our enterprises ever since. The thinking system we invested in was Aristotle's 'analytics', and we made the choice around the era of the Enlightenment, which ushered in what we today call the Scientific Age. That decision has proven so sweeping that it now monopolizes what most people characterize as 'thinking.' Thinking processes are dominated by the culture of the sciences, and you get no better evidence of this than our universities, the home of thinking, where any subject must position itself as a science to be taken seriously. Traditional approaches to strategy sit fairly and squarely at this table of logic and Science.

What few people realize is that Aristotle conceived two thinking systems, not one. We made the big mistake of just buying one, and allowing it to monopolize the whole territory of thought. We should have bought them both, and used them as partners. Instead we have only one thinking tool in our hands and we are using it for all the wrong purposes. Here is how it happened.

Aristotle was the first person to codify thinking into a system. He did this for a reason: he lived in perhaps the most dramatic social experiment of human history, the invention of democracy by the Greek leader **Kleisthenes** around 450 BC. This political system did what no other had tried to do: it delivered decision making into the hands of human beings. Prior to that, regimes were governed by the king or the gods. That meant that no matter how sophisticated they might have been in terms of Engineering or Mathematics, they were not sophisticated about human reasoning, especially where decision making was concerned. Clearly, Kleisthenes' political reforms created a great need to codify the processes by which humans think and can arrive at 'truths.' If ever there was a do-it-yourself manual, this was it! Ordinary humans were playing god in Aristotle's Greece.

The Logic Road

In answer to this demand, Aristotle invented the great 'truth making' machine of logic, and he brilliantly described it in his books on the *Analytics*. The heart of the machine was the 'syllogism,' and it dominates the works: if a=b, and b=c, then a=c. This formula could take inputs and compute them into truth claims that were universally true and incontrovertible.

In one brilliant essay, Aristotle laid down the path for deductive reasoning that has dominated the western mind for the last 300 years. With it, we have built what I call the 'logic road,' and it carries pretty much all of our intellectual traffic these days. The reason for its appeal is not so much the method but what it offers – control and certainty. If I can pull apart any system into its working parts and then explain it in cause-and-effect relations, surely I will be able to fully know the truth about this system. That knowledge will give me control; there will be no surprises, and I will be in the box seat. And with control I will also get certainty: I can predict outcomes and guarantee results.

The logic road convinced us more than it convinced Aristotle. He was always uneasy about the inputs into the system. He was confident that his inference-making engine worked well, but what if we could not trust the inputs? He never answered that question to his satisfaction (consider the last two pages of his *Analytics,* where he confronts this worry); but centuries later, two great minds conspired to apparently clean up the inputs question.

Firstly, **Galileo** pioneered the use of numbers to represent reality. Rather than represent the data of the universe as fable or story, he turned all its mystery into numbers – cold, hard, concrete numbers. Then **Descartes**, who hated uncertainty and ambiguity, elevated Mathematics to the head of the table as 'the only true Science.' Descartes famously hated the 'soft' humanities and declared that only numbers were unambiguous and 'true.' With this they conspired to patch up the inputs question and thus 'logic' became apparently water tight.

The logic road underpinned the era of Science, which delivered us technologies and made the Industrial Revolution possible. The Revolution delivered us untold wealth and capitalism, and sitting at the end of this beneficial trail lays modern management and its strategic processes, deeply indebted to the logic road. But the logic road has run into all sorts of trouble, mainly because it has failed to deliver on its main promise of control.

I often say to management groups that I work with, "We have never had so much information available to us as we have today, so who feels we have never been more in control of our world and our destiny?" Nobody does. So what has gone wrong?

The Second Road

For the answer, we can begin by going back to Aristotle. He was smarter than we were in rushing in and over-investing in his logic product. He significantly limited the application of his analytics engine to a certain domain of truth: he called this domain 'where things cannot be other than they are.' By this he meant the realm of Natural Science. If you have a truth question concerning the realm of nature or any realm where things do not change, by all means use the logic road. But he said that this domain was not the only domain for truth making. There was a second domain which he characterized in the memorable phrase, 'where things can be other than they are.' By this he meant the whole domain of human decision making, where we in fact 'play god' and determine alternative futures.

For this second domain, Aristotle conceived an entirely different thinking pathway that combined invention, judgment and decision wrapped up in a social process of debate. He called

We cannot analyze our way one inch
into the future, for the simple reason that
the future does not exist yet, so it is not
there to analyze.

this process 'rhetoric' or 'dialectic', and I call it the Second Road to truth. Aristotle described it just as fully, as his analytic engine in various books including the *Rhetoric* and the *Topica*. The critical difference between the two roads is always best understood by the different domains of question that they address: rhetoric was the road by which humans designed alternative futures; analytics was the road by which we diagnosed what already exists.

As **Richard Buchanan** of Carnegie-Mellon University has brilliantly demonstrated in a series of landmark essays, design is the modern rhetoric. The significance of this cannot be overstated: if strategy is in fact a design process, it has been using an incomplete tool kit to date.

Human beings do not analyze their way into the future. In fact, we cannot analyze our way one inch into the future, for the simple reason that the future does not yet exist, so it is not there to analyze. Let me demonstrate this to you quite simply. At the heart of the logic road lies the idea of proof and empirical reasoning. This is hard wired into our culture by the common challenge, "Prove it!" If we cannot 'prove' a hypothesis, we are undone.

Suppose I propose a dream for our organization in which I imagine an alternative situation, different from and much more desirable than the present situation. When management challenges me to "prove it!" I cannot do this, for the simple reason that my dream lies in the future and thus is beyond proof. Yet if I am so challenged and I reply, "Sorry I cannot prove it...but I believe it!" I would feel weak and defensive in most organizational cultures. The reason I would feel so defensive is that our whole paradigm is dominated by the analytic system – and it is out of this dominant thinking system that the challenge to 'prove it' flows.

The Power of Argumentation

If we cannot analyze our way into the future, how do we move ahead? The answer is 'by arguments,' and it is the art of argumentation that lies at the heart of the Second Road.

Arguments are the engines by which humans create alternative futures. The great Roman leader, **Cicero**, was an avid follower of Aristotle and quite possibly the greatest rhetorician of all time. He claimed that all human civilization was built on the pathway of rhetoric and memorably imagined uncivilized tribes arguing their way out of caves and into villages. Picture the first natives to start the argument:

"We don't have to keep sheltering high up in these caves forever. I reckon we can live happier lives way down by the river close to the water and our hunting grounds."

"So how do we do that, praytell, without freezing to death in the winter months?"

"Good question, but I have this idea – let's call it a 'hut' – which we could make out of the timber from old trees..."

"You are always dreaming, you fool...but the idea of huts has some attraction...take it further for me."

In that dynamic of argument lies the whole momentum of progress, according to Cicero: if Cicero's cave dwellers used Aristotle's logic road to improve their lives, they would still be there today analyzing the rock structures of caves. But they are not, because the human genius for argumentation enables us to craft alternative destinies.

Every strategy is an argument, every plan is an argument and every design is an argument. The concept of 'argument' opens a door onto a new landscape of tools and pathways to craft strategy and make it the 'design' process that it naturally is.

Following are three critical elements of the Second Road tool kit that have proven transformational for the managerial groups I have worked with. I name each with both a classical term of rhetoric and a modern term of management.

1. Agency (Corporate Intent)

The first element of a compelling argument is 'agency.' In the scientific process, you aim to keep people out of it: we are taught

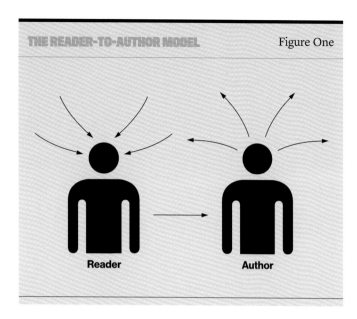

Reader   **Author**

to be 'objective' and not bring ourselves into the thinking process. This confines the scientific thinking process to being merely cognitive. In the Second Road, the opposite is the case: we humans become the 'causes' that create 'effects.' We must become 'agents' if we want to change things. This repositions strategy as an act of the will, not just of cognition. Strategy crystallizes the corporate will. This fundamentally changes how we view strategy: it is as much a matter of the will as the intellect.

However, most people don't feel like agents, and the modern organization does not help that feeling with its emphasis on compliance, hierarchy and command/control relationships. If we want to get people to design their futures, our first task is to emphasize their 'agency.' They must feel that the world is not an accident, nor is it 'determinate': it is putty in their hands and they are its authors.

There are two stances we can take into life, as indicated in **Figure One**. We can see ourselves as 'readers' in which case we believe that someone else 'writes' the text of life and our job is to read it. Ironically, the more educated we become, the more we feel like readers, since most education is framed in the analytic paradigm and literally enforces a disposition of 'readers' on the students. The alternative disposition sees us as 'authors': life is a canvas and our job is to write the story, not read it.

I ran a workshop recently for the leaders of a major newspaper organization with a great past but an uncertain future in the online world. They had pages of analysis before them, and most of it was depressing. We began the workshop by asking, "Do you believe that this organization has a credible future? Is it worth the effort of creating a strategy or do you feel that long term decline is really inevitable?" The question surprised them and evoked a spirited and open discussion for two hours. When we finished they agreed that there was a hopeful future, and it lay in nobody's hands but their own. They had moved from being 'readers' to 'authors.'

2. Possibility (Invention)

The second element of a compelling argument is 'possibility.' True design is the art of invention, not analysis. You cannot analyze your way to invention. So how do we do it? Whereas analysis is a process that works like a formula, invention is an art that works like a forge. We must melt down fixed ideas and views, allow them to swirl around and then shape them into new combinations. The process is one of immersion and emergence, not analysis. Sound strange to you? Watch a painter paint a landscape or a poet exploring ideas and you will see it happen in practice. This is design thinking at work. It does not work like a spreadsheet.

In my work I try to stimulate this kind of thinking by shifting the dynamic of the strategy process from documentation to conversation. Most strategic processes rely far too heavily on documentation; but documents were not made to generate ideas, they were made to codify and communicate them. Furthermore, documents are primarily an individualistic tool, not a social one. People write documents alone and they read them alone. Conversation is different: it is a melting pot of ideas – a living, organic process. It is a perfect way to generate possibilities and create arguments.

My team and I have mapped the conversation process in an image we call the 'Design Wave™' (see **Figure Two**). Arguments are developed by advancing topics across this wave. Things start out foggy, but then crystallize as we transform confusion into arguments that can mobilize action. But conversations need some structure, or they will unravel and achieve nothing. We do this by using the *writing process* (rather than documents) to structure the dialogue. Good writers explore ideas by sketching them with maps and models. We create virtual design studios where groups start with a blank sheet and 'write' their strategy by a process of dialogue. We shape and guide the energy that the conversation creates by mapping and modeling in real time on an electronic

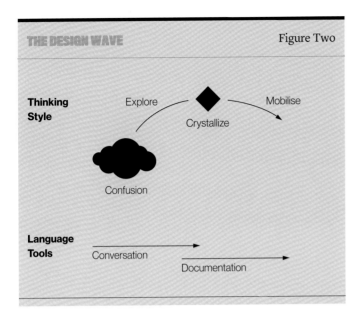

Thinking Style

Explore   Crystallize   Mobilise

Confusion

Language Tools

Conversation

Documentation

---

whiteboard. This effectively transforms the group into designers who are using heavily right-brain tools of visualization, modeling and prototyping ideas.

If I could turn on a video camera and show you one strategic conversation that we facilitated recently for instance, you could have watched Australia's aboriginal leaders design a way forward for our indigenous community that aims to rewrite 200 years of sorry history. You would have seen the swirl of dialogue melt down fixed positions and transform them into new possibilities. Immersion and emergence happened before our eyes. The Second Road is not just theory for us; it is an art of action. And rhetoric was not a theory for Cicero and his friends. It was an art of action and design.

3. Persuasion (Community of Action)

The third element of an argument is 'persuasion.' In the scientific road, persuasion is not the goal – proof is. In the Second Road, persuasion is the goal because the aim of the argument is to mobilize people to create a new future. This has two significant consequences for strategy as design. Firstly the criteria of a good strategy changes; we cannot look for the 'right' strategy, we must instead look for the 'compelling' strategy. Good arguments compel belief. The second consequence is that an effective strategy process will not just produce a 'plan', it will produce a community of action: that is our real goal. Nothing is stronger than a persuaded community: they will create alternative worlds.

A New Theory of Language

Underpinning this whole Second Road of rhetoric/design lies a fundamental new belief about the nature of language. In the analytic paradigm, language is descriptive. It is a tool to put labels on the world. Its role is passive: it merely enables communication. Little wonder that the analytic world has now passed the baton of power to Mathematics as the underpinning tool of trade.

The rhetoric road operates from a fundamentally different and emerging belief that language creates new realities, it does not just describe them. If I name a situation as 'hopeless', that will create hopelessness; if I name a situation as 'promising', that will create promise. In this view, language is an agent of design.

Design begins with language that creates proxies for alternative futures long before they exist in material form. Viewed that way, language is the raw material we use to create our current and future realities. The Second Road builds arguments or designs out of the playground of language; the first road of analytics has narrowed the whole playground to the skimpy perimeter of empirical reasoning and spreadsheets.

In closing

My work always takes me to groups facing uncertain, often troubled, prospects. They have a choice: 'keep operating as normal and let the future happen to us' or 'design our world.' In every case, a tool kit comprised only of analytic tools would have been at least inadequate, or at worst, counterproductive.

Design offers organizations a new paradigm of thought and a whole set of practices that can revolutionize how we 'do' strategy, and more ambitiously, how we build great organizations. The tool kit outlined herein does not stop there in its implications: it is relevant to the worlds of education, social design and human enterprise everywhere. *R*

Tony Golsby-Smith is the founder and CEO of Second Road Pty Ltd. He has worked with the Australian Tax Office to introduce design thinking into the tax system – the first major attempt in the world to design a national system actively using design methodologies.

A longer version of this article appeared in the *Journal of Business Strategy*'s special issue on design and business, published in May 2009.

Design Thinking:
On its Nature
and Use

While it is less understood than scientific thinking, design thinking has characteristics of great value to teams dealing with complex, ill-formed problems.

by **Charles Owen**

THE HANDIWORK OF HUMANKIND has finally begun to impress itself on the global environment and on us, its inhabitants. It is news to no one that current rates of resource consumption cannot keep up with population growth as it exists. By 2050, world population is virtually certain to increase by half again from its present seven billion – with all that means for our dwindling resources. Coupled with that, it is now clear that global warming is fact, and its growing control over Earth's climate and weather systems will unpredictably complicate problems already made serious by population pressures.

While the road ahead seems dark, there is hope: a profusion of new technologies is emerging, many with the potential to alleviate the problems induced by population growth. Key to the use or misuse of these technologies are the decision processes employed by those in power. History has shown that political decisions do not always favour the best interests of all, and when critical factors include information not easily understood by decision makers, that information may be disregarded or not even considered. The stakes are now too high for critical information to be unheard or ignored.

Science advisors have long been included among high-level governmental advisory staffs. How their advice is valued, however, has varied with the problem context, and political interests have almost always trumped scientific advice. More than ever before, scientific advice requires serious consideration.

But another kind of thinking deserves equal attention: design thinking is in many ways the obverse of scientific thinking. Whereas the scientist sifts facts to discover patterns and insights, the designer invents new patterns and concepts to address facts and possibilities. In a world with growing problems that desperately need understanding and insight, there is a great need for ideas that can blend that understanding and insight in creative new solutions.

Finders, Makers and Applied Creativity

A sensitive observer might notice an interesting thing about creative people: they tend to work in two different ways. Those who work in the first way might best be called 'finders.' They exercise their creativity through discovery and are driven to find explanations for phenomena not well understood. In professional life, they usually become scientists or scholars and are responsible for much of our progress in understanding ourselves and our surroundings.

Those who work in the second way are 'makers,' and they are equally creative, but in a different way. They demonstrate their creativity through invention. Makers are driven to synthesize what they know in new constructions, arrangements, patterns, compositions and concepts that bring tangible, fresh expressions of what can be. They become architects, engineers, artists – designers – and are responsible for the built environment in which we live and work.

Given the fundamental process differences between how finders and makers think and work, it is reasonable to believe that other factors might similarly reveal differences among professional fields and, therefore, help to define the nature of design thinking.

One such factor is the content with which a field works. A conceptual map can be drawn to address both content and process factors (see **Figure Two**). Two axes define the map: separating it into left and right halves is an Analytic/Synthetic axis that classifies fields by process – the way they work. Fields on the left side of the axis are more concerned with 'finding' or discovering; fields on the right with 'making' and inventing. A Symbolic/Real axis divides the map into halves vertically, according to content or realm of activity. Fields in the upper half of the map are more concerned with the abstract, symbolic world and the institutions, policies and language tools that enable people to manipulate information, communicate and live together. Fields in the lower half are concerned with the real world and the artifacts and systems necessary for managing the physical environment.

A sampling of fields illustrates how the map differentiates between fields (see **Figure Three**). The five chosen are highly recognizable with well-defined disciplines and well-understood differences. Every field has component elements in each of the four quadrants. What distinguishes one field from another is the degree to which a field positions its 'centre of gravity' away from the centre

into the quadrants, and the direction that positioning takes. In Figure 3, fields close to the centre are more 'generalized' with respect to the axes; fields away from the centre are more 'specialized.'

As a field that is heavily analytic in its use of process, Science is farthest to the left. Its content is also more symbolic than real in that subject matter is usually abstracted in its analyses. There are elements of Science, however, that are synthetic in process (as, for example, in Materials Science or Organic Chemistry), and it can deal directly with unabstracted, real content, particularly in the Natural Sciences.

Law, as a generalized field, is located higher on the map, concerned extensively with the symbolic content of institutions, policies and social relationships. It is also positioned more to the right, as a significant portion of its disciplines are concerned with the creation of laws and the instruments of social contract. Medicine, in contrast, is sharply lower on the content axis, vitally concerned with the real problems of human health. On the process scale, it is strongly analytic; diagnostic processes are a primary focus of medicine. Art is high on the content axis, strongly symbolic, and almost evenly divided on the process scale, still more synthetic than analytic, but very much involved with interpretation of the human condition.

Design in this mapping is highly synthetic and strongly concerned with real world subject matter. Because disciplines of design deal with communications and symbolism, it has a symbolic component, and because it requires analysis to perform synthesis, there is an analytic component – but Design is a field relatively specialized, and specialized nearly oppositely to Science.

Fields, of course, are just the tops of hierarchies, and the hierarchical nature of their subject matter opens a door to the examination of relationships among elements at finer levels of detail. For almost any field, a case can be made for movement to the left or right based on the variety of detailed interests the field subsumes, but absolute positioning is not what is important in this kind of mapping: relative positioning is. It provides a means for comparing multi-field relationships with regard to the two important dimensions of content and process.

Values and Measures

Science is driven by the need for understanding. To achieve this goal, it values correctness, in the sense that theories can be evaluated for whether they are correct, as best can be determined with current data. It also values thoroughness because understanding must be thorough to remove uncertainty. Testability is valued because closure demands that theories be tested and determined to be correct or incorrect. These values (and others) find expression in measures that expand the essence of the value into tools that can be incorporated directly or indirectly in frame-of good citizenship. Measures such as just/unjust, right/wrong, complete/incomplete, appropriate/inappropriate and fair/unfair draw out the evaluations appropriate to the field (see **Figure Four**).

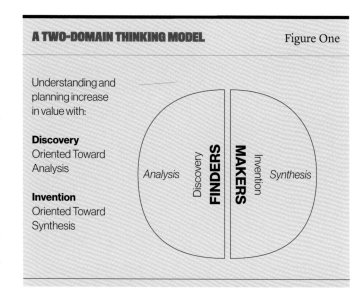

A TWO-DOMAIN THINKING MODEL — Figure One

Understanding and planning increase in value with:

Discovery
Oriented Toward Analysis

Invention
Oriented Toward Synthesis

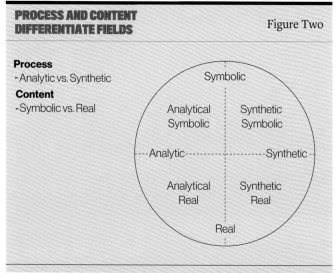

PROCESS AND CONTENT DIFFERENTIATE FIELDS — Figure Two

Process
▸ Analytic vs. Synthetic

Content
▸ Symbolic vs. Real

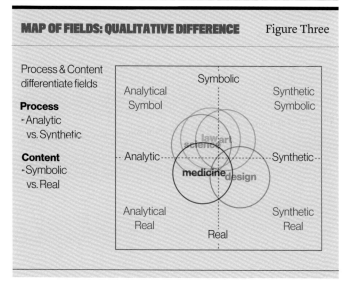

MAP OF FIELDS: QUALITATIVE DIFFERENCE — Figure Three

Process & Content differentiate fields

Process
▸ Analytic vs. Synthetic

Content
▸ Symbolic vs. Real

Figure Four

Field	Need/Goal		Values	Measures
science	understanding		correctness thoroughness testability	true/false correct/incorrect complete/incomplete
art	expression		insightfulness novelty stimulation	provable/unprovable thought-provoking/banal fresh/stale
law	justice		thoroughness appropriateness fairness	exciting/boring just/unjust right/wrong
medicine	**health**		effectiveness correctness	appropriate/inappropriate fair/unfair
design	form		cultural fit appropriateness effectiveness	works/doesn't work fits/doesn't fit elegant/inelegant better/worse sustainable/unsustainable

Art, quite different in this kind of analysis, derives from the need for expression. Values such as insightfulness, novelty and stimulation highlight important aspects of expression as it is regarded today, and measures such as thought provoking/banal, fresh/stale and exciting/boring particularize these for the criteria to be used in the production and criticism of art.

Medicine shares much with Science, but has its own need for being in maintaining, promoting and regenerating health. Among its values, correctness is critical for diagnoses and procedures, and effectiveness, a value strongly shared with design, is relevant when something is better than nothing. Measures include correct/incorrect, works/doesn't work and better/worse.

Design exists because of the need for form. The form giver, in the broadest use of the term, creates order. Because the world of design is the world of the artificial, the values of design tend to be ones associated with human needs and environmental needs created by human actions. Cultural fit is associated with aesthetic issues; appropriateness targets the wide range of physiological, cognitive, social and cultural human factors; and effectiveness gauges functionality and utility. For cultural fit, good measures are fresh/stale, fits/doesn't fit and elegant/inelegant; for appropriateness, appropriate/inappropriate and works/doesn't work (from the human factors perspective) are helpful. From a utility perspective, works/doesn't work, sustainable/unsustainable and better/worse measure effectiveness.

Seen through the lens of their underlying values, differences among fields become clearer and more understandable. As a case in point, a major difference between Science and Design lies in the difference between 'correctness' and 'effectiveness' as important measures of success. Correct/incorrect (or true/false) is appropriate for a field in which there can only be one 'true' answer or correct explanation for an observed phenomenon. Better/worse is appropriate for a field in which multiple solutions can be equally successful because the conditions for judgment are culturally based.

From all this, it is easier to see why a combination of Science and Design thinking is better than either alone. While both are valuable, together they bring the best of skeptical inquiry into balance with imaginative application. Because both are well served by creative thinking, we will now look at the general characteristics of the creative thinker.

Characteristics of Creative Thinking

Despite considerable speculation, the nature of creativity – what makes one person creative and another not – and the creative pro-cess itself remain elusive. Nevertheless, a number of characteristics have been identified that can be useful in contemplating the nature of creative thinking and, in particular, creative design thinking.

In a special issue of *Kaiser Aluminum News* some years ago, editor **Don Fabun** assembled characteristics of the creative individual culled from the observations of a number of thoughtful writers. While they are not all-inclusive, they provide a good start for assembling a catalogue:

Sensitivity: a propensity for greater awareness which makes a person more readily attuned to the subtleties of various sensations and impressions.

Questioning attitude: an inquisitiveness, probably imprinted in early home training that encourages seeking new and original answers.

Broad education: an approach to learning instilled from a liberal education that puts a premium on questions rather than answers and rewards curiosity rather than rote learning and conformity.

Asymmetrical thinking: the ability to find an original kind of order in disorder as opposed to symmetrical thinking that balances everything out in some logical way.

Personal courage: a disregard for failure derived from a concern, not for what others think, but what one thinks of oneself.

Sustained curiosity: a capacity for childlike wonder carried into adult life that generates a style of endless questioning, even of the most personally cherished ideas.

Time control: instead of being bound by time and schedules, creative individuals use time as a resource – morning, noon and night – years, decades – whatever it takes, unbound by the clock.

Dedication: the unswerving desire to do something, whatever it may be and whatever the obstacles to doing it.

Willingness to work: the willingness to continue to pursue a project endlessly, in working hours and so-called free hours, over whatever time might be required.

In 1976, psychiatrist **Silvano Arieti** thoroughly reviewed what was then known about creativity. From his study, several additional characteristics can be included:

Fluency of thinking: word fluency – the ability to produce words containing specified letters or combinations of letters; associational fluency – the ability to produce synonyms for given words; expressional fluency – the ability to juxtapose words to meet the requirements of sentence structure; and ideational fluency – the ability to produce ideas to fulfill certain requirements.

Flexibility: the ability to abandon old ways of thinking and initiate different directions.

Originality: the ability to produce uncommon responses and unconventional associations.

Redefinition: the ability to reorganize what we know or see in new ways.

Elaboration: the capacity to use two or more abilities for the construction of a more complex object.

Tolerance for ambiguity: the capacity to entertain conflicting concepts for periods of time without the need to resolve uncertainties.

Mihaly Csikszentmihalyi, a renowned psychologist and anthropologist at the University of Chicago, sees the creative individual in terms of 'pairs of apparently antithetical traits that are often both present in such individuals and integrated with each other in a dialectical tension':

Convergent *and* divergent thinking: divergent thinking to generate ideas; convergent thinking to tell a good one from a bad one.

Playfulness *and* discipline: exploring ideas widely and lightly, but surmounting obstacles and bringing ideas to completion with doggedness, endurance and perseverance.

Fantasy *and* reality: breaking away from the present without losing touch with the past.

Extroversion *and* introversion: seeing and hearing people, exchanging ideas, and getting to know other peoples' work to extend interaction; working alone to fully explore and master abstract concepts.

Humility *and* pride: humility in the awareness of those who worked before, the element of luck involved with achievement, and the relative unimportance of past achievements in comparison with a focus on future projects; pride in the self-assurance associated with accomplishment.

Masculinity *and* femininity: 'psychological androgyny' enabling the best traits of bold, assertive masculinity to be combined with the best traits of sensitive, aware femininity.

Conservatism *and* rebellious iconoclasm: being able to understand and appreciate a cultural domain and its rules, while at the same time being willing to take risks to break with its traditions.

Passion *and* objectivity: passion in the attachment and dedication to the cause or work; objectivity in the ability to stand apart, detached, to evaluate quality impartially.

Suffering *and* enjoyment: the heightened highs and lows that come with intense involvement and sensitivity, both to observed quality and to what others think.

Csikszentmihalyi notes that these conflicting traits are difficult to find in the same person, but "the novelty that survives to change a domain is usually the work of someone who can operate at both ends of these polarities – and that is the kind of person we call creative."

Many of the above characteristics are not qualities to be taught: at best, they are natural personality traits that can be recognized where they exist or noted in their absence; but many can be developed or encouraged.

Characteristics of Design Thinking

Creativity is of major importance to design thinking, as it is to science thinking and thinking in any field. But as is true for each field, characteristics other than creativity are also important. I would nominate the following as key aspects of design thinking:

1. Conditioned inventiveness: creative thinking for designers is directed toward inventing. Designers tend to be more interested in the 'what' questions than the 'whys' of interest to the scientist. Design creativity thus complements scientific creativity, but it brings to invention a concern that what is produced not only be inventive, but be so within the frame-

> It is easy to see why a combination of science thinking and design thinking is better than either alone: together they bring the best of skeptical inquiry into balance with imaginative application.

works of human-centred and environment-centred measures governing the designer's efforts.

2. Human-centred focus: Science and, to a slightly lesser extent, Technology have few built-in governors. That is to say, as in the Arts, exploration proceeds where discoveries direct. Design, on the other hand, is client-directed. Design thinking must continually consider how what is being created will respond to clients' needs.

3. Environment-centred concern: in recent years, design thinking has acquired a second, omnipresent client: the environment. Present-day thinking puts environmental interests at a level with human interests as primary constraints on the design process. Sustainable design is one very noticeable result. The ultimate value of human-and environment-centredness is a guarantee that the best interests of humankind and environment will be considered in any project.

4. Bias for adaptivity: in recent years, the emergence of adaptive processes in manufacturing and information technologies has greatly reinforced a practice historically followed by some designers: the design of adaptive products able to fit their users' needs uniquely. Design thinking today has accepted that concept, approaching problems with the view that, where possible, solutions should be adaptive – in production, to fit the needs of users uniquely; and throughout their use, to fit users' evolving needs.

5. Predisposition toward multifunctionality: solutions to problems need not be 'monofunctional.' Designers routinely look for multiple dividends from solutions to problems, keeping the big picture in mind while focusing on specifics.

6. Systemic Vision: design thinking is holistic, treating problems as system problems with opportunities for systemic solutions involving mixes of hardware, software, procedures, policies, organizational concepts and whatever else is necessary to create a holistic solution.

7. View of the Generalist: common wisdom holds that success will come more readily to those who choose to specialize early and plan their training accordingly. Design thinking, to the contrary, is highly generalist in preparation and execution. In a world of specialists, there is a real need for those who can reach across disciplines to communicate and bring diverse experts together in a coordinated effort. For inventive creativity, the wider the reach of the knowledge base, the more likely the creative inspiration.

8. Ability to use language as a tool: language is usually thought of as means for communication, but for designers it is also a tool. Visual language is used diagrammatically to abstract concepts, reveal and explain patterns, and simplify complex phenomena to their fundamental essences. Mathematical language is used to explore 'what if' questions where feasibility may be established by approximation – by calculations not exact, but close enough to support an idea. Verbal language is used in description where explanation goes hand in hand with the creative process, forcing invention where detail is lacking and expressing relationships that are not obvious visually.

9. Facility for avoiding the necessity of choice: the job of the decision maker is to choose among alternative proposals – usually the products of different problem-solving approaches. Design thinking takes the view that making that choice is a last resort: before moving to choice-making, the designer looks for ways to 'have your cake and eat it too.' The optimistic designer, however, searches the competing alternatives for their essential characteristics and finds ways to reformulate them into a new configuration. When this process is successful, the result is a solution that combines the best of both possible choices.

10. Self-governing practicality: in very few fields is there the freedom to dream that is expected in design. The best design thinkers understand this and learn to govern 'flights of fantasy' with a latent sense of the practical: the flight is to the outer reaches of what can be conceived; the tether is to ways that the conceivable might be realized. This is embedded in a style of thinking that explores freely in the foreground, while maintaining in the background a realistic appraisal of costs that can be met and functionality that can be effected.

In closing

Together, the characteristics of design and science thinking form a set of complementary thought processes able to add considerable strength to the advisory task. The ability to provide design thinking in an advisory capacity will require an evolution in design education and design research. For design education, new programs must be designed that bring the best of design thinking into the new context of policy planning. New content will be necessary; new processes must be developed and taught; and new ways of working will have to be learned.

It will be worth doing. **R**

Charles Owen is a distinguished professor emeritus at the Illinois Institute of Technology's Institute of Design, where he has taught design thinking since 1965.

A longer version of this article appeared in the January 2007 edition of *Design Research Quarterly*, published by the Design Research Society.

Building
Shared Understanding
of Wicked Problems

Interview by **Karen Christensen**

CogNexus Institute founder Jeff Conklin explains why the Age of Design requires a new approach to problem solving that is built on a foundation of shared understanding.

You believe that we are in the midst of a shift from the Age of Science to the Age of Design. Please explain.

In the Age of Science, the job of Science was to describe the universe. Once we had created a good description of the natural world, we could begin to exercise control, and the path was opened for technology – the art of harnessing, controlling and transforming our world. In the last century, organizations have borrowed heavily from the ethos of Science and technology: the goals of 'management science' were to describe (or predict) the future and control it. In the Age of Science, facts legitimized decisions – indeed, they were the only acceptable basis for decisions and actions. The goal of problem solving was to find the right answer, and the problems to which organizations devoted themselves were generally 'tame' ones: they may have been complicated and involved hundreds of people and years of effort, but the problems themselves were not wicked. The problem definition was well understood (i.e., 'build a bridge across the widest river in the world'), the stakeholders were few, the constraints stable, and in the end, there was a concrete result that solved the problem. In this fading epoch, organizations rewarded individuals for predicting and controlling their environment; people worked separately, using a linear process, to gather all the facts so that they might formulate the right answer and deliver it for implementation.

Those days are gone. In the emerging paradigm, the Age of Design, something new is happening, and those who excelled in the former paradigm are no longer succeeding as they once did. In place of prediction and control, we seem to have nothing but chaos; in place of individual efforts, the problem-solving process is now clearly social; in place of basing decisions on facts, we base them on stories that give us a more coherent sense of meaning. In place of finding the 'right answer', we seek to gain a shared understanding of possible solutions. The skills and knowledge that were so important in the Age of Science are still important, but they are no longer sufficient. The focus of our activities has shifted to creation.

Whereas description is about *what is*, creation is about *what might be*. It is an organization's ability to learn and innovate that now provides the greatest competitive advantage. Employees are being asked to throw off the shackles of past ways of thinking and doing, to think for themselves and invent new ways to increase customer satisfaction or decrease costs. In the Age of Design, getting something done depends on your social skills and your network, both formal and informal. Unfortunately, we are babes in the woods in the Age of Design, and the nature of our tool set is quite primitive.

Discuss the relation between 'problem understanding' and 'solution formulation'.
When I first started out, the implicit assumption was that problems were stable and well defined, and most of the work in any major project involved coming up with the solution. The process of working out a solution was understood to be fundamentally linear – a sequence of steps which, if followed, would result in a successful outcome. Today, there is increasing awareness that a shared understanding of a given problem cannot be taken for granted, and that the absence of buy-in about a problem's definition, scope and goals can kill a project just as surely as faulty implementation.

Organizations are beginning to embrace the idea that these two aspects of projects – problem understanding and solution formulation – are not distinct phases, but rather different kinds of conversations that must be woven together from beginning to end. Problem structuring is a critical aspect of the design process that takes into account the diversity of goals, assumptions and meanings among stakeholders. At the heart of this new understanding of organizational life is the recognition that project work is fundamentally social, and that communication among stakeholders must be managed and nurtured in order for the social network to cohere into a functioning entity. What is missing from our 'social network tool kit' is an environment or 'container' in which stakeholders can collectively step back to see the big picture.

You believe that the two most intense forces impacting organizations today are wicked problems and social complexity. Please explain.
When design theorist **Horst Rittel** first started writing about wicked problems, he characterized them as having 10 or 11 properties, which I think can be pared down to six essential ones (see **Figure One**). But in our post-modern world, things have become even more complex, and problems now take shape within a social framework that agrees that something is a problem. For a long time, there's been a model – a pre-understanding – that what organizations needed to do was 'identify the problem' and then systematically work to develop a solution and appropriate implementation. What Rittel said is, it's just not that easy. Problem understanding is actually the more important and evasive part of the process.

The social complexity aspect of it is that you have different stakeholders with strongly-held beliefs about what the problem is. Dealing with wicked problems is not at all a matter of coming up with the best answer; rather, it's about engaging stakeholders in a robust and healthy process of making sense of the problem's dimensions. The current situation with respect to global warming and energy policy is a great example: people from the developed world have one set of views about what needs to be done, and the developing world has a completely different set of views. Nobody 'owns' the problem, nor has a clear idea of how to work out the answers. Because of social complexity, solving such a wicked problem is fundamentally a social process. This same kind of dynamic exists in a microcosm in most organizations around their critical strategic problems. As a first step, the distinction that the problem you are facing is wicked can help you get a handle on the fact that it will require a different style of leadership and a different approach.

You have said that "when you combine wicked problems and social complexity, you get fragmentation." Please explain.
Fragmentation is a condition in which the stakeholders in a situation see themselves as more separate than united. The fragmented pieces are, in essence, the perspectives, understandings and intentions of the collaborators, all of whom are convinced that their version of the problem is correct. It is clear today that the forces of fragmentation are increasing, challenging our ability to create coherence, and causing more and more projects to flounder and fail. The antidote to fragmentation is shared understanding and shared commitment.

How do you define 'shared understanding'?
The 'Holy Grail' of effective collaboration is creating shared understanding, which is a precursor to shared commitment. If you accept that the crux of effective action is agreeing on what the problem is, then the challenge for organizations is coming to a shared understanding about what their particular dilemma is. Plenty has been written about how to get people 'on board' and create buy-in for a strategy; but the business of how to craft shared understanding – a deep and robust understanding of the circumstances – hasn't been well understood. Shared understanding means that the stakeholders understand each other's positions well enough to have intelligent dialogue about their different interpretations of the problem, and to exercise collective intelligence about how to solve it.

The best way to grasp shared understanding is to consider what happens when it is missing. If you think about where teams or projects have failed, you often realize that what was missing was a shared understanding about what the process was going to be, or what the fundamental problem was to begin with, or the dimensions of the problem. There may have been a lack of shared understanding about roles and responsibilities, or there might have been a specific issue around which there was a lack of understanding. There are many aspects to shared understanding, and there is no shortcut to creating it. Any way you slice it, it entails heavy lifting, and you have to roll up your sleeves and have the hard conversations in order to expose where shared understanding is missing.

Design theorist Horst Rittel defined wicked problems as having six characteristics:

1. You don't understand the problem until you have developed a solution.
Every solution that is offered exposes new aspects of the problem, requiring further adjustments to the potential solutions. There is no definitive statement of 'the problem': these problems are ill-structured and feature an evolving set of interlocking issues and constraints.

2. There is no stopping rule.
Since there is no definitive 'the problem', there is also no definitive 'the solution.' The problem-solving process ends when you run out of resources such as time, money or energy, not when an optimal solution emerges.

3. Solutions are not right or wrong.
They are simply 'better/worse' or 'good enough/not good enough'. The determination of solution quality is not objective and cannot be derived from following a formula.

4. Each is essentially unique and novel.
No two wicked problems are alike, and the solutions to them will always be custom designed and fitted. Over time we can acquire wisdom and experience about the approach to wicked problems, but one is always a beginner in the specifics of a new wicked problem.

5. Every solution is a 'one-shot operation'.
Every attempt has consequences. This is the 'Catch 22' of wicked problems: you can't learn about the problem without trying solutions, but every solution is expensive and has lasting consequences that may spawn new wicked problems.

6. There is no given alternative solution.
A host of potential solutions may be devised, but another host are never even thought of. Thus it is a matter of creativity to devise potential solutions, and a matter of judgement to determine which should be pursued and implemented.

You believe that most of today's problems have a significant 'wicked' component, even if it doesn't appear at the outset. Please explain.

One criticism of the notion of wicked problems is that you can't do a diagnostic that identifies a problem as 'definitely wicked'. There are degrees of wickedness. What is clear is that the notion of business-as-usual that we inherited from the industrial era is a manufacturing-based, linear process-oriented approach, and if you are locked into that view, you will miss out on all the deeper problems. That's what a lot of the attention to innovation is really about: it's about being able to get outside of the limited framework of business-as-usual and sense and reflect on the bigger situation. Any time you do that in today's environment, you're looking at a wicked problem, because you're confronting fundamental problems of identity: who is our company? What is our direction? What is our market? Who is our customer? These fundamental issues are always present, but it's very easy to avoid them by focusing on immediate problems that are more tractable.

Two common organizational coping mechanisms are routinely applied to wicked problems: *studying* the problem and *taming* it. Please discuss.

While studying a novel and complex problem is natural and important, it is an approach that will run out of gas quickly if the problem is wicked. Pure study amounts to procrastination, because little can be learned about a wicked problem by objective data gathering and analysis. Wicked problems demand an opportunity-driven approach: they require making decisions, doing experiments, launching pilot programs, testing prototypes, and so on. One corporation I worked with, struggling to decide between two very different strategic paths for the future,

studied and discussed the two options for so long that, by the time they implemented their choice, the chosen option was no longer viable.

Taming a wicked problem is a very natural and common way of coping with it. Instead of dealing with the full wickedness of the problem, people simplify it in various ways to make it more manageable and solvable. While it may seem appealing in the short run, attempting to tame a wicked problem will always fail in the long run. The problem will simply reassert itself, perhaps in a different guise, as if nothing had been done; or worse, the tame solution will exacerbate the problem.

What first steps can people take to better handle wicked problems?

There is no quick fix. Our education and experience have prepared us to see and solve tame problems, which is why wicked problems sneak up on us and create so much chaos. In times of stress, the natural human tendency is to find fault with others. If we step back and take a systemic view, we can see that the issue is not whose fault the mess is – the issue is our collective failure to recognize the recurring and inevitable dynamics of the mess. **R**

Dr. **Jeff Conklin** is director of CogNexus Institute, based in Napa, California, and the author of *Dialogue Mapping: Creating Shared Understanding of Wicked Problems* (Wiley and Sons, 2006). He has worked on shared understanding with the World Bank, the United Nations, NASA, AOL, Verizon, BP and others. For more, visit cognexus.org.

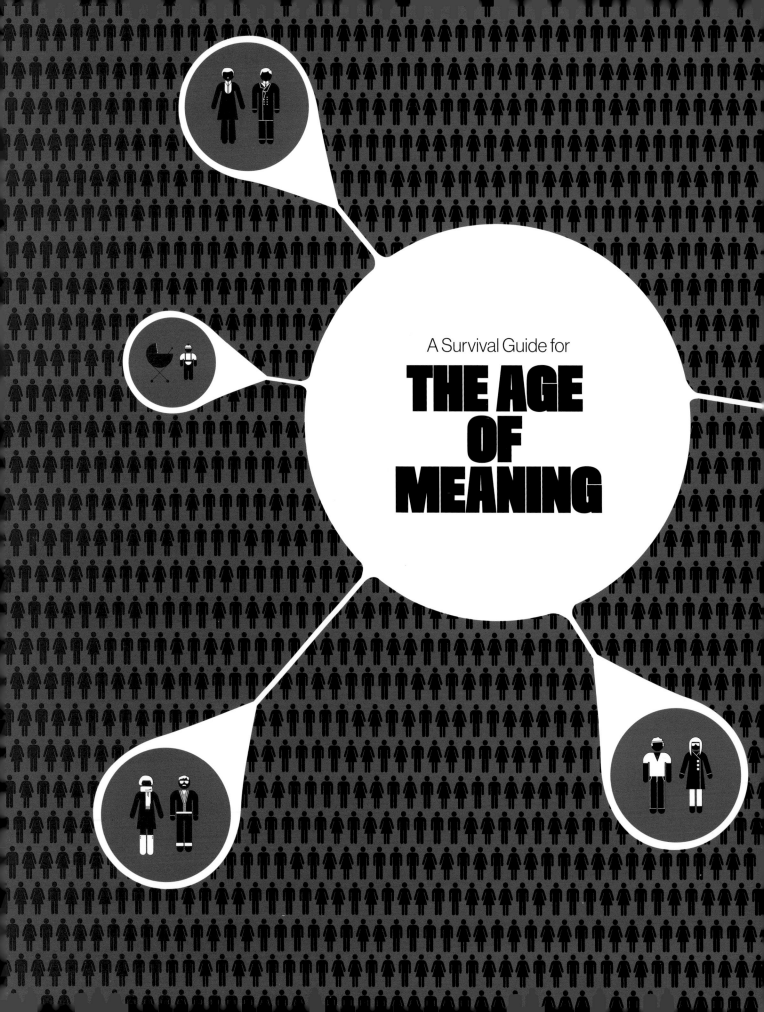

A Survival Guide for

THE AGE OF MEANING

It's time for companies to push the 'pause' button, dig deep, and commit to the 'tribe' of consumers that is the best match for what they have to offer.

by **Sohrab Vossoughi**

RECENT ECONOMIC TURMOIL HAS FORCED COMPANIES around the globe to re-evaluate their core business strategies. In order to move forward and thrive – indeed, to survive – organizations have to carefully consider how to remain relevant going forward.

The power shift from companies to consumers in recent years has been undeniable. Globalization and the Internet have killed our affair with the mass economy – with mass production, mass markets and mass marketing. The consumer-driven world of segmented media and markets that has emerged calls for new terms of engagement.

It seems like just yesterday that a successful, sustainable business was a one-size-fits-all, mega-hit brand that could be efficiently replicated around the world. Think **Starbucks**: Wall Street sang its praises and shares rose from $11.06 in 2000 to $35.42 in 2006. But somewhere between the original handful of stores in 1982 and the over 15,000 in 43 countries today, the company's strategy went from grass-roots to gimmicky.

Like so many other companies, Starbucks suffered from 'efficiency-syndrome', which occurs when a mass-produced brand attempts to be everything to everybody and in the process, dilutes its offering, its appeal and thus its value. In 2008, Starbucks shares fell to $13.58 in July and then $7.17 after September's stock market turbulence.

Gone are the days when the master brand was king and companies were customer-focused only to the extent that customers generated sales. More than ever before, today's savvy, choice-fatigued and cash-strapped consumers crave meaningful connections with brands that allow them to be more-authentically themselves.

Brands are now defined by consumers, not 'positioned' by companies. My colleagues and I have dubbed this new era 'The Age of Meaning', and it is imperative for business people to understand the new rules of engagement that come along with it.

In the Age of Meaning, a strong brand creates
value and competitive advantage only when
it delivers a compelling, holistic experience that
is authentic, unique and relevant.

Where We've Been

Curious about how we arrived at this point in business history, my colleagues created an 'authenticity timeline' to illustrate the evolution of the marketplace, business values and consumers' deepening desire for authentic engagement.

The timeline begins with what we call the *Age of Representation*, when advancements in manufacturing technology allowed people to create near-identical products. The invention of the steam engine in the late 1700s launched the Industrial Revolution and marked the beginning of the era of mass production. This era included **Ford**'s Model T and America's first planned community. Modern production methods made the American dream of owning a single-family home affordable to millions, and business was finally able to accommodate the basic needs of the masses with relative ease.

Next came the *Age of Simulation* from the mid-1950s to the 1980s, when manufacturing excellence and know-how helped industry evolve from meeting people's needs to satisfying their desires. This was the realm of fantasy, of making 'dreams come true'. The opening of **Disneyland** in 1955 marked the start of this epoch, followed by the rise of adult playgrounds like Las Vegas. The era of the 'knock-off' had arrived, and China, Japan and Taiwan became hotbeds of low-price, high-volume manufacturing. This is the era that valued mass efficiency – 'make as many products for as many people for as little as possible'. Market share, efficiency and quality were its measures of success.

The late 1980s and early 1990s marked a quantum shift in global marketplace dynamics as companies undertook re-engineering efforts to make themselves more efficient in order to compete globally. The first Web site went online, initiating the 'flattening' of the world and empowering consumers with choices and the ability to expose insincere brands and institutions. The turn of the century brought a U.S. recession, the Internet boom and bust, myriad corporate scandals and 9/11's terrorism, leaving people searching for meaning. The Web answered the call with sites like **epinions** and **YouTube** and in 2006, *TIME* voted 'YOU' the Person of the Year. Consumers were now empowered to satisfy their every whim with goods from around the world, and then blog about their experiences online.

In the last ten years, we have entered the *Age of Meaning*, where abundance and transparency have created a demand for authenticity. Consumers now seek brands they can trust, and they won't – because they don't have to – accept anything less. The efficiency-minded, technology-driven mass economy has been replaced by an Experience Economy controlled by consumers. Core technologies and skills have become commoditized, and time-to-market has shrunk from two years to six months or less.

In the Age of Meaning, a strong brand creates value and competitive advantage only when it delivers a compelling, holistic experience that is authentic, unique and relevant. Recent behaviour on Wall Street has only deepened this trend and amplified the desire for authenticity and meaning on Main Street. Consumers will only put their limited budgets behind brands whose values and products are aligned with their own altruistic goals.

A Shift in Values

In December 2008, *Brandweek* reported on a study by **MS&L Worldwide**, conducted in partnership with **GfK Roper** that examined some of the corporate values today's consumers find most important and the effects of such perceptions on maintaining long-term business. One of their most striking findings was that "while price and quality may be the primary purchase influencers in tough times, in the long run, it is *values* that matter the most." Seventy-seven per cent of consumers in the U.S. said they either strongly agreed or somewhat agreed with that statement.

Starbucks exemplifies a company stalled at the crossroads of the Age of Simulation – when efficiency reigned – and the Age of Meaning, where effectiveness reigns. Having set out to design a 'third space' for its customers, Starbucks went on to repeat that experience around the world. By its own admission, it soon lost sight of who it was and what its customers wanted. Automated espresso machines made coffee-making more efficient, but at the cost of handcrafted beverages served with the care and engagement of the barista. Couches were replaced by coffee tables and chairs, dismantling the 'third place' feeling in favour of a fast-food feel. Merchandising ran amok and food, music and book clubs diluted the 'Starbucks story' until the experience felt like little more than a kit-of-parts that could be put together by anyone, anywhere. Word spread like wildfire on the Internet, helping to prompt Starbucks' fall from grace.

What the Age of Meaning requires is a distinct priority shift from *efficiency* to *effectiveness*. Customer equity, rather than market share, is the new measure of success. This is an era characterized by intimate conversations with select consumers; by meaning-rich experiences that foster a sense of empowerment and belonging; and by design thinking that artfully crafts experiences that extend to every touch point of a brand.

What is effective – i.e. meaningful – for your tribe and unique and authentic to your brand is now far more valuable than being bigger, better or more efficient than your competitor. Here are a few approaches to consider when such effectiveness is your top priority.

1. Create Meaning

Effectiveness means doing what is right for your brand and for your tribe. Companies must be willing to define or redefine the relationship with their tribe in terms that are meaningful and relevant.

The 95-year-old **Clorox** company owns a handful of brands that aren't necessarily known for their environmentalism – S.O.S. Pads, Formula 409 and Liquid Plumber, to name a few. CEO **Don Knauss** joined Clorox in 2006 from **Coca-Cola** and began to shift attention to environmental concerns like greener packaging and monitoring their carbon footprint. The company's Green Works cleaning supplies line was a response to the evolving desires of its customers. Clorox hit the bull's eye, and in the first year alone enjoyed $40 million in sales.

Green-business guru **Joel Makower**, who consulted with Clorox on the launch of Green Works, describes the evolution of the company's new green brand on his blog, makower. typepad.com. He talks about how Clorox market research identified a "consumer market they dubbed 'Chemical-Avoiding

Naturalists' – consumers who wanted greener cleaners but felt the incumbent products didn't work well, came from brands they didn't know or trust, were too expensive and weren't always available where they shopped."

Jessica Buttimer, Green Works' director of marketing, described the opportunity as follows: "We were actually in a perfect position as a company. We had the Clorox brand; we had these distribution channels and great relationship with **Walmart**; we had the science to make an efficacious product; and we had the scale to charge just a 20 per cent premium, instead of the usual 100 per cent premium." Listen closely: this is the language of effectiveness.

In just eight months, Green Works sold $3.4 million worth of glass cleaner, compared to $1.1 million sold by **Seventh Generation** and $947,000 by **Method** over a full 12 months. Green Works' effect on the market has been so dramatic that in November 2008, Seventh Generation initiated a product redesign in response to the threat to their market supremacy and the extreme change within the sustainable products market in general. In the meantime, Clorox has effectively engaged a new generation of Clorox brand consumers and bolstered the green cleaning products market for a wider audience.

2. Less is More

Effectiveness also means considering practices that may have previously seemed antithetical to business success, like harnessing growth. For example, when sales were expected to surpass their projected target, **Toyota** decreased production on its Scion model. This protected the 'specialness quotient' and helped the product maintain, or even increase, its value.

Toyota clearly understands that one of the secrets to creating meaning lies in limiting the size of its success. Not only does bigger not necessarily mean better, it could mean the death of a brand. In 2006, the *Wall Street Journal* reported that the Scion was on track to beat its 150,000-car-a-year sales goal by 25,000 vehicles. "This is a big reason why Toyota surpassed **DaimlerChrysler AG** to become the No. 3 auto maker in the

Effectiveness means tailoring niche – rather than mass – brands that are relevant to your tribe.

U.S. in sales. But instead of riding that momentum to increase sales even further, Scion plans to throttle back production to keep sales from going above 150,000 vehicles next year. This is part of its marketing strategy to keep the brand special and, above all, cool."

This rule also applies to the total number of a firm's product offerings. **General Motors** has recently come under fire for the 'bigger, better, and more' mentality that fueled its eight-brand, 70-model offering. While the company may have been trying to efficiently match different consumer segments or tribes with multiple brands and model options, the strategy was about as effective as throwing spaghetti onto the wall to see which strands stick. Meaning is rarely made from demographic data alone, and GM would have been better served by understanding its tribe's deepest cravings and designing just a select few, relevant products.

In a December 2008 article titled "At GM, Innovation Suffers for Profits," the *New York Times* reported that GM finally acknowledged that it had too many brands and it would scale back its offering to just four core brands – Chevrolet, Buick, GMC and Cadillac. The profit-over-innovation strategy is a pure efficiency mentality, and GM ran its business on an 'earn it or cut it' philosophy. For example, it cut back on an early hybrid offering, the EV1 electric car (too expensive) and a minivan (why would people need minivans if they had station wagons?) before either innovation had a chance to prove itself in the market.

Unique, custom, personalized and sustainable: these are the primary values in the Age of Meaning. When combined with a nuanced understanding of the hearts and minds of the tribe, businesses will be well on their way to a strategy of effectiveness.

3. Take a Platform-based Approach
Effectiveness means tailoring niche – rather than mass – brands that are relevant to your tribe. The key is to leverage back-end effi-

ciencies for front-end success, similar to technology platforms that are leveraged to run countless software programs. Clorox's Green Works is a successful platform-approach, utilizing the same back-end systems (distribution channels, production methods) and established brand equity to produce a new product targeted to a specific audience. The 'price to play' is therefore significantly less and, if done effectively, can only pay off.

Urban Outfitters is another such success story. The clothing retailer, which also owns **Anthropologie** and **Free People**, knows what it does best – merchandise and lifestyle brands that empower its tribe(s) to be more authentically themselves. Anthropologie's customer, for example, is not a roughly-sketched demographic or price-point niche, like, say, GM customers or those targeted by the **Old Navy**, **Gap** and **Banana Republic** continuum. Nor does the company expect to sell a selection of products to everyone with a 'one-size-fits-all' approach. Instead, it demonstrates its understanding of the tribe by digging deep into the subtleties of the psychographic profile of a specific type of 30-something, married woman. Anthropologie stores are an extension of her adventurous, bohemian-chic self that doesn't get as much play when juggling a career and kids. Anthropologie's retail environment is an artful rendition of a French market, creating an air of discovery and whimsy. It tells a simple story and stays true to its brand DNA. For this, the average customer spends over an hour in the store and spends close to $80 per visit.

Urban Outfitters and Free People are equally zeroed-in to their respective tribes. *Women's Wear Daily* reports that all three stores are selling between $800-1,000 per square-foot. The company leverages the same back-end systems, but tailors each brand experience with care. Urban Outfitters' recent announcement that it is considering additional concepts is further evidence of effectiveness thinking.

In his book, *ZAG: The #1 Strategy of High Performance Brands*, **Marty Neumeier** calls the Urban Outfitters model a 'house of brands' and compares it to the 'branded house' model (i.e. Starbucks). For Neumeier, the advantage of a house of brands is that each one is "free to fight its battles on its own terms, unfettered by the meaning of the parent brand." The advantage of the branded house, he explains, is that "all products and services can share the same budget, customer and market position." However, it also runs the risk of getting bogged down by trying to be everything to everybody.

In the Age of Meaning, when the rate of change seems to only accelerate, a 'house of brands' has the ability to be more nimble and respond to shifts in consumer needs and market trends. Platform innovation, for example, can create an ecosystem of partner brands. **Apple** makes only four iPod products, but there are more than 3,000 products that other manufacturers and brands create around them. Companies can enrich the experience of their brands by extending utility, borrowing status or quickly leveraging new trends.

The key to success, however, lies in a company's ability to create relevant experiences for their targeted tribes: a 'House of Brands' can only achieve success if it is a House of *Meaningful* Brands.

4. Consistency is Key

Effectiveness means that the brand experience is extended to every touch point – what we call a '360-degree experience'. There is no experience-killer worse than a story being told from only one aspect of a customer's interaction with a company. There may be a great product or service hiding in there, but if customer service or a Web site doesn't extend the brand experience, the brand is invalidated and there is a high risk of losing the customer. Every aspect of the brand must reflect the desires of your tribe.

Apple, of course, is the master of a platform-based, 360-degree effectiveness strategy. The story of Apple is told in every single detail of the experience, from elegant package design to the genius bar in Apple stores to their ads that say 'Apple' in a way that

only Apple can say it. The Apple tribe continues to fall ever-deeper in love with the company that woos them with such care. Apple continues to produce a limited number of products that allow their tribe to more authentically be themselves; contrast this model with **SONY**, which produces hundreds of different products each year, only a handful of which are real profit makers. Every Apple product has a story and a meaning behind it, as well as a profit margin that is the highest in its industry. Clearly, an effectiveness mindset pays off.

In closing

During a recent conversation with leaders of a major food company, a senior executive said to the group, "In the early 2000s we became the most efficient food company in the world; but so have our main competitors. What now?"

In the end, every efficiency strategy has a natural limit, because it can be imitated. Competitors can leap-frog your business in a matter of months. What is truly effective – i.e. meaningful for your tribe, unique and authentic to your brand – is inimitable.

It's time for organizations to push the pause button, dig deep and commit to their true DNA and to the tribe that is the best match for what they have to offer. Such effectiveness should be at the top of the agenda for every CEO today, and it should not stop there. Time should be set aside at regular intervals – every six-to-nine months – to take stock of trends and of the tribe's shifting behavior, attitudes and values.

Change. Adapt. Innovate with soul. And worry about efficiency only after it is completely clear how to be effective. It will be hard work, but the potential payoff is great, and the Age of Meaning requires nothing less. *R*

Sohrab Vossoughi is the founder and president of Ziba, a leading design consultancy based in Portland, Oregon, whose clients include Microsoft, Whirlpool, 3M and P&G.

Companies prosper when they tap into a power
that each of us already possesses: empathy.

THE EMPATHETIC ORGANIZATION

By **Dev Patnaik** and **Peter Mortensen**

IN 1986, MANAGER Jack Stack and 12 co-workers staged a successful buyout of **Springfield Remanufacturing Center** from its parent company, **International Harvester**. The engine rebuilder had been losing money to the tune of $2 million a year, and Stack and his team believed that they could revive the moribund unit. Realizing the need to make massive operational changes, they revamped SRC's system for financial reporting and decision making. In the process, they helped spawn a management revolution: open-book management.

Stack and his colleagues realized that the only way to successfully make a multitude of changes quickly was to enlist the help of every person in the company. Every employee needed to think and act like an owner. They needed to understand the business consequences of their actions and make better decisions. To

> People in companies with a widespread sense of empathy possess a shared and intuitive vibe for what's going on in the world that helps them to see new opportunities faster than their competitors.

achieve this, each employee was taught how to read the company's financial statements, including all the numbers that were critical to tracking the business's performance.

Then the managers made the books public: Stack posted the company's financials on the breakroom walls, in handouts, and on the computer network. Training courses and regular meetings taught everyone what the numbers meant. Suddenly, a machinist on the shop floor could see the effect of finishing a part faster, reducing raw material, or shaving some time off of a job. The results were astounding: SRC's sales grew 40 per cent a year in the first three years, and operating income rose by 11 per cent. When other manufacturers heard of SRC's turnaround, they too overhauled their decision structures. By 1995, *Inc.* magazine had devoted an entire issue to the phenomenon called open-book management.

As successful as open-book management has been, it's clear that numbers aren't everything. Short-term financial success doesn't prevent a firm from being blindsided by new threats, especially in a fast-moving sector; operational efficiency doesn't guarantee a firm's ability to discover and leverage new ways of providing value to the customer; and acumen alone can't mobilize a large group of people. For today's companies, value creation depends on knowing as much as they can about the people they serve. More complex than providing an open book, creating value for people requires the creation of an open *channel* to the outside world.

Empathy = Growth

Companies prosper when they tap into a power that each one of us already possesses: empathy, the ability to reach beyond ourselves and connect with other people. Human beings are intrinsically social animals. Our brains have developed subtle and sophisticated ways to understand what other people are thinking and feeling. Simply put, we are 'wired to care'. We rely on this instinct to help us make better decisions in situations that affect the people around us.

Unfortunately, this instinct seems to get short circuited when we get together in large groups. We lose our intuition, our gut sense for what's going on outside of that group: corporations become more insular; colleges start to feel like ivory towers; and political campaigns take on a 'bunker mentality'. This sort of isolation can have disastrous effects, because institutions depend on the outside world for revenues, reputation and votes.

By contrast, people in companies with a widespread sense of empathy possess a shared and intuitive vibe for what's going on in the world that helps them to see new opportunities faster than their competitors, long before that information becomes explicit enough to read about in the *Wall Street Journal*. They have the courage of their convictions to take a risk on something new, and the gut-level intuition to see how their actions impact the people who matter most: the folks who buy their products, interact with their brand, and ultimately fund their 401(k) plans. That intuition transcends what's traditionally referred to as market research.

A widespread sense of empathy starts to influence the culture of a place, giving it a sense of clarity and mission. People spend less time arguing about things that ultimately don't matter. Empathy can even start to ensure more ethical behaviour in a way that no policies and procedures manual ever could.

The Open-Empathy Organization

The idea of creating an Open-Empathy Organization is to build and propagate a system of human information. It's about every member of an organization having a first-hand sense of what people need, how their company solves those needs, and how what they do as individuals can add or subtract value. When employees can see that their daily activities have an impact on people outside the company, they often become inspired to create more positive impacts.

Most of us are reasonably good at figuring out how to make each other happier, but those instincts can't kick in if we can't see the people we're trying to help. Widespread empathy restores that connection. That's why, just as with open-book management, people in Open-Empathy Organizations make better decisions. When they can see who they're really working for, they know why their work matters and how to do it better. Instead of realizing how finishing a project faster will make the company more profitable, people in Open-Empathy Organizations know exactly where value resides in the world of customers and potential customers.

In our research at Jump Associates, we've had the chance to meet a few such organizations. **Harley-Davidson** fills its headquarters with tangible reminders of the shared story of motorcycle riding. Everyone who works at Harley need only look around them to understand exactly what riders genuinely value. Likewise, **Nike** has built an entire culture to celebrate the potential for athletic greatness in each of us. **IBM** helps its customers keep their information technology up and running, which is why the company stays as close as possible to its business clientele. The company uses its services division, direct sales force and online portals to connect employees with customers on a daily basis.

For these companies and others like them, empathy is an intangible-but-important asset, and a significant engine for growth. Open-Empathy Organizations outperform their competitors and consistently add value to the top line because they understand how the work they do affects the people they serve. Generating widespread empathy throughout a company requires the active involvement of senior leadership. It can demand changes in how employees are trained; what facilities look like; or even how managers are incentivized.

The goal is to improve the thousands of decisions people make every day. This might sound like a daunting undertaking, but any company can take steps in the right direction with a few small changes. Organizations that make empathy an *easy*, *everyday* and *experiential* part of the way that their employees work will succeed in making empathy widespread.

1. Make it Easy

Open-Empathy Organizations depend on having employees at all levels who are genuinely interested in other people. This can be difficult, especially since no one likes to take on a bunch of extra work. Everyone has enough to do as it is – mandating ethnographic field research visits for all employees simply adds to their workload. Open-Empathy Organizations don't make their employees work hard to develop empathy for their customers – they provide lots of easy ways to interact. Although every business needs to walk many miles in the shoes of its customers, few have the time or budget to travel thousands of miles to take that walk. Here are some tips for developing empathy in your organization:

Use the language of your customers. One straightforward way to determine the level of empathy that an organization has is to listen to the language it uses. It's easy for corporations to develop language and behavior that distances themselves from their customers. In fact, the more successful a company becomes, the more likely they are to be removed from "customer segments," "consumers," and "purchasing decision makers." One company even refers to candy bars as "filled bars with inclusions."

Open-Empathy Organizations instead always talk about their own work using the same terms that their customers do. Cars should be called "cars," not "C-class Vehicles." Chairs should be called "chairs," not "seating." And, more than anything, candy

THE EMPATH-O-METER   Figure One

😃	😐	😦
High Empathy	**Striving**	**Low Empathy**
Commerce Bank	BP	Citibank
Harley-Davidson	Clorox	Delta Air Lines
IBM	Hewlett-Packard	Kraft
Microsoft Xbox	Intel	New Balance
Netflix	Procter & Gamble	Schick
Nike	Steelcase	Samsung
Patagonia	Sony	Sears/Kmart
Virgin	Target	Unilever

bars should be called by their right name. By doing that, any organization can get a little closer to their customers.

Dress like your customers. Another easy way to reflect the outlook of your customers is to dress the way they do. Target stores used to get this right. Target shoppers tend to be middle-class folks with an appreciation for both style and low prices. When they shop at Target, they wear the casual, fashionable clothes sold at the retailer. Target corporate headquarters used to be the same way. It wasn't unusual to see executives wearing the same clothes that they helped put on the shelves. That changed in 2004 when Target created a strict dress code requiring formal business attire.

Changing the dress code created two obstacles to empathy. First, Targeteers no longer looked like their customers. Second, and more important, they now had to shop at other stores to buy clothing that was more suitable for work. Local newspapers even noted a marked increase in sales for menswear stores serving Target employees in need of sharper clothes. By becoming "more professional," Target lost an easy way to walk in the shoes of their customers.

Use your own products and services. Ask your employees to use the company's own products. Mail-order video rental service **Netflix** gets this right. When you start as a new coder, marketer, or even line worker at Netflix, you're given a DVD player if you don't own one. As an employee, you also get a free subscription to the company's service. As DVDs begin to arrive in your mailbox at home, you experience what all Netflix subscribers experience. You learn how to change the order of the films that you want to watch on your online queue, you anticipate the arrival of new discs, and you learn how to repackage the discs to ship them back to Netflix. People at Netflix don't have to wonder what it's like to be a Netflix customer: they are customers, too. Subscribing to their own service allows everyone at Netflix to see constant areas for improvement and to envision new services to add value to their existing offering.

2. Make it Everyday

At first, the novelty of empathy-building activities can make the initiative seem special, a break from the usual routine. That's a bad sign. Open-Empathy Organizations avoid the kind of "big empathy-building events" that leaders love to kick off. While they can create a lot of excitement, these one-off events rarely have lasting impact. It's far more important to insert empathic information into the workplace on a daily basis. To really stick, empathy needs to be part of the everyday routine: accessible, quick and a constant presence.

Get senior leadership to model behaviour. One of the most essential characteristics of an Open-Empathy Organization is a leadership team that demonstrates empathic behavior in its everyday work. For example, when **David Neeleman** was the CEO of **JetBlue Airways**, he flew around the country several times per week. But he never flew on executive jets or in first class – he rode in coach class on regularly-scheduled JetBlue flights. Once the plane reached cruising altitude, David would get up and join the flight crew to pass out snacks and drinks. When the plane landed, he would pitch in to clean the plane after the flight. This first-hand exposure to his offering and his customers provided David with a strong sense of empathy. More importantly, his visible activities were well-known throughout the company, and people at all levels replicated his interest in the company's customers. Even now that he has left JetBlue, David's commitment to develop empathy for his customers has set the tone for the rest of the organization.

Hire your customers. There is no more effective way to get closer to your customers than to have them come to work alongside you. Every single day, you will have the opportunity to learn about the people you serve just by chatting with a co-worker. Better still, all such employees have a great intuitive sense for customers. Years ago, upon realizing that it didn't understand a generation of kids who had grown up with PCs, cell phones, and the internet, **Casio** hired teenagers to help design its products. This gave the company instant, actionable feedback from its target group. Using the same logic, **The Container Store** figured its best holiday retail employees would be the same folks who regularly bought holiday products. The company sent invitations to its best gift-wrap customers to help sell wrapping paper and other holiday items and was greeted with an overwhelmingly positive response.

Surround yourself with empathic information. The final key to making empathy an everyday part of working is to fill the workplace with information about the company's customers. We came across a good method for making empathy an everyday part of working several years ago while visiting semiconductor giant **Intel**. The company has a robust ethnography team that conducts extensive interviews with ordinary people in their homes to figure out what sorts of devices Intel and its partners should create next. But Intel is a large company, and the ethnography group is small. To widen its impact, the group translates what it learns about people into end-user 'personas' – fictional people whose demographics, personality traits, and habits are based on those of real people the team has met. Such personas can provide touchstones in the product development process, but they wouldn't have any impact at Intel unless people read them. That's why Intel's ethnography group has created a unique method for spreading personas throughout the organization. The team has hit upon one of the rare moments when people sit down and have some time to themselves: in the bathroom. Intel posts the personas inside restroom stalls, where they're easy to access and read. After all, people are going to spend time there anyway. Why not help them learn something in the process?

3. Make it Experiential

Finally, it's important to make empathic information experiential. The emotional centers of our brains aren't easily triggered by Excel spreadsheets. Open-Empathy Organizations work to create ways for employees to interact with customers and environments for themselves. Sometimes that means encouraging employees to get out into the world. Other times, it means bringing the outside world into the office.

Routinely visit real customers. Too many leaders only understand their customers in the form of market research about their purchasing habits. They don't know them as people. Open-Empathy Organizations instead encourage employees to regularly meet the actual folks that they serve. When **Lou Gerstner** became IBM's CEO in 1993, he launched 'Operation Bear Hug' to meet this goal. The program required each of his 50 top managers to meet with at least five of IBM's biggest customers in the span of three months. Managers weren't supposed to sell product in those meetings. Instead, they were to listen to customer concerns and think about how IBM might help. All of those executives' 200 direct reports then had to do the same thing. Gerstner demanded short written reports on the outcomes of each Bear Hug meeting, and he personally read every single one. As a result of this process, Gerstner saw the opportunity to dramatically grow IBM's business by moving into professional services, a shift that restored the once-beleaguered firm to profitability and growth.

Bring the outside in. Many companies are insulated to what life is like for their customers. Open-Empathy Organizations blur the line between the company and the rest of the world. One great way to do this is by finding ways to bring the outside in. Gardening tools company **Smith & Hawken** does a great job of

The first steps are simple: take the
way that you already work today and add in
experiential activities that put you
in the shoes of the people you serve.

this. Everyone in the company is required to take rotations work-ing in the garden – to literally get down in the dirt. It's the compa-ny's way of helping its employees develop a better gut sense for how real gardeners view the world. The gardening program helped Smith & Hawken create an empathic connection that helped employees quadruple the company in size and expand from a mail-order business into one of the fastest-growing retail companies on the planet.

Communicate through high-bandwidth media. Though it's easy to boil down information about customers' lives to a single bullet on a PowerPoint slide, Open-Empathy Organizations recognize that too much gets lost in the process. Instead, they rely on storytelling, video, and even immersive spaces to communicate data about the people that they serve. No one does this better than Nike.

A major brand in the United States, Nike is also a big name in Japan, a notoriously difficult market for American companies to crack. Experiential empathy has made this possible. At the beginning of a project for Japan, Nike designers visit the country in person to gain inspiration by hanging out with teenagers. The designers see their homes, go to school with them and get a sense for what cool means to them. Upon returning home to Beaverton, Oregon, designers recreate the environments they've visited overseas: they build rooms that look like the teenagers' bedrooms they saw in Japan, right down to the posters on the walls and the colour palette of the furniture. They even turn on the same Japanese TV shows that teenagers there like to watch. These rooms serve as an immersive space to help design-ers and marketers create offerings for Japan. They sketch, brainstorm, and debate a product's look or positioning while immersed in the world of the people they want to connect with. This way, even someone who didn't go to Japan can experience what they missed.

Use consumer-insight people as coaches, not experts. Consumer insight departments are often the keepers of information about the people a company serves. By contrast, in Open-Empathy Organizations these folks act as coaches and facilitators who cre-ate opportunities to learn about customers for everyone else in the organization.

Procter & Gamble exemplifies this principle. In 2001, it cre-ated the 'Living It' program, in which the consumer insight division arranges for managers and other employees to live for a few days in the homes of lower-income consumers. The same group also developed 'Working It', which allows employees to work behind the counters of small stores to see consumers up close and personal. On numerous occasions, P&G employees have come up with breakthrough ideas for products in response to needs that they discovered through time spent outside of the organization. While these experiences are set up by the insights department, the people who go through them work in every func-tion and at every level of the company.

In closing

Creating an Open-Empathy Organization entails a long-term process of organizational change. But the first steps are simple: take the way that you already work today and add in easy, every-day, experiential activities that put you in the shoes of the people you serve. Companies can begin to change by filling just one wing of the building with fresh air. If even a single unit develops widespread empathy, that group's enthusiasm for the people it serves can spread to everyone else in the company.

Over time, any organization can learn to hear what people outside its walls are talking about, feel what they are feeling, and see the world through their eyes. Open-Empathy Organizations see the world as it really is: rich with life and overflowing with unseen opportunities to grow. ***R***

Dev Patnaik is founder and CEO of Jump Associates, a San Mateo, California-based growth-strategy firm. **Peter Mortensen** is a Strategy Lead at Jump. They are the co-authors of *Wired to Care: How Companies Prosper When They Create Widespread Empathy* (FT Press, 2009).

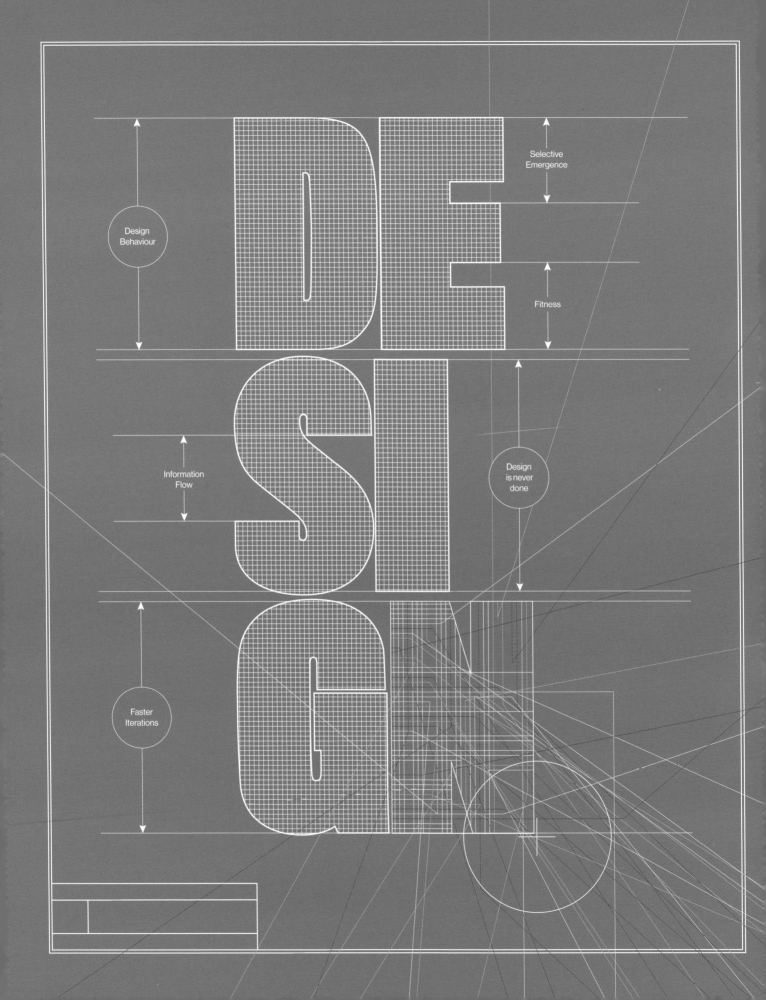

From Blueprint to Genetic Code:

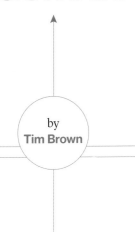

by
Tim Brown

The Merits of an Evolutionary Approach to Design

Like everything else in life, design is evolving, forcing us
to give up the very essence of the Newtonian notion
of design: the blueprint.

LIKE MOST DESIGNERS, I am quite comfortable with the notion of designing simple things. I can pick up just about any object and tell you how it was made, and I could probably have a reasonable crack at designing an equivalent of it, even though I'm not a particularly technical person. That's because it is possible to defini-tively know everything important about a simple object: we can know its form, the market for it, and the best method of manufac-turing it. We might even know what to do with it when people are finished using it. The traditional design process entails figuring all of this out beforehand and 'making it so' in the world.

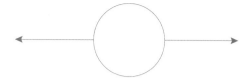

Unfortunately, as the world's problems have become more complex, the traditional design process has been challenged. Many of the products and services created today are more like complex systems than simple objects; they often involve a confluence of software, hardware, and human behaviour. And as systems evolve, so must our knowledge of systems design.

Take urban planning, for instance. Look around your city and you will see countless examples of the unintended consequences of a failure to understand a complex system. That's because a traditional design process was likely used to create the sub-par products and services, and cities are like organisms – they evolve. It is very difficult to create a 'planned' city, as Chinese leaders are currently finding out through their attempts to create fully planned, top-down, large-scale cities.

In traditional attempts to design a service, we 'script' the service, creating a 'user experience blueprint' that attempts to describe everything that will happen to the customer during the experience. For a hotel, for instance, this would include everything from what the lobby looks like to what the check in service is like. Attention to all these details leads to a relatively complicated script, which makes us confident that we have covered all the bases. The problem is, even when we get these scripts right, it's amazing how often things go wrong.

From Newton to Darwin

As designers become more involved in solving the world's wicked problems, an ability to deal with complexity becomes all the more important. In my view, this indicates a paradigm shift for the world of design, because it demands a shift from thinking about the world in the way that **Sir Isaac Newton** encouraged us to think about it, to the way **Sir Charles Darwin** thought about it. Let me explain.

Newton's world was based on the assumption that we have an ability to predict the world based on actions in the present. When we think this way, it encourages us to be top-down in our activities, to be predictive, to believe that we can imagine a complete system. I would argue that the complexity we often face today requires us to think more like Darwin, who encouraged us to think about constant evolution, emergent change, and the notion of unpredictability on a large scale, even if we understand things on a small scale.

As designers and as leaders, I believe that we need to start emulating Darwin a bit more and to stop emulating Newton. Following are some possible aspects of a more Darwinian approach to design.

1. We should give up on the idea of designing objects and think instead about designing *behaviours*.

Behaviours are about the interrelationships between people and the objects that exist in the world around us. To illustrate the difference between designing an object and designing a behaviour, take a look at this image:

This sign can be found on trains in Europe – a vain attempt to encourage the male of the species to create less mess in the public toilets. But because it is simply an instruction, it doesn't work very well; anyone who has used a train toilet knows all too well the degree to which it doesn't work. About 25 years ago, the fellow who managed the airport in Amsterdam had a much better idea:

He realized that if you printed a fly on the urinal – in just the right spot – you would give people something to aim at. And when you give a man something to aim at, he actually does a remarkably good job: this approach has reduced the mess in urinals by up to 80 per cent. That's what it means to design a behaviour.

2. We need to think more about how information flows.

If you talk to people at the **Santa Fe Institute**, or read any of their books, you will learn that a key characteristic of a complex system is that the more complex a system is, the more information flows through it. If this is true, then we ought to be thinking more about these information flows when we are designing complex systems. In fact, before we work on designing a better solution, we need to get better at understanding the complex system *as it is today*, and what information is already flowing through it.

For example, Harvard's **Nicholas Christakis** has studied the relationships between people with respect to their health, and one of the conclusions he has come to is that if you are in a network of obese people, you are *three times more likely* to be obese yourself. Conversely, if you are in a network of non-obese people, you are three times more likely to *not* be obese. This is a very important insight for design: that the behaviour of those around us significantly effects our behaviour. Intuitively we might know this, but we don't necessarily always think about it when we're designing systems.

3. We must recognize that faster evolution is based on faster iteration.

The faster we do things, the faster we learn and the faster we improve. The natural world deals with this truth very well. The reason viruses evolve so fast is that they reproduce every few minutes, which is why we have such a hard time keeping up with them. In contrast, humans evolve (i.e. reproduce) every 20 years or so, and in general, business is more like humans than it is like a virus. How can we make a business more like a virus? One way to move in this direction is to accept that we cannot know all the answers before we do things.

We recently worked with **State Farm Insurance** in the U.S. to launch Next Door, which provides coaching and financial advising to a new generation of customers. Next Door is a place for customers to come and learn about insurance and financial services, and at the same time it's a place for State Farm to learn about them. The idea that we can launch things *simply to learn from them* is quite useful when we're thinking about increasing the reproductive pace of iteration in business.

4. We must embrace selective emergence.

So far, natural biological systems appear to be way ahead of us in dealing with complexity, but we do have one advantage over them: with biological systems, all of the improvements are random – they are based on mutation. There are some *guiding prin-ciples* perhaps, but there is no *guiding intelligence*. We humans have the benefit of potentially using the best of both when we design something.

There are technologies out there that are already doing this – enabling us to use the idea of selective emergence to rapidly iterate things while nudging and guiding them towards some outcome that we want. For example, 'genetic algorithms'. In software today it is quite common to build algorithms that reproduce themselves; certain rules are applied, but you don't know in advance what the optimal version of that piece of code is going to be. Evolution gets you to it, and all you've done is apply certain rules to nudge it in the right direction. This idea can be applied in fields as varied as engineering, design and art.

The strange looking thing pictured below is called a *strandbeest*. These remarkable structures were created by Dutch sculp-

tor **Theo Jansen**, and you can find them walking up and down the beaches in Holland. Made out of PVC plumbing pipe, they are 'self-articulating' – they move on their own. Jansen used a genetic algorithm to create the 'hip' and 'foot' joints. He didn't know in advance what the right ultimate solution was, so he designed an algorithm and it kept iterating and iterating until it created the most efficient foot and hip mechanism to make these sculptures walk on their own. I believe we should be using this approach more often in design. We are already seeing it done in architecture, where architects use a similar kind of technology to create the facades of buildings – the ones you see that often look much more organic than a traditional structure.

As designers, we need to remember our relationship with science a little bit more. We're often very good at exploration

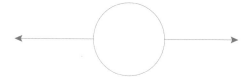

or divergence – asking questions without any real sense of a hypothesis. But I think we also need to relearn some good scientific methodology. Doing so will enable us to ask more of the right questions, come up with better hypotheses, design effective experiments and most importantly, share our learnings.

5. We need to focus on fitness.

Biological systems naturally focus on fitness; at its core, that's what evolution is all about – striving for fitness, whatever the environmental context might be. All kinds of biological systems do this; but what is the equivalent of fitness in business and in design?

I believe one way of thinking about fitness in the organizational realm is the concept of *purpose*. Organizations that have a clear purpose tend to be able to design in a less top-down way. Many years before **Apple** took over the world, **Steve Jobs** spoke to his people about "being insanely great," telling them: "What you create has got to be so good that you are shocked that you could actually create something that good." This became the driving purpose of the organization, and it allowed many more people to contribute to the greatness of Apple than would have been the case if there were no such purpose. Imagine an organization that didn't have this purpose, but still had a Steve Jobs in it; it would have been impossible for him to achieve what he achieved. I believe that his incredible vision *plus* an organization that believed in the notion of being *insanely great* are the keys to Apple's success.

6. We must accept the fact that *design is never done.*

In the architectural world, there is a notion of 'life after the open house.' Architects see all sorts of perfect photographs of buildings just at the moment when they hand it over to the client, but very rarely does anyone see photographs of what happens afterwards. I think this is natural, and I do the same thing: I design a product and I take a perfect picture of it, before the manufacturers get their hands on it, never mind the user. This is that moment when the 'thing' is closest to my vision, and it's when I think I'm done with it. Of course, this is a ridiculous notion, because in truth, it is now in the hands of users, where it will be adapted and used for things that I didn't expect it to be used for.

In the world of video games, particularly in online games like *World of Warcraft*, design is going on all the time. Yes, there is an environment that was created, but the design of behaviour – of the events, the characters – all of this is done by users who are, in effect, *participating in the design*. I believe that design is going to look much more like this in the future, rather than the idea of unveiling a pristine 'thing' that we hand over to people.

Evolutionary Organizations

Embracing a more evolutionary approach to design can do more than enable us to create better products and services: I believe that we can use these ideas and principles to tackle some of the most important challenges of our time. In the field of chronic health problems, for instance, we're beginning to see opportunities to hand control over to patients and enable us to design behaviours for ourselves that help to manage chronic disease. As a result, we're starting to get past the idea that our bodies are mysterious 'black boxes'. For example, there is a scale that comes out of Europe that does something very simple: each time you weigh yourself, it sends the data to your iPhone. Over time, you can build up a clear picture of the relationship between your behaviour and your weight, because you get to see it on a graph. Such devices could measure all sorts of things, potentially allowing us to equip people with the means to change their behaviour.

Another way of changing behaviour is to put the tools of design themselves into the hands of people delivering services. We've been working for several years with **Kaiser Permanente**, teaching nurses and doctors and technicians how to use design thinking to improve patient care, and Kaiser now has its own consulting group made up of nurses who have become expert at this. They go around to hospitals working on different problems, creating wards and hospitals of the future. Already, they've had some great success in increasing the efficiency of shift changes for nurses.

At IDEO we are particularly interested in applying design to issues of poverty. While it's still early days, we are finding that the way to have the most impact is to give people tools rather than designing an end product. For example, we've been working for some time now on sanitation issues in Ghana, designing a low-cost toilet for people's homes. The problem is, even if you design the lowest-cost toilet possible – in this case, about $30 – it's still too expensive for most families. We looked at things like micro-finance to deliver the service, but what we found is that the really important design unit here was a service business model. The model allows room for entrepreneurs to set up service businesses where they rent toilets out to people and come to empty and clean them on a daily or weekly basis. The lesson we learned: the important part wasn't the design of the toilet itself, but the whole business system around it.

We recently worked on a project with the **Bill and Melinda Gates Foundation** to create a Human-Centered Design Tool Kit, which is really a field guide for design for not-for-profits and NGO's. It includes tools that enable them to understand their users

> If you want to be involved in the 'participation economy', our old notions of designing in a controlled way just don't make sense anymore.

better, to create ideas through prototyping, business model design, etc., and we've had some interesting success with it. Already, the tool kit has been downloaded over 70,000 times and it is being used on projects ranging from creating a new maternal hospital in Nepal to working with a cooperative of weavers in Rwanda to water distribution management systems in Malawi and hand-washing stations in Vietnam.

In an effort to scale all of these efforts up, last September we launched **IDEO.org**, which is a sister organization to IDEO and a not-for-profit design organization that works on social innovation initiatives. Unlike IDEO's core business – where we're hired to solve problems for clients by designing new services or products – we're doing something quite different with IDEO.org: we're looking to build out the capacity for design in the social sector. This is a space where giving up control is necessary: if you want to participate and be involved in social networks – what I think of as the 'participation economy' – our old notions of designing everything in a controlled way just don't make sense anymore.

Evolving as an organization means listening to not only your clients, but to what's happening in the world around you. Our clients would often say to us, "You talk about how we should use innovation to disrupt ourselves, but how are you disrupting *yourselves*?" We thought about this for some time, and asked questions like, "What if we could solve problems collaboratively via a global network?" Basically, what would happen if IDEO had 50,000 people working on design challenges instead of the few hundred working within our walls?

We came up with **Open IDEO**, which is a platform for tackling social innovation problems. We do this in conjunction with various non- profits and sometimes with companies, as well. For instance, we teamed up the **World Wildlife Fund** and **Sony** on one challenge, and **Unilever** is helping us out on the sanitation challenge in Ghana. At the moment we have about 25,000 people in the design community working on projects in 178 countries.

We are already seeing businesses getting launched through Open IDEO, and we're seeing some really interesting ideas going back into the organizations that sponsor projects. But more importantly, we're learning a huge amount about how collaborative design might happen in the future.

In closing

Like everything else in life, design is evolving, and in many ways we are being forced to give up the very essence of the Newtonian notion of design: the blueprint, which personifies control and defining every outcome of the design process.

Instead of focusing on designing blueprints, I believe there is something that better represents what we should be designing going forward: genetic code. At one level, genetic code represents the biological view of design I have described, because it is an 'instruction set' for biological behaviour. But more importantly, it represents the idea that code is only the beginning of something: it sets off a series of behaviours, but you can't know the ultimate outcome in advance.

While most of us don't understand how to work with genetic code, we have already begun to understand how to work with a different type of code: software code. The design and engineering of software has changed quite radically in the last 10 years to be much more 'open-ended' than it used to be. In a sense, this is a metaphor for how we as designers – whether we are industrial designers or designers of businesses – need to behave and work going forward. *R*

Tim Brown is CEO and president of IDEO and the author of *Change By Design: How Design Thinking Transforms Organizations and Inspires Innovation* (HarperBusiness 2009). He blogs at designthinking.ideo.com

2

How Design Fits Into the Modern Organization

WHETHER YOU WORK FOR A HOSPITAL, a bank or a small startup, I can say with certainty that design is a capability that can benefit your organization. That's because everything that surrounds us is subject to innovation, as Roger Martin has stated.

There are a variety of ways to put design to work for you. In a world where cognitive diversity is more important than ever, one obvious way is to include a trained designer on your team, which will bring a unique way of thinking and problem-solving to the table. Designers are expert at challenging the questions being asked and the constraints being discussed, and in my experience, they can often identify unexpected solutions that eliminate tradeoffs.

Another approach you can take is the one we took at P&G, which is to teach the design thinking methodology to people throughout your organization. The fact is, you don't have to be a trained designer to practice design thinking. Learning these skills will improve the problem-solving ability of any team, and enable them to identify new opportunities and big ideas.

A third approach you can take is to pull out the components of the design methodology that make the most sense for your organization. For instance, embracing the concept of prototyping can drive value creation for many organizations. At its core, prototyping is a tool for improving customer insight, which is invaluable in and of itself; but it also does something very powerful: it gives people a license to try things, and to fail. When you develop something and you call it a prototype, people understand and expect that it's not finished yet, which gives you the license to *fail*. People don't like to say they've failed or made mistakes, but everyone is happy to say, "Well, that was just a prototype; I'm learning." In my experience, this alone can be an invaluable addition to any organization.

One of the biggest lessons I've learned over the years is that, if you tell people you want to introduce them to design thinking, they are likely to have a negative bias towards it. My team learned pretty quickly not to tell people about the 'wonders' of design thinking: instead, we *showed* them: we demonstrated the methodology, the thinking processes and how it works, using real-world business problems.

The late-great Peter Drucker once said that, "The mission and purpose of every business is to satisfy the customer." In our complex and information-saturated world, we often lose sight of this. Leaders tend to focus on questions like, "What should we do next?" rather than, "What does my customer need?"

The concept of design will bring you back to your customer, every single time. And if you want to create value these days, that is where you have to be.

Claudia Kotchka served as Vice President of Design Innovation and Strategy at Procter & Gamble from 2001 to 2008. She retired from P&G in 2009, completing a milestone-filled 31-year career. Currently, she advises Fortune 500 companies on wide ranging aspects of innovation, design and culture change.

Embedding Design into Business

Firms everywhere are realizing they can jump-start growth by becoming more design-oriented. But to generate meaningful benefits from design, they will first have to change the way they operate along five key dimensions.

by **Roger Martin**

THE TOPIC OF DESIGN is hot these days. Wherever you look, there are cover stories, conferences – you name it, if it's design-related, people are talking about it. Firms everywhere want to revolutionize themselves by becoming more design-oriented. They look wistfully at the stupendous growth that the iconic iPod provided for previously-stagnating **Apple**, and are hopeful that design can help them create their own version of the iPod and restart their growth engines.

Unfortunately, it's not as simple as hiring a Chief Design Officer and declaring that design is your top corporate priority.

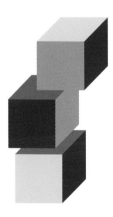

To generate meaningful benefits from design, firms will have to change in fundamental ways to operate more like the design shops whose creative output they covet. To get the benefits of design, firms have to embed design *into* – not append it *onto* – their business.

Design organizations vary significantly from traditional firms along five key dimensions: flow of work life; style of work; mode of thinking; source of status; and dominant attitude. Left unchecked, the stark contrast between traditional firms and design shops on these attributes will impede any attempt by traditional firms to become more 'design-oriented'. Let's examine each characteristic in turn.

Flow of Work Life

In traditional firms, the flow of work life is organized around permanent jobs and ongoing tasks. 'Vice-president of marketing' is a permanent position with a set of tasks that are considered ongoing, without finite duration: managing the annual advertising plan; setting marketing budgets; coordinating with sales; reporting quarterly on share trends to the CEO, etc. The vice-president of marketing is rewarded primarily for fulfilling these ongoing responsibilities consistently and adroitly. By and large, colleagues mirror this flow of work life.

In design shops, the work flow is radically different. The world is made up primarily of projects with defined terms. Designers are used to being assigned to a given project with a specific deadline; when the deadline comes and the project is completed, it disappears from sight, and the designer moves on to other projects, each of which also has a fixed duration. Designers get used to 'mixing and matching' with other designers on ad hoc teams that are created with a specific purpose in mind. They view their careers as an accumulation of projects, rather than a progression of hierarchical job titles.

Dropped into a traditional setting with a 'permanent job' defined by the performance of an ongoing set of tasks, a designer will feel completely alienated from his or her 'normal' way of operating, because design thinking and work requires a different flow of work life than is common in traditional firms. Indeed, it could be argued that traditional firms actually fool themselves by attempting to portray jobs and tasks as 'ongoing' and 'permanent', when in fact, the majority of work life is naturally a set of projects, each of which has its ebbs and flows. Many managers complain that because they are constantly 'fighting fires', they can't seem to get their 'real jobs' done; but I would argue that they have a skewed sense of reality, and that the fire-fighting they are called upon to do is probably more 'real' than the set tasks associated with their 'real job'.

Style of Work

Traditional firms have a style of work that is consistent with the ongoing, permanent tasks that characterize their flow of work. Roles tend to be carefully, if not rigidly, defined, with clear responsibilities for each individual laid out and economic incentives linked tightly to those responsibilities. Individuals are typically much more adept at describing 'my responsibilities' than they are at describing 'our responsibilities'. They are inclined to work away at these responsibilities, refining and honing outputs before sharing a complete, finalized 'product' with the appropriate individuals. For example, the SVP of marketing will be inclined to toil away on the

Designers may not be able to prove
that something *is* or *must be,* but they
nevertheless reason that it *may be –*
and this style of thinking is critical to
the creative process.

annual marketing plan, refining and adjusting it until it is 'perfect', and only then presenting it to the CEO, who will hopefully agree.

In a design shop, the style of work is much more collaborative. While there is likely some hierarchy within teams, projects are typically assigned to teams rather than to individuals. A design team is mandated to come up with a design solution *together* – explicitly *not* as individuals. And throughout the process, the team is expected to interact with the client by bringing them into the design collaboration.

Because of this collaborative atmosphere, the work style also tends to be *iterative* – the opposite of waiting until something is 'right'. This involves prototyping, honing and refining through multiple iterations with the client. Architect **Frank Gehry** is famous for this style. When his first design for a project goes public, it is typically greeted with a firestorm of protests for its inadequacies on a number of dimensions – making clients, users and observers extremely nervous, because they generally work in traditional organizations in which nothing sees the light of day until it is 'right'. They can't imagine that Gehry is only *beginning*, and that even though he is a brilliant expert, he wants to get valuable feedback for the next iteration (which won't be final either, by the way.) Indeed, 'final' only emerges many iterations into the future.

When traditional firms hire designers, their managers often find designers disappointing because, like Gehry, they bring them prototypes for feedback instead of final products. Unfortunately for the designers, these managers think they are seeing a final product, and when judged by that standard, the product is patently sub-standard and the designer is considered incompetent.

Mode of Thinking

Traditional firms utilize and reward the use of two kinds of logic: *inductive* – proving through observation that something actually works – and *deductive* – proving through reasoning from principles that something *must be.* For example, a retailer may study the cost structure of all of its outlets to determine which has the best cost position in order to set, inductively, a cost target for the whole chain. Or a consumer packaged goods firm can use its engrained theory – i.e. 'build market share and profits will follow' – to deduce the appropriate action in a given situation. However, any form of reasoning or argumentation outside these two forms is at a minimum discouraged, and at the extreme, exterminated. The challenge is always, "Can you prove that?", and to prove something in a reliable fashion means using rigorous inductive or deductive logic.

Design shops also use and value inductive and deductive reasoning. Designers induce patterns through the close study of users and deduce answers through the application of design theories. However, they also encourage and highly value a third type of logic: *abductive* reasoning. As described by Darden School of Business Professor **Jeanne Liedtka**, abductive reasoning is the logic of *what might be.* Designers may not be able to prove that something *is* or *must be,* but they nevertheless reason that it *may be* – and this style of thinking is critical to the creative process.

When **Bill Stumpf**, head of his own Minneapolis-based design shop, and **Don Chadwick**, head of his own design shop in Santa Monica, designed the award-winning Aeron chair for **Herman Miller**, they had lots of detailed consumer research from which to apply inductive reasoning and robust sets of design principles to consider deductively. But their reasoning processes

The source of status and pride in design organizations derives from solving 'wicked problems' – problems with no definitive formulation or solution, whose definition is open to multiple interpretations.

went well beyond the inductive and deductive: they imagined what a chair of the future *could* look like, and how that chair could forever change the way users would think about office chairs. Could they prove any of it in advance? No. In fact, when users first saw the chair, it received a decidedly chilly reception – but only because it looked like no other chair they had ever seen.

In short order, users warmed to the Aeron chair, because Stumpf and Chadwick had indeed created a product that no consumer could have described, but that nonetheless met their unarticulated needs and sought to be better than anything that came before it. Despite bearing a price tag double the prevailing level for a high-end ergonomic office chair, the Aeron became the best-selling office chair of all time and a must-have for board-rooms everywhere. Among other accolades, it won the award for the best design of its decade. None of this would have happened without the design shop sensibilities that fostered Stumpf and Chadwick's abductive reasoning.

Source of Status
The primary source of status in traditional firms is the management of big budgets and large staffs. When executives have the occasion to boast about themselves, they are inclined to refer to the number of people for whom they have direct responsibility and/or the bottom line that they deliver each year – i.e., "I run a 5,000 person organization and our bottom line this year will be $700 million." And of course, bigger is always better!

In a design shop, one would be hard-pressed to find someone bragging about big budgets or large staffs. If anything, the bragging would be about how small and elite the shop is. The source of status and pride in design organizations derives from solving 'wicked problems' – problems with no definitive formulation or solution, whose definition is open to multiple interpretations. This reality is confirmed from looking around the office of any star designer: desks, credenzas and shelves likely display the world's best designs – the ones that have solved the most difficult design challenges in the most elegant fashion. Designers become known for their great solutions, whether it be the Apple mouse, the Bilbao Guggenheim Museum, or the **Nike** swoosh. These designers enjoy the highest status inside their firms and across their industries, and as a result, everyone in the design field seeks to earn status through tackling and solving wicked problems.

Dominant Attitude
The dominant attitude in traditional firms is to see constraints as the enemy and budgets as the drivers of decisions. The common argument is, "We can only do what we have the budget to do." If only budget constraints could be relieved, these managers seem to imply, so much more would be possible. As a result, 'budget constraints' are pegged as the reason why a product's packaging is cheap-looking, or a product is late to market, or its range is too narrow. 'The budget' – arch enemy of the traditional firm manager – simply makes it impossible to do any better.

By contrast, in design shops the dominant mindset is, "there is nothing that cannot be done." If something can't be done, it is only because the thinking around it hasn't yet been creative and inspired enough. For **Buckminster Fuller**, the problem of buildings getting proportionally heavier, weaker and more expensive as they got larger in scale was not an intractable problem: it was only intractable until he designed the geodesic dome, which gets proportionally lighter, stronger and less expensive as it gets larger in scale.

For design shops, constraints are never the enemy. On the contrary, they serve to increase the challenge and excitement-level of the task at hand. In fact, given the source of status in these organizations, constraints actually increase the level of a problem's 'wickedness', making its potential solution that much more rewarding. Hence designers are disinclined to say, "That simply cannot be done," or, "We don't have the budget for that". Instead, they are inclined to say: "Bring it on!"

The Journey from Appending to Embedding

It is both unrealistic and unproductive to think that traditional firms will ever transform themselves completely into design shops. There are reasons why even leading international design shops are tiny by corporate standards. However, given today's design-centric environment, traditional firms can – and should – make subtle but important changes in their values to embed and meaningfully exploit design, rather than append it as nothing more than the latest management fad.

The linchpin of the required change lies with 'wicked problems'. Traditional firm values result in assuming away wicked problems as the product of immutable constraints with which the firm must live: managers avoid working on wicked problems because status comes from elsewhere, and concentrating on ongoing tasks crowds out working on and thinking about wicked problems. Even if a wicked problem is taken on in a traditional firm, the lack of appreciation of both abductive reasoning and iterative/collaborate work make it less likely that it will be tackled productively.

If instead, traditional firms recognize that wicked problems represent their biggest opportunities for value creation, they will be spurred to see that tackling them requires a project-based approach – and that the important role of projects in firm life must not be ignored, but rather protected from the tyranny of ongoing tasks. They will be more inclined to assign their best and brightest to tackle 'wicked projects', which will signal that solving wicked problems is a very high status activity. And by recognizing these issues explicitly as 'wicked problems', the firm – and those assigned to tackling the problem – will be more inclined to recognize that abductive logic and iterative/collaborative processes are necessary, given the wickedness of the problem at hand.

Firms that truly want to embed design into their fundamental operations need to wade into – not avert their eyes from – wicked problems. The response to these problems must be "bring it on," rather than "nothing can be done." Wading into wicked problems using the approaches described herein will provide the catalyst to introducing key design shop characteristics into a traditional firm. And as some of today's most successful companies have shown, infusing an organization with these principles can pay big dividends in terms of value creation. *R*

Roger Martin is Dean, Premier's Research Chair in Productivity & Competitiveness and Professor of Strategic Management at the Rotman School of Management. He is the author of eight books, most recently, *Playing to Win: How Strategy Really Works* (Harvard Business Review Press, 2013), co-authored with A.G. Lafley. In 2011, he placed sixth on the Thinkers50 list, a bi-annual ranking of the most influential global management thinkers.

A focus on design translates to
a focus on customers' true needs
and unarticulated aspirations,
ultimately creating better-informed,
more nimble companies.

THE EVOLUTION OF THE

DESIGN-INSPIRED ENTERPRISE

by **Gabriella Lojacono** and **Gianfranco Zaccai**

IN THE LITERATURE ON DESIGN, product development and innovation, the word 'design' refers to many things: a creative art, a phase of product development, a set of functional characteristics, an aesthetic quality, a profession, and more. In the lexicon of more and more companies, however, the word has come to denote the totality of activities and competencies that gather all relevant information and transform it into a new product or service.

Design is now understood as a core activity that confers competitive advantage by bringing to light the emotional meaning products and services have – or could have – for consumers, and by extracting the high value of such emotional connections. This evolution is creating the *design-focused enterprise*, an organization that uses consumer-centered product development to move quickly and effectively from intimate customer knowledge to successful product and service offerings.

Much has been written about design's ability to increase productivity, product performance and the value of the emotional connection with customers, but little about design's contribution to an overall better understanding of the consumer. There has been discussion of the role of consumer knowledge in driving innovation, but not of the practical techniques for letting consumers' unspoken, often unconscious, needs and desires emerge and for infusing such insights into all functional teams.

Nevertheless, consumer-centered product design is an emerging best practice in many industries, particularly those characterized by practical products that hold no emotional appeal; in which competition is based on increasingly less profitable attempts to cut cost or improve performance; where once-distinctive products are becoming commoditized; or where there is little room left for product innovation.

Among these best practitioners, design is viewed as the art and science of putting all the pieces together – technical, financial, operational and emotional. As most companies already lavish quite a bit of expertise on the technical, financial and operational aspects of what they do, it is this equal focus on the emotional connection with customers that stands out as novel. This newly co-equal dimension influences and informs the others, producing new and unexpected results.

These companies still have strong technology, operations, marketing, research and manufacturing competencies, but these are guided by an organization-wide, shared understanding of who their customers are and how the design of their products or services can best shape the customer experience.

Traditional consumer research – surveys, focus groups, etc. – asks people what they want. However, while customers can reliably express their preferences for incremental improvements in existing products and services, they cannot reliably express their higher-order needs and aspirations, which may call for radical redesign or for entirely new offerings. Although these higher-order aspects are what form the basis of a customer's emotional connections to any offering, the customer himself may deem them irrelevant, insignificant or even embarrassing, or may simply not be conscious of them. Because traditional consumer research is unlikely to bring such insights to light, it often provides technical, marketing and operational departments with inadequate information and debatable strategic objectives, resulting in rejection by the marketplace. Design-focused companies, on the other hand, use design research to glean such insights that help guide them to a profitable emotional connection with their customers.

For example, when **Procter & Gamble** sought to provide a better way to clean floors, it discovered that its customers did not wish for better mops but to have clean floors without mopping. P&G took the 'mopless floor' fantasy seriously and developed the very successful Swiffer line of dry and moist cleaning tools.

BMW found that drivers of its high-performance cars were not stressed by high-speed driving but by parking, so the company integrated proximity sensors and an acoustic signal to assist drivers in parking. Interestingly, BMW realized that a completely automatic system would have been an affront to the pride its customers take in their driving skills. It correctly determined which emotional connection to make and which one not to violate.

When **Master Lock Co.** learned that its customers were not as interested in its locks *per se* but on the possessions the locks protected, it switched tactics from selling padlocks as hardware to selling *security* for specific possessions. Similarly, **Sunbeam Products Inc.** (now known as **American Household**) discovered that people who bought its Coleman barbecues associated the brand with fond childhood memories of camping. The company changed the focus of its marketing from highlighting the product's performance to reinforcing the pleasant memories it evokes.

Methods of Design Research

It has been shown that front-end activities, such as brainstorming, which precede the detailed design, prototyping, pilot production and manufacturing ramp-up of a new product, can powerfully influence the outcome and significantly determine downstream costs. But brainstorming and concurrent development have to be informed by customer values and aspirations. In a design-focused enterprise, the front-end activity is design research, a systematic process for understanding the consumer's unexpressed needs and desires, then envisioning and testing new ways to meet them.

The best practice in design is to integrate people from different backgrounds into a design research team. For example, when **Johnson Controls** wanted to develop an electric room thermostat for hotels, the company assembled a design research team of technical consultants, architects, hotel managers, building managers, HVAC installers and hotel guests. The team's task was to gain firsthand insight into the customer's world and what specific products or services meant to them. Multidisciplinary teams are even more effective when the team is made up of multidisciplinary individuals who can mentally juggle the trade-offs among the competing goals of various disciplines. When ergonomics says one thing, the company culture says the opposite and customers say something else again, multidisciplinary individuals can integrate the three disparate sets of clues into an optimal solution.

In the cases we observed, design research teams started with a variety of *ethnographic techniques*, watching and recording

Testing prototypes with consumers is nothing new, but design researchers make sure to do so in a real-life context.

what people do in real life. They followed consumers into stores to watch them buy padlocks, into their homes to watch them mop floors and even into their bathrooms (via videocamera) to watch them take showers. This provides an understanding of the environment in which the product will be used. For instance, by observing customers in their homes, **Cambridge SoundWorks** learned that men who buy premium audio systems like to display them in their living rooms, whereas women would rather hide them behind plants or furniture. In an attempt to appeal to both sexes, the company launched its Newton Series in 2001, which featured powerful speakers designed to blend in with living room furniture. It became the company's most successful product up to that point.

Design research also employs *psychophysiological techniques* such as biofeedback, eye tracking, vocal analysis and facial coding to understand the emotions underlying observable behaviour. By correlating physiological characteristics such as heartrate, brainwave level, skin response or body position with a person's preferences, researchers can design the offering to maximize the desired physical responses.

Brand personification is another technique used to make hidden values and emotions perceptible. When Master Lock asked consumers to associate their current classic padlock with a person, the name most often mentioned was **John Wayne**; when they were asked to associate it with another product, the frequent answer was a military Jeep. Asked with whom or what they equated Master Lock's prototypes of innovative new concepts for padlocks, consumers most often named **Arnold Schwarzenegger** and the Humvee. When the company created a promotional campaign to launch the new locks, it was informed by these associations.

Testing prototypes with consumers is nothing new, but design researchers make sure to do so in a real-life context. Thus, Master Lock's design research team observed customers using prototypes of the new padlocks on their own luggage, toolboxes, gun cases, garden gates and trailer hitches.

Methods of gathering data can be compared in terms of their degree of customer involvement. Some traditional methods, such as brainstorming, are entirely internal. Surveys involve consumers, but the consumers can only answer what they are asked and can only express what they consciously know. Focus groups allow more freedom of expression but still cannot probe the unconscious. Design research, by observing consumers buying and using products in real life with no external guidance, offers the highest possible consumer involvement. Skilled observers have a chance to see nonverbal evidence of unconscious feelings.

Skipping design research can be costly. For example, high-end German automobile manufacturers were stunned when U.S. customers would not buy cars without cup holders. While drinking coffee in the car seemed unthinkable to Europeans, it wouldn't have taken much design research to learn how important it is to U.S. car buyers. The manufacturers, forced to retrofit, created some of the most complex, expensive, unreliable and least-user friendly cup holders ever produced.

Design research findings are not typically in the form of data and reports but are instead stories and characters, often captured on video. Such findings resemble and evoke real experience more powerfully than data and reports can, vividly conveying the desired emotional connections between people, products and services, and they help a company to triangulate these findings with appropriate technologies and economic objectives.

When the findings have been gathered, there are a number of techniques that help the researchers interpret them:

Issue mapping. Identifying all the stakeholders and decision influencers involved with ordering, stocking, displaying, promoting, buying, using, servicing and disposing of a product or a service helps to paint a fully dimensional picture of its impact and interaction with consumers and the marketplace.

Metaphors. Having consumers suggest similar products or scenarios, as Master Lock did, can help consumers express their

Design research findings are important tools for building organization-wide identification with the customers' needs and aspirations.

emotional connection to a particular product, while stimulating researchers to think along new lines. A good metaphor may end up as part of the design to communicate the emotional connection to the consumer.

Consumer archetypes. Personifying the typical consumer can be enormously helpful in keeping everyone's thinking focused on the emotional connection to consumers. The archetype can be a real person or a composite creation. For example, **AMF Bowling Worldwide** used archetypes to help make sense of an extremely broad potential target market for a major product development. Facing a mature market in the United States, the maker of equipment and furniture for the bowling alley industry set its sights on overseas markets, where bowling often has novelty and even significant prestige and where the penetration of bowling centers is still very low. AMF assumed that it needed to design for those markets specifically, and it embarked upon user-centered design research. However, the research revealed that regardless of market, the distinguishing characteristics among bowlers had to do with why they bowled: for competition, to perfect their game, for the joy of participation or for the sense of occasion. These archetypes allowed AMF to efficiently develop a product system that had global applicability.

Work-flow mapping. The visual mapping of the steps an individual takes to complete a given activity has been a standard technique for 75 years, but it can reveal new insights and opportunities when combined with the other techniques listed here.

Storytelling. Creating storyboards, associating imagery and other techniques can be used to elicit feelings and aspirational insights from consumers.

Bulletin boards. By taping, pinning and hanging all sorts of objects and information related to a project on the walls of a meeting room, design research team members can immerse themselves in information. Being literally surrounded by inputs in a room can cause designers to make connections among elements that might have initially seemed unrelated.

Building Design Focus Into the Organization
Corporate strategy is often shaped by macrodata – industry trend analysis, competitive analysis, technology assessments, demographics – and carried out by specialists focused on quarter-to-quarter sales, technical invention, measurable performance and operational efficiency. These individuals are often in separate departments that do not communicate well with each other, and the voice of the customer is often drowned out by the voices of various departments. In contrast, the findings of design research become important tools for building organization-wide identification with the customers' needs and aspirations, keeping everyone's eyes on the same prize. As people develop, manufacture, stock or maintain a product, they are much more likely to keep in mind a real person who they've watched in a video washing his car, or putting her kids to bed, than on a page of market survey results.

At Master Lock, video ethnography, in-context interviews and early conceptual sketches and models were integrated into a presentation for the proposed new segmentation. This made the rationale for the resulting strategy far more tangible than any written description or statistical data could have done. Each market segment was represented by a consumer archetype: real people who the researchers had met and with whom people in R&D, manufacturing, sales and finance could naturally empathize.

Companies can use this technique to communicate their connection with customers to important outside stakeholders, from **Walmart** buyers to Wall Street investors. In a risky and unusual move, Master Lock shared its presentation and prototyping with selected mass-merchant buyers. By allowing Master Lock to 'tell a complete story', this approach won the buyers' enthusiasm and collaboration, and it garnered the company valuable time during which key buyers agreed not to reduce their shelf space despite their declining market share.

Even with such vivid communication tools, it is necessary to continually repeat the message so that it sinks into the fabric of the organization. Once organization-wide empathy is achieved, however, every aspect of the organization can add value to the emotional connection. Not only can the traditional design areas of product, packaging, point of purchase, corporate communication and the Web site be coordinated to meet consumer needs and aspirations, but engineers can find ways to meet those needs and aspirations while still delivering function and performance.

In fact, implementing a design-inspired strategy tends to provoke some redesign of the company itself. Once Master Lock realized how much could be accomplished with its new approach, it took steps to embed consumer-centered product design at all levels. Rather than simply selling hardware to hardware buyers, the sales and marketing groups were reorganized and staffed to serve different market segments, such as automotive and recreation. Product, packaging, point of purchase, corporate communication and the Web site became coordinated, supporting the segmentation strategy with messages and visual languages appropriate to each consumer archetype. Engineering became responsible for increasing perceived value as well as actual performance. Manufacturing developed more flexible channels for getting more new products to market sooner without compromising quality or efficiency. The company also became more open to incorporating outside innovation that complemented its design-inspired strategy.

The successful practice of customer-centered product design varies from one design-focused company to another, but the companies we observed have many of the above-discussed best practices in common. They also all saw the value in, and had the capability of, making as many mistakes as possible in the front-end phase, when they could learn the most at the lowest risk and cost.

For example, Master Lock's first foray into the automotive market was the production of an innovative steering-wheel lock.

Although the company's reading of the market potential was accurate, it misjudged the obstructive power of an entrenched competitor. Master Lock was able to quickly change course and pursue a new customer in the same segment that had already been identified by its existing design research – the trailer owner. With customer archetypes and video clips imparting to all parts of the company the common image of a consumer for whom the trailer means 'freedom and security', and whose worst fear is that the trailer might be stolen, Master Lock had enough focus and cohesion to rapidly develop and introduce a unique trailer lock. This successful entry into the automotive market gave Master Lock a position from which it was later able to successfully reintroduce its steering-wheel lock.

In closing

Design-focused companies don't get everything right the first time, but they can make quick course corrections due to the depth of their customer insight and their techniques for rapidly and vividly conveying new ideas to all parts of the company in order to put that knowledge into action.

In a world in which consumers cannot always convey and may not always know what would delight them, design-focused companies are best equipped to glean the information through careful and imaginative observation, to respond accurately, quickly and flexibly and to define and lead rapidly-evolving markets. *R*

Gabriella Lojacono is a professor of business administration and design management at Bocconi University, Milan. **Gianfranco Zaccai** is president and Chief Design Officer of Continuum.

Even in seemingly 'hostile' territory, it is possible
for design thinking to prosper – if leaders
embrace the challenge by employing techniques
from the design thinker's toolbox.

by **Roger Martin**

DESIGNING IN HOSTILE TERRITORY

BROADLY SPEAKING, value creation in the 20th century was about taking a fundamental understanding of a mystery – a *heuristic* – and reducing it to a formula – an *algorithm* – so that it could be driven to huge scale and scope. As a result, many 20th-century organizations succeeded by instituting fairly linear improvements, such as reengineering, supply chain management, and cost controls. The success of **McDonald's,** **Dell** and **Walmart** depended not so much on superior products, but on a superior process.

As evidenced by the success of **Apple, Google, Amazon** and others, competition is no longer in global scale-intensive industries; rather, it's in non-traditional, imagination-intensive industries. The 21st century will be characterized by the production of elegant, refined products and services that delight users with the grace of their utility and output. And as a result, business people must think and become more like designers – more 'masters of heuristics' than 'managers of algorithms'.

Before organizations can even think about generating meaningful benefits from design, they must first address a hidden trade-off that is being made within their walls on a regular basis: the one between 'reliability' and 'validity'. The paradigmatic shift taking place in economic value creation requires individuals and organizations to move away from an obsession with *reliability* and towards creating a welcoming environment for *validity*.

A reliable process is one that produces a consistent and predictable result, over and over. To enhance the reliability of any process, one has to reduce the number of variables considered and use quantitative, bias-free measuremer n the other hand, to increase the validity of any process, one must consider a wide array of relevant variables. Of course, we would like a process that has both high validity and reliability – and up to a point, it's possible to get more of both, simply by being more thoughtful and less sloppy. But ultimately, reliability and validity are at opposite ends of a spectrum: more reliability requires fewer variables and therefore less validity, and vice versa.

Design's Bias Toward Validity

How does this trade-off relate to design, and why should it matter to today's business leaders? Design possesses an inherent bias toward validity. Great designers seek deep understanding of the user and the context, which entails the consideration of many variables. They don't limit their considerations to aspects that can be thoroughly quantified; they worry less about whether they can replicate a particular process – and more about producing a valid solution to the problem before them.

Entrepreneurs – who are essentially designers of business models – have a similar approach. They start out with new-to-the-world ideas that they believe in, but typically can't prove. They value judgment, experience and gut instinct – and in this way, they are highly validity-oriented. But as a successful entrepreneurial venture grows, it acquires outside investors and a board of directors, and it begins leaning more towards reliability. With ever-bigger bucks at stake and more scrutiny of investment de-

cisions, the growing organization increasingly values processes that are quantitative, analytical, and bias-free. Variables that are difficult to measure quantitatively – feelings, relationships – get dropped.

It's not that organizations don't like or want great design; it's just that when a validity-oriented design comes to an important corporate decision gate, the reliability-oriented question inevitably gets asked: "Can we prove this will work? How can we be sure?"

Typically, the answer is no, it can't be proven, and we can't be sure. Nobody could prove before **Herman Miller** launched its Aeron chair that it would succeed at all, let alone become the most successful office chair of all time. And so design often gets undermined, subdued, or killed without explicit intent – a victim of the corporate bias toward reliability.

If an organization wants to enjoy the benefits of design in its products, services, processes and business models, it must go considerably beyond simply hiring designers or declaring itself to be design-oriented. Its leaders must take responsibility for safeguarding validity. If they don't, the natural inclination towards reliability will win out. The questions people ask, the proof they demand, the way they treats failure – each sends a signal as to whether design thinking is 'safe' or not. If their questions are all about the most readily-quantifiable numbers, and if the standard of proof is high and numerically-driven, and if failure is treated as indicative of incompetence, employees will understand that their organization values reliability over validity.

If, however, a leader's questions probe the trickier *qualitative* aspects of a decision along with the hard numbers; if she utilizes a balanced standard of proof that takes into account the complexity of the issue at hand; and if she treats failure as an unfortunate consequence of living in a risk-filled world, then she will signal that she balances the need for reliability with the desire for validity. And she will foster design thinking.

The Validity vs. Reliability Battlefield

A friend who works for a large wireless provider complained to me recently about the impossibility of taking a design approach

What are the user's greatest hopes?
What keeps the user up at night?
What are the minimum acceptable conditions
for the user to embrace a design solution?

in his 'design-unfriendly' organization. He recently put forward a new approach to customer service designed to dramatically enhance retention, and it was shot down in flames by, of all things, the 'Corporate Customer Innovation Committee.' "Roger," he bemoaned, "You write all this stuff about business design, innovation and creativity, but unless managers have a CEO who aggressively promotes design, they will be squelched."

I can feel his pain, and I empathize with him; but do I sympathize? Not really, because he is thinking about the question from a design-free perspective and expecting a design-friendly outcome that is just not going to happen, much as I might wish it for him. The bottom line is, you don't need anyone's permission to think like a designer. But there are five things you need to do if you want to be effective in a design-unfriendly organization.

1. Take 'Design Unfriendliness' on as a Design Challenge

This is the essential starting point. A key tenet of designers is that constraints make the challenge more exciting and rewarding, and hence the absence of a design-appreciative CEO is not a constraint about which to complain. To be sure, it is a constraint. But to a designer, a constraint is an important signal – a signal of the presence and centrality of a design challenge. And that challenge was not, in my friend's case, the design of a customer retention enhancement. The real and highest-order challenge was the design of a way for the Customer Innovation Committee to get itself comfortable enough with a proposed new initiative to take action on it.

The non-designer's approach is to imagine the task as creating a nifty way to enhance customer retention, while averting his eyes from the constraint of creating an idea that is compelling to the Customer Innovation Committee. This is what I call 'narrow perfectionism': if you ignore the trickiest constraints and define victory narrowly, you can always achieve victory and blame someone else – i.e. the Innovation Committee – for the failure to produce beneficial action.

In contrast, the design thinking manager would hone in on the most difficult constraint – 'design unfriendliness' – and integrate that constraint into her design approach. This of course makes the challenge bigger and more complicated, increasing the

possibility of failure – all of which does nothing to deter a true design thinker; in fact, it attracts them even further to the challenge.

2. Empathize with the 'Design-Unfriendly' Elements

The only way to design a compelling solution for a user is to understand that user in a positive way. If the Customer Innovation Committee can only be understood by my friend as 'a bunch of ultra-conservative, gutless Luddites', then the key insights to designing a compelling solution for them will be hidden. It is almost impossible to design something compelling for a person whom you don't respect or attempt to understand. The architect's filing cabinet full of never-built plans for houses designed for clients he viewed as 'philistines' are testament to the limitation of disrespecting your user. The architect consoles himself with the brilliance of his design, without having any better explanation of its still-born fate other than "the client had no appreciation of architecture." The same holds for credenzas full of unused strategic plans from strategy consultants and book shelves full of unpublished manuscripts for the 'next great novel'.

In contrast, the design-thinking manager attempts to achieve a deep understanding of the user in order to uncover the greatest range of options for creating a compelling solution. What are the user's greatest hopes? What keeps the user up at night? What are the minimum acceptable conditions for the user to embrace a design solution? How much risk is the user willing to absorb?

Crucially, each of us has a choice of answering these questions either with *empathy* or *disdain* for the user. The non-designer sees what keeps the user up at night as the desire to 'keep his proverbial ass covered'; while the design-thinking manager sees what keeps the user up at night as the desire to protect his employees from the consequences of a reckless decision. The latter form of understanding enables the designer to probe what constitutes a reckless decision versus a 'sensibly-aggressive decision', and hone in on a sensibly-aggressive decision – from the user's standpoint. Because the non-designer has no idea where the user draws the line between 'sensibly' and 'recklessly' aggressive, she will create a solution that inadvertently lies in the reckless zone, and will be rejected out of hand.

The best tool available is analogy:
crafting a story that takes an existing idea
in operation elsewhere and shows how it is
similar to the novel idea being proposed.

3. Speak the Language of Reliability

In order to empathize, one needs to communicate. The problem is that 'design-unfriendly' and design-oriented people speak different languages. The former speak the language of reliability, putting a high priority on the production of consistent, predictable outcomes. They frequently use words such as 'proof', 'regression analysis', 'certainty', 'best practices', and 'deployment'. Design-oriented people speak the language of validity, putting a high priority on producing outcomes that delight users, whether they are consistent and predictable or not. They frequently use words such as 'visualization', 'prototyping', 'beta-testing' and 'novelty'.

The latter words quite simply terrify the members of a design-unfriendly organization; they don't really understand what they mean to the designers, and the way in which they do understand them runs in direct opposition to the things they hold near and dear to their hearts. These design-oriented words connote danger, uncertainty and guess-work; things that encourage, if not compel them to say no.

If a design-oriented person is indeed embedded in a design-unfriendly organization, she is going to have to wait a very long time for the organization to learn the subtleties of her language. It is incumbent on her to learn the language of the majority – the language of reliability. This will enable her to do the best as possible to describe her ideas in reliability-oriented language. It simply won't cut it to say, "I know that no one has ever tried this before, but I think it is going to knock the socks off our customers!"

I should know: I vividly remember working as a relatively young consultant for a gigantic bank on a private banking strategy for its high net-worth customers. My team came up with a breakthrough idea based on insights about the customers that the bank had never considered. In due course, we were given an audience to present our proposed strategy to the bank's CEO and his six direct reports. They listened attentively. At the end, the COO asked one question: "Have any of our competitors ever done anything like this?" Revelling in the unique brilliance of our solution, I enthusiastically responded: "No, not even close!"

I was too young, foolish and design-insensitive to realize that my answer put the final nail in the coffin of our idea. That was 1988; it is small consolation that I have recently observed several banks utilizing the approach we laid out almost two decades ago.

4. Use Analogies and Stories

What tools can help bridge the 'language gap'? It is difficult to provide 'proof' or 'certainty', even if a design-thinking manager appreciates that those words loom large in the reliability lexicon. The best tool available is analogy: crafting a story that takes an existing idea in operation elsewhere and shows how it is similar to the novel idea being proposed – not exactly the same, but similar enough to provide the proverbial 'trail of bread crumbs' from the analogy to the new idea.

So rather than either exalting the complete novelty of the design idea or throwing-in the towel because it simply can't be proven with certainty, admit that while it has elements of newness, it also looks a lot like x combined with a little of y, both of which have been working for some time. Had I had more empathy with my banker clients and understood the language of reliability, I might have responded to their query, "None of our domestic competitors have done this; but a variant of this approach has been used by some of the best-performing European private banks for some time now. It isn't exactly the same, but it bears important similarities. And recall, our bank has succeeded in the past when it taken an idea from outside our home market and introduced it here."

This approach doesn't eliminate the risky appearance of the idea, but it helps the receivers formulate a reliability-oriented argument to themselves. And in the end, in order to take action, they will need to convince themselves that the idea falls into an acceptable range of reliability.

5. Bite Off as Little a Piece as Possible to Generate Proof

Even with careful use of language and employment of analogies, 'proof' remains the biggest problem for design thinkers. They simply don't traffic in it – at least not 'before-the-fact' proof of the sort reliability-oriented folks crave. Designers simply can't prove in advance that their ideas will work in the way that a reliability-oriented executive can prove that he sold $800 million of product in the latest fiscal year. As a consequence, a big part of the task facing the design-thinking manager in a design-unfriendly environment is to generate bits of 'proof' on the way to the full deployment of the design idea.

Design-oriented managers don't like this notion. Typically, they want approval of their whole idea, because it feels to them that any parsing or phasing of the solution will destroy its integrity. That may have appeal to the designer, but that approach once again averts eyes to the real design challenge – how to bring the idea to life in a somewhat hostile environment.

It may not be entirely comfortable, but a whole industry – venture capital – has figured out this approach. The entrepreneurs that venture capitalists finance are validity-oriented designers: they attempt to come up with new-to-the-world products or services, which they believe will be smash hits, but they can't prove this in advance. Each one would love the venture capitalists to see exactly what they see and generously fund the entire project from start to finish. But since the wacky days of 1998-2000, that rarely happens. The venture capitalists, who feel the need to be more reliability-oriented on behalf of their investors, dole out the venture financing in little dollops, with each round contingent on increasing levels of 'proof' that full deployment of the idea in question will be a big success.

Like venture-capital-backed entrepreneurs, design-thinking managers living in 'design-unfriendly' environments need to develop the capacity to create roll-out plans for their ideas that help their organization ratchet up its confidence, one step at a time.

In closing

Certain corporate departments – including powerful ones like finance – are more insulated from direct market pressures and can more easily slide into deep reliability. Strict numerical proof is required before anything can happen; finance provides the templates for analysis, sets the burden of proof, and anything that can't be strictly quantified is unnecessarily risky.

Every organization needs a strong finance function – and human resources, product development, legal, etc. – but its leaders need to understand that they can't let finance or any other division run roughshod over validity, or they will unknowingly drive design thinking out of their organization. That's why an additional task for today's CEO is to act as the 'CVO' – Chief Validity Officer – in order to protect and nurture a design culture.

While my aforementioned friend would love to be given the latitude to think design thoughts and experience no friction in bringing them to life in his organization, reality is rarely going to be so idyllic. However, neither he nor others in his situation need to assume that it is impossible for design thinking to survive in seemingly hostile territory. Design thinking can prosper if managers in my friend's position embrace the challenge of designing in hostile territory. *R*

Roger Martin is Dean, Premier's Research Chair in Productivity & Competitiveness and Professor of Strategic Management at the Rotman School of Management. He is the author of eight books, most recently, *Playing to Win: How Strategy Really Works* (Harvard Business Review Press, 2013), co-authored with A.G. Lafley. In 2011, he placed sixth on the Thinkers50 list, a bi-annual ranking of the most influential global management thinkers.

Opportunity Maps can help leaders make choices about what to do
and what *not* to do, charting a path for future growth.

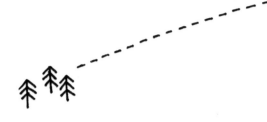

MAPPING THE FUTURE IN UNCERTAIN TIMES

by Alonzo Canada

ON PAPER, ROB MCEWEN WAS AN UNLIKELY CHAIRMAN and CEO for Canadian mining company **Goldcorp, Inc.** With a background in finance, the small, soft-spoken man with the neatly-trimmed moustache preferred meticulous tailoring to industrial machinery. But despite his appearance, McEwen was a prospector at heart: he had a fascination with gold and grew up hearing tales from his father about miners, prospectors and grubstakes at the dinner table. So smitten was he with the industry that he ham-

mered out his own template for what he thought a 21st-century gold-mining company should look like, despite never having worked for one. In 1989, he made the leap, stepping into a takeover and becoming majority owner of under-performing Goldcorp.

Some called him crazy for buying what was regarded as a rust bucket of a company. At the time, the gold market was depressed; the mine's operating costs were inflated and the miners were perpetually on strike. McEwen even received a death threat; but he stuck with it, because he believed the business had a promising future. "The Red Lake gold district had two operating gold mines and 13 former mines that had produced more than 18 million ounces combined," he once said. "The mine next door had produced about 10 million ounces; ours produced only 3 million." McEwen believed that the high-grade ore that ran through the neighboring mine was present in parts of the 55,000-acres he owned – if only he could find it.

To turn around his dream company, he needed to find new sources of value within his existing business. He had to make some very big decisions about where to dig, and he couldn't afford to be wrong. Inspiration struck him one day at an MIT seminar, where he learned about open-source code, wide collaboration and the story of the increasingly-popular **Linux** operating system. McEwen realized that if he could attract world-class talent to the problem of finding more gold in Red Lake, they could potentially transform Goldcorp's geological data to reveal the most promising places to dig. He didn't need to get lucky: he needed new ways to see where value was hiding on his property.

The rest, of course, is history. McEwen launched the Goldcorp Challenge in March 2000, splaying the company's proprietary geological data to the world. More than 14,000 scientists, engineers and geologists from 50 different countries downloaded the data for virtual exploration. The winner of the contest was a collaboration by two groups in Australia, **Fractal Graphics** and **Taylor Wall & Associates**, which together developed a powerful 3D graphical depiction of the mine. Goldcorp drilled four of their top five targets and struck gold on all four. This new way of looking at the business laid the foundation for McEwen to restructure Goldcorp, increasing its market capitalization from $50 million to more than $13 billion and growing its share price at a 40 per cent compound annual growth rate.

When McEwen bought Goldcorp, it was failing largely because it was unable to see where true value resided on its property. Its existing maps were insufficient, because they simply articulated previously-made discoveries, which had obvious limitations. As **Albert Einstein** once said, "the definition of insanity is doing the same thing over and over again and expecting different results." In order to renew growth at Goldcorp, McEwen needed a fundamentally-different way of seeing the world. His approach of pooling experts to solve his problem is widely celebrated as a benefit of using an 'open innovation approach'. Less-often discussed is the output from Fractal and Taylor Wall: the team crunched, reconstituted and synthesized mountains of geologic data into a wholly-new map that revealed promising new mining targets. In short, they created a map focused on finding value, rather than on verifying existing data, and in the process, they helped McEwen make savvy bets on the future growth of his company.

Mapping in Uncertain Territory

Though few executives outside of the mining industry actively dig to find new growth for their business, virtually every company's future depends on pursuing bold new ideas with an uncertain payback. Just as Goldcorp couldn't grow until McEwen redrew his existing maps, leaders seeking growth must look beyond what is commonly known to reinvent their core business, develop adjacencies and target 'white space' opportunities. They need to see the world differently than their competitors by reframing their market landscape to discover previously-hidden opportunities; and, they need a differentiated strategy with a roadmap on how to target those opportunities over time.

At **Jump Associates,** we are often asked to help executives create new businesses or reinvent existing ones. Such challenges are inherently unpredictable: it is simply impossible to guess what the next big business will be. In response, companies take a variety of approaches to pursuing organic growth. Some take pains to avoid pioneering new categories, waiting for competitors to validate that an idea has legs; others become hopelessly incremental, creating new products and services only if they are clear extensions of existing lines. More cavalier companies simply launch as many new things as they can, waiting for something to stick.

We have found that the best way to manage the inherent uncertainty of innovation is to take a page from McEwen's book and look beyond the existing data to find out where value truly resides for your business. One of the most effective methods for doing this is to create an Opportunity Map – a visual representation of a business landscape that guides future strategy by synthesizing met and unmet consumer needs, emerging discontinuities such as cultural and technology trends, both direct and indirect competitive activity, and internal and external competitive competencies. Synthesizing all of this data helps innovation teams separate the handful of opportunities that they *should* target from the dozens they shouldn't. In short, it helps managers make better decisions – both in larger questions of long-term growth strategy and on more short-term concerns about whether a new product category is worth entering.

It's useful to think of an Opportunity Map as a book with chapters: each chapter is a layer of data on the map that visually and verbally articulates a larger narrative about what's important to a firm, its customers and its short- and long-term growth opportunities. While there are no hard-and-fast rules for how many data layers to include or which kinds of data are most important in an Opportunity Map, we have found a few to be particularly useful.

1. Begin With a Foundational Framework
Start with a 'foundational framework' that defines the boundaries and fundamental dynamics of your firm's business land-

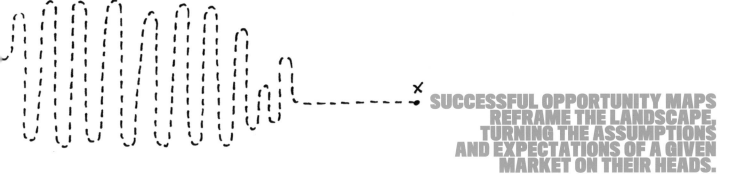

scape. Spatially map opportunity spaces as 'islands in an ocean.' Next, create a layer that captures existing and potential solutions, future technology trends, direct and indirect competitive offerings, and analogous points of view within the landscape. To see beyond technology and the competition, consider creating a layer formed of descriptions of consumer needs, behaviour and activities. Finally, your map will be most actionable if you add a layer that captures, plots, and contextualizes the central firm's capabilities and existing and future initiatives.

The structure and dimensions of the foundational framework define the boundaries and describe the forces that shape a landscape, embodying a point of view about what is important to a firm and its customers by emphasizing customer needs and market categories that are relevant and excluding those that aren't. Such spatial plotting of opportunities also allows a firm to see the relationships between opportunities and more effectively ascertain their promise. Unlike an atlas, this is not a map of the world. For example, if a firm were making an Opportunity Map for business travel, it may or may not include hotels, luggage or airlines. These choices depend on what type of business your company is in.

2. Develop 'Thick Descriptions'

Without any underlying thinking, opportunity mapping risks becoming an exercise in graphic design. To avert this, accompany the foundational framework and its opportunities with 'thick descriptions' that synthesize what the data means. *Thick descriptions* is a term coined by cultural anthropologist **Clifford Gertz**, who said that in order for human behaviour to make sense to an outside observer, a thick description is necessary to explain not just how people act, but the *context* for their behaviour. Each opportunity on the map should include thick descriptions that synthesize consumer needs, existing competitive and analogous solutions, consumer behaviours, cultural trends, technology trends and competitive activity. Just as each opportunity area is spatially plotted on the map, the contextual data is plotted as well, providing further detail about commonalties and interrelationships.

3. Perform Strategic Evaluation

Good data alone does not make for a useful opportunity map; it is just as important to layer in key strategic criteria. After all, there is no such thing as a universally-ideal opportunity. Getting into digital music players and distribution in 2001 turned out to be a brilliant move for **Apple**, but it would have been a disaster for **Honeywell**. In order to properly assess their potential, opportunities must be evaluated on firm-specific criteria such as brand fit, strategic alignment, barriers to entry, strength of need, competitive activity, use of leverageable assets and existing capabilities. Similarly, it's important to understand where on the map the direct competition will play, both in the short term and in the long term. This isn't just about the competition's current and future offerings, but also their brands, messaging, marketplace positions and key activity systems that might give them advantages. This continued layering of data can clarify how a firm can best compete, making certain to play to its own strengths – and not those of its competitors.

Reframing Your Landscape

Successful Opportunity Maps reframe the landscape, turning the assumptions and expectations of a given market on their heads and enabling an organization to follow a clear, differentiated approach. A reframe is much more than an insight or an interesting nugget of data: it constitutes a fundamental shift in thinking about how the world works by not only shedding light on a situation but invalidating previous models. Armed with the right reframe, companies can discover new value in almost any market.

The discount retail sector provides an example. This industry has long been focused on living up to its name by selling cheap stuff. **Walmart** has become the largest company on earth by finding ways to drive out cost in everything it sells, building a competitive advantage that no one can match – though that hasn't stopped other retailers like **K-Mart** from trying, much to their peril. The only large discount retailer that has responded effectively to the rise of Walmart is **Target**, and the reason for this is quite simple: Target is the only company that has a fundamentally different view of discount retail than Walmart's. Despite its broad appeal, Target views its business through the lens of one very important person, a single 'ideal guest:' she's a 35-year-old suburban mom with two kids who needs to look out for value but aspires to give her family much more than what a rock-bottom price might offer. Everything Target does seeks to delight this woman, from its house-branded products to the design of its stores to the vendors whose stuff it puts on shelves, which together constitutes a reframing of the market.

Walmart has won by saying people should get what they buy at the lowest possible price; Target has managed to find its own way to thrive by saying that although low prices are important, discount retail is actually about getting more out of everyday household goods than mere functionality. That's a very different view of the industry – and one as hard to copy as Walmart's legendary efficiency, because it plays to Target's core strengths in marketing, design and trend spotting.

Bridging Needs and Solutions

Economics is governed by the principles of supply and demand. Innovation is also governed by fundamental laws, but very different ones: *needs* and *solutions*. Let's say you're looking for ways to improve store efficiency, and you observe that a clerk is having trouble getting boxes from a high shelf. You might conclude that he needs a ladder, but a ladder is merely one of many possible solutions to his need to reach the boxes. You could also lower the shelf, raise the floor, give him flying shoes, or encourage him to grow a few inches, to name but a few. Reaching a box is a need; a ladder is a solution. Significantly, needs outlive solutions. Therefore, when considering the long-term potential of the market, it is critical to understand both the needs you're serving and the solutions that will be profitable and viable today and in the future. For this very reason, a good Opportunity Map accounts for present-day solutions while also grounding concepts for future development in needs that will persist over time.

At a recent corporate retreat for the venerable venture capital firm **Kleiner, Perkins Caufield & Byers**, partner **Bill Joy** presented what he called 'the map of grand challenges'. This chart of multi-colored squares tracked the firm's progress in identifying and investing in key categories of green energy technologies, including transportation, energy efficiency, electricity generation, energy storage and more. These were the existing solutions that met current needs for sustainable energy. Joy also left blank spots on this chart that hinted at new technologies that should be possible in the near future. These spots were the needs that current solutions could not yet meet.

Because Joy's map synthesized both needs and solutions, it has come to represent a rough conceptual outline for the future clean energy economy. The firm now uses this map as its playbook, investing in promising start-ups with nascent solutions and stimulating universities and laboratories to create new technologies in order to meet critical unmet needs. Basically, if your green-tech idea could solve one of the blank challenges on Kleiner's map, they're interested in talking to you; if not, it's a much harder pitch for their investment.

Defining Both the Island and the 'X'

What good is a treasure map with no X on it? It's about as useful as a piece of paper that has an X on it but no drawing of the surrounding island. Good Opportunity Maps include both 'fields of interest' (large possible areas for investment and development) and points (specific ideas for offerings and businesses.) This not only provides an overview of the realm of possibilities, it highlights where to concentrate efforts for the greatest return.

For decades now, it has been apparent that clean technology and alternative energy had the potential to become remarkably lucrative fields. **BP** made its first investments in solar energy in 1973, but the promised 'big green ship' still hasn't come in. The last half-century is, instead, littered with the detritus of countless ambitious projects that promised to propel the economy and save the earth at the same time. Forty years later, breakthroughs are still in short supply. How could this be? Perhaps the answer is that past green-technology efforts have been too broad and too ambitious. Companies have had maps that show them the islands where a green economy might one day be built, but they don't have the Xs marking the spots where treasure is buried.

GE has been one of a very small handful of large corporations that has driven measurable growth through its investments in green technologies and alternative energy generation, and it has done so remarkably quickly. In 2005, the company announced Ecomagination, a major initiative to tackle the big challenges of sustainability that have vexed so many others. But GE didn't merely declare that it was going to the island of green technology. CEO **Jeff Immelt** very carefully noted the specific targets most appropriate to his organization's strengths and capabilities. Specifically, he started with efficient lighting (literally the company's founding business), hybrid locomotives, lower-emission aircraft engines, and highly-efficient wind turbines. Following this targeted approach within the vast landscape of environmental possibility, GE has rapidly realized returns from its Ecomagination investments. By next year, after just five years, it expects those efforts will constitute more than $20 billion in revenue, nearly 15 per cent of the entire company's contributions. By creating a map containing both the islands and the Xs, GE has turned the perpetual money sink of going green into, well, green.

Defining Your True Competition

Executives often live in fear of being blindsided by their competition. Unfortunately, many traditional strategic frameworks are inadequate to anticipate possible game-changers, in large part because they focus heavily on existing activities. It is doubtful that anyone applying **Michael Porter**'s Five Forces Model to the passenger rail industry circa 1874 could have guessed that their most threatening substitutes would turn out to be automobiles and flying machines. Opportunity Maps, by contrast, synthesize a wide variety of data on both current and future activity, making them particularly effective at identifying potential moves from incumbents and new entrants. Moreover, a focus on needs and cultural phenomena means that seemingly unrelated competitors aren't missed. This knowledge can lead a team to discover unique insights about how it might best address such competitive threats through direct competitive moves or strategic partnerships.

Several years ago, the Explore team at **Nike** was given the mandate to help the larger organization become not just a shoe company, but a *sports* company. The team met the challenge by creating a map to identify its most promising opportunities, defining a strategy for growth and setting first steps toward a future vision. The team ascertained opportunities beyond shoes, like sunglasses, watches, MP3 players and sports apparel. The data on their Opportunity Map included consumer needs, societal and technology trends, and their usual competitive set of **Puma, Adidas** and **Reebok**. To maximize the map's utility, however, the team also considered indirect competitors like **MTV**, who had a competing opinion about what kids should do after school: Nike wants you playing sports, and MTV wants you to sit in front of the tube. Because the team also looked at indirect competing points of view, their work led Nike to consider opportunities that it might have otherwise overlooked, such as new partnerships that marry sports and digital entertainment, including the wildly successful Nike+iPod platform.

Charting a Path to a Better Future

Long-term opportunities are seductive. After all, they're bigger bets, which means that they carry significantly greater potential rewards than ideas with a closer horizon. Of course, this also means that they carry far greater risks, cost more to develop, and don't show results for a longer period of time than most organizations find acceptable. As such, it's rarely a good idea to focus exclusively on far-out new ventures, just as it's a bad idea to pursue only the opportunities that are easiest for your organization to develop given existing strengths and capabilities.

Successful Opportunity Maps don't just help companies see which opportunity areas they should develop, they allow them to set a clear, phased path from the current state of affairs to a new long-term strategic position. This is one advantage to making a visual map – it literally depicts far-off opportunities as being further away from your current position. Moreover, it shows how success in a few key near-term opportunity areas can set you up to get the most out of more audacious long-term goals.

The **San Diego Zoo** recently took on several initiatives to explore new opportunities for growth. Working closely with Jump, the Zoo defined more than a dozen new opportunities that would potentially strengthen its business model while increasing its impact as a global conservation and education leader. Some of these were extremely 'close in', such as using the Zoo as a showcase for sustainable technologies and leveraging the Zoo's unique skills to provide consulting and research services in the emerging field of Biomimicry. These were made immediate priorities, and the Zoo began executing upon them virtually from the day the project ended. But promising as they were, these close-in ideas did not, on their own, constitute a strategic vision for the Zoo's future. Instead, they were territory to immediately expand into before stepping toward more ambitious opportunities that would be nearly impossible to develop today.

Rather than leaping to the biggest prizes, Opportunity Maps create a clear sense of priority and a set order for development. With a good map, an organization can get a clear sense of why it is going after certain ideas today, and why it is ignoring dozens of other interesting ideas.

In closing

Any way you slice it, charting a path to a better future is an act of faith. Rob McEwen had a hunch that there was hidden value on Goldcorp's Red Lake property, and Fractal Graphics and Taylor Wall & Associates remodeled the existing data and redrew the map to discover where to dig. Like McEwen, leaders must navigate uncertainty by following the courage of their convictions about what is best for their company and the customers it serves.

Forging such conviction can be challenging when sifting through the tangle of choices pertaining to a firm's future prospects, but Opportunity Maps can help leaders navigate this complexity as they chart a path to future growth for their company. Ultimately, hunches must be substantiated and insights discovered so that the organization is clear about why it chooses to do some things and not others – the very essence of strategy. *R*

Alonzo Canada is SVP of Strategy for the Technology practice of Jump Associates, a leading growth strategy firm in San Mateo, California. In addition to consulting with executives at a variety of S&P 500 companies, he teaches design methods at the Hasso Plattner Institute of Design at Stanford University.

by **Peter Coughlan** and **Ilya Prokopoff**

MANAGING CHANGE BY DESIGN

Coupling design and business expertise creates a capacity to envision and realize futures that are both desirable for stake-holders and viable for organizations.

WE READ EVERYWHERE ABOUT rapid and constant change and, therefore, the increasing unpredictability of the future. And yet, we have seen little in the way of tools and methods to manage that change effectively and proactively. The tools of traditional business planning start with the assumptions that maintaining the current state is the best strategy, and that incremental growth is a satisfactory outcome.

But what if we can no longer base our future business on what has happened in the past? We believe that organizations might look to tools from the field of design to help business managers both get in touch with their customers' (and other stake-holders') unarticulated needs and desires, and to intentionally imagine and create futures based on the one thing that seems to remain relatively stable even in times of great change: human behaviour. When made a part of an organization's work processes and competencies, design tools enable the organization to embrace change as a normal part of managing its business.

Tools for Change

A recent health care client of ours was engaged in long-range planning activities that included the introduction of a multi-story patient care tower, to be completed in seven years.

Shortly after finalizing plans for the building, one of the hospital's core specialty groups severed ties to the hospital in order to open up an integrated-service facility literally across the street from where this new tower was to be erected. This move, coupled with a drop in the cost of core medical technology, procedural changes that dramatically reduced the required length of stay in a hospital, and shifts in consumer demand and expectations about how care could be delivered, suddenly rendered obsolete any plans based on the hospital's past.

Looking at alternative data from what managers are typically exposed to, hospital leadership might have seen that the drivers behind this change were evolving requirements for patient care – for example, competitive pressures, technology, and human resource issues. However, the data that management had at its disposal – customer survey and employee satisfaction data – indicated general satisfaction with the services provided by the hospital; it did not reveal what problems, if any, customers had with the current services, or what they might have preferred if given a choice. No amount of examining the past could have prepared hospital leadership for this dramatic turn of events.

What could management have looked at to make a better guess about their future? And once it understood its present condition, how could the hospital have come up with an appropriate plan for getting to the future? Below, we describe three tools from the designer's tool box that we have found to be particularly effective in helping businesses manage change.

1. Contextual Observation

Effective design (whether incremental or radical) begins with a clear understanding of the problem to be solved. In order to help formulate problem statements, designers look to people's behaviour for the data they need. Specifically, designers use observational research methodologies to reveal latent needs that can form the basis of change initiatives. They do this by going out and looking at people engaged in everyday activity. Designers observe, take pictures, ask questions about the here and now. They discover what people specifically like and dislike about their work or play, what pictures they have in their heads about how a process works, how they have invented ways to work around a particular problem, and what ritualistic behaviour they engage in during a given activity. In short, they look at what is commonplace and familiar, and they reveal the ways in which it is unique, allowing them to break through existing assumptions and acceptance of things as "the way it's always been done," so that new opportunities for change can be explored.

Some common methods we use to help our clients 'see the familiar in un-familiar ways' include:

- mock journeys, in which we simulate the experience of a customer, or someone else for whom we are designing;
- shadowing those involved in a process to note their everyday behaviours, use of tools, communication patterns, and so forth;
- expert walk-throughs to quickly understand complex processes;
- spatial observations, to absorb the atmosphere of a location, observe behavioural patterns, and look for evidence of 'everyday workarounds' or innovations that may indicate unmet needs; and
- day-in-the-life surveys, to get stakeholders to take note of their own surroundings and behaviour.

We are always surprised by how difficult it is for managers, who typically have extensive quantitative and qualitative data at their disposal, to 'see' their reality, because the data have been stripped of the emotional content that forms the basis for the most compelling change initiatives. Giving people a different way of seeing that reality helps them to articulate their unmet needs or desires. For our health care client, getting them to shadow a day-in-the-life of a doctor, or to walk in the gown of a patient, gave them a much clearer sense of what was and wasn't working in the system. Seeing data captured from everyday reality (as opposed to data captured from a satisfaction survey) helped them to understand the vast number of opportunities to create new services or to improve existing ones, to retain customers and doctors alike.

2. Human-Centered Frameworks

System-level problems are hard to solve. In organizations of any size, people often complain that the organization has "a life of its own," or that "change is impossible," in spite of the fact that people can usually identify what is not working. The reason for this is simple: although most systems have evolved over time from something small and simple to something larger and more complex, their growth has not typically been managed in a holistic way. The design of the system is no longer contained in the head of a single individual or group – rather, it is emergent across multiple individuals or groups. Incompatibilities or even conflicts are no one person's or department's responsibility. It is simply that different parts of the same system have been optimized for their own local goals, resulting in silos that are hard or impossible to stitch together seamlessly.

Designers create frameworks so that they can simplify and unify design opportunities in order to conceive of possible futures and make sure that all the parts and pieces that compose

EXHIBIT A: PATIENT-CARE DELIVERY MODEL
CLIENT: SSM HEALTH CARE'S DEPAUL HEALTH CENTER, BRIDGETON, MISSOURI

SSM Health Care approached IDEO with a vision to develop a new patient care model at the **DePaul Health Center** that will ultimately provide the foundation for improved services. Realizing that hospital services influence the well-being and care of people, DePaul aspired to provide innovation for a comfortable patient experience. To achieve this, IDEO explored the hospital's space usage, technology, services, and staffing and then developed design concepts for a new patient care delivery system.

The IDEO team worked onsite at DePaul's facility to fully research the opportunities for innovation. By brainstorming, observing, interviewing, and actually living as a DePaul patient, they visually 'mapped' the patient-journey process, documented DePaul's procedures from patient check-in to recuperation. Visualizing the journey helped IDEO identify current challenges, such as moments of confusion, and helped the Center recognize that these 'moments' were actually 'translation points' where new designs could have significant impact.

IDEO provided DePaul with a framework to create its new patient care delivery model and developed concepts to support the new model. In addition, the designers worked closely with a cross-functional team from DePaul to prototype and begin testing some of the design solutions. By learning the basic steps of process innovation and receiving a rough implementation plan, DePaul can now further refine and actualize the design concepts.

Amongst the changes proposed by IDEO: valet parking; 'frequent flyer cards' that detail regular returnees' needs and preferences; self-registration; a patient hotline for instant connection to staff who can act as a system translator; pod-like staff work spaces that keep caregivers closer to patients; a 'family healing area'; and vending machines in waiting areas that dispense bandages, over the counter analgesics and other temporary discomfort relievers.

Place of Practice
Places of practice, like the radiology suite at left, are dedicated to facilitating the staff's most efficient and best work for the patient. While primarily serving system goals, there are numerous simple opportunities for important translation to occur which can greatly impact the patient experience.

1. Patient Journey Punch Card
Carried with the patient and updated by staff, this allows for a simple graphic way for the patient to know where they've been and what is coming next.

2. Patient Garment with Information Badges
Additive badges allow the staff to get a brief history of the patient visually.

3. Modal Diversion
Patient has automatic control over simple things in their environment – everything from important information to a personal soundtrack accompanies the patient on their journey.

4. Information Transfer Doorway
A place for a simple log of patient interactions, patient photos and useful tools facilitate the doorway as a translation zone. Eventually information transfer can happen wirelessly.

5. Patient Hotline
A patient Hotline allows for instant connection to staff who can act as a systems translator. All mediated staff interactions happen through the phone because it is a familiar interface.

6. Patient Manuals
Customized patient manuals which track the patient journey based on their specific illness can allow for the possibility of in depth information at any point.

7. Staff Cross-Training
Anyone coming in contact with the patient has the minimum knowledge necessary to answer simple questions and help in basic matters.

The **Mayo Clinic** has developed a worldwide reputation for practicing cooperative, patient-focused medical care for people with some of the most severe forms of illness. At Mayo's three primary outpatient facilities in the U.S., physicians and health-care practitioners combine their skills and experience in team fashion to help solve people's medical problems in a way that puts the patient first. To enhance service provision, Mayo invited IDEO to help turn an internal medicine wing into a laboratory for improving the patient-provider experience. The new venture is known throughout Mayo as the SPARC Innovation Program, which stands for See, Plan, Act, Refine, and Communicate.

IDEO began by observing how patients interacted in waiting areas and exam rooms, and how they worked with doctors, nurses, and staff to navigate the health care process. They provided the Mayo team with a basic template for creating service delivery innovation - a systematic process that includes how to brainstorm new ideas for using the space, rapidly prototype novel service delivery designs, and use customer observation and direct feedback to refine solutions.

Supporting patient-physician communications is one way in which Mayo and IDEO worked together to put the process into action. The team devised a simple and flexible design for the internal medicine corridor that allows for more informative, comfortable, and guided interactions among staff and patients. Physically, the team turned the wing into a four-zone 'moving journey' through which patients proceed.

The first stop is the Service Home Base, an inviting locale that provides visitors with resources for planning their trip through Mayo. This area can be used in various ways, and Mayo plans to develop it into a highly visible information hub that displays literature about the clinic. Sectioned waiting spaces can be used as a tool to explore new designs in better accommodating individuals who want privacy, or families who need to spread out.

The Visitor-Facing Hub is the second destination, allowing patients to choose the type of service they need – be it drop-in and pick-up, check-in, or in-depth information. The flexible set-up enables the eventual use of clear graphics that will give visitors easy and quick access to precisely the information they require – without long waits or hassles. A frosted glass wall allows translucent views into behind-the-scenes areas, enhancing the sense of friendliness and accessibility and making innovation processes and practices as visible as possible to Mayo customers.

In the Preparation Service Area, providers take patients' vital statistics and offer educational consultation in advance of their meeting with the physician. Half-rooms provide flexible modules that can be easily outfitted for a variety of purposes. Architectural features such as special lighting and translucent barriers enhance the sense of service and intimacy.

Finally, patients enter Innovation Central, where exam rooms feature outside walls that are used as storytelling boards to convey patient information and movable interior panels that can modulate between privacy and open space. Furniture and space are configured for collaboration and can accommodate large-group communication.

The wing will remain a section of the clinic where staff and physicians can continually develop new processes for improving service delivery. Over the long term, Mayo anticipates that the SPARC program will generate innovations to enhance patient satisfaction, make more efficient use of physician time, and add a new dimension to the Mayo Clinic's mission of putting the needs of the patient first.

---

these futures are coordinated with one another. Frameworks are powerful because they can be used to generate a coordinated set of ideas or opportunities, and later, to evaluate the degree to which a current set of offerings satisfies user needs and reflects an organization's intentional view of the future.

Frameworks reintroduce a holistic viewpoint to an organization and allow it to refocus on its reason for being: to provide value to customers, employees and other stakeholders. For our health care client, we developed a framework that consisted of a 'patient journey' that helped them to understand that the patient views their experience as a contiguous process, unaware of how the organization is structured to deliver care.

For example, patients do not understand why, each time they move to a new location in the hospital, they are asked the same set of questions. From a hospital perspective, redundancy of information collection ensures accuracy and safety (and reflects the reality of non-integrated IT systems). However, from a patient's perspective, it creates an experience laden with frustration and lack of trust.

3. Rapid Prototyping
Rapid prototyping helps people to experience a possible future in tangible ways. These include rough physical prototypes of products or environments, or enactments of processes and service

Prototyping gives an organization license to explore hunches that may in turn give more clarity to the problem statement.

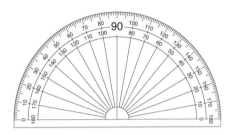

experiences, as well as the internal infrastructure and business plans that will be required to deliver them. It allows a very low-risk way of quickly exploring multiple directions before committing resources to the best one. Prototyping is commonly used in design development to explore details of how a product, service, or experience will be manifest. It externalizes the project team's thinking, allowing for quicker convergence and more useful feedback from stakeholders. This feedback is based in the reality of an experience, rather than in an interpretation of a description of that same experience.

When organizations go about developing their strategies, they typically define both the problem statement and a proposed solution at the same time, as a means for getting approval and resources to move forward. Rapid prototyping gives an organization license to explore hunches or directions that may in turn give more clarity to the problem statement. It also helps them continue to be mindful of the possibilities of creating systemic solutions.

Faced with the challenge of improving the hospital's dining experience, our health care client used rapid prototyping to quickly explore ideas that allowed patients and family members to eat whenever they wanted to. One of the ideas that came out of this exploration was a concept for a mobile 'minibar' that could be ordered and stocked appropriately. In the process of testing this idea, the team discovered and resolved issues around ordering, fulfilling, and maintaining the minibar. They also discovered that this particular solution affected multiple parts of the system, from patient room design to admissions processes to food service design. A simple prototype allowed the hospital to surface these issues and solve them all at the same time, resulting in a more unified experience for patients.

In closing

Increasingly, our client organizations come to us expressing a wish to be "more innovative." We interpret this as a request to be better able to face change. While design continues to be seen as a specialized expertise, we have found that the tools of design are learnable and applicable to challenges that business managers face every day. When we couple design process experts (with no vested interest in perpetuating the current way of doing things) with business content experts (who are looking for ways to think differently about their area of expertise), we create a capacity to envision and realize futures that are both desirable for people and viable for organizations.

The challenge remains for business schools to find ways of integrating design thinking into their curricula, and for design schools to expand the purview of design to include not only products, services, and experiences, but the organizational means by which they are created and supported. *R*

Peter Coughlan and **Ilya Prokopoff** are Partners at IDEO, based in Palo Alto, California.
This excerpt appeared by permission and is originally from *Managing as Designing* edited by Richard Boland Jr. and Fred Collopy, ©2004 by the Board of Trustees of the Leland Stanford Jr. University. All rights reserved. Reprinted by permission of Stanford University Press, www.sup.org

by **Jeanne Liedtka**

How 'Design Catalysts' Conquer Growth Gridlock

'Catalysts' succeed by freeing themselves from growth gridlock, and they are as distinctive for what they *don't* do as for what they do.

LIKE MOST MANAGERS, you probably have some ideas about how to grow your organization. You may even suspect that one or two of them could turn into something big. Unfortunately, you don't have the data to prove that any of your ideas will be needle-movers, and the numbers guys insist on proof before any corporate support can come your way. A believer surrounded by professional doubters, you spend your time trying to convince them, while the window of opportunity closes.

If this sounds familiar, you are caught in 'growth gridlock' – a frustrating place where the corporate entrepreneur's optimism and need for speed collide with the organization's skepticism and need for control. The executives at headquarters demand growth, but don't give you the tools to enable it. If you manage to find it despite them, you're soon fighting the bureaucracy that they've constructed around you.

Despite this prevailing environment, my colleagues and I knew there *had* to be people out there who had 'cracked the code' and achieved growth: ordinary managers making important contributions to their organizations' objectives. Managers who were fighting growth gridlock and *winning*. We recently completed a three-year research project that focused on the role of operating managers in achieving organic growth.

It seemed to us that potentially-significant opportunities for innovation and growth were being ignored – in particular, opportunities for creating better value for customers by leveraging existing capabilities and technologies. This type of innovation, we believe, is the responsibility of *everyone* in the organization, not just the executive team and the experts in R&D. We began our research with some fundamental questions: who are the managers that lead these kinds of growth efforts? What experiences do they bring to the task? And how do they crack the corporate code to discover opportunities?

We asked University of Virginia alumni, recruiters and executive education participants to nominate a growth leader who they personally knew, assembling a pool of 225 candidates from firms as diverse as **Best Buy**, **Dell**, **Dow Chemical**, **NBC**, **UBS** and **Pfizer**. From this pool, we identified an initial group of 25 individuals who had achieved significant, organic top-line growth.

We interviewed these managers in-depth, asking them to share with us a particular initiative they had led – one that they felt represented their approach to fostering organic growth. What we discovered is that growth is not necessarily the result of far-sighted corporate strategies or radical new products and technologies. Obviously, these can help, but more often than not, sustainable growth is driven by operating managers whose leadership initiates a near-chemical reaction that generates significant top-line results.

The Design Catalysts
Often acting without substantial corporate support, these extraordinary 'catalysts' showed themselves to be masters at leveraging existing resources to spark growth by creating better customer-value propositions. Who they are, how they think, and what they do combine to ignite growth in their organizations.

Consider **Kurt Swogger** at **Dow Chemical**, who accepted the challenge of growth in a business so bad that even the consultant hired to value it for sale told him not to take the job. Kurt took it anyway, and grew it into one of Dow's top performers and a model for innovation. Then there's **Clay Presley**, who arrived at his new job at **Carolina Pad** to find a failing paper company that used its out-of-date manufacturing facilities to serve second-tier retailers with a 'paper by the pound' mentality that gave new meaning to the term 'commodity'. Clay now runs a company that is seen by major retailers such as **Wal-Mart** as the go-to firm for high-end designer school supplies.

My team and I use the word *catalyst* to describe these growth leaders, because catalysts drive action. But there's more. In Science, the term refers specifically to an agent that is *required* to activate a particular chemical reaction. In other words, catalysts don't just make things happen: they make things happen that

Exploring new opportunities always involves making decisions under conditions of uncertainty – raising the challenge of how to take data from a known past and connect it intelligently to an unknown future.

would not happen at all without them. They accomplish this by reducing the barriers that would, under normal circumstances, prevent a reaction.

Try putting a lit match to a pile of sugar. Nothing happens, because igniting sugar requires more heat than a single match (or even a lighter) can provide. So it stays just sugar, no matter how many matches you throw at it. But put just a little cigarette ash on top of the sugar and see what happens when you strike that match: a desktop inferno ensues, all because of a small bit of ash.

The 'sugar' is already on your table, perhaps along with a ton of spent matches. Your leadership can catalyze it. And here's the crazy part: nothing else has to change to make this possible – except you. Customers can have the same needs they've had all along; competitors can continue to do what they've been doing. Nothing *external* is needed to create growth. You can ignite it from the inside when you adopt the ways of seeing and behaving that I'll talk about here. It sounds like magic, but it isn't.

Catalysts often start out in the same place as everyone else, without superior information, capabilities or customer contacts, but then they go on to accomplish extraordinary things. What they do is not rocket science, but it *is* counterintuitive to what many managers have been taught. Catalysts succeed by freeing themselves from the shackles of business-as-usual in their companies: they are as distinctive for what they *don't* do as for what they *do*. They don't, for instance, 'think big', 'let the numbers speak', or segment their market according to some set of meaningless demographic descriptors. They don't even rely on focus groups.

Imagine that.

Obstacles to Growth

Catalysts' crack the growth code by recognizing that internal organizational factors are even more of an impediment to growth than market conditions and competitors. There's not often much you can do about market conditions or competitors; you can, however, do a lot to navigate within your own organization more successfully.

That's the good news. The bad news is that most organizations don't make it easy. They often have two seemingly natural impulses that gridlock growth which, together, can be toxic to growth.

Sin #1: Worshipping at the Altar of Analysis

Organizations are designed for stability: shareholders expect it, employees and communities like it, and customers depend on it. And stability depends on the rigorous collection, analysis and use of information. In this environment, it's managers who know how to wield information – to analyze, validate, and justify the use of corporate resources – who succeed. Proceeding without solid data, without the analysis to back-up an idea, is a sin.

But there are limits to the power of analysis. Exploring new opportunities always involves making decisions under conditions of uncertainty – raising the challenge of how to take data from a known past and connect it intelligently to an unknown future. It involves, to borrow a phrase from historians **Richard Neustadt** and **Ernest May**, 'thinking in time': figuring out how to connect what you know about the past to think constructively about a new future. As they point out:

"The future has no place to come from but the past; hence

the past has predictive value. But what matters for the future in the present is departures from the past, alterations, changes, which prospectively or actually divert familiar flows from accustomed channels."

Subjecting new growth initiatives to validation through the kind of rigorous analytics that established organizations crave creates a fundamental problem: since the data we need about the future doesn't yet exist, we have to make it up. Until we act, data from the past is all we have to help us think about the future. Challenged by their organization's professional doubters to *prove* – using today's data – their theories about some not-yet-existing business, managers create phony numbers based on extrapolations from the past, plus predicted diversions. Everybody involved knows the game being played, so they demonstrate their savvy by cutting the projections as they pass by. By decision time, somehow the opportunity doesn't look 'big enough' to move the needle anymore.

This is a BIG problem, because the second sin in many organization is being small.

Sin #2: Believing That Only Big Is Beautiful

People running organizations like big ideas. This makes sense, because limiting the number of initiatives under way increases headquarters' ability to sustain a clear focus. Opportunity costs are high, and moving the needle is hard; chasing lots of new business ideas simultaneously seems like a mistake. But some unsavory realities get in the way of this apparently solid logic:

Reality 1: If an opportunity is big and obvious, chances are that somebody else has already seen it.
Reality 2: Human beings (customers, in particular) are terrible at envisioning things that don't already exist.
Reality 3: If you insist on home runs, chances are you won't get many singles (*or* many home runs).
Reality 4: When the ratio of *resources invested* gets too far ahead of *knowledge possessed*, bad things happen and heads roll.

Particularly tragic is the 'triple threat' mentality that we often find in well-funded industry-leading companies. According to this mindset,

1. We want big payoffs only: no small projects need apply
2. Let's do it ourselves: partners are a problem
3. Let's keep it secret: even from our customers

When these attitudes are allowed to drive the development of new business initiatives, the result is usually expensive fiascos. This approach keeps real learning out of the effort until it is almost too late – by fully designing offerings in the absence of real customer engagement and bringing production capacity on-line without demonstrated market demand.

Fighting Growth Gridlock

Picture midtown Manhattan at rush hour: throngs of people anxious to get somewhere; cars idling, fumes spewing, frustration building. Maybe you can see growth possibilities in this scenario and maybe you can't – but it doesn't matter much, because you can't make any progress on them anyway. You're not going anywhere anytime soon, because you are caught in the congestion caused by the conflict between corporate's need to control the existing business and your need for the freedom and resources to grow a new one. If there's any activity at all, it's usually in the form of PowerPoint presentations and meetings and lots of horns blaring. Hard to mistake that for progress, though it does chew up plenty of time and energy. After all those exhausting meetings, you haven't moved an inch.

It is counterintuitive but true that you cannot ease traffic gridlock by building more highways: the new ones only fill up again. It is also true that the people who run the transportation system can relieve congestion somewhat by better timing the lights, designing more effective traffic flows or discouraging the volume of cars. You can hope for that. But there's not much you can do about any of those things as you sit idling, tapping out *Bohemian Rhapsody* on your steering wheel.

What you can do is figure out other ways of getting where you want to go. In our research, catalysts showed an alternative route to producing growth – not the path of the entrepreneur or the traditional path of the corporation, but a third route that is built on six lessons which, taken together, allowed them to break through growth gridlock.

Lesson 1: Don't look up, look in

Growth begins with you. Not with corporate. Not with the market. Not even with customers. The first lesson from Catalysts is that who you are – how you are 'wired' – really matters. Across the board, Catalysts are restless and impatient with the status quo and endless analysis. For them, idling is just not an option. They hate standing still. Failure is forgivable; *not trying* is the ultimate sin.

But it's not all about attitude. Their pasts matter. Kurt Swogger was able to break through the growth gridlock at Dow not just because he had the guts to try, but because he knew every nook and cranny of his organization. Trained as an engineer, he branched out early and worked in just about every function – manufacturing, marketing, R&D – and in products ranging from Saran Wrap to agricultural chemicals. By the time he took over the polyolefins and elastomers (PO&E) business, he'd just about seen it all. The same was true for Clay Presley. He had been a CPA who audited small businesses for years before moving into the stationery business. A unique combination of attitude and experience seems to hardwire the Catalysts' ability to see and chase opportunity successfully.

Lesson 2: The monkey isn't on your back, it's in your head

How growth leaders *think* also matters. The first step in easing gridlock is to escape the 'Mother, may I?' mentality – to get over the belief that your every move must wait for an approving nod from corporate. If you want to crack the code, stop complaining about the monkey on your back and worry about getting rid of the one inside your head. The solution isn't *them* thinking differently – it's *you*. Catalysts don't like asking for permission or forgiveness. They don't like *asking*, period. They don't wait for corporate to change the rules – they elect to play a different game all by themselves.

Many managers are programmed to think 'the corporate way', to seek certainty and rely on data to predict and plan. That approach works well when you're running an existing business where you know a lot, but it is deadly in the world of growth, where what you *don't* know is far more important than what you do. Growth is all about uncertainty and how you work with it. Prediction and analysis have a place in this world, but you're in trouble if they are the *only* tools you've got.

Sure, Catalysts like **Jim Steiner** at **Corning**, a former corporate controller, can run numbers with the best of them when they need to. But they avoid taking unnecessary risks, and relying on prediction is one such risk. So Steiner started with capabilities he already had in house, found a partner to ante up the capital to produce his new product instead of asking corporate for money, got commitments from his biggest customer, **Texas Instruments**, early in the process, and managed his potential loss to what he could afford – just like successful entrepreneurs do. Catalysts tap into the capabilities and the network of relationships they already have, and in the process, they don't merely make lemonade out of lemons – they make daiquiris.

Lesson 3: It's not rocket science – you just need to reframe

A big contributor to deer-in-headlights paralysis is the misconception that a genius-like flash of brilliance – a big disruptive idea – is necessary for growth. It isn't. However, you do have to go *looking* for growth: unlike life, it doesn't just happen while you're making other plans. The good news is that, if you can learn to see differently, it is *already there*. You just need to change your perspective to find it – a process that we call 'reframing'.

Clay Presley at Carolina Pad reframed how he looked at his business and came up with the idea of fashion notebooks for teenage girls. Not exactly rocket science. **Jeff Semenchuk** at **Pfizer Consumer Products** climbed into his customers' heads, took an array of products that the company already had, packaged them in portable sizes, and let everybody from business types to soccer Moms customize them into their own 'portable medicine cabinets'. Both of these turned into very significant new businesses. These innovations and others like them are neither the dramatic breakthrough kind nor the 'tweak a bit here and there and raise prices' kind. They are *genuine* innovations, but are usually built around enhancements to existing value propositions.

Lesson 4: Learn to juggle with beanbags

Once you come up with a concrete opportunity to create better value for your customers, you've got to figure out how to *move* on that idea. The traditional route: form a committee, start gathering data, run some proforma P&Ls, maybe even hire some high-priced market research firm to help you assess the idea's potential. After you've done the analysis, focus on a big launch that will catch your competitors off guard.

We've got a better idea. Try starting with beanbags instead of flaming torches. If you're a novice at this growth stuff, you're much less likely to get burned. Launch it small and focus on learning what works. Place some small bets fast: find a customer – maybe just a single one, and try to sell them something, even if it's just a rough prototype. Enlist some advice from your supply chain. Internally, find a team of seasoned performers to give it real attention. Think of your new business as a hypothesis to be tested.

To accomplish this, you'll probably need to build a 'protective bubble' that lets you escape detection by the corporate radar, at least until after there is a level of success that you *want* to be noticed. A bubble that lets you focus your energy on learning in real time from real customers, rather than filling out budget requests; a bubble that lets you call the baby ugly if it turns out to be ugly. Then, when you're confident that you've got the winning recipe figured out, ramp it up with a vengeance.

We call this process a 'learning launch'. Learning launches focus on placing small bets fast (a passion that all catalysts share) while minimizing risk, accelerating learning and generating insights quickly from direct market experience. A learning launch is definitely not a test; it's an *art* that requires developing some new skills, thinking deeply about some stuff you probably ignore, and committing some unnatural acts (by corporate, not decency, standards).

Lesson 5: Lead them, don't love them

Catalysts are not superheroes. They don't try to go it alone, and neither should you. A key factor in their success is their ability to assemble and motivate high-performing teams. They refuse to settle for B-team players, and they are somehow able to combine two seemingly-opposing forces: setting high expectations and holding people accountable for delivering results and at the same time, engaging their passion. Catalysts take risks with new business ideas, but not with people. In fact, they won't hesitate to remove any team member who isn't delivering. Yet the people who work for them describe these tough bosses as caring, motivating and inspiring.

Lesson 6: Speed thrills

When the five lessons above come together, they produce the last tool in the Catalysts' tool kit: *speed*. Speed is their mantra. Growth leaders not only create growth but also accelerate the entire growth process. They put some ash on the pile of sugar, and they give everybody who works for them a match. Through it all, their obsession with speed drives a surprising and powerful array of consequences.

This isn't your father's version of speed that we're talking about here. This is speed as *learning velocity*, the ultimate Trojan horse. In the daylight, it looks reassuringly familiar to corporate as a source of competitive advantage. After all, who could argue against speed? Yet what it actually does is unleash a decidedly-subversive force under cover of darkness. You can't care about speed and go about business as usual; and you can't get there without aligning all of the pieces we've already talked about.

In closing

My colleagues and I immensely enjoyed meeting the design catalysts and hearing their stories. They have taught us a tremendous amount about how to lead growth in large organizations, how to escape growth gridlock and have the best of both worlds.

The good news is that potential growth leaders exist within every business, waiting to be unleashed. I am hopeful that our findings will enable you to crack the growth code in your own organization and begin your journey – to find the Catalyst in you. *R*

Jeanne Liedtka is the United Technologies Corporation Professor of Business Administration at the University of Virginia's Darden School of Business and the former chief learning officer at United Technologies. This article is an excerpt from *The Catalyst: How You Can Become an Extraordinary Growth Leader* (Racom Communications, 2011), which Jeanne co-authored. Her most recent book is *Solving Problems with Design Thinking: Ten Stories of What Works* (Columbia University Press, 2013).

INFORMING OUR INTUITION

DESIGN RESEARCH FOR RADICAL INNOVATION

Radical innovation requires both evidence and intuition: *evidence* to become informed, and *intuition* to inspire us in imagining and creating new and better possibilities.

By **Jane Fulton Suri**

THE TERM 'RESEARCH' shows up in the context of design and innovation in multiple guises, not all of them positive. For some people it connotes 'data collection' – looking to the past and present but not to the future; for others it's simply a required step before coming up with ideas; for yet others it's a filter that rejects promising ideas before they've had a chance to evolve.

The truth is that research can be an immensely positive force in the innovation journey. But to derive value from it, we must be willing to complement, challenge, and evolve many of the approaches and practices that traditionally prevail.

Starting out as a human-sciences graduate, I believed passionately that research could help us reach a better understanding of people – their needs, desires, habits and perceptions – and that this would lead to better decisions about what and how things get designed and put into the world. I still believe this today, but I now have a much more nuanced perspective of what it takes and have come to understand that different challenges require different approaches.

New Kinds of Innovation Challenges

At the beginning of my career I worked on projects that involved influencing the design of things that already existed: urban housing in Scotland, motorcycles, power tools, washing machines, and elements of public transit systems. Effective research in such cases relies upon carefully gathering and analyzing existing evidence. By looking at current behaviour in existing situations, at records of sales, at complaints and incidents, and by asking people about their desires, problems, and preferences, it wasn't hard to find good ways to innovate by incrementally improving the existing designs.

Later, in the early 1990s at **IDEO**, I was given the chance to work on things that were completely new to the world, such as some of the first digital cameras, and medical processes and devices that neither doctors nor patients had experienced before. I also began to conceive and develop new offerings aimed at specific groups of people – educational games for children, a new kind of drink for athletes, and tools and services for people travelling on vacation.

These days, many of the innovation challenges we face in the workplace are framed in an even more open-ended way:

- How can we leverage the value of this brand to increase its reach?
- Here's an amazing new technology – what applications would be good business opportunities?
- There hasn't been real innovation in our industry for a decade or more – what can we do to change that?
- We already own this market category – what's going to be our 'next big thing'?

Responding to such challenges involves a more radical kind of innovation than that required to improve something that is already familiar. In this more radical context, it is much less clear what kinds of innovations might catch on and how new offerings might influence people's future habits, which presents a different challenge to research: how can you find out what is going to matter to people if it doesn't yet exist? And this new thing that you might develop (but that doesn't yet exist) – how do you discover what kind of people it might appeal to?

In cases such as these, effective research is not just about analysis of objective evidence – there isn't any directly applicable data anyway; it's also about the synthesis of evidence, recognition of emergent patterns, empathic connection to people's motivations and behaviours, exploration of analogies and extreme cases, and intuitive interpretation of information and impressions from multiple sources. This type of approach is now often referred to as 'design research' to differentiate it from purely analytic methods. At its core, design research is about informing our intuition.

The Role of Intuition

In innovation projects – particularly those that are more radical in scope – discovery and decision making cannot rely exclusively on analytic processes. By definition, as soon as we start to think ahead to future experiences and how people might respond, we

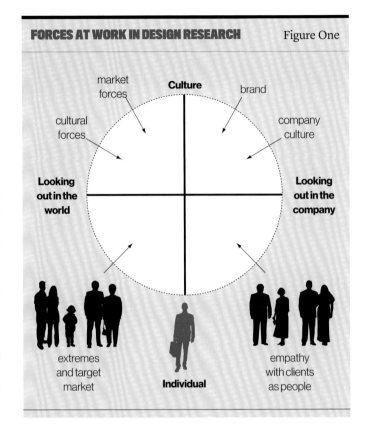

FORCES AT WORK IN DESIGN RESEARCH   Figure One

begin to draw upon our intuitive and interpretive abilities. We begin to imagine and empathize.

Of course, imagination and empathy can also run into realms of fantasy. As **Malcolm Gladwell** reminds us in *Blink: The Power of Thinking Without Thinking*, intuitions can be spot-on, but they also can be misleading and, sometimes, simply wrong. Imagination, empathy and intuitive leaps – so important in innovation – also need to be informed by experience and tempered by continual doses of reality.

Design research both *inspires imagination* and *informs intuition* through a variety of methods with related intents: to expose patterns underlying the rich reality of people's behaviours and experiences, to explore reactions to probes and prototypes, and to shed light on the unknown through iterative hypothesis and experiment. Innovation projects have different scopes and different starting points, ranging from the incremental – enhancements to known offerings in a known market with well-understood consumers and usage patterns – to the more radical, in which the intent is to create new offerings for which there is not yet a market or established behaviours.

Innovation is an activity that socially and emotionally affects everyone involved. Teams, investors, and sponsors all have a lot at stake. During the innovation journey, we must be willing to apply creativity, energy, and enthusiasm to an uncertain venture that has the potential for significant impact on our personal future and the success of our business. In addition, we need to stay motivated, curious to explore, yet responsible about investing time and materials. Positive outcomes can't be guaranteed, but everyone needs confidence and reassurance along the way. It's not realistic to expect blind faith and optimism to carry this process forward.

Sources of Confidence

As a reaction to inevitable risk and uncertainty, many organizations establish consumer research processes as a way of deciding what programs to support, and many employ methods that have been optimized to assist in decision making about incremental innovations. For incremental innovation, by definition, there is a history of actual market performance against which to calibrate new concepts, so it makes sense that we assess ideas using processes and objective pass/fail criteria that have proven to be good predictors in the past.

Unfortunately, these same processes often work against our ability to innovate effectively in more radical ways – to create 'disruptive' innovations. As **Clayton Christensen** writes in *The Innovator's Solution: Creating and Sustaining Successful Growth:*

> Not surprisingly, disruptive ideas stand a small chance of ever seeing the light of day when they are evaluated with the screens and lenses a company uses to identify and shape sustaining innovations. Companies frustrated by an inability to create new growth shouldn't conclude that they aren't generating enough good ideas. The problem doesn't lie in their creativity; it lies in their processes.

Processes that are good at instilling confidence when it comes to directions for incremental innovation can be inappropriately limiting and personally discouraging to more radical innovation efforts, in which many variables are unknown or unknowable. It is heartening to see organizations like **Hallmark**, **Herman Miller**, **Intel**, **Motorola**, **Procter & Gamble** and **Whirlpool** actively developing and applying design research methods as they strive for more radical innovation and for more empathic and intimate understanding of consumers.

Integration and Engagement

Design research is most valuable when it is treated as integral to the innovation process rather than as an external activity. To inform intuition, it is important to have team members actively interpret the richness of evidence and discoveries as they emerge. Research that brings rich information will provide not just facts, but insights and possible reasons behind the facts. Even seemingly bad news – that we have been considering something that seems to be a fruitless opportunity or a concept with serious flaws

To be done well, design research demands that everyone involved be prepared to grapple diligently with ambiguity and nuance. It asks us to bring creative energy to the synthesis of confusing and conflicting information.

– can serve as inspiration for new and better ideas, instead of signaling a depressing failure. With richly understood bad news, we can adjust our assumptions and perhaps see a new opportunity to move in a more fruitful direction. A huge opportunity for learning is missed when research phases are simply tacked on to a program as 'safeguarding' or when research activities are outsourced to a separate team.

To be effective, decisions informed by design research demand a much higher level of personal commitment and engagement at all levels within an organization than do judgments based purely upon hard facts and objective data. Design research often means changing the way work gets done. It means getting out of the office, being where customers are, becoming aware of and sensitive to social trends and the broad ecology of stakeholders, rolling up our sleeves to try out unfamiliar things first hand.

The largely qualitative and interpretive nature of design research is its strength, but this also makes it potentially vulnerable to invalid or ill-founded conclusions. In order to be done well, design research demands that everyone involved be prepared to grapple diligently with ambiguity and nuance. It asks us to bring creative energy to the synthesis of confusing and conflicting information, to be willing to challenge and adapt our own and our colleagues' interpretations, and to stress-test these interpretations both with other points of view and in the harsh light of relevant evidence, even if such evidence is not statistically-proven fact.

This degree of direct involvement often brings another advantage to the design and innovation process – that of creating common ground and shared perspectives among people representing multiple functions within an organization, in ways that have seemed previously unachievable. Enabling teams to share raw evidence and create meaningful frameworks, principles, goals, criteria, and priorities together energizes movement forward with much more enthusiastically supported ideas and greater confidence. In this way, successful design research first requires, then perpetuates, forms of cultural transformation in organizations that enable radical innovation to thrive. What, then, does it feel like to make this kind of commitment to informing our intuition?

Design Research in Practice

Let's get more specific about what it actually means to conduct design research. Typically, research processes used in new product development combine multiple objectives into a single exploration. A survey tool, for example, may be constructed both to seek out consumer insight about opportunities and to field a sample-size that enables statistical estimations of scale. Or a series of focus groups may be used to explore both the appeal of an early idea and the size of the potential market.

For known markets and offerings, this approach seems to work reasonably well. But in research for radical innovation, compromising the potency of a single research objective leaves important questions unanswered: we know what people say they want, but do their behaviours really support this? How can we use the best of our half-baked ideas to create a better, more integrated experience for consumers? How can we assess the likely size of an opportunity if we have nothing to directly compare it with?

In research for radical innovation, there's great value in separating these objectives – distinguishing the types of questions we want to answer and creating appropriately-tailored tools to apply at different points throughout the innovation process.

Design research addresses three different kinds of questions with respect to innovation:

- **Generative:** gaining insights and opportunities – research that provides human-centered insight, revealing new ways of framing opportunities and inspiring new ideas.
- **Evaluative or Formative:** learning and refining – research that provides continual learning throughout the process to determine the what, how, and to whom of the offering.
- **Predictive:** estimating potential – research that helps to estimate the scale and potential of an opportunity even when most variables are unknown.

Here's how design research contributes in these three areas – and where there are important gaps to be filled.

1. Generative design research

Generative research involves looking for emergent patterns, challenges, and opportunities that can be addressed by innovation. The intent is that ideas about possible new offerings are informed and inspired by in-depth understanding of people's aspirations, attitudes, behaviours, emotions, perceptions, processes, and motivations within their prevailing and evolving social, cultural, and technology context. Crucially, it is about interpreting this understanding to inspire new perspectives that disrupt current conventions and ways of seeing things.

Here's an example from a project for an airline: innovation team members, in addition to shadowing specific passengers and observing their behaviours throughout an airplane journey and asking crew members and passengers to keep a trip diary of their mood and significant events, also reported on their own trips of various kinds. Later, the team worked together as a group, integrating insights from these direct sources with more traditional forms of market research, technology, and other trend-related information relevant to travel and analogous services, to create a framework for thinking about the air-travel experience. This laid the foundation for innovation opportunities around specific service and physical design, in this case related to seating and baggage in particular.

2. Evaluative or formative design research

Evaluative or formative design research is essentially an iterative series of 'learning loops.' In design research, ideas don't stay intangible or ambiguous for long: they are given form, whether as sketches, models, stories, videos or other kinds of prototypes. In this context, a prototype is simply a visible or tangible representation of an idea, to be thought of as a probe or thought-experiment; it is not a full-fledged pilot or a preproduction version of the real thing. And although evaluation involves an element of testing of ideas, it is less about validating and filtering the ideas than it is about providing ongoing guidance in the uncertain innovation endeavour.

Evaluative design research is about building confidence by addressing questions and uncertainties *as they arise.* Frameworks, ideas, and concepts are shared in various ways as prototypes from very early (even in insight-gathering phases) to late in the process in order to learn from other people's reactions, and to check, revise, and refine assumptions.

Rather than treat evaluative research as a formal and objective test, it is often more fruitful to engage with participants in a spirit of co-discovery, even co-design, in which input is valued for whatever insight it brings, whether or not it reflects well on the concept. Treated more openly as an interactive design session, evaluative research can result in valuable dialogue that engages the best of participants' critical thinking and creativity. For example, in designing a new class of surgical instrument for use in the operating theater, some very significant breakthrough ideas were evolved via hands-on prototyping and evaluation sessions in which surgeons interacted with engineers and other team members around a simulated surgical setup.

3. Predictive design research

How confidently can we really predict whether a radical innovation will be a success? Predictive research refers to those research activities that are concerned with looking ahead to estimate the potential of future opportunities and ideas, primarily from the perspective of their business viability. This type of research is much less well-charted territory for design research. Designers need to be more creative in finding good ways to work through these business questions, both in helping to define potential markets and in determining the viability of ideas. There is tremendous pressure to provide estimates of business potential to guide decision making about innovation, including its most radical forms.

In-market experimenting seems to offer great potential to radical innovation in enabling accessible, rapid, and considerably lower-risk and lower-cost learning than would a full-fledged launch. For example, **Bank of America** has been able to make great strides in both learning and innovation by reconfiguring several of its fully-operating branches in Atlanta to run live experiments on multiple service innovations, with real employees serving real customers in real time. A similar approach is exploited on an even larger scale by **Google**, through Google Labs, which has multiple experimental projects running at once and takes full advantage of the nature of hosted software to allow early launches – frequently updated in response to what is learned from users – of what effectively become eternal beta versions of their offering.

In closing

Both a personal and an organizational mind-shift are required to get comfortable with the emphasis that design research places on informing our intuition. Like many people in our culture, my formal education placed higher value upon received knowledge than upon personal discovery. But the longer I practice design and innovation, the more I am convinced that true learning comes not only from ready-processed data, but also from concrete sensory evidence and direct subjective experiences that have the power to capture our imaginations and achieve new understanding.

Design research demands commitment from innovators to reach new levels of understanding about what matters to the people we want to connect with. For radical innovation, we need both evidence and intuition: evidence to become informed, and intuition to inspire us in imagining and creating new and better possibilities. ***R***

Jane Fulton Suri is a Partner and Creative Director at IDEO, based in Palo Alto, California. She is the author of *Thoughtless Acts: Observations on Intuitive Design* (Chronicle Books, 2005).

**Concept
Visualization**

**Empathy & Deep Human
Understanding**

**Strategic Business
Design**

TURNING
DESIGN THINKING
INTO
DESIGN DOING

by **Heather Fraser**

The principles of design can be applied to generate breakthrough thinking over incremental thinking. Here's how to get started.

DESIGN IS ONE OF THE HOTTEST TOPICS in the business arena in recent years, dubbed the new driver of innovation and a new competitive weapon. It has even received its due at Davos, where the **World Economic Forum** has featured programs on the value of design as a means of unlocking breakthrough ideas [including sessions led by Rotman Dean **Roger Martin**.]

Imagine if everyone could get in on what the world's leading innovators are discovering; we would no doubt see more value and less waste – of energy (human and otherwise), time and money. But before design can impact human and economic value to its fullest potential, it must be translated into an accessible, 'doable' program. Those who are intrigued by design need to be able to grasp its core notions and begin to put its principles and practices into play, with a long-term conviction to shifting their culture by driving the philosophy throughout the entire organization.

Whether your goal is to develop new products or services, a new way of marketing to your customer, or to reinvent your entire business model, 'design thinking' holds valuable clues as to how to get to bigger ideas, faster and more efficiently. And while there are many methods for fueling innovation, the principles and practices behind design are so intuitive and have such a pedigree of success, it is hard to question their value.

The purpose of this article is to translate inspiration into implementation by highlighting the learning and practices of those who have discovered how to turn *design thinking* into *design doing*.

The core principles and practices behind all great design can be broadly leveraged into general problem-solving and the reframing of opportunities.

Design vs. Design Thinking

Most people associate the word 'design' with a physical manifestation of form and function – an aesthetic that appeals to the discerning user, a form that creates a satisfying user experience, a physical and emotional 'journey' for the user in spatial terms, or an engineering accomplishment that makes the concept viable technically and economically. All of these are valid and valuable interpretations of design, relating to the craft and technical expertise of the design field that helps to create human and economic value for the world.

But beyond these dimensions, the core principles and practices behind all great design can be more broadly leveraged into general problem-solving and, most importantly, the reframing of opportunities in a strategic sense. This is what is often referred to as 'design thinking'. Design disciplines of all kinds (engineering, architecture, graphics, industrial design and others) teach things not typically taught in business and management schools. When we study the ways the 'design world' thinks and makes stuff, there are patterns that emerge in terms of mindset and method that are just as valuable to business and not-for profit endeavors as they are in the design realm.

In fact, any organization on a mission to create economic and human value – be it a federal government agency or a well-established commercial enterprise – can harness the power of design thinking to drive true innovations. Is it all about creativity? No. Creativity is technically the *ability* to create something new. Design is about the process of making or *doing* something new. And that's where design is more aligned with innovation on a grand scale: it is not an *attribute*, it is fundamentally about *action*.

The process of 'design doing' is not about establishing a new set of rules; it is about a fundamental shift in culture – a reframing of the collective mindset and methods of working that infuses your culture with the spirit of innovation in a way that is consistent and sustained.

The Mindset Defines the Conditions

The first step is to extract the 'attitude' behind design. There have been scores of great articles written about the mindset of those who design, all pointing to some inspiring characteristics that most of us admire and would willingly embrace under the right conditions. The most notable themes fall into three general traits: open-minded collaboration, courage and conviction.

1. Open Up: Design doing is a non-starter without open-minded collaboration. This means everyone on the team needs to be receptive to everyone and everything in order to achieve something worthwhile. Openness requires not only a commitment to 'working together', but also an earnest receptiveness to new ideas (good and bad), an interest in every new insight -- whether it fits your preconceived paradigm or not, and an allowance to imagine the possibilities of what could be, no matter how unreasonable or infeasible ideas may seem. Designers get a charge out of new insights, new ideas, new partners and new possibilities. They feed off of new insights and effectively build off the ideas of others, embracing both the friction and fusion that comes with intense collaboration.

2. Go out on a limb: The right emotional circumstances will inspire courage to experiment and play with new ideas. Great design does not come without risk-taking and trying new things, with the very strong possibility of failure. **IDEO**, one of the world's greatest innovation labs, has countless stories of where a really 'bad' or 'crazy' idea became the germ of a brilliant concept. How often have we heard someone ask, "What if it doesn't work?" or claim, "If I do that I may get fired." Creating a culture of courage is not just about making people brave enough to go out on a limb, it is about creating the right conditions in which brave and intelligent people can perform – conditions of integrity, trust, and tolerance for risk-taking. All of these are related back to open-minded collaboration, as integrity is the root of trust, which is the fuel for collaboration. If you don't create an open-minded environment, even the most courageous individual will not succeed.

3. Don't give up: No great design is realized without conviction. Conviction is the absolute unwillingness to give in to constraints and obstacles. Rotman Dean **Roger Martin** states that the single biggest attitudinal driver in breakthrough success is a mindset of "no trade-offs" – an attitude of those who dive into the 'wicked problem' and see constraints as a juicy challenge rather than a reason to give in and settle for less.

While there are many important emotional conditions under which design thinking can flourish, without these three elements, innovation through the practice of design will never get off the ground. The psychology of the individual and collective is the first foundation for success.

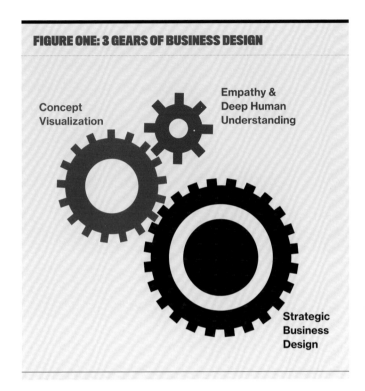

FIGURE ONE: 3 GEARS OF BUSINESS DESIGN

Concept
Visualization

Empathy &
Deep Human
Understanding

Strategic
Business
Design

The Methodology – Gearing Up

With the right emotional conditions in place, the next step is to DO something together, focusing on a few core components rather than a litany of rules, process maps and formulas. There are many tools and techniques in design, but for design to become culturally embedded in an organization, three 'forces' have to converge: a deep user understanding; multiple prototyping; and strategic business design. At **Rotman DesignWorks**™, we call these forces 'the three gears of design'.

What most well-established companies do as a matter of practice is begin by examining their 'big gear' – the existing business model. This tried-and-true exercise focuses largely on how to make the most of their current capabilities and capacity – naturally, as this is where their capital and salaries are invested. Most 'growth initiatives' take the form of line extensions and expansions; concepts are developed, and then tested with the consumer they know in a certain way for specific products or categories. If research suggests incremental sales with minimal investment risk, it's 'all systems go'. This is a very responsible way to stretch more out of your current activity system, with largely incremental results.

Then there's the 'breakthrough route', where innovation really thrives. If you begin with the user and set out on a path to look at the broader context of their lives and activities, you will suddenly see a whole new set of opportunities to be tapped. The Illinois Institute of Technology's **Institute of Design** has developed an ethnographic methodology for understanding the user's 'activity' (versus product usage) that reveals a whole new set of opportunities and helps set new criteria for innovation. If you develop a deeper understanding with a broader lens, you open yourself up to new possibilities. Witness athletic performance brands like **Adidas** moving into the fashion arena and iPOD's redefinition of mobile entertainment.

The next round is to build on those new insights and criteria to develop 'outside the dots' concepts – exploring many new and even seemingly crazy ways to deliver bigger, broader user value. The 'design key' in the concept development process is to create and consider a variety of ways to deliver against your criteria through multiple-prototype exploration, with an open mind to feedback and reconfiguration along the way. With user feedback, you can continue to narrow your options and create the concept that is most distinctive and creates the most value for your user, perhaps tapping into a need or opportunity that no one (including the user) had even recognized or articulated: that's breakthrough. The computer mouse for **Apple** was perfected by IDEO following extensive prototyping and iteration in order to meet the seemingly impossible requirement of 'increased reliability at 10 per cent of the original cost of the **Xerox** version'. Similarly, concept cars are unveiled at auto shows to generate customer feedback and further refine the design.

With the 'big idea' in hand, you then take on lever three, strategic business design, to model a unique system of 'strategic hubs' and 'supporting activities' that will not only deliver value to the user, but also competitive advantage and profit to you. Pushing the concept through to a point that it is viable and profitable is not easy; this is where the 'no trade-offs' attitude pays off. It requires a lot of hard work and many iterations, but every team behind a great breakthrough will tell you that their conviction and collaboration pushed the project through to fruition. **Southwest Airlines**' activity system has allowed it to become one of the most innovative providers of consumer value in a highly-competitive industry, becoming a sustainable competitive advantage that other airlines have attempted (in vain) to mimic.

For each of the three gears, there are many tools and techniques that are used by great design teams, but the depth and rigour behind each gear cannot be compromised. Moreover, it is never a clean and linear pass-through process; it is very iterative. It's not about using a restrictive set of rules – but instead creating the right conditions under which some core pillars (user – idea – business model) serve as the touch points throughout an iterative development process. It is about liberating oneself and the team from the constraints of early perfection and

It's about liberating oneself and the team from the constraints of early perfection and not being preoccupied with getting it right too early.

not being preoccupied with getting it right too early, so that you limit your possibilities. What companies find when they practice iterative prototyping – be it a product concept or a business model – is that they work their ideas through earlier and faster, leveraging the experience and perspective of senior management – rather than waiting until all of the I's are dotted and T's crossed to get their approval.

Design Principles Pay Off
When the conditions are ripe for innovation and the general principles and methodology of design are put into play, it is remarkable how big and broad the impact can be.

Following are some wide-ranging examples that demonstrate how 'design doing' can deliver breakthrough results in any field.

Life-Saving Packaging: Target's Prescription Bottle. In 2004, insightful designer **Deborah Adler** set out to completely overhaul the standard decades-old prescription bottle which created no end of problems with patient compliance and health risks due to medication mistakes. With a deep understanding of who took medications and how, she designed a remarkable new package to take the anxiety and risks out of medicating. **Target Pharmacies** embraced her design and took on the challenge of working to refine the concept into a viable reality. The U.S. Surgeon General wrote that this may very well be the single biggest breakthrough in prescription care in decades. This is a fantastic example of how something 'generic' and functional can create both competitive advantage and offer immeasurable user value – from holding pills to saving lives.

Operational Transformation: Boeing. Fraught with operational issues and the need to build a new manufacturing plant with an eye to improving the operational and organizational challenges of its past, Boeing and its architectural firm **NBBJ** decided to put design thinking to work in its broadest sense and create a 'democratic' workplace where blue-collar workers and white-collar en-

gineers, sales, and corporate people work side by side with the product (Boeing 737) at the core. The new workplace, opened in 2004, was infused with the design message of collaboration and the idea that every individual was important, with the focus on the product rather than the process. Real and quantifiable improvements were noted: plane unit costs were decreased, resolution times shortened, and the number of 'flow days' in the factory for final assembly reduced by 50 per cent. Results demonstrate that you can improve operational effectiveness by understanding your employees as customers and design space for both operational and cultural transformation.

Communications Design: Viagra. In 2001, Viagra held the leadership share in its category. The challenge was that the market was 'contained', for the simple reason that men were not consulting their doctors about their condition. By understanding the holistic experience of the sufferer from the stage of 'denial through to revival', **Pfizer** implemented a program that connected to and guided the sufferer through every stage of their journey, using a multitude of channels and tactics to empathetically transform a passive patient into an active patient. The results – an unleashing of patient/doctor dialogue and a surge in prescriptions – demonstrate that these same principles can also be applied to breakthrough market development and communications planning.

Seven Steps to Successful Design Doing
Following are some tips to consider upon committing to 'design thinking' as a means of dialing up innovation and increasing the odds of sustained success:

1. Make a long-term commitment: Design thinking is not a one-shot vaccine; rather, it's an 'innovation fitness program' that puts an organization on top of its game. It is not an 'event', it is a way of thinking, communicating and doing every day. **GE**'s strong track record of investing in management practices that push for continuous product and business model improvement have made this organization an innovation behemoth.

2. Build it into your corporate/organizational strategy. Design is not just a 'tactic'; in order to succeed, it needs to be part of your organizational strategy – from top to bottom, across all areas of expertise. **Samsung**'s embrace of design at all organizational levels has allowed it to move from a commodity producer to a brand leader. In the U.S., it now regularly trounces **Sony** and **Panasonic** in sales.

3. Assign a leader, but don't limit it to a function. Innovation through 'design doing' involves everyone. It is not just the "design department" or the "innovation team" or the "marketing function" – it should inspire and impact every corner of the organization. Teams need to be singing from the same song sheet. **Claudia Kotchka**'s appointment as head of Design Strategy at P&G served to inspire and institutionalize design across the 100,000-strong organization, making it one of the most innovative and consumer-centric corporations in the world.

4. Collaborate & internalize it. Don't hire someone to do it for you, collaborate with experts who will do it *with* you and inspire/teach you along the way. As with physical training, consider hiring a 'design trainer' or 'coach'.

5. Inspire, don't legislate. It's not about establishing a new set of rules: It's about a cultural shift toward fewer rules, deeper values, and stronger principles. It's a new way to think, not just about projects but the way you work together day-to- day to solve problems and create breakthrough opportunities. One only has to see the power of inspiration in fueling corporate 'brand' cultures like **Clearnet** (now **Telus**), Apple and **Medtronic**. Design thinking can inspire in much the same way.

6. Feed it and reward it. If all of the above conditions are met and 'design doing' is set in motion, the organization will make design a way of life and build its own momentum. Much as design is part of an organization's innovation strategy, it also needs to be part of its cultural development program and reward system in order to be validated. **3M**'s strong 'culture of innovation' rewards creativity at every organizational level and has made the company a leader in delivering breakthrough solutions throughout much of its history.

7. The future starts today. While a sustained shift in culture takes time to gain traction, it is important to get started, think big about the future, and implement what you can today.

In closing

It has become evident that organizations can no longer count on quality, performance or price alone to sustain leadership in the global marketplace. Design has clearly emerged as a new competitive weapon and key driver of innovation. Leveraging the power of design across all aspects of a business can establish and sustain an organization's unique competitive advantage.

By consciously fostering the right kind of emotional environment and following the seven guidelines outlined here, your organization will be well equipped to translate inspiration into implementation. *R*

Heather Fraser is the co-founder of Rotman DesignWorks™ and Adjunct Professor of Business Design at the Rotman School of Management. She is the author of *Design Works: How to Tackle Your Toughest Innovation Challenges Through Business Design* (Rotman-UTP Publishing, 2012) and recently opened a business design consultancy, VUKA Innovation.

DECISIONS BY DESIGN:
STOP DECIDING, START DESIGNING

When tackling the most abstract and ambiguous challenges, 'design thinking' can lead to more effective decisions.

by Colin Raney and Ryan Jacoby

AS A LEADER, YOU ARE LIKELY FACING a set of unprecedented challenges. You might find yourself in markets that are increasingly competitive, comprised of customers who are highly discerning or downright fickle. You're also likely leading a fast-changing workplace, where the ground rules seem to shift beneath your feet. The world is changing so rapidly, you may be wondering how you'll be able to find new ways to grow and sustain your business. Which new products and services should you offer?

We believe that when you find yourself in such a situation, you may be better served to approach your problems less as a manager and more as a designer. In other words, stop *deciding* and start *designing*. In recent years, designers have been applying their skills to a host of problems that have been traditionally associated with business strategy and approached through analysis.

With this shift has come the realization that a design-based approach, or 'design thinking', is well suited to tackle some of the most complex challenges out there.

A first step is for managers to understand the differences in the ways they and designers go about solving problems. Managers tend to follow a very analytical process. Usually, they make decisions by understanding all of the available options and rigorously determining the best path forward. In contrast, designers tend to prototype and iterate ideas, learning as they go and often developing new ideas along the way. [Rotman Dean] **Roger Martin** has contrasted 'business as usual' and 'business-by-design', and **Richard Boland** and **Fred Collopy** have contrasted a 'decision attitude' and a 'design attitude'. The net result of these investigations is that the more ambiguous and uncertain

Designers use art, metaphors, analogies and other elements
to provoke inspiration around form, function, feel and experience.
Through this process they break the decision down while
simultaneously giving themselves new options.

the problem, the more suitable design thinking seems to be. The foundational reason is that in a creative process, there aren't automatically a handful of constrained options to analyze and choose among. Instead, the playing field is often broader and the possibilities may appear endless. To make sense of all the options, designers *design their way through the problem.*

Design thinking is showing up in businesses everywhere. Leaders of entrepreneurial online services have built companies that 'live in beta', constantly allowing them to evolve their offerings. Meanwhile leaders of established companies are reshaping their organizations to create flexible, adaptable businesses capable of fluidly changing with the market. In a sense, these leaders are developing organic, breathing decision-making machines that balance exploration and execution.

If you're not learning how to do this, you may be missing out. In this article we will share stories about where the value of this approach has revealed itself and explore how a designer's approach can help any business leader enhance the decision-making process in their organization.

How Designers Think

To understand the designer's mindset, it is important to examine how they approach problems. Imagine a furniture designer tasked with creating a chair. The designer would begin with a brief that details what they are to create. The brief could have an extremely tight focus: it might call for an office chair that supports 300 pounds, offers comfortable seating for long durations, includes adjustable arm and chair height with breathable fabrics. Oh, and a weight less than 20 pounds and a manufacturing cost no more than $50. Briefs of this nature can run pages and pages in detail. However, even with all these details, it is impossible to

visualize from the beginning what this chair might look like, or how it might operate. Within this one challenge lie literally thousands of interlocking decisions.

Collectively, all of these questions together are too big to digest, so the designer leaps headlong into the process and begins creating. First, she looks for inspiration, collecting ideas and expressions that help her think. Designers use art, metaphors, analogies and other elements to provoke inspiration around form, function, feel and experience. Through this process they are breaking the decision down while simultaneously giving themselves new options. Very soon, the designer will begin to create prototypes to understand how certain parts of the chair will work, what it will feel like, and how it will look. Through experimentation and iteration, designers formulate a deeper understanding of their options. Over and over, they refine their ideas; building and rebuilding, they winnow small decisions down until they arrive at the final object. This is design thinking in action.

For designers, the process of building, prototyping and trying things *is* the decision-making process. Instead of boiling down a problem to one large decision, designers make lots of *little* decisions, learning as they go. As they build and learn, something interesting happens: through the iterations, the best option often reveals itself and other less-appropriate options fall by the wayside. By trying things, designers navigate large decisions through smaller trials. Constraints and prototypes help reduce risk and convert decision-making meetings from consensus-building slogs to collaborative, invigorating critique and build sessions. This subtle but significant change in the decision-making process can lead to new avenues that didn't exist at the beginning of the process.

Taking this process and applying it in a business context can yield amazing impact. While the situation for most managers will no doubt be quite different from our chair example, design thinking can help crack all sorts of tough problems. In our own work we've prototyped services that combat teen pregnancy, airport security checkpoints to help TSA improve security, and medical devices that help carry organ donations. Instead of chairs, you might envision teams of people creating all sorts of prototypes to understand the problems they're facing and making decisions they hadn't originally conceived. They could be designing products, services, brands or even organizations.

Building to Decide

Designers are known for their prototypes. Automobile designers' clay models and architects' blueprints and scale models are products of their decision process. Our colleague **Diego Rodriguez** put it perfectly when he said, "A prototype is nothing other than a single question, embodied." By building rough and rapid prototypes we can ask the questions that ultimately inform our larger decisions.

Prototyping doesn't always mean creating something physical. Almost anything can be prototyped, and many of today's most successful organizations make it a habit to prototype all the time. You've likely noticed this behaviour in online services. **Amazon**, **Google** and others routinely experiment with parts of their offering to evolve the whole experience. Amazon, for instance, tests new page layouts and interactions with a subset of their users and gauges their response. This style of 'in-market prototyping' is how Google became synonymous with the idea of 'living in beta.' Google is constantly experimenting and trying new things. These days, most start-up web services embrace this approach, but all manner of organizations can apply this type of thinking to their own challenges. For example, **Trader Joe's**, the grocery chain, is constantly adding to and removing from their private label product lines. Nothing is sacred, and the experience is always evolving.

We often refer to a prototype in the context of an unproven theory or technology, but the act of prototyping can also be helpful when making larger, more complicated decisions. Many times with complex decisions, people fall victim to the *availability bias* and other decision biases. They think they understand potential options and outcomes, when in reality, the impacts are far too complex to conceptualize. Prototyping in these instances can actually help reduce risk. The act itself invites you to begin with what you can try, breaking down big decisions into smaller, more manageable ones. By prototyping, you're no longer judging from the sidelines; you're 'in the game' understanding how individual moves will affect the larger outcome.

Recently, an IDEO design team travelled to Ghana to introduce a new product to a new market. While the new offering was pretty common in the U.S., it was uncommon in Sub-Saharan Africa, so the team was trying to understand how people would react to it. Was it desirable? What price might they pay? How might they buy it? In this situation, they had no consumer reports to analyze and no comparable products to benchmark. The team's leader, **Jocelyn Wyatt**, had to start *building* before she could start *deciding*, so she and the team started designing. They set up a stand in a local market and began offering the product. Over the course of the day, they tried all types of experiments – different sizes, prices, messaging and packaging. By day's end, they had a much better understanding of the space and how to move forward. By approaching the problem with a design mindset, the team grasped how the various components of an offering would work together and how the product could be sold. In effect, they had prototyped a business.

Upon returning from her trip, Jocelyn and her team were refining the different components of the service when they realized that the investment required for the micro-franchisees to start the business was more than most people could afford. The money could be gathered over time, but saving just wasn't common for the potential franchisees. Using what they had learned about the local environment, Jocelyn began to prototype a complementary credit system. She knew it couldn't be anything fancy, so she designed a system that could be run almost entirely through text messaging, a note pad and a pencil. Realizing that the service alone wasn't enough is a key insight that she might not have had if she had designed from her desk. By building things to gain deeper understanding, she and her team got farther, faster and discovered some major landmines that could have spelled disaster down the road.

Embracing Constraints

In a business-as-usual environment, there is a common refrain around 'enough': not enough time, not enough resources, not enough data. However, designers know that additional time, money and resources often cause even more problems than they solve. Things look different in a design-thinking context. Designers are inspired by constraints: what they aren't afforded actually gives them something to work with. If a product can only cost a certain amount of money, the designer must make different choices of what materials to use; if a website must service millions of users, that will influence how it is designed. Constraints are a critically-important stake in the ground, as they create an agreement around what exactly is being designed.

Utilizing design thinking, leaders can use constraints as a challenge to run small, contained experiments to gain a better understanding of 'what could be'. Prototyping is a powerful exercise, but you must have constraints; if you try too many things at once, you won't learn as much. Culturally, this keeps the costs of failure low and encourages more experiments. The more prototypes you build, the more you will learn; and the more you learn, the more the answer to the problem at hand will begin to reveal itself.

Turner Interactive might not seem like a likely candidate for embracing constraints. For the past ten years, most media companies have invested heavily to establish online offerings; few however have managed to earn any direct returns. In 2006, a team within Turner, led by an executive named **David Rudolph**, took a different tack when exploring potential web offerings and businesses. Instead of assembling a grand strategy and pouring millions of dollars into execution, Rudolph's team stayed small and experimented. According to the *Wall Street Journal*, he challenged his team to conceive and implement a new business concept in just 30 days. Rudolph told the journal: "The goal was to say within the company that it doesn't take years to go from idea to launch."

One of the concepts Rudolph's team developed involved broadcasting college sports directly over the Web to loyal fans. With college sports, big teams and big games get regular coverage on television, but fans of smaller teams often have to follow their favorites by listening to the game online or by following post-game reports. Turner developed an offering that filmed these games and broadcast them over the web to paid subscribers. To start, they chose the Atlantic Coast Conference (ACC). To understand if the project could be profitable, Turner established a tight production budget; each game had to be filmed and broadcast for around $1,000 (an order of magnitude less than a normal broadcast) with only four cameras (representing a $35,000 initial investment). If the service couldn't be profitable, they'd kill the project. Amazingly, it took just 40 days to not only conceptualize the service, but also launch it, just missing their deadline.

After a few iterations, the experiment showed signs of success. By September of 2006, Turner launched an offering that allowed subscribers to watch any game in the ACC conference online. According to the *Wall Street Journal*, "Turner would not

WHEN *DESIGNING* MAKES MORE SENSE THAN *DECIDING*

- You have a goal, but many possible ways to achieve it (i.e. many 'right answers')
- Conversely, you have a goal, but no clue how to get there (a 'foggy problem')
- You know very little about the people or situation you hope to serve (distance from the problem)
- You have a finite set of options/choices and many moving variables (moving target and 'shifting sands')
- You're designing a new-to-the-world offering that doesn't compare to anything else (high uncertainty)
- Your personal reputation or job is on the line (high stakes)
- The right person to make the decision knows the least about the issue (hierarchy challenges)

WAYS TO START DECIDING BY DESIGNING

- Test your early scenarios quickly, with real users in their environment
- Challenge yourself to design a solution under extreme constraints
- Use concrete, provocative prototypes to uncover new learnings
- Strive to create two or three new options beyond those you considered previously
- Make sure you are eliminating options as you create them

disclose how many subscribers it had, but executives said that the service is averaging a couple of hundred viewers per event with popular basketball games drawing a couple of thousand viewers." By creating real constraints, the team arrived at an outcome that wouldn't initially have seemed viable or possible. The idea of filming and broadcasting a sports event for $1,000 seems really difficult, and even more so is the prospect of getting enough viewers pay for event. Figuring out if there was a real business to be had in less than two months was downright audacious.

Compare the cost and timing of Rudolph's approach with a typical product development process. If you design more and strategize less, you too can actually learn faster, invest less and make more informed decisions.

Evolution Through Design

Arriving at decisions through design thinking has implications beyond the working team. By urging teams to prototype and experiment frequently, traditionally-hierarchical organizations start to behave in new ways. Because decisions are made through action, meetings start to look more like 'build sessions'. Decisions can become more evidence-based rather than political or argumentative. Team members often spend more time with customers because they have prototypes that help them solicit feedback. In this sense, people begin to build things in order to have conversations, instead of having conversations to build things.

The very act of prototyping an idea creates empathy for users and a conversation in the organization. Leaders can experience what it's like to be a salesperson; marketers might begin to understand the challenges of developing a product. This process engages stakeholders in a completely new capacity, making them part of the conversation.

From our experience, such involvement can create transformational moments for an organization. We recently worked with a large company to help design a loyalty strategy for the organization and offerings for their customers. On the surface, the concept of 'loyalty' might seem straightforward, but there are myriad strategies that companies can pursue. For example, some use strategies that are weighted to appeal to customers' sensible sides, like frequent-purchasing programs, while others create loyalty through deep emotional connections, like **Apple** and **Whole Foods**. For our client to be successful, they would need to agree on how to approach and deliver on a very abstract concept. To actually get a product and service launched, they'd have to have alignment across all the functional groups responsible for delivering the service on the right strategy. In their culture, buy-in was critical.

To design an appropriate strategy, we spent time understanding what loyalty meant and what it could mean to the company's customers, the competitive environment and the organization. However, we didn't wait to start designing. We began to prototype very tangible elements of a loyalty offering right away, creating examples of rewards programs, customer experiences and even sample communications/advertising that represented potential ways 'loyalty' could manifest itself for the company and its customers. We used these prototypes as discussion prompts with customers to test the boundaries of what

was desirable, possible and probable. We didn't set out to decide on the absolute right answer; rather, we *started designing* to better understand the space.

This approach wasn't just useful for customer research and offering design. Our goal was to make an extremely abstract notion concrete right away for the organization, too. Because we started designing, we were able to engage a broad set of stakeholders in a concrete conversation about 'what was wrong' and 'what was right' with each concept. Normally, the organization would have discussed the abstract notion of a 'loyalty strategy' – and this was certainly occurring as we started the program; but with concrete prototypes in hand, the nature of the conversation accelerated and shifted from *opinions* to *building*.

There is no quicker way to get somebody talking than to throw out a bunch of prototypes and say, 'tell me what you like' or 'what would have to be true for this concept to work?' Do it with just one option and you've got a bloodbath on your hands, but do it with many options and we guarantee you'll have a really amazing discussion. The prototypes and options create a platform for group understanding, enabling you to refine your options, identify new ones, understand risks, and find a shared understanding of what a 'good' solution would look like. If we had solely attempted to come to a consensus or decide on an agreed-upon definition of loyalty, we would not have been able to navigate such an abstract space as quickly. By designing our way through the problem, we were able to get there faster and move quickly to more refined programs and services.

In closing

There will always be a place for robust analysis in business; but by seeking constraints, creating options, engaging people in the decision-making process with prototypes and iterating, leaders can design their way through some of their most vexing problems. Given the complexity of the situations facing today's leaders, we believe it's the best option you've got. **R**

Colin Raney is a Business Designer and Boston Location Director at IDEO. **Ryan Jacoby** helps companies conceive and build growth businesses. He's based in New York.

When it comes to generating business growth by bringing new things into the world, the stakes are high, and risk is everywhere.

by **Diego Rodriguez** and **Ryan Jacoby**

Embracing Risk to Learn, Grow and Innovate

IT'S EASY AND SEDUCTIVE TO SAY that entrepreneurial business people always forge ahead, risk be damned. However, the glamour of bold action is often stymied by the specter of risk. New offerings may succeed in the market, but more often, they fail. Competitors may outwit you. Careers may hang in the balance. Taking bold risks does not feel safe. But to seek out 'zero risk' is to commit to doing nothing.

How does one move ahead and create growth in such an environment? There is a better way. We applied the design process to this challenge, and set out to understand how designers approach risk.

What we found is very encouraging. In the world of 'design thinking,' acknowledging risk is the first step toward taking action, and with action comes insight, evidence, and real options. To increase their odds of innovating routinely and successfully, today's organizations need to learn to live with risk the way designers do.

The Designer's Approach to Risk
Risk, in the traditional business sense, is an assessment of the downside that might result from taking a particular action. If the perceived level of risk is too high, people working within a business-

People who employ design thinking know that amplifying risk is a way to create more evidence of what works and what doesn't.

as-usual paradigm look for a less-risky alternative, or even forego action altogether.

We've found that this traditional, negative definition doesn't exist in the lexicon of most designers. For them, risk isn't a measure of 'the downside'; instead, it is a measure of upside and opportunity. If the risk isn't great enough, designers might well ask themselves, "why bother?"

Insight #1: Designers don't seek to mitigate risk. They embrace it, even amplify it.

Yoda was wrong. When it comes to working with risk, trying is as important as doing. Consider what **Owen Rogers**, a designer who has worked at **IDEO** for over a decade, told us. Speaking to a set of experiences gleaned from hundreds of client engagements, he summed up how designers approach risk: "For a designer, trying is more coveted than success. The real risk isn't failing, it is not trying." Trying is a statement of optimism, and a person, a team, or even an entire company grows more by acting than by standing still.

In the worldview of a design thinker, failure is the best way to clear the fog to see a path to success. With its diminutive wheels and bug eyes, the first generation **Toyota** Prius looked odd, and its performance was nothing to write home about. Competitors said it couldn't possibly be profitable. A failure? By conventional standards, yes. But if we had taken Toyota's view, we would have seen it not as a failure, but as an experience absolutely necessary to creating the second-generation model, which is by all accounts a remarkable success.

Designers see risk not as something static, but as a dynamic element, as yet another design variable. Amplifying risk is a way to increase the amount of information one receives from experiments and prototypes. An IDEO industrial designer told us, "On every project, we have our hands on a 'risk dial'; we have designers on one side pulling it toward the red line, and our clients and their systems on the other side pulling it toward the safe zone." In his mind's eye, there is a glossy, black-anodized aluminum risk dial, and his "goes to eleven." Such is a design thinker's thirst for learning that they actively seek out failures, and even intentionally increase the frequency at which they occur. They then trumpet those failures, rather than hiding them, knowing that the feedback they receive will put them ahead in the long run.

Which brings us to our next insight.

Insight #2: Designers take risks to learn.

All of this might sound scary to someone who practices 'business-as-usual.' Are designers all about the adrenaline rush? A clue can be found in what we heard from **Madison Mount**, who co-leads IDEO's work in the food and beverage arena: "I'm slightly addicted to risk. If I'm not taking risks, I feel uncomfortable, because I'm not learning." Designers aren't hooked on adrenaline: they are hooked on learning, and embracing and amplifying risk is a way to learn. The more you try, the more you learn; and the more you learn, the greater the likelihood that you can design a new and better experience for a user. Designers want to have a meaningful, positive impact in the world, and they recognize that taking risks is the way to get there.

So if you were to poke your head inside the door of a 'business-by-design' organization, would it look like a scene out of *Mission Impossible*? Would designers be riding motorcycles with scissors in their hands or setting things on fire to see what happens in the name of positive impact? Not exactly. There's something keeping the paramedics and firetrucks away. That force is an approach to innovation that regular readers of this magazine know well: design thinking.

Insight #3: Designers embrace risk, but their process of thinking mitigates it.

Design thinking uniquely combines conscious risk taking with structured risk mitigation. This is a fascinating paradox: designers embrace risk, but the way they think mitigates it. Each of the three behavioural building blocks of design thinking – empathy, prototyping, and storytelling – serves to simultaneously embrace and mitigate risk.

Empathy. Design thinking starts with people and looks for evidence of desire. This is one of the most fundamental ways to mitigate risk. Why? Because marketing things that people don't want increases one's risk of failure substantially. Ask yourself, what is the bigger risk: placing a bet on a value proposition that customers are asking for either latently or directly, or investing in an idea that springs from the cloistered assumptions of a conference room deep within your company?

In a recent innovation project, design thinkers from both IDEO and a bicycle-manufacturing client listened deeply to what potential customers said and felt. The conclusion they arrived at was not at all what they expected: instead of a desire for more technical 'extreme' biking experiences, what non-consumers of modern bicycles truly desired was a simpler, more joyful biking experience. And so they designed a much simpler experience, at the root of which is a bike that eschews complex, over-serving product features in favor of a simple foot-operated brake and an automatic gearbox. Risky? Yes, but only relative to the ingrained bias of the bicycling industry.

Prototyping. Design thinking encourages you to gather feedback long before an idea, concept or story is 'finished.' A prototype, in the hands of a design thinker, is finished when it can teach them something. The goal of prototyping is to accelerate feedback and failure. Failing indicates that you haven't quite yet nailed the experience, and suggests what you might try next. Prototyping lets you find problems, but it also teaches you to 'let go' of ideas that aren't fruitful. Failure due to sins of commission (as opposed to those of omission) is not a personal indictment, but an incitement to go out and create another prototype.

Imagine what could have been if the creators of **Iridium**, a global mobile phone service, had approached their challenge of orbiting 77 geo-stationary communications satellites from a prototyping mindset. In addition to the service being expensive, a severe drawback of Iridium was a lack of user satisfaction with the phone handsets, which were bulky and didn't work well inside of buildings – both fundamental value-proposition flaws. In the end, Iridium's $6-billion-dollar system was not viable, resulting in a fire sale for $25 million. Could the Iridium team have used prototyping to uncover these and other system flaws while they were still actionable? We're not technical experts in satellite deployment, but with the optimism that comes with a design thinking approach, anything can be prototyped. The real risk lies in not doing so.

Storytelling. Crafting and telling simple, emotional, concrete stories is a critical part of the design thinking approach. Focusing on storytelling ensures that the essence of the value proposition is communicated and understood in a way that allows people within an organization to learn and act. This essence is what **Chip Heath**, co-author of *Made to Stick*, calls "command intent." Telling stories that people can internalize is a way to reduce execution risk – they will execute with a common vision in mind. In the absence of data and direct execution experience, well-told stories might be the only way to inspire action and ensure that all parts of an organization are on the same page.

Recently **Len Wolin**, a senior director of program management at **Ritz-Carlton**, was looking for ways to "bring a little something extra out of each hotel that would help to make the experience personal, unique, and memorable." An IDEO team worked with his organization to create a set of 'scenography' workbooks meant to help each individual hotel create localized service experiences, such as a warm, personalized check-in process or a 'big night in.' These workbooks outlined the key elements of experience scenes using a series of photos that told an evocative story. The key was to communicate the principles driving the Ritz brand experience without prescribing the solution for individual hotels. Storytelling like this created broad corporate alignment and encouraged local creativity all at once, a wonderful formula for effective execution.

Getting Started

No matter your context, a design thinking approach can help you deal with risk in a more productive, generative manner. Here are seven ways to get started:

1. Cultivate an unreasonable obsession with desirability

As we mentioned earlier, beginning with real people and what they need and value is the most fundamental way to mitigate risk. Design thinkers look for evidence of human desire and needs via an unreasonable (by business-as-usual standards) obsession with 'what is desirable.'

Why did the Mini become a best-seller for parent company **BMW** (financial success) as well as the iconic 'hot-hatch' of the 21st century (brand success)? If you look at the competition, it

As you create something new to the world, simple conversations with lead and expert users might tell you more than what any detailed survey could tell you.

wasn't the fastest option, nor was it the most reliable. But the Mini cornered the market on desirability on three counts. It's 'I've-seen-you-before-and-you're-a-cute-rascal' styling grabs us viscerally, it's a hoot to drive, and masterful reflective design in the form of cheeky billboards and interactive magazine ads convinced our brains that we'd be better humans if we owned one. The Mini is the product of an unreasonable obsession with desirability. You can cultivate your own desirability chops by using these three experience elements from **Don Norman**'s book *Emotional Design* – visceral, behavioural and reflective – to analyze the offerings and services in your own life that make you happy.

2. Become more comfortable acting on your informed intuition

In a speech at Harvard, **Andy Grove** made an important point about the relationship between risk and intuition, saying "I think it is very important for you to do two things: act on your temporary conviction as if it was a real conviction; and when you realize that you are wrong, correct your course very quickly." When faced with a risky decision, and lacking complete data which would only be available at some point in the future, a design thinker decides based on their informed intuition. Design thinkers use their informed intuition and personal evidence to reduce the likelihood that they embark on a journey of solving the wrong problem. Designers know that waiting for perfect data is often the riskiest move of all.

It's not as hard as you think to begin to shape and form your own informed intuition. As you create something new to the world, simple conversations with lead and expert users might tell you more than what any detailed survey could tell you. When it does come time to begin looking for explanatory data, uniqueness may be more important than liking or purchase intent.

3. Prototype, prototype, prototype

We believe a key measure of the effectiveness of any innovation system is the time it takes to arrive at a first prototype. Be it **Paul MacCready** crashing and building and crashing his human-powered Gossamer aircraft in rapid succession, or the crew at **Pixar** creating incredibly-rough videos of movies like *Monsters, Inc.* months and years before the start of final production, quickly iterating prototypes is a signature way to mitigate risk by giving you 'risk-killing' information.

To put this into action, take that challenging project that has you worried right now and list five or six assumptions you have about potential solutions. Now build something that helps you test one of your assumptions. That something could be a physical model, a quick video showing what the human experience would feel like, or even a reverse income statement. Then walk next door (or to the next cube) and put it in front of your colleague (or your spouse or your mother). What did you learn? Repeat this process again and again.

A key metric: how long is it taking to get feedback on your Big Idea from another human being?

4. Think big, but start small(er)

Think big, but use constraints – such as schedule, headcount, and scope – to learn more about what it will take to execute your big-picture value proposition without spending big-picture amounts of energy, money and time. Designers love constraints because they give them a toehold, a place to get traction, even in the most slippery of ascents. Limiting the scope of your initial efforts (without losing site of the vision you're heading toward) is an effective way to prove viability. And limiting scope makes it easier to prototype, which, in a virtuous cycle, accelerates feedback about which constraints to keep applying energy against. In the end, it's less risky to scale a viable proposition than it is to try and make viable an operation already at scale.

Design thinkers at **Turner Entertainment Group** in Atlanta have been thinking big but acting small in order to bring a disruptive business model to market. **David Rudolph**, a Turner development executive, challenged his team to create an in-market prototype of an Internet-based 'television' business to satisfy the rabid desire of **Atlantic Coast Conference** basketball fans to watch untelevised games. However, they had to do it for less than $35,000 in fixed costs and $1,200 per game. The result? Each of Turner's small experiments can be cashflow breakeven after only a few months of existence. Focusing only on business viability plus customer desire instead of on getting big was a risk; but it enabled Turner to learn a lot about their customers and their own business model.

5. Treat money as a positive constraint

Money is just another constraint, but it's such an important one that we had to give it its own billing. Money is the grease, yet paradoxically, having less of it can make things move faster and seems to also help brains think more clearly. **Jaime Lerner**, a renowned Brazilian architect, urban planner, and mayor of Curitiba, says that "creativity starts when you lose a zero from your budget." To boost usage of the Curitiba's public transit system, and without access to piles of money or time, Lerner created a lottery which used bus fare as lottery tickets.

Treating a lack of money as a positive constraint helps strip away the fatty financial insulation that success builds up. Leaner budgets are less risky because they make it harder not to act.

6. Make a list of the best things that could happen

Ross Mayfield, CEO of **Socialtext**, is a Silicon Valley entrepreneur with an interesting approach to formulating strategy. "As a planning exercise, I always try to ask two questions: 'How could we take more risk?' and 'What risk can we take that creates the greatest amount of options?'

As we saw earlier, with Markus Diebel's 11-digit risk dial, people who employ design thinking know that amplifying risk is a way to create more evidence of what works and what doesn't. When Ross Mayfield thinks of ways to take more risk, he's actually reducing the long-term risk of his venture by uncovering the kinds of long-term business opportunxities that are the lifeblood of a thriving organization. He creates real options, because this risk-embracing activity puts you in to the flow of opportunities he would not have known existed without thinking through risky scenarios.

7. Seek challenges

Organizations are but groups of people, and in our work at IDEO we see over and over a direct correlation between the design thinking abilities of individuals and the innovation quotient of the organization they belong to. It is hard for an organization to be pushing itself to the edge of its capabilities and learning if its people are not adept at living with risk.

The ideal situation for someone trying to be innovative is one that balances clear, achievable goals with just enough task challenge so that there's a real risk of failure – enough to light their fires of creativity. Design thinking is the methodology individuals can hang on to in order to navigate challenges and risk. As they do so, they will learn and grow, and in their personal growth is the wellspring of creativity and innovation to feed larger innovation efforts.

In closing

In business as in life, we all seek to reduce and manage risk, but we also need to grow and innovate. The best way to achieve both is to embrace risk while also mitigating it.

At a personal level, design thinking is a life skill that gives us the tools to recognize risk and act in ways that mitigate it so that our dreams – big and small – can come true. For organizations, this approach provides a consistent and proven way to structure challenging innovation initiatives so that they become less risky. We can't all be designers, but we can use aspects of design thinking in our lives to embrace, amplify and mitigate risk in order to create lasting value for ourselves and our world. **R**

Ryan Jacoby helps companies conceive and build growth businesses. He's based in New York. **Diego Rodriguez** is a Business Designer and Partner at IDEO, based in Palo Alto. In addition, he is a Consulting Professor at the Plattner Institute, also known as Stanford's 'd.school'. For more, read his influential blog about design thinking at www.metacool.typepad.com.

Illustration by **Hennie Haworth**

The Future of Retail: From Revenue Generator to R&D Engine

Tough economic times and emerging technologies
are prompting consumers to change their
buying behaviour, and smart retailers are responding
with innovative in-store offerings.

by **Dana Cho** and **Beau Trincia**

OUR TOUGH ECONOMIC TIMES have hit traditional retailers hard, particularly in North America. **Circuit City** and **Borders** have filed for bankruptcy; **Ann Taylor** and **Home Depot** have closed hundreds of stores; and **American Apparel** is reportedly millions of dollars in the red, to name but a few. The official reasons for these failures range from overly-aggressive expansion strategies to unfortunate investment decisions – but, in reality, a big driver of this retail upheaval is old-fashioned belt-tightening.

Financial uncertainty is prompting consumers to change their buying behaviours. Enabled by new technologies, shoppers are now using mobile phones to comparison shop on the fly, access in-the-moment promotions, and consult friends or family before buying anything.

As the ways in which people make purchase decisions multiply, retailers of all kinds are at a crossroads. One of the key reasons for operating a bricks-and-mortar store – building a strong,

Customers today want retail
to be less about well-orchestrated
brands and carefully rehearsed
answers and more about transparency,
authenticity and passion.

distinctive brand experience – no longer seems relevant. Thanks to the rapid rise of social media and corporate transparency, consumers now wield tremendous influence in shaping retail brands and are growing increasingly skeptical of overly-slick store designs, clerks and marketing messages. The once-dependable competitive edges for bricks-and-mortar retailers are eroding, which means they can no longer afford to assume any inherent advantages over their online competitors.

For instance, store owners have long believed that the 'thrill' of shopping – that visceral, emotional rush that people get when touching or interacting with a product before they buy it – would uphold their popularity. But e-commerce Web sites are disproving this axiom by generating similar excitement online with concepts such as 'flash sales' and 'social shopping'. For example, **GILT Groupe** offers its members daily flash sales, which feature luxury goods in low quantities for an extremely limited time, giving people only a few minutes to make purchase decisions. The site, which launched in 2007, now has a valuation of US$1 billion. Meanwhile, **Svpply** has built a social network around shopping, letting its users track trends, including the items their friends buy. Its popularity has grown seven-fold since its introduction in late 2009.

As online retailers slash shipping times and costs to next to nothing, bricks-and-mortar retailers can no longer depend upon instant gratification as a competitive edge. Online giants **Zappos** and **Amazon** now send purchases overnight at a discount and provide second-day service for free. The success of these tactics suggests that virtual storefronts can be at least as effective as physical ones, if not more so. So, how can bricks-and-mortar retailers survive – and thrive – as consumer attitudes and buying habits change?

They could, of course, expand their online presence, and many are doing just that. But a few leading-edge companies are also challenging long-held industry beliefs and re-examining how they use their *physical* presence. These retailers are discovering that the sales floor presents them with opportunities to develop more open relationships with shoppers that help them better understand their audience and create an inspiring experience that drives customer loyalty.

Although digital channels may be better positioned to provide short-term transactional value, bricks-and-mortar stores still give retailers the best space in which to establish long-term connections with customers. Let's look at how a few companies are shifting their mindsets and moving from driving transactions to encouraging inspiration and discovery; from featuring 'expert staff' to 'informed enthusiasts'; from targeting shoppers to targeting product owners; and from focusing on revenue generation to R&D.

From Driving Transactions to *Encouraging Inspiration*

The focus on convenience, straightforward navigability and seamless transactions in the name of making in-store purchases as easy as possible runs counter to what consumer behaviour tells us. During the 2010 holiday shopping season, 48 per cent of consumers who used a smartphone in some way said they purchased goods in retail stores, while nearly as many – 45 per cent – bought items online via computer. However, the majority also said that, regardless of how they ultimately acquired the product, they had visited an actual store to browse. This suggests that although consumers often opt for the convenience of digital channels to make purchases, bricks-and-mortar stores continue to play an important role in the shopping journey – primarily where product discovery and inspiration are concerned.

The types of products purchased online versus at retail stores also varies. Shoppers are increasingly off-loading mission-based errands, or the acquisition of commoditized products (i.e. household staples) to other channels. This gives traditional stores both room and permission to be less about enabling convenient, seamless transactions and more about inspiration, discovery and serendipity. Stores could focus more intently on enticing browsers, using the physical space to convert exploratory shoppers, who arrive with little to no intention to buy, into potential buyers, who may make a purchase in the store or through another channel later.

J.Crew's Liquor Store provides a prime example of doing exactly that. J.Crew opened its first men's clothing store in 2008 with the goal of inspiring exploratory shoppers – people who weren't current customers of the brand. At the time, J.Crew's menswear had little following, and the retailer sought to raise its profile through a dedicated storefront. It took over a historic watering hole in New York's TriBeCa neighborhood, and rather than focus on packing in as many items into the 935-square-foot store as possible, J.Crew kept the bar's atmosphere intact, stocking shelves with bottles and filling the room with vintage furniture and non-J.Crew brands such as **Timex**, **Red Wing** and **Mackintosh**.

Retailers who believe in conventional wisdom would consider this a waste of precious floor space that could have been devoted to as many sellable brand-specific products as possible. However, J.Crew's goal was to *raise awareness* of its men's line – and pique the interest of potential customers. The concept appears to be working: J.Crew has subsequently opened three more Men's Shops, and although the company declines to provide sales figures for individual stores, CEO **Micky Drexler** recently told investors, "We are beyond thrilled with the performance of our stand-alone men's stores." J.Crew earned $44.7 million in the first quarter of 2010, up from $20.4 million during the same period a year ago. In addition, its chief menswear designer, **Frank Muytens**, was ranked among the top in his field in *GQ*'s 2010 Best New Menswear Designers competition.

Using physical spaces to drive inspiration rather than transactions isn't limited to the retail industry. In 2010 **Crédit Foncier**, a mortgage lender in France, invested in a high-profile store in Paris's Opera district to inspire people to want to own a home. Most lenders make in-person visits from prospective borrowers as perfunctory and short as possible, gearing information toward people who plan to buy a home in the near future. In contrast, Foncier Home targets anyone who might be thinking about home ownership – even if it's just a long-term goal or dream. The store includes a café, where people can meet casually with a real estate agent while looking over residential listings. It also includes a section with information about renovations and remodeling – services that Foncier Home doesn't yet offer but are an exciting, aspirational aspect of home ownership. Although the company sells nothing tangible and has no real need to maintain a large retail space, Foncier is banking on the notion that a discovery-based experience such as the one made possible in its flagship store will encourage more people to become home buyers. And when they do, Foncier Home will be top-of-mind as the go-to lender. Crédit Foncier expects this concept to drive growth in the future and has plans for expansion.

From Expert Staff to *Informed Enthusiasts*
Powered by social media, peer recommendations are gaining ground in power and influence. In a recent survey, nearly eight out of ten people said they trust peer recommendations *above all other sources of information*. Yet retailers are still pouring billions of dollars into service training on a workforce that routinely sees 50 per cent turnover each year. The fact is, as consumers rely on friends, social networks and other independent resources for expert information, the role of the store associate is shifting dramatically.

The *new* purpose of a retail store lies in its ability to represent an organization's actual culture and values, captured and rendered by its sales associates. Customers today want retailers to be *less* about well-orchestrated brands and carefully rehearsed answers and *more* about transparency, authenticity

and passion. Store associates, therefore, need to evolve from 'expert staff' into informed brand enthusiasts who are proud of their organization.

How might a retailer and its sales associates reveal a brand's organizational values? Consider the UK department store **John Lewis**, which operates on a partnership model that makes every employee a partial owner of the business. Not surprisingly, because they are partners who share in the company's profits, employee engagement and retention are high; compared with others in the industry, John Lewis staff stays on the job twice as long. The store's hiring practices de-emphasize retail experience; what counts in recruitment is *behaviour*. "You can train anyone to do things," one partner told the *Guardian UK*. "But nobody can teach someone how to *be*."

"We ask not only that you do your day job, but that you play an active role as an owner," a member of the partnership board explained in the same article. "That you engage with your colleagues and work with them in thinking through what will make the business successful. Our shareholders aren't passive and distant ... they have lots of opinions." And those opinions are voiced through democratic channels: the chairman and board run the company's commercial activities, but an 82-member partnership council elects nearly half the board (which could, if needed, fire the chairman). The partnership council is elected primarily through a network of forums representing every department of every company store. So, the board looks after the partners; the partners look after the customers; and the customers spend money in the store. For John Lewis, this 'virtuous circle' works well: in the depths of a global financial downturn, John Lewis has turned an operating profit of 20 per cent, and customer satisfaction remains high.

The shift from being an *expert* to being an *enthusiast* – someone who believes in the brand and organization they work for and can speak passionately about the products at hand – has less to do with scripted service and more to do with organizational design. In the John Lewis example, hiring, governance and accountability create a foundation for empowered, engaged and impassioned associates. Many leading-edge U.S. retailers have taken similar personnel-oriented approaches. Perhaps the best known is **Apple**, which transformed consumer technology retail with its retail stores. For the Apple Store's tenth anniversary 're-fresh' this year, the company invested heavily in supporting its enthusiastic store associates with service-enabling technology rather than in a redesign of the bricks-and-mortar interior.

From Targeting Shoppers to *Targeting Owners*
Retail stores have traditionally been designed for shoppers with the intention to buy and, perhaps as a result, retailers have long depended on in-store marketing and communications to sell the quality and other worthy attributes of their products. Under the new paradigm we are describing, bricks-and-mortar retailers have an opportunity to acknowledge the value of the *product owner*'s role as a brand ambassador and key influencer on other shoppers.

In a study conducted by social-networking site **myYearbook**, 81 per cent of respondents said they had received online advice from friends and followers related to a product purchase, and 74 per cent of those who received such advice found it to be influential in their decision. Meanwhile, 90 per cent of online consumers trust recommendations from people they know; and 70 per cent trust the opinions of unknown users. The 'owner' or existing user of a product, then, can be the most powerful influencer of all.

As a result, designing the bricks-and-mortar store for the consumer who already owns your products (versus the consumer who is shopping) can have profound effects on a brand. By focusing on participation in the store – through education, trials and membership experiences rather than marketing, promotion and sales – retailers are positioning themselves for a longer-term, more open relationship with customers, helping them successfully evolve with the 21st century.

We would argue that the very future of retail depends on this ability to make stores participatory and desirable to an owner audience. One retailer that 'gets' this is **American Girl**, based in Middleton, Wisconsin, which draws owners of its customized dolls back into stores with a Doll Hair Salon where kids can get makeovers for their dolls, have repairs done and socialize with other owners at the same time. This presents an obvious opportunity to sell new accessories, too, but more importantly, the stores can passively evangelize the doll experience: when girls and parents tell their friends and family about their positive experiences onsite (which often have nothing to do with buying the original doll), they bring new owners into the fold.

Likewise, **Nike**'s branded stores pull in repeat visits from owners via its Nike+ Run Clubs, which meet at designated shops worldwide. Building on its platform of performance-tracking products and Web site, Nike+ is now the largest running club in the world, with more than three million members. In 2009 alone, membership grew by 50 per cent. Athletes of all skill levels train together and are privy to product trials and expert clinics. Nike motivates owners to use its products as a group, and the group inspires other curious runners to join them – and buy Nike gear – through camaraderie and knowledge-sharing. Taking the concept a step further, in 2010, Nike opened its first 'category experience store' dedicated solely to the sport, Nike Running Stanford, in Palo Alto, California.

From Revenue-Generator to *R&D Engine*
The paradigm shift we are describing questions, at a fundamental level, the role of the physical store in a retail organization's business. As the channels to buy continue to multiply – from new e-commerce models to mobile-phone payments – traditional retailers face more competition than ever before. If consumers can buy anything anywhere at anytime from anyone, bricks-and-mortar stores needs to derive new meaning and value for their business in order to remain a strategic asset.

Fortunately for bricks-and-mortar, not all channels are created equal, and the traditional retail store maintains an important edge over the digital realm: the physical space provides a direct, personal connection with consumers. Smart retailers have begun using the storefront to foster relationships with people, which means going beyond selling products or presenting a well-orchestrated brand experience to understand existing and potential customers and their needs. In short, they are using the retail floor as a platform for learning.

These retailers realize that developing a new offering behind the scenes until it is exactly right is a slow strategy that doesn't

Smart retailers have begun using the storefront to better understand existing and potential customers and their needs.

allow for quick adaptation in a rapidly-shifting market. Instead, they 'beta test' new offerings and experiences and quickly pivot the offering on the fly as dictated by actual customers. For example, at the height of the recession, **Urban Outfitters** opened an experimental store in Los Angeles called **Space 15Twenty**, which aims to attract – and study – customers other than its typical college student. Brand collaborations with Santa Monica bookseller **Hennessey + Ingalls** and New York vintage shops **What Comes Around Goes Around** and **Generic Man** act as magnets for people who don't typically shop at Urban Outfitters. In a sense, it's a store for *tomorrow's customer*, rather than *today's sales*. The store is an investment in market reconnaissance, rather than solely a means toward hitting revenue targets and achieving profitability; its primary goal is gathering customer information from which Urban Outfitters can learn.

While recession has hit some retailers very hard, in the first quarter of 2010, Urban Outfitters saw a 72 per cent increase in profits. CEO **Glen Senk** credits creativity and experimentation. "We don't go about revenue and profit as a goal. Rather, we focus our energies on the customer experience: innovating, making beautiful products, really pushing the limits of our brand expression and constantly refining how we operate. Revenue per square foot is the result of that focus, rather than the starting point or motivation."

The threshold where companies interact with customers can be a leading element in driving innovation, rather than being the last thing they consider. In August 2011, **State Farm** opened its doors to a new retail venture called **Next Door**. In contrast to its other locations, Next Door's purpose isn't solely to sell products. Instead, it offers personal financial coaching,

classes and community space – all for free. It's self-described as 'an open-source learning lab and community space' – no catch, no sales pitch. Why? While Next Door helps people work toward their goals, State Farm learns more about what consumers want and need, and how it can help. The store employs an on-site research analyst whose job it is to learn about the needs of the community and translate those needs into meaningful, actionable insights for the company. The store, then, is a channel for consumers to shape and influence the organization's strategic direction.

In closing

The future success of retailers may depend greatly on their ability to challenge what the industry has simply accepted as true: that a brand experience is crafted by the design and messaging around a physical experience, and that a store's primary purpose is to *sell*. Increasingly, traditional retailers are openly questioning the role that the physical store plays in their business strategy – and opting to use these spaces to effect long-term change over short-term sales growth. We believe this is a great way to solidify long-term customer loyalty and provide shoppers with that increasingly-important window into an organization's soul. **R**

Dana Cho is a Partner at IDEO in Palo Alto, California. **Beau Trincia** is an Architect and Interaction Design Lead at IDEO.

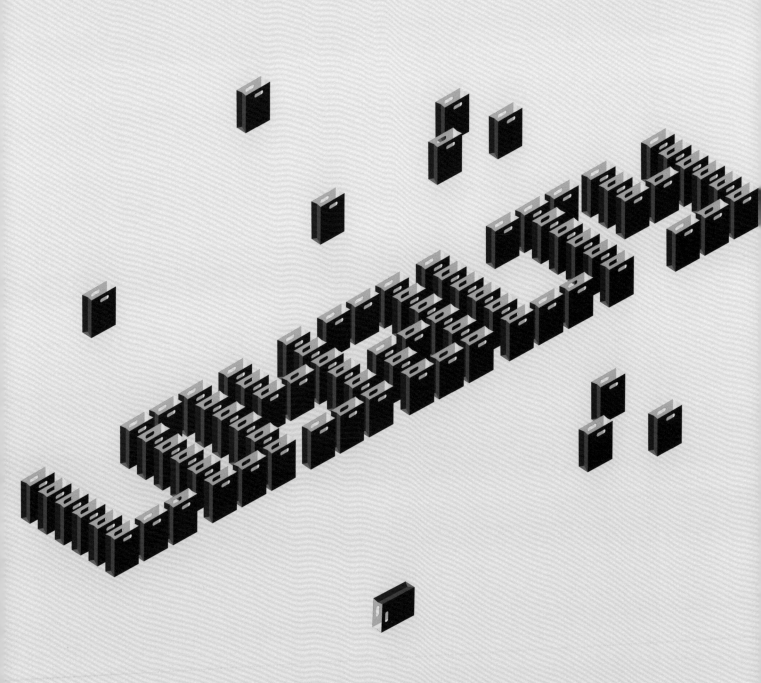

by **Jeremy Alexis**

Loyalty By Design:
Using Design to Create Fiercely Loyal Customers

Cultivating fiercely loyal customers requires ambition
and risk-taking, but will ultimately provide your company
with valuable and sustained relationships.

IT IS A COMMON OBSERVATION: As soon as the plane lands, at least half the passengers quick-draw their BlackBerries to check their e-mail and voicemail. The device responsible for this behaviour is sometimes mocked as a 'crackberry' or 'an extra appendage.' Some may see this as a sad commentary on modern business life, but it is also evidence of fiercely loyal customers.

Most of the quick-draw artists on the plane will also likely be members of the airline's frequent-flier program. Whereas the BlackBerry derives loyalty from an easy-to-use interface, consistent service, and a robust device design, the airline derives loyal-

ty from a complex and expensive reward program that includes call centers, free product giveaways, and sophisticated accounting practices. A study reported in *Brandweek* showed that offerings such as the **BlackBerry** (along with similar products from **Samsung** and **Palm**) and **Google** have the most-loyal customers, while companies such as, for example, **American Airlines** have increasingly *less*-loyal customers.

The companies at the top of this survey share a set of common factors: they offer products and services that are easy to use and address a holistic set of customer needs. In other words, they are *well designed*. This evidence suggests that traditional levers for creating loyalty (reward programs and contracts) are easy to copy and increasingly less effective, and that companies that depend on them should look to new, more-powerful levers to build better relationships with their customers.

The Ongoing Quest for Loyalty

Creating loyal customers remains a goal (often articulated as the most important goal) of most companies. Estimates put the number of books on customer loyalty in the thousands. In North America alone, companies spent $1.2 billion on loyalty programs in 2003, and this number is increasing. There are more than 8,600 supermarkets, 50 airlines, 30 phone companies, 20 hotel chains, and dozens of credit cards that offer loyalty programs. However, according to **McKinsey & Company**, organizations often underestimate the full cost of setting up loyalty programs, and then, even if sales increase, the program may actually result in losses.

In addition, companies spend a great deal on technology to help them manage their customers – with less than stellar results. In 2004, North American companies spent $10.9 billion on customer relationship management systems. However, only 28 per cent of companies that implemented a CRM system last year believed it led to any improvements.

Despite these efforts, and not including customers of outliers like Google and Samsung, consumers are increasingly less loyal to brands and products. For example, food retailers will lose up to 40 per cent of their new customers in three months, and only about 10 per cent of customers are 100 per cent loyal to certain consumer products.

In a nutshell, modern customers are less loyal, and loyal customers are less profitable, than most companies estimate. Much of this can be attributed to increased choice and availability of information. However, we should not overlook the fact that many organizations have incomplete and old beliefs about loyal customers (see **Figure One**). This evidence begs the question: Should companies be concerned about creating loyal customers and, if so, what tools can a thoughtful design manager employ to build more sustained and mutually beneficial customer relationships?

The answer is deceptively simple. A company's goal should be to create completely satisfied customers through a more thorough understanding of their needs and through distinctive offerings. According to research conducted for Harvard Business School by **Thomas O. Jones** and **W. Earl Sasser**, "To a much greater extent than most managers think, completely satisfied customers are more loyal than just satisfied customers." Traditional loyalty efforts produce customers who are only marginally loyal, and they make it easy for customers to switch to competitors. In contrast, completely satisfied customers become fiercely loyal customers, exhibiting the qualities that were once assumed common for all loyal customers. But this class of customer loyalty can be difficult to cultivate; it requires an integrated approach of design, development, sales, and marketing, and it cannot be achieved with a standalone program.

RETHINKING BELIEFS ABOUT LOYAL CUSTOMERS	Figure One
Old logic: loyal customers...	**In reality: loyal customers...**
Cost less to serve	Have higher expectations from your organization and your offering
Will pay more for your offering	Experience helps them to get the best price from your organization
Are receptive to cross selling	Are very sensitive about your organization taking advantage of their loyalty for marketing and price increases
Will create positive word of mouth buzz for your brand: they will market it for you	Are not reliable marketers, and do not always present accurate and positive messages

Figure Two details the six available levers for creating customer loyalty. The three levers on the left are the more common strategies. Customers (both consumer and B2B) are becoming more adept at avoiding lock-in; it is not a desirable condition from a user's point of view. These levers operate under the false assumption that programs can change and control customer behaviour. Although the programs may see initial success, customers will soon learn how to extract the maximum value from them while contributing limited value and loyalty.

The three levers on the right create more-sustained, fiercer loyalty, and they reinforce and enhance customer behaviours. Not surprisingly, the levers on the right benefit the most from integrated design efforts, which suggests that design managers have a more important role in building customer loyalty than is generally accepted.

To create fiercely loyal customers, companies will often employ several levers simultaneously. To illustrate this point, we'll look at two examples: **Walmart** and **Apple**.

Exhibit A: Walmart

Among retailers, Walmart's customer base is second in loyalty only to that of **Target**. The company has created a sophisticated system of partner relationships and logistics that provide its customers with consistently low prices, and customers are loyal to Walmart because of the favourable economics created by these systems. In addition to price, Walmart has created a close emotional connection with its customers. Despite stories of labour and sourcing issues, most of them are fiercely loyal to the brand. Walmart uses design strategically, creating a brand

THE SIX LEVERS FOR BUILDING CUSTOMER LOYALTY

Figure Two

	1. Loyalty Programs	2. Contracts	3. Limited Choice	4. Distinctive Solution	5. Emotional Connection	6. Favourable Economics
Source of loyalty	Repeat purchase builds rewards	Obligated, early termination results in fee	Other choice is nothing	Solve best for customer needs	Customers are aligned with/ buy into brand	Best economic proposition
Example	AA advantage	Cell phone contracts	Utilities	Total Merrill from Merrill Lynch	Apple	Walmart
Challenges	• Expensive • Easy to copy • Customer loyal to program, not brand	• Can create adversarial relationship with customers • Can lead to complex accounting	Subject to privatization and monopoly regulation	• Complex to manage • Requires constant updating	Requires deep customer knowledge	• Hard to manage • Can lead to low profits
These levers:	• Modify customer behaviour • Can easily be copied • Create marginal, temporary loyalty			• Build on/leverage existing behaviour • Are difficult to copy • Create sustained loyalty		

and a store environment that is aligned with the beliefs and values of its core audience. That audience is attracted to simple, uncomplicated signage and merchandising, and a store look that embodies economy.

Exhibit B: Apple

Apple is especially instructive in this case, as it would be difficult to identify a brand with more-loyal customers. This high degree of loyalty results from the application of multiple, but well-integrated, levers. Apple has honed and strengthened this emotional connection over the years. The company also offers its customers unique solutions, such as the iTunes/iPod system. Customers are loyal to the iPod because it made digital music easy to use. Other digital music systems required users to understand a dizzying array of file extensions, to log on and establish accounts with several service providers, and ultimately to live with a device that was not an attractive or desirable object.

A Guide for Creating Fiercely Loyal Customers

As noted above, design and design thinking (both within the internal team and with consultants) can play a critical role in customer loyalty efforts. A design team's core value lies in developing economical and user-centered solutions and/or creating emotive and meaningful brand experiences, which ultimately are responsible for creating the most loyal customers. **Figure Three** details how design efforts can be employed as part of the three most powerful levers.

So far, we have shown that traditional loyalty efforts will not create completely satisfied, and thus fiercely loyal, customers.

We have also argued that design is well positioned to create this new class of loyalty. The challenge remains for design managers to articulate this argument within their companies and then to build an integrated approach to employ more effective loyalty levers. When implemented properly, these efforts will create customers who:

- Are more accepting and accommodating of product launches that require further iteration and refinement
- Will be instrumental in moving your offerings from early adopter to early majority markets
- Can become partners in your innovation and development efforts

Although implementation at your company will vary based on culture and industry, the following guide outlines a four-step process for defining the appropriate levers, design interventions, and organizational strategy for creating fiercely loyal customers.

1. Shift mindset from 'lock in' to 'lock out';
2. Diagnose the current level of customer loyalty;
3. Identify the appropriate levers and interventions;
4. Collaborate on an implementation strategy.

1. Shift mindset from 'lock in' to 'lock out'

The first step is both the most important and the most challenging. It requires you, the design manager, to immediately shift the focus, first of your team, and eventually of your future collaborators, to the correct path for achieving customer loyalty. Most loy-

Lever	Potential Design Interventions
Distinctive Solutions	• Conduct design research to understand unarticulated and unmet needs. • Develop product platforms that address a comprehensive needs set. • Conduct usability testing to ensure offerings are best in class for usability and usefulness.
Emotional Connections	• Conduct design research to understand customer values, aspirations, and passions. • Develop brands that communicate emotion and feeling, not just functional value. • Develop products and communications that customers covet and desire.
Favourable Economics	• Conduct usability design studies to understand which elements of the current offering can be shifted to customers, reducing costs and complexity. • Seek innovative fabrication and sourcing models. • Assess product and service design with intent to reduce unnecessary components and complexity.

alty programs are based on a *company-centered point of view*, and they attempt to lock customers in to services and offerings.

When a company takes a customer-centered point of view, which is ultimately required if you intend to create completely satisfied customers, the corporate focus needs to change. The goal of the loyalty efforts should be to provide products, services, and communications that are so compelling and distinctive that customers do not even consider switching, essentially 'locking out' competitors and substitutes.

Although initially challenging, this change in focus will be liberating. Most of the people in your organization will not disagree with this suggested change (there are few companies that do not give at least lip service to "putting the customer first"). However, despite their agreement in principle, many of your colleagues will not be converted until they begin to see change and results. It is critical for the design team to remain vigilant, positive, and dedicated to the effort during the uncomfortable period between initial agreement and full buy-in based on results.

2. Diagnose the situation

Once your colleagues agree in principle, the design team should begin an analysis of the current situation. The team should gather data to help answer the following questions:

- How loyal are our current customers?
- What levers do we employ to build their loyalty?
- How effective are these levers?
- How loyal are our competitor's customers?
- What levers do they employ?
- Do our competitors do anything related to loyalty that we wish we did or wish we could do?
- What can we learn from companies in other industries?

Much of the loyalty data may already exist. However, it is important to understand the methods used to collect the data and the objectives of each study. Loyalty studies, like any good piece of research, need to limit bias. Often, these studies can be biased to show loyalty being stronger than it actually is. Ideally, you want to be able to identify customers who are not satisfied, somewhat satisfied, and highly satisfied, and the drivers behind each segment's current state.

3. Choose the right levers

Your situation diagnosis will help your team to understand what gaps need to be filled in order to create more loyal customers. Your study will also likely reveal opportunities created by your competitor's myopia or company-centered focus on loyalty. Now, your team can select and then detail the appropriate levers.

Set realistic and appropriate goals. Your team should be sensitive to the presenting condition and position of your customers. If you have identified that the majority of your customers fall in the lower range of *somewhat satisfied* or even *not satisfied*, it may be difficult to move all the way to *fully satisfied* with one set of interventions. In fact, these customers may prefer your organization to focus on getting the basics right before they will become more loyal. It is critical to set goals that are appropriate for your customers and that can be achieved by your team. This is truly a case where it is smarter to under-promise and over-deliver.

Identify existing and new organizational capabilities. Your selection of levers should be aligned with your organization's capabilities. So, if your company does not have the sourcing and logistics capabilities to deliver low-cost offerings, selecting favorable economics as a lever may not be the appropriate choice. There may be some instances in which the team identifies new capabilities that need to be developed or nurtured. This will require additional collaboration and resources; developing a new capability is a strategic decision.

Use multiple levers simultaneously. As noted earlier, several levers should be employed for maximum impact. Ideally, these

THE PROFIT-SATISFACTION MATRIX — Figure Four

	Not satisfied	Somewhat satisfied	Highly satisfied
Profitable customers	Start by getting the basics right to build initial loyalty.	Conduct research and apply appropriate levers to build satisfaction and loyalty.	Monitor and adjust efficacy of levers to ensure ongoing satisfaction and profitability.
Break even customers	Provide incentives for customers to become more profitable and satisfied or to exit.	Apply appropriate levers and pilot alternative business models.	Shift cost/service burden to customers.
Unprofitable customers	Develop incentives to steer these customers to different offerings and services.	Prototype and pilot alternative business models.	Shift cost/service burden to customers.

levers will be mutually reinforcing. For example, if you choose to deliver the lowest price to achieve favorable economics, you should also be able to create an emotional connection with your customers based on offering them a low price – this should be a key benefit for your customers.

4. Develop an integrated approach

With a set of interventions defined, your team can now begin to plan the implementation with other disciplines and functions. To the extent it is possible, you can include a broader coalition during development, but at this point it is critical to move efforts to a larger, more cross-functional team.

At the core of this integrated approach is the idea that customer loyalty is not created by a standalone program but is the result of orchestrated efforts of marketing, sales, product development, and strategy.

It is critical at this point to create a coherent business argument for loyalty. Despite the common sense and clear benefits of creating completely satisfied customers, there will no doubt be individuals in your organization that still require convincing. A tool for making this argument and for engaging skeptics is the profit/satisfaction matrix illustrated in Figure Four. This tool integrates your design-focused research, which segmented customers according to loyalty, with research that likely lives in the finance department and details which segments of customers are most profitable.

Combining these data into a single model will require some cleaning and modification, but it will create a common tool to help guide and shape a robust strategy. This model also will force a much-needed collaboration among design, marketing, sales, and finance. What is important is that this model will move the customer loyalty conversation to a strategic level of the same rank as profitability. Although not always acknowledged, profitability and customer loyalty have a mutually reinforcing relationship:

- If you just focus on creating profitable customers, without trying to make them completely satisfied, your competitors can easily poach these highly valued customers.

- If you just focus on creating "completely satisfied" customers, without understanding profitability, you may rack up losses serving them.

Depending on the nature of your business, it may be possible to put individual customers (likely in a B2B environment) or customer segments in each cell in the model. Figure Four lists strategies as appropriate for customers or customer segments in each cell.

In closing

All companies want to create fiercely loyal, profitable customers. This can be achieved only through rethinking existing logic about customer loyalty and loyal customers, integrating loyalty efforts with offering development, marketing, and sales, and close collaboration between the strategy and design functions within the organization. Cultivating fiercely loyal customers requires ambition and risk-taking, but will ultimately provide your company with valuable and sustained relationships. **R**

Jeremy Alexis is the director of interdisciplinary education at the Illinois Institute of Technology and a senior lecturer at IIT's Institute of Design, where he teaches a capstone workshop class for graduate design students. He is also the faculty lead for the Institute of Design's executive education practice.

MIND THE GAPS

THE CHALLENGES OF USING DESIGN TO SCALE SOLUTIONS TO WICKED PROBLEMS

WHILE PROBLEMS OF ALL SHAPES AND SIZES can benefit from creativity, it has become an article of faith that 'wicked problems', in particular, require highly creative solutions that span boundaries and organizations. And as more of the critical issues facing our society – from sustainability to chronic disease – are being classified as *wicked* (or at least extremely stubborn), the prominence of design thinking continues to grow in the public sphere, expanding into areas heretofore unexplored by designers.

I have watched this unfold first-hand in my work at **frog**, where we have seen a rapid expansion of interest from organizations such as the **United States Agency for International**

In trying to solve our biggest problems, four obstacles often come between creative approaches and large-scale implementations.

by **Robert Fabricant**

Development and the **State Department**, both of which have embarked on initiatives to integrate design thinking into their programming. As a result of such partnerships, 'social innovation' has moved into the lexicon, with programs popping up simultaneously at business and design schools around the world.

Paul Polak – a pioneer of low-cost irrigation technologies in Bangladesh and other developing countries – first exposed me to the link between *design methods* and *social innovation* in 2006. Paul believes that products that meet user needs are a significant, underappreciated market for customers living on less than $1 a day. His organization, **International Development Enterprises (IDE)**, has created products ranging from treadle pumps to low-cost drip irrigation systems by using design methods including direct observation of user needs followed by rapid cycles of iteration and prototyping in the field.

The success of organizations like IDE has led to a belief not only in the power of human-centered, participatory approaches, but also to a belief that these efforts will generate an expanding portfolio of solutions from which the best can be identified and scaled to solve a host of wicked problems.

Treadle pumps and microfinance programs have become the design icons of social innovation, positively impacting millions of lives. As **Judith Rodin**, president of the **Rockefeller Foundation**, has pointed out, "solutions to many of the world's most difficult social problems don't need to be invented, they need only to be found, funded and scaled."

Unfortunately, very few social innovations have achieved comparable scale. Why? As **McKinsey**'s **Steve Davis** writes (in the online journal *What Matters*):

> " Unlike in the private sector, where successful product innovations have a clear process for gaining market share, the best social innovations are not necessarily widely adopted. The 'iPods' of poverty alleviation and literacy have likely been invented and put to use by small organizations in some corner of the globe, but there is no market for identifying these breakthrough ideas and ensuring widespread adoption."

Imagine a world where wicked problems were more easily tamed, allowing us to pull solutions off the shelf to meet the needs of under-resourced populations around the world. The good news is that, through a myriad of business model competitions and fellowship programs, social venture capitalists have become adept at identifying disruptive innovations with the potential to achieve scale – in theory. Yet due to some significant 'design gaps', very few have been able to achieve scale in practice.

Gaps to Achieving Scale

Over the last six years, under an initiative called Mobile Mandate,

my colleagues and I have committed significant time and resources to collaborations that leverage the social impact of design, and along the way, we have gained a healthy respect for the value and limitations of design in this space. One thing we have noted is that it is easy for designers to underestimate the gaps that exist between prototype and implementation, and in the case of wicked problems, these gaps are particularly daunting.

In my experience, four obstacles often come between creative approaches and large-scale implementation. While my examples come primarily from our work in the social sector, the observations and recommendations that follow are broadly applicable to wicked problems in any field.

1. The Systems Gap

Six years ago, **Pop!Tech** (an 'innovation accelerator') gathered a group of collaborators at frog to tackle one of the most severe and intractable health issues in the world: HIV in South Africa. A combination of cultural barriers and political neglect had created an epidemic of massive proportions in KwaZulu Natal, with infection rates estimated to be 40 per cent and co-infection with TB and multi-drug resistant TB widespread. Often, by the time people reached the healthcare system, it was too late in the disease cycle for effective care.

We had some great ideas to start with and a shared belief that we could change the dynamics of the situation at scale. Together, we incubated an initiative called Project Masiluleke, which focused on solutions that sit largely outside the traditional healthcare infrastructure. Our first step was to sketch out a new model for reaching people at every stage – from awareness to treatment and follow-up. Our discussion was guided by the sort of design frameworks that we use for commercial clients like **Disney** and **GE**. Within a few hours we had mapped out a systematic strategy and agreed upon the problem space by hypothesizing potential solutions.

The first result was a mobile-messaging system that alerted people to get tested and follow up with treatment. Simple solutions like these are crucial to build the necessary credibility to catalyze system-wide change. Today, the Project Masiluleke messaging service touches between one and two million South Africans a day. It has encouraged more than three million people to reach out for help in the last three years. Without this simple, concrete result, we might not have remained so committed to the initiative. The mobile messaging service has already traveled far, and is now implemented in other African countries by our partner, **Praekelt Foundation**.

In today's world, designers and investors often feel that the more systematic the approach, the more likely the solution is to succeed and scale. But while we often operate under the assumption that the *system* is the transportable part, what we learned from this experience is that it is usually the *discrete pieces*

In the end, it might not be a product or service that will scale the best, but the *process of engagement itself* with different participants in an ecosystem.

that travel more easily and are crucial in building support in new communities on the path to scale.

We are seeing the same thing in our work with **UNICEF**'s innovation team on Project Mwana. This initiative focuses on early infant diagnosis of HIV and has pioneered a system to return lab results to clinics via text messaging. This concept came out of several days of workshops that UNICEF's innovation team lead in Zambia with key stakeholders. The creative process played a key role in the early inception as well as the design and prototyping of the pilot solution. This simple solution is now going to scale in Zambia and will likely be exported by UNICEF to other countries.

Summary of Contributing Factors:
• Designers love systems, so systems thinking can be a great tool for alignment and shared understanding in the space of wicked problems. However, systems are contextual and conditional: they are not as scalable or transportable as we would like to think.
• The potential for impact is often greatest in the parts, not the sum. The discrete parts are easiest to measure and are most replicable.
• Simple solutions and quick 'wins' are crucial to build the necessary credibility to catalyze system-wide change.
• Systematic solutions often take too long to realize, bogging down smaller-scale innovators and entrepreneurs in a single market or community and preventing more discrete solutions from traveling to other locations.

Recommendation #1: Decompose large systems into their component parts to look for the individual pieces that are the most effective and efficient. Create a smaller set of discrete innovations that can be re-combined to suit the needs of different contexts at small scale to deliver widespread change.

2. The Discipline Gap
I was recently invited to a strategy planning session for the **mHealth Alliance**, an initiative hosted by the **UN Foundation**. The session brought together a number of major funders who were investing in innovative approaches to public health with leading mobile tech entrepreneurs. Such approaches have proliferated over the last few years, making it the ideal ground to test **Steve Davis**' hypothesis. That is, funders should be in a great position to pull the best mHealth innovations off the shelf and bring them to market at scale around the world. The good news is that many of these organizations *are* funding similar, even redundant, efforts in areas like HIV and maternal and child health. The challenge is that they are often unaware of what each other is doing, and lack a fundamental language for describing and comparing different solutions and implementations to figure out what really works.

There is clearly a role for design here. Designers are particularly adept at drawing connections between different efforts and visualizing patterns. But finding solutions to wicked problems is not as simple as merely mapping them out. Even with people who share the same cultural reference points, it takes time to unpack different initiatives to identify both the common and unique components of even a simple solution like our mobile messaging service. Most projects involve a much more diverse community of participants with different cultural perspectives and local knowledge.

The great strength of creative solutions is the willingness to prototype and iterate. But for these very same reasons, it can be hard to retrace your steps, and the very skills that make creative thinking so effective can initially hold you back. Creative partners like to continually iterate, particularly in the space of wicked problems, making stable solutions hard to identify and document. Designers are not likely to take the time to capture and describe the components of a solution adequately so that others can follow along and 'steal' the best parts; and imaginative solutions are hard to describe and normalize when many contextual variables are at play. Plus, the social knowledge and shared understanding that drives creative approaches is hard to capture for new stakeholders who didn't participate directly in the process.

Compounding the situation is the fact that funders often look for validation and measurement before they will invest in documenting and scaling a solution, creating a catch-22. Failures as well as successes need to be captured and disseminated, but often they are not, preventing the best hybrid solutions from propagating, as Steve Davis rightly points out.

Summary of Contributing Factors:
· Creative solutions are hard to describe and normalize, due to their many contextual variables.
· The social knowledge and shared understanding that drives creative approaches is hard to capture for new stakeholders who didn't personally participate in the process.
· Creative partners like to continually iterate, particularly in the space of wicked problems, making stable solutions hard to identify and document.
· Too much learning is being lost as we tackle wicked problems, because failures are not often documented. It is equally important to document failures as it is to document successes.

Recommendation #2: Invest equally in the definition and documentation stages so that solutions can be normalized and compared, even if the solution is a failure. This is another reason why it pays to focus on smaller, more discrete solutions, as they are easier to describe and compare (see Recommendation #1).

3. The Evidence Gap
One of the key achievements of design in the social sector has been to increase appreciation for the value of direct engagement with end users to better understand needs and collaboratively shape solutions. Many design collaborations begin with just that – working on a small scale with local partners and social entrepreneurs to rapidly develop and test new approaches. But all too often, funders and policy makers in fields like public health discount this sort of 'qualitative' and participatory research.

In 2009, I was participating on a panel at Harvard Business School's Social Entrepreneurship Conference, when a skeptical audience member raised the topic of measurement. The only designer on the panel, I was pleased to be armed with some fairly detailed stats on our work in South Africa. Our Project Masiluleke data showed a tripling of volume into the **National Aids Helpline** that could be directly correlated and attributed to our service.

Information technologies that are central to many social innovation initiatives in areas like mobile health are a natural place to gather quantitative evidence around feedback and engagement, building credibility with funders to invest in scale efforts. But while they are compelling, these stats generally reflect engagement and feedback – they have not been connected to any specific health outcomes, which can take years of study in an area like public health. While valuable, they do not fully address the 'evidence gap' raised by funders and policy makers.

The evidence gap cuts two ways: many interventions that have demonstrated measurable impact through traditional measurement and evaluation (M&E) studies, like mosquito nets, have hit barriers to scale due to lack of engagement and adoption. Large scale NGO's like UNICEF generally classify this under the category of 'demand generation', often seen as an afterthought in their programming – like a commercial company looking to 'market' its products once development is complete. In the space of wicked problems engagement, awareness and adoption are not something you can afford to take for granted; they are integral to scale. Given the dynamic nature of these problems and the complex social and behavioural dimensions to any solution, qualitative feedback must be a continual part of the design process.

Summary of Contributing Factors:
· Qualitative design methods are good for gathering early feedback in problem definition and solution development, which can build credibility before impact can be directly proven and correlated. However, designers usually continue to iterate on the solution, making measurement and evaluation difficult, particularly when facing wicked problems that may not have an obvious control group.
· Scale is not just important for the delivery model, it must be a focus of the demand model. Demand generation is a great weakness of many efforts, making qualitative research essential throughout the process.

Recommendation #3: Develop a more agile model of M&E that takes better advantage of qualitative feedback as well as real-time measurements of engagement, awareness and adoption through integration of information technologies. Look at these additional forms of qualitative feedback not just as precursors to more formal M&E, but as critical components to the continued iteration and optimization of solutions to wicked problems in the social sector. And look for opportunities to better correlate qualitative feedback with impact measures to better understand how the two interrelate.

4. The Solution Gap

In the realm of wicked problems, we cannot and should not expect shrink-wrapped solutions – even if the solutions emerged from a highly creative, collaborative and iterative process. This can be difficult for organizations, which make high profile investments in creative collaborations with designers, and for senior stakeholders, with too much faith in the power of design thinking, to accept. One 'failure', and they will often scrap the whole endeavour.

The fact is, organizational engagement takes time. In working with **iTeach**, our front-line partner in Project Masiluleke, we have witnessed an amazing willingness to apply a creative approach to many different challenges. We have seen first-hand, for example, the ability of an organization with strong community outreach skills to adapt those skills very successfully to design activities such as observation and concept testing. iTeach has set up an entire video-based usability lab in its limited facility to foster the design process, and we are now investigating whether we can achieve similar results in a much larger organization like UNICEF.

Ultimately, scale itself may be the wrong goal, particularly when it is used as an excuse not to engage locally and understand specific cultural needs. In the end, it might not be a product or solution that will scale the best, but *the process of engagement* itself with different participants in an ecosystem.

Summary of Contributing Factors:
• Don't assume that a solution can be imposed from the outside. Instead, involve and empower the community in shaping solutions to meet their needs.
• The design process remains mysterious to many and hence, can be intimidating. The fact is, much of design is common sense.

Look to leverage existing capabilities such as community outreach that can be expanded to support design activities.
• Take the time to pick the design partner that is best in tune with your organizational culture. Make sure you have a partner within the organization who is involved throughout the end-to-end process.
• Set the right expectations with internal stakeholders and champions so that they do not expect immediate success and are willing to see failures and mistakes as integral to the process.
• Insist that stakeholders participate directly in design activities to increase their level of commitment and appreciation for the messy aspects of the design process.
• Understand and assess barriers to openness early in the process.

Recommendation #4: Focus on building a sustainable network of partners within the communities you seek to serve. Understand that the design process – even if it leads to ideas that might not immediately prove to be successful – can help to strengthen connections between various stakeholders and increase their buy-in on an ongoing basis.

In closing

Design can play a critical role in opening up new ways of approaching wicked problems. But as we turn our attention to problems of scale, we must acknowledge that design is but one ingredient in an overall strategy. Organizations looking to integrate design into this solution space would do well to mind the gaps that exist between pilot and implementation, particularly in the social sector. Embracing the recommendations outlined herein can serve to guide collaborations moving forward and increase the chances of achieving large-scale impact. **R**

Robert Fabricant is the vice president of creative at frog, a global innovation consultancy, where he is charged with helping to extend frog's capabilities into new markets and offerings for clients like General Electric, Pepsi, Nike and Chrysler. He also leads frog's Design for Impact initiatives, which focus on transformative opportunities to use mobile technologies to increase access to information and accelerate positive behaviour change. You can follow him on twitter @fabtweet.

When attempting to solve wicked problems, creative thinkers must design systems that influence people's behaviour on a mass scale.

Designing Systems
at Scale

by **Fred Dust** and **Ilya Prokopoff**

WANDER INTO MISSION PIE, a corner café in San Francisco best known for its namesake baked goods, and the place looks familiar enough. The 10 or so wooden tables, all in close proximity, are filled with pie-eating, warm-beverage-sipping customers. Some people chat, while others read leftover newspapers or peck out e-mail messages from their laptops. Swap the pie for bagels, and you could be in another San Francisco café. But stick around awhile, and the peculiarities of Mission Pie become apparent.

First off, roughly half of Mission Pie's 14-person staff is young – *really* young. But they're not the usual grad-school Lit majors or aspiring musicians working in so many of the city's eateries. They're either current or former students from Mission High, a nearby public high school with 68 per cent of the kids eligible to receive free and reduced-cost lunches. San Francisco native **Karen Heisler**, Mission Pie's owner, is largely paying the kids to understand where their food comes from and its impact on their bodies, their neighborhood and the world at large.

There's a surprisingly complex system behind a slice of Mission Pie's plum frangipane or mixed-berry tart. Mission Pie is part of a larger system: **Pie Ranch** is a 27-acre parcel about 90 minutes from the café and well positioned above the historic

Too often, solutions for big problems are subdivided into component parts. When designing systems at scale, we must consider the whole ecosystem that needs to be engaged.

Steele Ranch. Named for its shape when viewed from atop a nearby ridge, it operates as an educational non-profit with the goal of inspiring urban youth to transform their relationships to food, and to work with their communities in building healthier local food systems. Not only does Pie Ranch supply the café with berries, pumpkins and apples, it welcomes the café's Mission High staff to work the land, contemplate the crops and sample the fresh food.

As both Mission Pie and Pie Ranch have found, the simple task of showing people where their food comes from and pointing to the impact of industrialized farming touches off all sorts of big system challenges, from obesity and education to sustainability and personal food-related attitudes and behaviours.

To design compelling, effective solutions for challenges of all sizes, an organization must consider the overarching system it hooks into. Heisler is a firm believer in the necessity of the human element – the community as a manifestation of the system. "Lose the human aspect," she says, "and the system falls apart."

In our work, we see system disconnects around us all the time. As networks grow and mutate, designers are forced to tackle issues of scale, legacy and influence. This reminds us that life is complex, and as designers, business people and other creative thinkers, we must resist both the seduction of simplicity *and* the safety of Byzantine networks that allow good ideas to fade and humans to be lost or forgotten.

When tackling major challenges, we think about 'systems at scale', which involves two distinct elements: designing systems that work and influencing people's thinking at mass scale. The best design solutions do both.

Balancing the Ecosystem

Every ecosystem is comprised of both micro and macro elements, and when any element gets out of whack, the rest of the system suffers. In too many cases, products and services are conceived to impact massive change, yet the offerings lack an awareness of their overall systems.

Consider, for instance, the Segway. The two-wheeled transporter didn't catch on for a lot of reasons, from cost and practicality to a mountain-high learning curve for use. Still, an overarching issue was that it wasn't intentionally designed to be a part of a larger-scale system; rather, it was an individual product at odds with a larger ecosystem. The Segway clashed with local road and sidewalk regulations and has yet to be approved by the **Food and Drug Administration** as a medical device, which would allow for expanded use in public spaces. Worse still, it didn't perform on the human scale – when it functioned, the rider still looked and often felt silly. How might creative thinkers at Segway have considered the broader range of real-world design challenges that could make or break the relevance of their new technology?

On the other end of the spectrum, there are examples of efforts that influence people's thinking, but are not complemented by the systems needed to make them succeed at a large scale. **Al Gore**'s *An Inconvenient Truth* is an interesting example. The documentary focused on educating people through a PowerPoint presentation about global warming. When Gore's road show took off in a way few expected – ultimately becoming the fourth-highest-grossing documentary film to date in the U.S. – the effort struggled to move from knowledge to action. The task at hand – lessening the impact of global warming – seemed, to many viewers, hopeless.

When the final credits rolled in Gore's slideshow, viewers were given a long list of small changes to make in their lives to offset global warming. For some, these suggestions felt too individually based and incremental, missing out on a proposal for a system-level solution as a complement. Gore and his team are now working to address the system at scale by bringing in more stakeholders from the governmental and business sectors.

Problem-solving for big systems often leads designers to ask tough questions: how can an organization turn its workers, partners and customers into believers, people who buy into the current system, yet continue to help grow it? How can an organization avoid making only incremental changes or giving in to the temptation of defining a problem as 'unsolvable' or 'inevitable'? How can we make changes that impact multiple organizations and ultimately solve really big problems? The following examples – hard-earned success stories – show the potential for what balanced ecosystems can achieve through human-centered design, sticky systems, and reciprocity.

Growing Influential Networks

Following are three approaches that specifically deal with the idea of humanizing big problems to influence people to change and grow influential networks.

1. Human-Centered Systems: Design for People, Not the System
The notion of designing human values into big systems isn't new. How-to business books the world over talk about building and maintaining that human connection. But often, the advice seems hollow, like a poster in the employee break room reminding everyone to smile at the customer. The point isn't to simply humanize a system, but to embed *specific* human elements within it.

One of our favourite success stories comes from an unlikely place: Bogotá, Columbia, a place typically known for corruption, violence and general indifference to chaos. In 1995, after 18 years in academia, **Antanas Mockus** was elected mayor of Bogotá, a position he held intermittently between forays into presidential politics until 2004. While mayor and in his subsequent work, Mockus showed a knack for human-centered design by putting himself directly into the mix. For him, this entailed literally bumping shoulders with the city's inhabitants and personally reaching out to them.

When Bogotá's water was in short supply, Mockus had himself filmed showering for local TV broadcasts, during which he turned off the water as he soaped. The goal? Get city dwellers to curtail their showers to less than 20 minutes. Show them, as Mockus explained, "that even in a very private space, your behaviour can be linked to a citizen's duty. You cooperate because of the fun of doing it." Within two months, people were using 14 per cent less water.

Humour as a human element can certainly be used as a generalized way of creating robust systems. But Mockus showed real genius in systems design when he incorporated more specific cul-

tural insight into his approach to changing human behaviour. In 1998, he hired 420 mimes to help calm traffic by standing at major intersections and poking fun at scofflaw drivers. In doing so, Mockus used a deep insight in the Columbian nature: the citizens of Bogotá were far more uncomfortable with being mocked than they were with being fined. Faced with public humiliation, albeit humorous, they opted to change their behaviour. Within the year, traffic fatalities dropped from 1,300 to about 600 in the city. "Mimes defeated pessimism," explained Mockus, adding, "Feel confidence in unexpected solutions."

Mockus' antics are more than one-trick wonders. They reveal a deep understanding of his constituents and a confidence to use humour, reality, and cultural insight to aid in big system change and more viral but profound behaviourial change. In short, he understands what it takes to design for impact at scale. Mockus shows the value of looking past what a system should simply accomplish to ask, What should the system *feel* like? In doing so, he brought the human into the mix in a way that had significant impact on the broader system.

Alas, Mockus' political career hasn't been a complete success: he has failed to win presidential campaigns twice, and it's fair to wonder how conscious he was of the system at the start of his city-turnaround campaign. Still, Mockus is clearly on to something, with his ability to build both a directed and an organic system and identify insights that can lead to behaviourial change. Enough so that the John F. Kennedy School of Government at Harvard brought him in as a visiting fellow at its Institute of Politics.

Professor **Jane Mansbidge** had him talk to her class "Democracy, from Theory to Practice." "He focused," she explained in the *Harvard University Gazette* in 2007, "on changing hearts and minds – not through preaching but through artistically-creative strategies that employed the power of individual and community disapproval." She added that Mockus "made it clear that the most effective campaigns combine material incentives with normative change and participatory stakeholding."

There is brilliance in this approach. As we design our way out of difficult problems, we need to harness influences that can become viral and, eventually, create ever-expanding loyalty and adherence that becomes organically self-sustaining and able to reach a broad range of stakeholders in a system. The citizens of Bogotá may have laughed when Mockus spoke while wearing yellow Spandex tights and a red cape, dressed as 'Supercitizen', but they listened. More importantly, many changed their behaviour.

2. Sticky Systems: Design for Scale

Solutions – not only people – can be trapped inside silos. Too often, solutions for big problems are subdivided into component parts: Let's make a system that solves this, or Let's get people to change their beliefs, so they do this. This approach rarely leads to robust solutions, and it can be counterintuitive, making people feel disempowered. When designing systems at scale, we must consider the whole ecosystem that needs to be engaged. With multiple networks within an ecosystem, shareholders need to understand – and buy into – the desired impact.

Functioning 'silos' can be effective at a particular task, but the overall system eventually threatens to bottom out or limp along (think back to Gore's *Inconvenient Truth*.) It is only by combining components into a whole that we see the potential for a solid, sustainable ecology – something we call 'sticky systems'.

The **American Red Cross** has long had an effective system for collecting donated blood, but it turned to IDEO when it recognized the need to improve its long-term influence with donors and become more proactive in attracting new and younger donors.

Many people outside the organization, Red Cross officials realized, didn't associate the organization with the donation process: rarely were donors seeking opportunities to give blood independently and directly to the Red Cross. Rather, they waited to be spurred into action by a local school or church blood drive. The individual donor experience became the chance to influence donors to give as though it were their jobs or personal passions. As IDEO worked with the Red Cross to gain greater emotional relevance with potential new donors, the question posed to donors shifted from "how much blood?" to "why I give." Everyone had a story to tell.

Putting human sensibilities at the center of the solution for scaling influence also allowed staff and volunteers to reconnect with their humanitarian mission, as opposed to becoming cogs in the system. Workers posted donor-generated "why I give" answers on walls and a Web site. Surprisingly, privacy wasn't an issue: donors wanted to share their stories broadly. The "Why I Give Campaign" became the centerpiece of a community-building experience that reminds donors that there's no need for a middleman when giving blood. As one donor from North Carolina explained, "It's great to find out why someone donates. It gives you more of a reason to donate yourself."

3. Reciprocal Systems: Connect by Sharing

Convincing people to give back to a system as a means of connecting to it is, in some respects, a telltale sign of system success. It can also be incredibly difficult to do. Yet, when the other key elements such as human-centered design and influential systems are working, it becomes possible. **Wikipedia** and other open-source systems certainly make it look seamless.

Best Buy is another example. With a complex ecosystem of 140,000 employees, hundreds of retail stores, and a legacy of more than 40 years, the company leverages the power of its scale, but the focus is not on consistency or predictability (though it generally delivers on these points.) Rather, it's on building simple systems that engage people in focusing their creative energy on making things better for themselves and their customers. It's an acknowledgement that no one person at the top will have all the solutions, and that people on the frontline want to do their best and contribute to the continual improvement of the whole.

Another interesting element of Best Buy's system is that it's been designed deliberately to be 'fuzzy' at the edges, to allow and encourage room for people to generate and try new ideas and to give back when and how they can. The scale of the organization is harnessed by creating venues and processes by which employees can see themselves as part of a local team that has global reach.

Best Buy's women's leadership forum, known as 'WoLF', shows this in action. **Julie Gilbert**, a senior vice president at Best Buy, started WoLF in 2004 as an innovation engine and employee resource group after noticing that women needed a loyal pack of cohorts who would help them advance and better engage female customers. At Best Buy, a 'WoLF pack' is a group of 27 people (25 women and two men) who come together from all parts and ranks of the company. Together, they network, brainstorm and focus on the fact that women make up roughly 45 per cent of all retail consumer electronic purchases in an industry built by men for men.

The WoLF packs have paid off. More than 20,000 female customers and employees have been pulled into the effort; the number of female job applicants has increased by 37 per cent; and female-employee turnover has dropped by 5.7 per cent. Quarterly events let participants volunteer their time back to society in the form of events and fundraising. WoLFs can also mentor individuals or packs in another part of the country, and their efforts have organically led to a job-share pilot program.

In the realm of systems at scale, WoLF exemplifies an ecosystem developed to a point in which each component can give back as a valued shareholder in the form of consumer information, new products and volunteer work. The quid pro quo or social contract for this kind of giving back must be carefully considered. Esteem, visibility, and pride of affiliation are the currency of being part of a WoLF pack, part of the community.

Wikipedia, as its founder Jimmy Wales explained in a TED Talk in 2005, wouldn't work if its editors were paid. The system benefits from people wanting to feel valued and employed to make a difference in the organization through an authentic, personal way that cannot be bought.

As these examples show, the forces around any endeavor result in its ultimate design. Oftentimes, in order to manage the complexity of what we chose to bite off in a project, we frankly leave much of the design to chance. As Mission Pie's Heisler suggests, the community – its people and all its components – is a manifestation of the system. The question isn't, Do organizations get the system they deserve? Rather, as a creative thinker, How can you design the system your organization deserves? Can you acknowledge and own your part in effecting and improving the overall organization, not just one element in a system filled with silos? The underpinning promise of a human-centered approach is that designers can rely on people and their

behaviours and the things that entice them to find large-scale solutions that fit with – and thereby change – the bigger world around them.

Let's face it: in order to take on the design of really big solutions, creative thinkers need to tap the most powerful (and most human) of design tools: optimism. By its very nature, thinking like a designer requires us to believe that we can change things for the better. Thinking like a designer keeps us from becoming stunned by the complexity and seeming impossibility of a goal. It also allows us to create a balance, from the big view to little view, and involve stakeholders, even those at the fuzzy edges.

Despite the relative early days of Mission Pie, Heisler is already working with a long list of individuals, from fellow Pie Ranch co-directors **Jered Lawson** and farmer/educator **Nancy Vail** to Mission High kids and the café's bakers, customers, and food distributors to more distant people working on emerging projects that borrow from Mission Pie's approach. Her plan to "lay out the landscape, so people can see the value of the system, the value of community-supported agriculture" allows for both freshly-baked pies on a daily basis and impact in the realms of education, health, and farming over time. The long view, optimism, and determination leads to systems at scale that work and adapt, while making their shareholders proud participants.

In closing

Systems at scale comprise a series of methods for directing behavioural change on a large scale by inspiring people to embrace a system as a shareholder. In a world increasingly plagued by wicked problems, this is one approach to tackling seemingly-unsolvable problems. ***R***

Ilya Prokopoff and **Fred Dust** are Partners at IDEO, in Palo Alto, California. Ilya co-founded IDEO's Transformation practice, which helps clients use the tools and methods of design to work in new ways to address the challenges of the future. Fred leads IDEO's Smart Space practice, the group responsible for helping clients with their strategic and innovation goals around space, real estate and communities.

BEYOND
STRATEGIC THINKING:

STRATEGY AS
EXPERIENCED

Achieving better strategic outcomes requires
an acknowledgement of the powerful roles of subjective
interpretation and experience in successful strategies.

by **Jeanne Liedtka**

HE IDEA THAT STRATEGY EXISTS within the realm of *thought* is pervasive. Grounded in the realm of the rational and the objective, this paradigm emphasizes the value of effective strategic rhetoric that defines powerful core concepts, provides clear guidelines for action and uses simple maxims to communicate vividly. It urges strategic planning processes that utilize conscious forethought, commit aspirations and plans to paper, generally include a strong quantitative component, stress effective communication and carefully measure and monitor outcomes. In short, it makes a great deal of sense.

Within this mindset, gaining employees' intellectual acceptance of a new strategy is seen as an early milestone in successful strategy implementation. The problem managers face is that this approach does not appear to be working very well: the gap between *strategic rhetoric* and *strategic action* remains frustrating.

Study after study demonstrates that the 'knowing-doing gap' is alive and well, and that many carefully-constructed strategies continue to be ignored or dismissed as irrelevant by the employees whose behaviour must change in order to make them work.

Clearly, knowing is not enough. In this article I will argue that *feeling strategy* must accompany knowing it. What does it mean to 'feel' strategy – to experience it in an emotional as well as a cognitive way? One thing is certain: it will require a fundamental change to our basic conception of what strategy is all about.

The Missing Link

Strategy's track record at translating its rhetoric into action fails to impress. A recent report by *The Economist* studied 197 companies and found that only 63 per cent of new strategies' promised returns were actually delivered. Consistent with these concerns, research on strategy practices as basic as the writing of mission statements – among the top-rated management tools employed over the last decade – continues to produce discouraging findings, including the lack of any substantial link between mission statements and performance. One researcher queried 356 managers in Europe, Asia and Africa and found that 82 per cent of their firms had mission statements but fully 60 per cent of managers interviewed did not believe that those statements reflected the reality of daily practice.

A primary culprit blamed for these failures has been strategic planning processes. Traditional approaches are alleged to stifle innovation and favour incremental over substantive change; their emphasis on analytics and extrapolation drive out creativity and invention. Many believe that such processes – seemingly detached from the reality of a fast-moving marketplace – produce plans that do not reliably lead to successful initiatives in practice.

I have come to believe that an even more fundamental and seemingly obvious cause may underlie the longstanding failure to align word with deed: nobody really *cares* about these strategies. Leaders must move beyond incorporating solid strategic thinking and effective communication in order to succeed: strategies must be *felt* as personally meaningful and compelling by the members of the organization who must adopt new behaviours in order to execute them. And thinking alone won't get you there.

Talking about a strategic intent as *experienced* raises some interesting issues. Perhaps most obvious, strategic intents are not tangibly real in any objective sense; rather, they are images or ideas of future states that are imaginary and abstract in the present. How, then can they be experienced? Answering this question is the challenge that lies ahead for today's leaders.

Consider the following quote from a manager at the **New York Botanical Gardens**, one of the oldest botanical gardens in the U.S., which had just completed a highly-successful planning process aimed at rejuvenating the institution:

> "At the time it was created, the plan was better than the institution. The plan was a view of *what we wanted to be*. As people came to understand and accept the plan, they came to embrace the Garden that they saw through the plan, rather than the Garden as it actually was, even though not much had actually been accomplished yet."

The pull of a powerful intent does not rest on delusion. The Gardens' stakeholders know that the future image specified in the plan does not reflect the current reality; they merely choose to act as though it did. This willingness to treat as 'real' what we know is not is prevalent in developed societies today. Consider the enormous popularity of 'reality TV', which has little to do with reason and rationality. Viewers are fully aware that only some aspects of what they are watching are real, and that others are not. Rather than being disappointed or repelled by this, they find that it enhances the experience for them, making it more, rather than less, real.

Similarly, sociologists studying the experiences of tourists note that 'pseudo-events' like battle re-enactments or re-created colonial villages complete with costumed guides, do not dismay tourists, despite being not 'real': on the contrary, they are generally preferred to museum displays that merely exhibit a set of authenticated 'true' historical artifacts.

As human beings, we seek out things that *feel real* to us – that combine reality and fantasy in a compelling way. Isn't that what strategic intent should be about? I would argue that strategy needs more 'costumed interpreters and re-enactors', rather than 'museum display space', because the more vivid and compelling the future image is – the more it is *experienced* as well as *thought* – the more effective the implementation will be. And we need to go beyond the faculty of reason and the power of slick communications to get there.

Contrasting Thought and Experience

I will now differentiate between the notions of *strategy as thought* and *strategy as experienced* by examining their respective aims, assumptions and the differing outcomes they produce.

Strategy as thought aims for intellectual acceptance by its audience. Grounded in a rational perspective, the strategy itself is seen as independent, existing detached from its social context, and as objectively real and unproblematically knowable by those stakeholders to whom it is presented. Its important qualities are that it work – that is, be functional – and that it be cognitively comprehensible and understood. Strategy as thought rejects the old notion that employees should act on a strategy based solely on faith in their leaders. Employees' own ability to think strategically – to understand the broader strategic intent and to adapt it opportunistically – is seen as important.

Strategy as experienced, on the other hand, works from the perspective of social construction – the idea that each of us interprets 'reality' through our own personal lens – and aims to achieve a satisfying authenticity. In studying the enormous popularity of reality TV, **Randall Rose** and **Stacy Wood** argue that what viewers seek is not truth *per se*, but that 'satisfying authenticity' that occurs at the intersection of the *objectively real* and the *desirable*.

Simultaneously grounded in the reality of current circumstances yet holding out promise of a better future, the idea of a strategic intent with satisfying authenticity is powerful and consistent with a view of strategy as narrative – a 'story' about an organization's desired future. If the story is perceived to combine reality with the desirable in a compelling way – rather than being merely intellectually accepted – its ability to motivate behavioural change increases dramatically.

We can see this at play in the Garden employee for whom the 'story' contained in the plan is personally desirable and therefore compelling – despite (or perhaps because of) the acknowledged reality that the Garden he sees before him today is a mess. If *strategy as thought* seeks to move employees beyond acting on faith in their leaders to understanding the strategy itself, *strategy as experienced* seeks to move them beyond such understanding to *caring* about whether it gets implemented. The catalyst that drives new strategic behaviour in the thought model is *goals*, while in the experience model, it is *desire*.

The Role of the Subjective

The mere creation and dissemination of a strategy – as embodied by the existence of a document or a slogan – does not assure its 'reality' to anybody but those who wrote it. Strategies are, by nature, abstractions: while they begin to take on form and concreteness when translated into words or symbols, such translation is insufficient for them to be experienced as 'real' by members of the organization not involved in their creation. As such, the Garden employee does not see the new plan as reflective of a vivid future reality simply because he or she *read* it: additional conditions must be met.

Progressing to the next step requires that the strategy win the competition for its audience's attention: it must *avoid being ignored*. What gives something the ability to draw such awareness? Decades of research by cognitive scientists demonstrate that the use of cognitive 'schemas' or 'scripts' dominates human sense making: most of us, much of the time, operate on 'automatic pilot'. Getting someone to actively pay attention requires the interruption of schema-driven processing. Something must stand out among all of the other messages competing for attention. Research shows that the dominant characteristic of the winners of our attention is that they are somehow 'interesting' to us. Sociologist **Murray Davis** demonstrated that the most attended-to theories in his field were valued *because they were interesting*, not *because they were true*. What made them interesting, he discovered, was that they combined the familiar with the novel: they engaged audience interest, not by stating the obvious, but by offering the possibility of something not-at-all obvious.

Researchers studying the business literature have found similar results: articles that readers deemed worth paying attention to were characterized as 'generating a particular balance of novelty and familiarity'. Translating this notion to business practice, consider the banality of much of the rhetoric of mission statements. Who sits up and takes notice of the exhortation to 'delight customers' anymore? Contrast this with the example of a Swiss bank's avowed intent that all customers could say, "I know my banker." This gets attention because it reverses the familiar concept of "we know our customer."

Returning to the Garden example, its leader captured the attention of his employees at the start of the planning process with the following statement: "We are a museum of plants, not a park." Both museums and parks were familiar concepts to employees – in fact, the Garden had been treated like a park for decades (complete with dogs, cars and picnics) and so it was intriguing to be told that they were not a park, after all. What was novel was the idea of becoming 'a museum of plants'. The familiar, while 'true', rarely disrupts schema-driven processing.

At the other extreme, the too-radical message – one that contradicts too much accepted 'truth' – is likely to be rejected as false out of hand. The 'artistry of the interesting' entails finding that point of optimal tension between the two that both engages attention and suspends disbelief. As a result, **Michael Tanner** has described great music as setting up expectations and then "pleasurably defeating at least some of them," and studies of

STRATEGIES THAT ENGAGE AT AN EXPERIENTIAL LEVEL COMBINE NOVELTY AND FAMILIARITY; THEY ARE INEVITABLY ABOUT CHANGE, BUT THEY ARE ALSO ABOUT WHAT WILL NOT CHANGE.

country music find that legends like **Hank Williams** were seen as both highly original and rooted in tradition. In a similar vein, noted architect **Frank Gehry** talks of the need to build 'conceptual handrails' into innovative designs – something stable to hold onto while you take in the new. Thus, strategies that engage at an experiential level combine novelty and familiarity to say something interesting. They are inevitably about change, but they are also about what will not change.

The ultimate catalyst for behavioural change as we move from *strategy as thought* to *strategy as experienced* shifts from *goals* to *desires*. Desire, not goal-directedness, is the true driver of behavioural change. **Bennett Helm** argues that cognition and its attendant goal directedness drive a "mind-to-world fit." When confronted with a disconnect between our cognitions and the world, we are apt to change our mind to fit the 'facts' of the world. Our desires, however, drive a world-to-mind fit: when confronted with a disconnect here, we are apt to try to change the world.

To summarize, *strategy as thought* emphasizes the effective communication of mission statements and plans; it utilizes conscious forethought to create these, and outcome metrics to monitor their implementation. *Strategy as experienced*, on the other hand, relies more heavily on dialogue-based strategic conversation as its foundation, with significant use of stories and metaphors, developed iteratively in an experimental approach. Rather than relying on outcome metrics as a control device, it finds sustainability in the energy produced by the process itself.

Following are the four key components of fostering *strategy as experienced* in your organization:

1. Invite Participation in the Conversation

The *strategy as thought* perspective often argues for broader inclusion in strategy making processes as a good thing – helpful to improving the quality of the strategic choices made and the commitment to operationalizing them. However, as strategy seeks to engage desire as well as reason, the *nature* of the inclusion matters. Engagement that builds caring requires asking employees to bring more than just their data and opinions into a

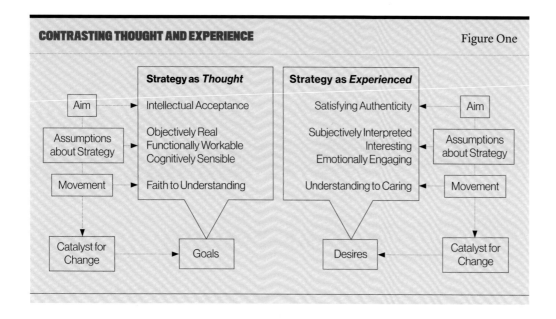

CONTRASTING THOUGHT AND EXPERIENCE   Figure One

Strategy as *Thought*	Strategy as *Experienced*

Aim → Intellectual Acceptance

Satisfying Authenticity ← Aim

Assumptions about Strategy → Objectively Real / Functionally Workable / Cognitively Sensible

Subjectively Interpreted / Interesting / Emotionally Engaging ← Assumptions about Strategy

Movement → Faith to Understanding

Understanding to Caring ← Movement

Catalyst for Change → Goals

Desires ← Catalyst for Change

---

conversation – the opportunity is to bring a set of possibilities that energize them into the search for the strategic intent, as well. **Peter Senge** and his colleagues have argued that the future lies latent within the organization already – in the minds of managers awaiting the opportunity to emerge. 'Presencing' is his term for creating a conversations in which this 'latent future' can emerge.

Creating desire necessitates inviting organizational members to be players, rather than audience. This 'backstage' region has full transparency and is without secrets, and is thus demystified. The 'front of house' region, conversely, is where the staged interaction between performers and audience occurs. To be 'one of them' is to be given access to the backstage – to be part of the production rather than the audience. Inclusion can come in many forms – including the written. But as the emotional component becomes key to translating something that is *understood* into something that is *cared about*, the written word is less powerful than the spoken. In addition, metaphorical language possesses the ability to be far more emotion-laden: analogies and stories are more compelling than analytical logic and reasoning. While conversations and stories cannot completely replace quantitative plans, they can make their content more compelling and vivid.

2. Acknowledge the Role of the Concrete

The vividness necessary to *strategy as experienced* also lies in the particular, and one of the primary roles of strategy making processes is to give form to ideas, to render the abstract concrete. While strategy gains its power from ideas, these abstract ideas must be translated into something meaningful at the local level – something concrete to move from thought to experience. Clearly, strategies do not spring fully formed into being. Similar to Pinocchio and the Velveteen Rabbit in the classic children's stories, strategies become more real over time and through interaction with them. In the interplay between the abstract and the particular, the conceptual and the material, a strategy comes to have personal meaning and value. By making the abstract concrete in a believable way, strategic intention becomes linked to the details of daily practice.

William James pointed out that the opposite of believing something to be real is not disbelieving it – it is *doubting* it. Strategic intents specify a hypothetical future, and as such, they can never be 'proven' to be true or false; what they must provide to be seen as real is not proof, but the absence of doubt. An interesting, meaningful, and valued intent may be doubted for many reasons – perceived under funding, missing critical competencies, or a lack of specificity, among them. To pass beyond thought to experienced, a strategy must offer substantive evidence that achievement of the intent is possible; it must translate abstract intentions into concrete images that guide action.

In the Garden's case, the abstract notion of a 'museum, not a park' becomes more concrete as actions seen as aimed at protecting the 'works of art' – the plants – are taken. Fences are built, and dogs and cars are prohibited – all tough and unpopular (with local neighbours) acts on the organization's part that both make the idea of museum more real and, at the same time, demonstrate that this time leadership really means to live their stated intentions.

3. Promote Experimentation

The process of *becoming* requires experimentation, a kind of prototyping: strategies move from the cognitive to the experienced through iteration, elucidation and ultimately, through hands-on engagement. **Henry Mintzberg**'s characterization of strategy as 'crafted' ought to be taken as literal, not metaphorical for strategy is embodied – the product of human hands as well as minds. Recent work in Cognitive Psychology has demonstrated the fallacy of the commonplace view that reason is disembodied, that the human brain functions independently of its host, the human body. Experience is physical as well as cognitive and emotional, and likewise, strategy must be made sensual, touchable, and viscerally accessible.

Strategy needs experiments – ways to iterate and manipulate concepts. Of course, this process is considerably more challenging

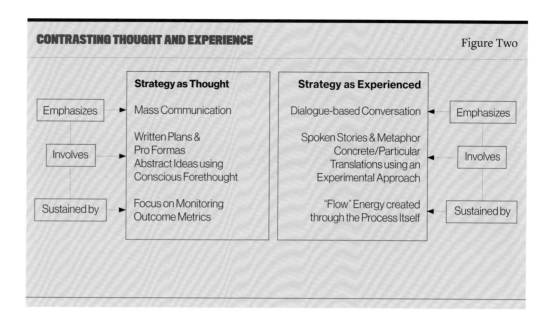

CONTRASTING THOUGHT AND EXPERIENCE

Figure Two

	Strategy as Thought	**Strategy as Experienced**	
Emphasizes	Mass Communication	Dialogue-based Conversation	Emphasizes
Involves	Written Plans & Pro Formas Abstract Ideas using Conscious Forethought	Spoken Stories & Metaphor Concrete/Particular Translations using an Experimental Approach	Involves
Sustained by	Focus on Monitoring Outcome Metrics	"Flow" Energy created through the Process Itself	Sustained by

for ideas and images than it is for physical products. Architects build models; product designers build physical prototypes; but how do strategies achieve similar vividness with images and ideas? This is one of the challenges to achieving *strategy as experienced*. **Donald Schön** argued that expert practitioners across many fields use thought experiments as their basic method of solving problems. The iterative processes of hypotheses generation and testing they use not only increase the likelihood of better solutions, they create opportunities for involvement that increases their tangibility as these hypotheses evolve into intentions.

'Serious play' has been offered as one approach for accomplishing this mental prototyping. **Michael Schrage** observes: "In order to have actionable meaning, the fuzzy mental models in top management minds must ultimately be externalized in representations the enterprise can grasp. Mental models become tangible and actionable only in the prototypes that management champions."

4. Move Beyond Outcome Metrics

One of the great truisms in management is that 'you can only manage what you can measure'. Measurement occupies a critical role in the strategy-as-thought perspective, as it does in virtually any discussion of good management practice around the implementation of new strategies. Of late, however, the weakness of relying solely on quantitative outcome measures is being recognized. Creativity, energy and engagement in the process can all be stifled by too single-minded an emphasis on outcome goals.

Scholars who study the concept of 'flow' – a subjective experience in which people report performing their best – argue for the possibility of a more sophisticated approach that would value the intrinsic rewards of the process itself and allow participants to better utilize tacit goals, standards and values to judge the quality of their work, consider the unique characteristics of a situation, adapt, and generate even goal-changing insights.

The idea of creating 'collective flow' is especially intriguing for strategy making processes. The potential is for the act of

engaging in compelling strategic conversations aimed at creating new futures to itself become a significant source of energy for sustaining the hard work of implementation. Such ongoing and iterative conversations, utilizing storytelling and the language of possibilities to engage and particularize, can do just that.

When the shift from goal-driven to desire-driven is successfully accomplished, attitudes shift along with it. 'Neglectful indifference' is replaced by 'passionate responsibility'. This is evident on the post-process reflection of a different Garden employee:

"All of the good things that have happened here might have come out of a process where senior managers got together and made all the decisions, but I don't think so. Even if they did, and even if the Gardens looked the same, it would feel a lot different. The ownership we feel – the investment that we all have in making the plan happen – that wouldn't be here. Neither would the patience that we developed in waiting for the things that my area has been promised in the plan."

In closing

The potential for both *better strategic outcomes* and *increased employee engagement* demands broadening our practices to acknowledge the powerful role of subjective interpretation and experience in strategy making processes. Such a shift will require courage and patience – two qualities that are in short supply in today's organizations. The rewards, however, may include finally locating the missing link between strategy's rhetoric and its execution, closing the gap between knowing and doing. **R**

Jeanne Liedtka is the United Technologies Corporation Professor of Business Administration at the University of Virginia's Darden School of Business and the former chief learning officer at United Technologies. She is the author of *Solving Problems with Design Thinking: Ten Stories of What Works* (Columbia University Press, 2013). This article originally appeared in *California Management Review*.

3

A Skill Set Emerges

 OVER THE PAST DECADE, my team and I have marveled as organizations of all types have gradually opened up their doors – and their minds – to design. The fact is, organizations are running up against issues that, increasingly, cannot be solved in conventional ways. The leaders we have worked with have displayed a strong desire for an alternative way to approach, tackle and resolve the challenges they face.

It's not just businesses: we've worked with plenty of non-profits and government institutions, and all of them are opening themselves up to design. These leaders know that, not only do we need a different *approach* to getting to solutions than we have used in the past, but we need solutions that are *more creative*, *more disruptive*, and that take us further than ever before. As we have watched our clients and their customers, a skill set has emerged, which falls into a series of four 'buckets'.

The first bucket includes skills associated with 'where ideas come from'. These are skills related to going out in the world and really *looking* and *studying* and *uncovering*. Ideas and insights don't fall off of trees for free: you've got to literally turn rocks over to find them. The skills required here include observation, careful listening, and questioning the obvious – challenging one's assumptions about even the most obvious, everyday things.

A second bucket involves skills around collaboration – the ability to work with people from different backgrounds, different fields, with different ways of thinking. The skills involved here foster a style and approach that leads to really active collaboration. It's about bringing out the insights that people have, engaging with the backgrounds and disciplines of other people.

A third bucket is to do with 'how ideas get developed'. These are the skills of making, of rapid prototyping, of going from an intellectual abstraction to something tangible. Whether you use skills of improv to act out a customer interaction or you build a cardboard widget that you can test with a consumer – the skills involved in rapid prototyping are very important. One of the most revelatory experiences for many of the business people we've worked with is just how quickly they can take an idea and make it *real* – if they give themselves permission to do that.

The fourth bucket involves the skills of getting something out into the world. These skills include engineering and manufacturing and all of the mechanics involved in launching an idea. But there's another piece to it, which is just as important: the 'politics' of implementation. And for this, you need great storytelling skills. This is something that the world's best innovators and entrepreneurs have in common: an ability to frame their idea in a way that makes sense to whoever they're trying to persuade.

Let's face it: the evidence before us is that our world is not going to get any less complicated or volatile. As a result, organizations have to be more adaptable and more resilient than ever before. As today's leading companies have shown, the key components of adaptation and resiliency are innovation, creativity and design.

Nature's solution to change has always been to create and evolve, and in my view, the smartest organizations will embrace this stance going forward.

Tim Brown is CEO and president of IDEO, the renowned design firm based in Palo Alto, California. He is the author of *Change By Design: How Design Thinking Transforms Organizations and Inspires Innovation* (HarperBusiness, 2009). He participates in the World Economic Forum in Davos, and his talks "Serious Play" and "Change by Design" appear on TED.com.

Developing

Design

Sensibilities

by **Jane Fulton Suri** and **Michael Hendrix**

Effective design thinking entails more than applying design methods. To produce the best outcomes, organizations need to develop – and trust – peoples' design sensibilities.

● **DESIGN THINKING IS RECEIVING** a great deal of attention as increasing numbers of innovative organizations succeed in solving complex problems by creative means. In doing so, many of these firms implement specific 'design methods' such as observational research, iterative prototyping and story-telling alongside more mainstream approaches. But as any professional designer will attest, design thinking entails much more than applying *methods:* to create value, methods must be applied together with design *sensibilities*.

Design sensibilities consist of the ability to tap into intuitive qualities such as delight, beauty, personal meaning and cultural resonance. Such subtle qualities are difficult to put into words, and thus are generally discounted in the workplace. Managers

schooled in analytic and rational decision making may find the idea of relying on their sensibilities uncomfortable. But when coupled with design methods, design sensibilities create the experiences and outcomes upon which successful businesses capitalize: clear distinction from competitors, lasting market impact and customer loyalty.

Cultivating Sensibilities
Innovation involves making multiple judgment calls about *what to express* and *how*, from a project's big strategic idea to the fine details of implementation. Sensibilities not only guide these decisions, they also ultimately influence how people experience the resulting product, service or brand. Will customers simply end up

getting something that 'works', or will they make an emotional connection with it – one that entails personal and cultural relevance and inspires future loyalty?

Take the case of Altoids mints, a favourite example of our colleague **Claudia Kotchka**, an accountant-turned-design thinker who spent more than three decades at **Procter & Gamble** and now works as a consultant. In the mid-1990s, Altoids turned a 200-year-old British stomach remedy into a leading global breath mint by reinventing its packaging (the now-iconic tin). Kotchka often uses this example to demonstrate the importance of design sensibilities to skeptical business teams.

She begins by holding up a tin of Altoids to highlight the product's many subtle design qualities – soft corners, rolled edges, nostalgic typeface, debossed graphics, crinkly paper liner, even the irregularly shaped and dusty sweets inside – that combine to create the product's appeal and sense of authenticity. Then, as chronicled in a *Fast Company* article, she enacts a more typical approach, which might have happened if, say, the pre-Kotchka P&G were to take over the brand:

"We're gonna get rid of this stupid paper – it's serving no functional purpose." She plops the tin on the table and picks up another product, unable to suppress a mischievous smile. "And this is what you get.'" Kotchka then reveals 'Proctoids', a box made of cheap white plastic from P&G's baby-wipe containers. With uniform beige ovals jammed into the container, fewer colours on the lid, and no paper, Proctoids taste like Altoids, but they look as appealing as a pile of horse pills. Gone is the pleasure people get when they buy Altoids. Gone, too, is the up to 400 per cent premium they pay. "That's what design is," she says. "That's what designers do."

Just as designers call upon their sensibilities to imagine and create an experience like Altoids, consumers tap into their sensibilities to enjoy it. Clearly, going beyond purely functional solutions to achieve emotionally-resonant ones takes more than analysis and measurement, but it also takes more than applying design methods. It takes design sensibilities – judgments informed by sharp intuition – to bring myriad subjective, complex and subtle qualities together into a meaningful whole.

Professional designers have invested considerable time and effort in practicing this kind of integration and refining their sensibilities in particular ways. In doing so, they become skilled at synthesizing different factors – what's viable, feasible, desirable, sustainable, etc. – and considering multiple permutations of potential design elements to reach an elegant, holistic solution.

How Designers See

Although every designer brings a unique perspective to the table, they generally engage with the world in similar ways. Keenly aware of their surroundings, their observations inform and inspire their work, often in delicate ways.

Professional designers hold a special responsibility because they are charged with both *sensing* opportunities for change and then *expressing* that change by manipulating elements to effect that change. The first of these responsibilities – *sensing* – is a way of looking at the people, places and things around us. For instance, have you ever tried to view the world from someone else's perspective? Perhaps you've taken a city tour with an architect, admired woodwork with the guidance of a skilled carpenter, or watched a movie with a video artist? In all likelihood, their observations were quite different from yours. Designers' perceptions reflect an awareness that our surroundings are created, and of the artistry that goes into their creation. Designers see physical, cultural and metaphoric relationships, such as the nooks and crannies where people naturally gather and the exposed spaces that people avoid, as well as the atmospheres (*welcoming* vs. *cold*) that those tendencies create. Designers notice the relative placement of graphical elements and materials in the form of an object and the sensations, memories (melancholic or joyful) and behaviours to which these give rise. In short, they are acutely aware of minute details and how small elements add up to a holistic experience.

Designers also bring a critical eye, detecting and sometimes becoming offended at designs that don't work – where details have been overlooked or dismissed as unimportant and thus undermine more positive possibilities. Perhaps it's a product package whose form and material contradict the verbal message it is trying to convey about freshness or simplicity; perhaps it's a hotel that intends to welcome guests at their journey's end with a calming experience, but instead sends them through a maze of unfamiliar distractions to find their rooms. Designers are able to reframe these misfires as opportunities to rethink the approach and carry through on a promise in a more effective, genuine way.

The second design responsibility – *expressing* – is a means of creating change by exploiting these perceptions. By valuing and sharing their observations simply because they seem beautiful, intriguing, offensive or amusing, designers enrich their intuitions. Their own subjective awareness of how particular attributes evoke a sense of beauty, intrigue, ire, or amusement informs the choices that they make regarding how best to express those qualities in any given design. In using *their* sensibilities, designers connect to *our* sensibilities and enrich our experience, even when we're not consciously aware of it.

Most professionals easily recognize the practical benefits of a product or service, but they often overlook the less-apparent qualities of an experience from which they derive pleasure, identity, and meaning. For example, while industrial designer **Jason Robinson**, a colleague of ours, was conceiving a new generation of surgical instruments, he met with various surgeons who would ultimately use these intricate power tools. "All the talk was focused on functional aspects of the procedure – that and the ergonomics of holding the tools," he recalls. "[They said] nothing about the way their tools represented them as professionals or said something about their technical skill and achievements."

Robinson describes later walking through the hospital's parking garage, where one surgeon's new top-of-the-line **Audi** caught his eye. Chatting with the doctor about this new purchase, it was clear to Robinson that the choice of car reflected an appreciation for quality and comfort, and pleasure in fine materials and precision engineering. Robinson considered other surgeons'

BALANCING DESIGN METHODS AND DESIGN SENSIBILITIES

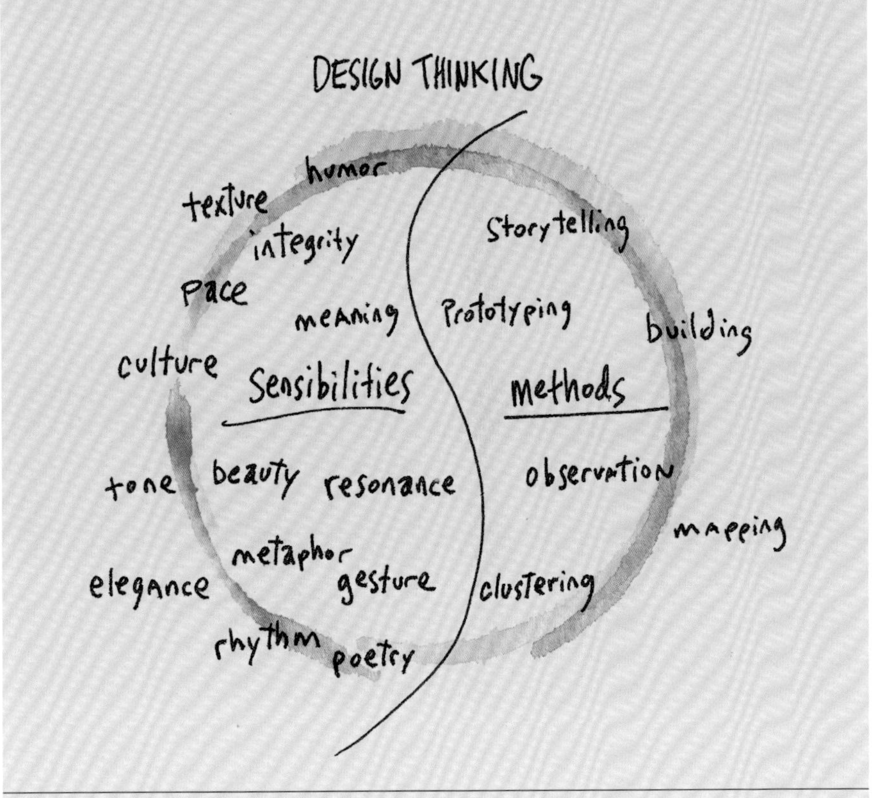

everyday experience of opening and closing the doors of their Audis and **Mercedes**. "It seemed obvious to me that they cared not just about the look and feel of the car, but how it made them feel about themselves," he says. "I thought about that a lot in selecting the materials and finishes for their work tools, certain that they would appreciate the same kind of qualities in their tools."

Designers use observation and prototyping methods of different kinds to help them figure out the best ways to express certain sensibilities. With sketches and models, they try things out to explore their effects, experimenting with physical elements (finishes, forms, fonts, materials) and control sensory inputs (contrast, rhythm, sound, space, pattern, pace) to determine what works and what doesn't. And, ultimately, they discover how to deliberately evoke particular feelings to support the desired experience.

Finding the right solution means experimenting with the right factors. This requires designers to choose, at a very detailed level, which of the many possible elements and qualities to explore – and how. At the same time, they must keep an eye on the bigger picture, from the context and meaning of an activity in people's lives and culture to the promise of a product, service or brand. Last but not least, they must synthesize all of the above into a highly resolved, integrated whole.

Sensibilities Make Good Business Sense

Design sensibilities can be realized in straightforward products, such as breath mints and surgical tools, or extended to much more complex challenges, such as the extension of a new service or brand that unfolds over time. Like skilled designers, successful organizations package their offerings as integrated wholes, fitting all the little details into a greater context that supports a meaningful experience and satisfies customers' senses.

Starbucks is a pioneer at this. You're probably familiar with the coffee giant's story and the effect it's had on **McDonald's**, **Dunkin Donuts** and multitudes of microroasters. Many competitors have tried to replicate Starbucks' success by adopting isolated elements of its customer experience: they sell better coffee made from better beans, or they change the colour palette of their retail environment; but they can't duplicate the magic of the integrated whole.

Starbucks' success is largely due to its ability to design for our functional and emotional needs, generating goods and services that we not only consume but have made part of our daily routines and personal identities. It has choreographed an elegantly resolved system of experience touch points, from manageable activities (like the design, sourcing and manufacturing of their products; distribution; pricing; and advertising) to less wieldy ones (like fan sites, community use, and a sense of place). It designed elements that defined multiple means by which the Starbucks experience could intersect with our lives.

Ironically, after its initial success, Starbucks temporarily fell into the same trap as its copycats: the company's aggressive pursuit of growth led to formulaic duplication that eventually prompted a cultural backlash and caused stock prices to plummet. In January 2008, founder **Howard Schultz** was reinstated as CEO and Starbucks appears to be back on track, thanks to tactics like cost-cutting and a return to its original design sensibilities. In a recent *New York Times* article about the rebound, Schultz uttered phrases like "the authenticity of the coffee experience" and "the theater of bringing that to life" in describing the Starbucks experience. He told *The Guardian* that his past mistakes included "a loss of the romance of coffee-making."

Reviving its design sensibilities for romance and theater, Starbucks opened **15th Ave. Coffee & Tea** in Seattle last summer. The boutique store aims to take the company back to its roots as a community-owned venue and to help it "re-learn" about itself. The space's design draws from its Pike Place roots –

Starbucks calls it "eclectic and raw" – and features repurposed materials from nearby abandoned buildings, shipyards and Starbucks outlets. The menu was changed to emphasize slow food and to include beer and wine. Now, when customers buy a cup of joe, they get a small-batch brew that tastes great, a story about history and economic fairness, a sense of place and community, access to peer-selected news and music, and a reminder of hometown success. The verdict is still out on whether these latest moves will quell the backlash from their missteps, but it's clearly a good start.

Wayfinding through sensibility is difficult in a management culture that measures progress by execution and results – typically numbers – as Starbucks has found. This is why it is so tempting to misapply design thinking and cling to design methods that focus on performance benchmarks. Yes, observational research and iterative prototyping produce quantifiable and tangible results and they are easily teachable. But without design sensibilities, design thinking runs the risk of addressing only functional concerns and falling short in issues of desirability. To address these subjective concerns, organizations must shift their focus

DESIGN SENSIBILITIES IN ACTION

Virgin America has differentiated itself from its competitors by providing customers with a rich set of experiences based on design sensibilities, such as luxury and style, which have been applied to its service scripts, amenities, industrial and environmental design and more. Its holistic approach is evident from the moment a passenger checks in.

Virgin's self-serve kiosks feature the same design aesthetic as the interiors of its planes. Each computer's glossy white chassis and glowing red interface foreshadows the seating and personal entertainment systems offered in the main cabin. When passengers check in, the kiosk prints credit card-size boarding pass for each one, VIP-style, which elevates the boarding process from an informational transaction to an event. While other airlines settle for a tissue-thin paper receipts, Virgin issues a permit that suggests travelers will be treated well on their journey.

At the gate, a pilot greets passengers in the waiting area while the gate agent announces that correct answers to his upcoming trivia questions will be rewarded with pre-boarding privileges. When it's time to go, a Virgin employee calls for late passengers in language that reveals sensibility: "We don't want to leave you," he says, not "The door is closing and you will be left behind."

Boarding is another signature moment. The end of the jet bridge reveals a violet and pink glow emitting from the cabin entrance. It's the first stage of the mood lighting that shifts throughout a six hour flight. Onboard, interactive touch screens at each seat enable passengers to order food, drinks and entertainment anytime, helping travelers feel as if they're flying first-class even when they're in economy. The leather seats are housed in a glossy white shell – remember the kiosk – that underscores style and VIP treatment. The tray tables are made

of the same material and emerge from their locked positions with a satisfying click. In the midst of these moments, it's hard not to be transferred to glamorous Hollywood depictions of space travel.

What Virgin is doing is not new: all airlines are trying to compete with better experiences. In such a commoditized industry, what else is there? However, how Virgin is doing this is new. Design methods tell you what to do, but design sensibilities tell you how. The traveling public is responding with approval – check out their four out of five star rating on Yelp.com. And though many factors contribute to financial results, indications are that this is translating into good business: the start-up airline posted a Q4 2009 operating profit and 40 per cent year-over-year revenue increase.

–Jane Fulton Suri and Michael Hendrix

from *what* to *how* and pursue meaningful connections with consumers. This will inspire functional and emotional design solutions that reach their full potential and inspire loyalty.

Developing Design Sensibilities

Obviously, expressing design sensibilities comes more easily to designers than to other professionals. As Claudia Kotchka told us in a recent conversation, "Designers speak a language that includes visual, tactile, multi-sensorial elements, and [they] are able to use these elements to say something that will evoke a specific kind of response. That's what designers go to school for."

We aren't proposing that you send your people to design school so they can learn to express their sensibilities. We are suggesting that you develop the design sensibilities of your employees as a business asset with two important benefits: more refined intuitions about the needs and desires of your customers and greater confidence in making intuitive judgments to resolve complex problems with well-rounded solutions.

We all have colleagues who embody certain sensibilities, from being a *stylish* dresser to a *gracious* host. We appreciate and are impressed by the fine distinctions they are able to make when buying a new suit or planning an important dinner party – and how their nuanced insights enhance our enjoyment. But in traditional business culture, intuitive abilities such as these are typically thought of as side or recreational interests, and their value in the context of people's work lives is often overlooked. We recently watched an executive do just that. During a client meeting, a vice president asked us how she might create a viral video campaign. Someone on her team volunteered that he had film experience and would love to contribute in some way. She dismissed his comment, and the conversation continued, even though he may have had valuable skills to apply. Why didn't his offer lead anywhere? The VP's perception of his abilities and contribution were constrained to *functional execution* rather than *enriching contribution*.

In her various corporate brand-development roles, **Ivy Ross**, executive vice president of marketing for **The Gap**, has excelled at cultivating the design sensibilities of her colleagues. Ross says one of the most important sensibilities "comes from seeing things deeply in the moment, really paying attention, and taking it in at a visceral level." At one point, Ross invited a guest to take her cross-functional team through a Japanese tea ceremony, with full explanations of each part of the ritual. She wanted to make them slow down and focus on the details, the relationships between elements, and the specific meaning of each. Her real intent, of course, was to help them become more attuned to noticing the details of everyday activities, objects, rituals and meanings.

In a similar vein, The Brand Academy at **BMW Welt** in Munich has a program to teach stakeholders about the car maker's brands and how they take root in culture. Its intent is to foster design sensibilities as they apply to particular markets. The Academy, led by **Hildegaard Wortmann**, vice president of product management for the X and Z Series, created an exhibition that includes rooms dedicated to communicating the brand values of BMW, Mini Cooper and Rolls Royce. Teams are guided through multiple workshops to attune their sensibilities, experientially and viscerally, to the core values of each brand. When asked how she pulled this off in a company known for an ultra-rational approach, Wortmann chuckled and said, "It took a lot of convincing." But convinced they were: the Brand Academy has been embedded as a core element of BMW's corporate curriculum for the last three years.

For those of us caught up in frantic pace of modern business, taking the time to encourage staff to develop and exercise their hidden talents may seem frivolous and over-indulgent. But when fostered and encouraged, employees' latent capabilities allow for more effective design thinking. Exploring and honing sensibilities is a powerful means to developing greater awareness of how your product, service or brand is experienced and to recognize opportunities for how it might grow.

In closing

Design sensibilities are essentially human sensibilities, although they are largely underdeveloped and undervalued in many traditional business settings. Like design methods, design sensibilities are learnable – although it takes encouragement, respect and discipline to fully develop them.

As demonstrated by innovations from Altoids to Virgin America, the key to design thinking is to balance methods with sensibilities. Investing in peoples' ability to make good judgment calls about the details that affect customer perceptions and experience makes good business sense. Design sensibilities enable managers to determine not only *what* to do, but *how* to do it. Combining design methods with strong design sensibilities is a sure way to avoid ending up with a box of mints that taste good, but that no one wants. *R*

Jane Fulton Suri is a Partner and Creative Director at IDEO, based in Palo Alto, California. She is the author of *Thoughtless Acts: Observations on Intuitive Design* (Chronicle Books, 2005). **Michael Hendrix** is an Associate Partner and Boston Location Director at IDEO.

1780

1810

Today more than ever, business growth requires an ability to see new possibilities, and seeing new possibilities requires new ways of looking at the world. Here's how to get started.

by **Sarah Rottenberg** and **Isabel O'Meara**

THE ART OF LOOKING

CHARLES AND RAY EAMES – two of the 20th century's most influential designers – are best known for their timeless furniture, which looks no less modern today than it did when they designed it more than 50 years ago. What is less known about the Eameses (pictured, left) is that they were also passionate educators who sought tirelessly to help people learn how to see their world anew.

Working with leading corporations, they created more than 60 films and slide shows for clients like **IBM**, **Boeing**, **Polaroid** and **Westinghouse**, visually communicating complex ideas in new ways. Charles once said that these projects were intended to give the viewer a 'new depth of vision', and as such, they proved invaluable, inspiring leaders to think beyond the status quo and envision new opportunities.

Today more than ever, business growth requires new ways of looking at the world. Unfortunately, all too often, we continue to look at the world in the same way we always have, only to be surprised and disappointed when we don't discover anything new. In this article we will attempt to enhance your ability to see possibilities that do not yet exist.

Seven Ways of Looking
The Eameses knew well that encouraging people to look at things anew – even from just *one* different perspective – can build up a capacity to see the world from multiple perspectives. For example, their most famous film, the 1977 masterpiece *Powers of Ten*, explores the relative size of things. In nine short minutes, we journey from an aerial shot of the hand of a man picnicking in

Chicago, to the Earth as seen from space 10^{+24} meters away, and then back down to view the hand at 10^{-16} meters magnification. The point is clearly made that what we see in our world completely changes, just by zooming in or out.

At Jump Associates, we have seen leaders in numerous organizations build this skill with deliberate practice. In our years of working with companies to create new businesses and reinvent existing ones, we have identified seven 'ways of looking' that have proven particularly helpful in helping people overcome their innate biases and build up the mental muscles required to drive sustainable growth.

1. Look at your own life.

Many companies have been founded based on a real-life stroke of inspiration. In the early 1990s, **Gary Erikson**, a long-distance cyclist and rock climber, had his epiphany during a 175-mile bike ride with a friend. Hungry from exertion, he started to eat an energy bar, but stopped short: it had no taste, poor texture and was generally unappetizing. He didn't want to eat another bite. Erikson knew he could do better. Back home, he developed and refined a new, tastier bar in his mom's kitchen, testing it on himself and his friends. Many years and many bars, later, **Clif Bar** continues to thrive.

Other founders have similar stories: **Scott Cook** developed the idea for personal finance software company **Quicken** while sitting at his kitchen table watching his wife struggle to balance their accounts; **Rebecca Matthias**, the founder of **Destination Motherhood** (formerly Mothers Work, Inc.), a chain of maternity stores, started the company when she was pregnant and couldn't find clothes to wear to work; and **Oxo** founder **Sam Farber** founded his ergonomic kitchen tools company after watching his arthritic wife struggle to peel a potato.

You don't have to be an entrepreneur to find business inspiration from aspects of your own life. **Microsoft** has done so repeatedly. Product manager **Trish May**'s frustration with the old ways of creating presentations led to the birth of PowerPoint; and when Microsoft wanted to build a platform for hardcore gamers, they hired actual hardcore gamers to design **Xbox**. Too often, as businesses grow and mature, we forget that our own lives can continue to inspire new opportunities. If you are your own customer, look at your own life. Get your colleagues to do the same. Institutionalize it, and see what happens.

2. Look through someone else's eyes.

While it is true that employees often represent a segment of their own customer base, most businesses grow and succeed by reaching people that are different from their founders and associates. As a result, we also need to take the time to understand people who are different from us, and see the world through their eyes. The Plastics division of **GE** had traditionally grown by expanding existing products into new segments and geographies. By 2005, they were running out of obvious places to go next. As they evaluated growth opportunities, the plastic fibers market rose to the top. This high-margin business focused on cutting-edge products like fire-retardant and bullet-proof materials. It was an attractive market, but it did have one entrenched player who would be difficult to compete with.

To define a successful market entry strategy with compelling competitive advantage, GE decided to try a new approach. For several months, a team visited with their potential customers (as well as their customers' customers) in the high-performance fibers market. Instead of talking about GE and asking the questions that were most pressing for them, the team listened, asked open-ended questions, and observed what went on in textile makers' offices and plants. They then spent time analyzing the stories to make sense of the culture of high performance textile manufacturers.

What they found was surprising. They expected to find operations-oriented managers focused on increasing margins, driving profitability and growing the bottom line. Instead, they found artisanal cultures, people as interested in figuring out what cool new things they could make from plastic fibers as they were in how to monetize it. One engineer told a story of pulling over on the highway during his commute home to gather milkweed and processing it into fibers at home in his garage, just to see what would happen.

GE had expected to invest heavily in infrastructure to get into this new market, developing its own cutting-edge materials to gain traction. Instead, it realized that the path to success wasn't in supplying textile manufactures with finished products, but in tapping into artisanal sensibilities and partnering with people to create new offerings.

Sharing prototypes, partnering closely with engineers instead of executives, and working with smaller companies as equal partners meant that GE executives and salespeople had to adopt a new way of working. But the results spoke for themselves. At the outset of the project, GE could not even get meetings with industry players. Their new approach won them a seat at the table, opened up the market and required less upfront investment. Ultimately, looking through their customers' eyes enabled the GE team to meet their five-year revenue goals in just 18 months.

Seeing the world from a new perspective sometimes requires getting out of the office and into the real world, meeting face-to-face with customers, consumers, and influencers. Talking to people isn't enough, though. To look through someone else eyes you need to listen and learn. This can help to build a widespread sense of what other people value and empower people throughout the organization to make better decisions.

3. Zoom out.
While looking closely at people's lives is a great source of inspiration, it's not the only way to shift perspective. We can also learn by looking at our businesses through the Eameses' eyes by zooming out. Take just one step backwards to see a wider frame of reference – the rest of the ecosystem connected to your business.

eBay's success is linked to its ability to zoom out in 1999. It saw the rise in online payments early on, and realized that offering its own online payment system would benefit both the bottom line and its customers. At that time, most eBay auctions were completed with paper checks and money orders. With online payments, eBay would speed auction closure for all merchants while removing a barrier for participation for the buyers. In May, 1999, eBay purchased **Billpoint**, a nascent online payment system.

Unfortunately, eBay's first foray into electronic payments was a failure: by the time Billpoint officially launched in the spring of 2000, **PayPal** was already firmly entrenched as the payment system of choice, beating out Billpoint 20 to 1. Billpoint never caught on, even with heavy promotion from eBay. But eBay didn't give up. They had the perspective to realize that owning a major player in online payments was the right thing to do. So in July 2002, eBay announced it would acquire PayPal. Eight years later, that vision and persistence is paying off. PayPal is growing, even in a bad economy: revenues are expected to double between 2009 and 2011, leading eBay's overall growth.

By zooming out, companies can look beyond their existing offerings to observe the entire value network in which they reside – and which new businesses will be critical to their future success. By focusing on the key enablers of an ecosystem, it's possible to spot promising acquisition targets, converging markets and white-space opportunities that are invisible under routine observation.

4. Zoom in.
Surprisingly, looking at a sideline piece of your business as a larger opportunity can be just as important as looking at the big picture. Sometimes, zooming in can be as beneficial as zooming out.

Stacy's Pita Chip Company was founded in 1997 by **Stacy Madison** and **Mark Andrus**. They first created Stacy's D'Lites, a food cart in Boston that sold sandwiches made on pita bread. The cart quickly became very popular, with such long lines that many potential customers walked away. To keep customers happy while in line, they baked their leftover bread into pita chips. Customers loved the chips and began asking the team to sell them in stores. Before they knew it, Madison and Andrus were in the chip business.

Running two businesses – the chip company and the food cart – soon became too much, and they had to make a choice. They realized that chips were more scalable, and decided to focus on that. By 2004, Stacy's had achieved nearly $30 million in national and international sales. In November of 2005, the company was purchased by **Frito-Lay**, a division of **PepsiCo**, and expanded to a wide variety of products that are now widely available. By zooming in on what their consumers genuinely valued, Madison and Andrus turned their little cart into a national brand.

> Ultimately, the number of ways that leaders can look at their businesses are infinite, limited only by the imagination.

Zooming in also led to the creation of **Viagra**, **Pfizer**'s blockbuster impotence drug. The drug was initially tested as a treatment for angina. Trials of the drug's effectiveness were disappointing, so the company was planning to shelve the product. However, volunteers began to report interesting side effects from the drug. Instead of a run-of-the-mill treatment for heart disease, Pfizer had stumbled onto a unique solution to impotence. By looking closely at the data its scientists had collected, Pfizer was able to zoom in on a new application for the compound.

The lesson: don't be distracted by the business that you *think* you are in. Instead, let yourself zoom in on the elements of your offering that are most valuable to customers.

5. Look at what you can borrow.

Taking a new perspective is especially challenging when an entire industry operates under long-held assumptions. We can get so stuck in the way things are done that we forget that other choices even exist. Borrowing great ideas from others can help you re-imagine your own business.

This was the case for the banking industry in the 1970s. At the time, banks were run more like government offices than like private companies. The hours were set for the convenience of the bankers, not their customers. Then, along came **Vernon Hill**. While in college during the late '60s, Hill worked at a bank and made loans to **WaWa**, **7-Eleven**, and **McDonald's** franchises. Meanwhile, he also started his first company, **Site Development**, which helped businesses find sites and work through community planning issues like traffic and zoning. His first client? McDonald's. Based on these experiences, Hill started a different kind of bank in 1973: **Commerce Bank** focused on service and convenience, just like the fast-food and convenience stores he'd been doing business with. The locations weren't branches, they were more like stores: they were open from 7:30 am until 8:00 pm; they opened 10 minutes early and stayed open 10 minutes late; and employees focused on customer service with a smile. Later, they introduced seven-day banking hours and real human beings answered the phone by the second ring, 24 hours a day.

The results were amazing: in the late 1990s and early 2000s, the bank opened an average of 30 'stores' a year. By 2005, its net income was $302 million, with assets of over $43 billion. In October of 2007, **TD Bank Financial Group** acquired Commerce in a deal valued at $8.5 billion.

6. Look within your organization.

While it is sometimes helpful to look outside of your organization, it can be equally illuminating to look more closely inside. While open innovation and technology transfer are useful tools for finding new ideas, companies sometimes forget to take lessons from other divisions or departments within their own organizations.

When developers at **Dentyne Gum** were launching a new product, they focused on creating an increased cooling technology that would deliver a more intense sensory experience than their previous products. As part of the product launch, the team wanted a new package that met two needs: contain moisture and differentiate the product on the shelves. At the time, Dentyne was owned by Pfizer, better known for medications than for making gum and candy. Dentyne took advantage of the opportunities provided by its sister company, and ultimately borrowed blister packaging from Pfizer's over-the-counter medication division. Dentyne Ice was born and quickly became a top-seller. By shipping in a blister pack, the product sent the message that it was more powerful than its competitors: it wasn't just gum, it was a cure for bad breath.

Of course, looking within your own walls isn't limited to looking for technologies. Sometimes an idea about how to go to market can be translated across brands. That's what sparked the creation of the **Progresso Light** brand. Progresso is owned by **General Mills**, a diverse food manufacturer that has robust capabilities in knowledge transfer. Noticing the long-term success of its **Yoplait** brand's light line, leaders at General Mills decided to apply the same strategy to Progresso – to great success. Progresso Light soups delivered over $100 million in retail sales in its first year.

Don't forget to look within to discover which under-leveraged ideas could be used in other parts of your company. We've seen our clients reap the benefits of looking within in two primary ways: creating internal networks that connect employees across silos, and providing incentives and recognition to those who do manage to transfer ideas and technologies within the organization.

7. Look for barriers.

Often, just finding a new way of doing things isn't enough to grow your business. Offerings must be compelling enough for customers to overcome traditional barriers to purchase – the cost of acquisition, the time to develop new behaviours, and the desire to hold onto what we already know. This is especially true for radically new businesses whose solutions don't always easily integrate into people's lives. Consumers almost always underestimate how good new technologies are, and companies almost always overestimate the benefits of their new products.

Solar energy holds the promise of a sustainable future, capable of eliminating most greenhouse gas emissions and reducing dependence on petroleum; it would even mean most consumers could stop paying a monthly electrical bill. But very few consumers have taken the step of installing solar arrays at home. The combination of solar panels' high cost, challenging installation and low curb appeal have so far prevented this technology from becoming mainstream. Worse, many homeowners' associations explicitly ban their members from installing rooftop solar arrays.

Acutely aware of the need for alternative energy generation, industrial designer **Peter Bressler** had an idea for overcoming these barriers. One day, he looked out from the window of a plane over miles of rooftops and wondered why they weren't generating electricity. He came up with an idea that could make solar energy an easier choice: integrating solar technology into existing roofing shingles. This would create a seamless design that overcomes the 'ugly factor' and mitigates some of the additional cost of installing solar panels.

Working on that idea in conjunction with **SRS Energy**, Bressler's firm **Bresslergroup** developed Sole Solar Tiles. The flexible polymeric material enables the panels to curve, bending into the structure of regular roof tiles. They can be used in place of regular tiles and can be installed by any roofing contractor.

It's a cost-effective, lightweight solution that makes collecting solar energy a simpler choice for consumers who are replacing their existing roof or building a new home.

Solar panels are an extreme example of a challenge that virtually all new products and services face: clearing the barriers to initial adoption. Unfortunately, most companies fail to recognize these barriers, and this mismatch in expectations has sunk many hyped technologies: the Apple Newton, WebVan and the Segway, to name but a few. If companies spent more time really exploring and resolving barriers to technology adoption, the chances for a successful launch would dramatically increase.

In closing

Ultimately, the number of ways that leaders can look at their business are infinite, limited only by the imagination. When we get stuck looking at our business primarily from one perspective – whether it be meeting this quarter's numbers or next year's projections – even embracing one new way of looking can be a challenge. But to lead effectively, it is imperative for CEOs to inspire their organizations to look at the world in new ways. The lasting benefits are a full innovation pipeline, unmatched market insight, and long-term sustainable growth. ***R***

Sarah Rottenberg is Associate Director of the Integrated Product Development Program at the University of Pennsylvania and a former directing associate at Jump Associates, a leading design firm based in San Mateo, California. **Isabel O'Meara** is the founder of Jetpack Consulting and a former Strategy Lead at Jump who teaches design research at the Hasso Plattner Institute of Design at Stanford.

Even if something looks effortlessly simple, it likely took
a great deal of effort to reach such a state.

by **Matthew May**

ZEN AND THE ART OF SIMPLICITY

WHEN OLIVER WENDELL HOLMES JR. SAID, "I wouldn't give a fig for simplicity on this side of complexity, but I would give my life for simplicity on the other side of complexity," he might well have been referring to the Zen aesthetic ideal of *shibumi*. This Japanese word is reserved for objects and experiences that exhibit all at once the very best of everything and nothing: elegant simplicity; effortless effectiveness; beautiful imperfection.

I first came upon this concept over 30 years ago through the best-selling spy novel *Shibumi*, by the late author **Trevanian** (the *nom de plume* of Dr. **Rodney William Whitaker**).

Trevanian's view paralleled Holmes's thoughts on 'simplicity beyond complexity': "*Shibumi* has to do with great refinement underlying commonplace appearances." Little did I know at the time that this idea would literally change my life and career in a meaningful way some 25 years later.

Midway through the course of what would eventually become an eight-year advisory retainer with the automotive giant **Toyota**, I found myself struggling to complete a unique-but-challenging assignment: to help identify and then design a way to teach the hidden creative process behind Toyota's uncanny ability to

When it comes to the structure and design of an idea – be it a product, service, strategy or experience – what isn't there can often be as powerful as what is.

successfully implement over one million inventive ideas each year. What made the assignment so difficult was the need to unite two distinctly different cultures – Eastern and Western – in a common approach, which entailed straddling two different ways of looking at the world.

In the midst of my struggle, someone anonymously gave me a little book of Chinese verse, entitled *Tao Te Ching*, circa 600 B.C., by Taoist philosopher **Lao Tzu**. In it, I found this snippet:

> Thirty spokes share the wheel's hub,
> It is the centre hole that makes it useful.
> Shape clay into a vessel,
> It is the space within that makes it useful.
> Cut doors and windows for a room,
> It is the holes which make it useful.
> Therefore profit comes from what is there,
> Usefulness from what is not there.

This ancient Eastern idea struck me as a completely different way of looking at the world. While it obviously wasn't new, to me it was radical: I suddenly realized that I had been looking at my problem in entirely the wrong way. As is natural and intuitive – at least for the Western mind – I had been focusing on *what was there*, and *what to do*, rather than on *what wasn't there*, and *what to stop doing*. By shifting my perspective, not only was I able to complete my project successfully, but I was also compelled to delve further into the singular thought that when it comes to the structure and design of an idea – be it a product, service, strategy or experience – what *isn't* there can often be as powerful as what *is*.

Tracing the Zen Aesthetic

What sets *shibumi* apart as a powerful design ideal is the unique combination of *surprising impact* and *uncommon simplicity*. It entails achieving maximum effect through minimum means, which, it turns out, is a universal pursuit that takes many forms: artists and designers use white or 'negative' space to convey visual power; scientists, mathematicians and engineers search for theories that explain highly complex phenomena in stunningly simple ways; musicians and composers use pauses in the music – silence – to create dramatic tension; athletes and dancers search for optimal impact with minimal effort; and physicians draw on the *Occam's Razor Principle* in an effort to find a single diagnosis to explain the entirety of a patient's symptoms, shaving the analysis down to the simplest explanation. Likewise, filmmakers, novelists and songwriters strive to tell stories with universal resonance that seem simple but that foster many different, uniquely personal interpretations. What these various forms all have in common, and what *shibumi* has at its core, is the element of *subtraction*.

Not only is the thought of subtracting something in order to create value a very different way of thinking (neuroscientists have shown using functional MRI scans that addition and subtraction demand different brain circuitry), it figures centrally in Zen. In order to appreciate the Zen sensibilities, it helps to have a rough sketch of their evolution from and incorporation into art, architecture and now commercial and corporate design.

As the Zen philosophy took hold in Japan during the 12th and 13th centuries, Japanese art and philosophy began to reflect one of the fundamental Zen themes, that of *emptiness*. In the Zen view, emptiness is a symbol of inexhaustible spirit. Silent pauses in music and theatre, blank spaces in paintings, and even the restrained motion of the sublimely seductive *geisha* in refined formal tea ceremonies all take on a special significance, because it is in states of temporary inactivity or quietude that Zen artists see the very essence of creative energy.

Further, because Zen Buddhists view the human spirit as indefinable by nature, the power of suggestion is exalted as the mark of a truly authentic creation. Finiteness is thought to be at odds with nature, implying stagnation, which is associated with loss of life. The goal of the Zen artist is to convey the symmetrical harmony of nature through clearly asymmetrical and incomplete renderings; the effect is that those viewing the art supply the missing symmetry and thus participate in the act of creation.

Renowned poet **Fujiwara Teika** maintained that "the poet who has begun a thought must be able to end it so masterfully that a rich space of suggestions unfolds in the imagination of his audience." Teika's work became a guiding force in the development of Zen thought in Japan, and his treatises on aesthetics are viewed by historians as the equivalent of universal handbooks on the philosophy of art.

The Core Principles of Zen
The question that remains is, how does this elusive quality come into being? In pursuit of the answer, let's take a look at the specific Zen design principles that frame and support the pursuit of *shibu-mi*, and then, at their practical applications to the design of business, work – and even life itself.

1. Koko (austerity)
The first principle is that of *koko*, which emphasizes restraint, exclusion and omission, embracing the idea that 'not adding' is a valid subtractive approach. The goal is to present something that appears to be spare, yet imparts a sense of focus and clarity. There is a wonderful photo widely available on the Internet of the young **Steve Jobs** (a Buddhist practitioner) circa 1982, sitting in the middle of the living room of his Los Altos house. There isn't much in the room, save an audio system and a Tiffany lamp. Jobs is sipping tea, sitting yoga-style on a mat, with just a few books around him – but the picture speaks volumes about the motive behind every **Apple** product designed under his command, and even helps to explain his aversion to buttons. Beyond the obvious fact that iPods, iPads and iPhones are virtually buttonless, rarely, (if ever) can Jobs be seen wearing a buttoned shirt. He even removes buttons from elevators in multilevel Apple retail stores.

The product designers of Toyota's youth brand, Scion, embraced the principle of *koko* when they created the fast-selling and highly profitable xB model. The small and boxy vehicle was made intentionally spare by leaving out hundreds of standard features in order to appeal to the Millennial Generation, who are prone to making personal statements by customizing their belongings. Sure enough, buyers commonly invested an amount equal to the purchase price to outfit their xB with flat panel screens, carbon fiber interior elements and high-end audio equipment.

Zen design lesson #1:
Refrain from adding what is not absolutely necessary in the first place.

2. Kanso (simplicity)
Kanso dictates that beauty and utility need not be overstated, overly decorative or fanciful and imparts a sense of being fresh, clean and neat. **Instagram**, a wonderfully simple and fun iPhone photo-sharing application founded by CEO **Kevin Systrom**, is a great example of *kanso* in software design and functionality. Instagram allows the user to snap a photo, choose a filter to beautifully transform the look and feel of the picture into a work of art, and quickly share it through social media. But Systrom's first iteration (called Burbn) was a feature-laden app lacking a simple value proposition, and thus had few users. By cutting out the clutter and paring it down into a streamlined app people could understand and have fun with inside 30 seconds, Instagram reached two million users in only four months, a rate of growth faster than **Facebook** and **Twitter**.

Zen design lesson #2:
Eliminate what doesn't matter to make more room for what does.

3. Shizen (naturalness)
The goal of *shizen* is to strike a balance between being at once 'of nature', yet distinct from it – to be viewed as being without pretense, without artifice, not forced, yet to be revealed as intentional rather than accidental or haphazard. When UK-based urban designer **Ben Hamilton-Baillie** goes about designing the kinds of 'shared spaces' found at Kensington High Street and Sloane Square in London, he is taking a page from the *shizen*-inspired high-traffic intersections in the Netherlands that have been redesigned to be void of traffic controls. In these shared-space intersections, curbs have been eliminated, asphalt replaced with red brick, and there are fountains and garden-like café seating right where you think you should drive. When you come to such an intersection, you have no choice but to slow down, have some human interaction, and use your intelligence. The result is an organic, naturally self-organizing order that leads to half of the accidents and nearly twice the vehicle flow. The only rule is driven by the context: first in turn, with all due respect to the most vulnerable. Such naturally emergent self-

Leaving something to the imagination
creates an irresistible aura of mystery,
compelling us to find answers.

organization is far better and more powerful than any control we could artificially impose. It's like looking at a crowded ice skating rink for the first time: it looks chaotic, but there is a natural order to things. "If we observed first and designed second, we wouldn't need most of the things we build," says Hamilton-Baillie.

Zen design lesson #3:
Incorporate naturally-occurring patterns and rhythms when designing a solution.

4. Yugen (subtlety, implicitness)

The principle of *yugen* captures the Zen view that the power of suggestion is often stronger than that of full disclosure: leaving something to the imagination creates an irresistible aura of mystery, compelling us to find answers. The seduction lies in what we don't know, and because what we don't know far outweighs what we do know, we are naturally curious and easily drawn to the unknown. What *isn't* there drives us to resolve our curiosity, and we will fill-in the information we deem missing in order to do so. Apple used *yugen* in its marketing strategy for the original iPhone which, in the months leading up to its June 2007 launch, was hailed as one of the most-hyped products ever to hit the market. To hype something, though, means to push and promote it heavily through marketing and media. Apple did the exact opposite: Steve Jobs demonstrated it at Macworld '07 just once, giving a masterful and tantalizing presentation a full six months before the scheduled launch. In between? Radio silence. No publicity, no leaks to the media, no price discounts, no demos for technology reviewers, no pre-ordering. There was essentially an embargo on official information, with only the Jobs demo available to reference online. The bloggers and Apple loyalists took over, interpreted and extrapolated, completed the picture as it were, and the iPhone 'tipped' before it ever went on sale, with over 20 million people expressing an intent to buy.

Zen design lesson #4:
Limit information to engage human curiosity and leave something to the imagination.

5. Fukinsei (imperfection, asymmetry)

The goal of *fukinsei* is to invoke the natural human inclination to seek symmetry. Nearly everything in nature is symmetrical – it's the predominant organizing principle of the universe. But because it's so prevalent, we often take symmetry for granted – until it's missing. To employ *fukinsei* is to convey the symmetrical harmony of nature by providing something that appears to be asymmetrical, so that the viewer must actively and creatively participate in completing the picture. **David Chase**, creator of the TV series *The Sopranos*, used this principle in the now-famous final episode. *The Sopranos* was an eight-year long series about a band of somewhat organized criminals in northern New Jersey run by one **Tony Soprano**. There was a great build-up to the final episode, made special because Chase himself wrote and directed it, and the audience would find out whether or not Tony would finally get 'whacked'. But the ending presented Chase with a true dilemma: if he killed Tony off, he would alienate half of his audience and squash his chances for a feature film; but if he let Tony live, he would disappoint the other half of the audience, because Tony was a really bad guy.

In the final seconds of the show – with 12 million people watching – just as something was about to happen, the screen went black. Credits rolled a few seconds later, and *The Sopranos* came to an end. People sat dumbfounded, cursing their cable provider for signal failure, or blaming a spouse for not paying the bill. No one saw it as *the* ending, but rather 'something gone wrong', because they were robbed of traditional story symmetry. The media uproar was deafening, with many calling Chase's decision a cop-out. Within 24 hours, though, Chase announced in a stroke of genius that everything one needed to know about the fate of Tony Soprano was embedded in that final episode; he had planted all kinds of clues. Within three days, another 25 million had viewed or reviewed the show, and not one, not two, but three distinctly-different endings sprang up on the Internet, each with a logical argument for why that ending was correct. By denying his audience symmetry, leaving the story incomplete and imperfect, and requiring audience participation to complete it, David Chase managed to triple his impact.

Zen design lesson #5:
Leave room for others to co-create with you, providing a platform for open innovation.

6. Datsuzoku (break from routine)

Datsuzoku signifies a break from daily regimen or habit, a certain freedom from the commonplace that often results in pleasant surprise and sudden amazement. Everyone knows the story of **Archimedes**' shouting "Eureka!" upon discovering volume displacement while taking a bath, and of **Einstein**'s *Theory of Relativity* coming to him in a daydream; but there are countless such stories of sudden genius. Car designer **Irwin Liu** sketched the innovative new lines of what became the shape of the first Toyota Prius after helping his child with an elementary school science project involving hard-boiled eggs; author **J. K. Rowling** was travelling on a train when the character of **Harry Potter** flashed in her mind; and **Shell Oil** engineer **Jaap Van Ballegooijen**'s idea for a snake oil drill came as he watched his son turn his bendy straw upside down to better sip around the sides and bottom of his malt glass.

These strange timings and random locations are not merely coincidence: neuroscientists now believe that the ability to engineer creative breakthroughs hinges on the capacity to synthesize and make connections between seemingly-disparate things, and a key ingredient is *time away* from the problem. Research shows that creative revelations often come when the mind is engaged in an activity unrelated to the issue being addressed, and that pressure is not conducive to creative thought. Recent findings demonstrate that the ultimate break – sleep – actually changes our mind's perspective unconsciously. Information is consolidated by a process taking place in the *hippocampus* during sleep, enabling the brain to effectively clear itself and 'reboot', all the while forming new connections and associations. The result can be new insight and the 'aha!' feeling of the legendary *Eureka!* moment.

Boston Consulting Group (BCG) recently ran a multi-year *datsuzoku* experiment in which members of a dozen four- or five-member consulting teams were required to take 'predictable time off' every week, defined as one uninterrupted evening free each week after 6 p.m. – no work contact whatsoever, and no BlackBerries. The downtime was awkward for many, nerve-racking for some, and a few even fought the idea, fearful of poor performance ratings or more weekend work. The goal was to teach people that you can tune out completely for a time and *still produce great work*. Within six months, internal surveys showed that these consultants were more satisfied with their jobs and work-life balance, and more likely to stay with the firm, compared to those who weren't part of the study. In addition, BCG's clients reported that these teams turned out better work, in part due to more open dialogue, and that the improved communication also sparked new processes that enhanced the teams' ability to work effectively. The experiment worked so well that BCG has since instituted it firm-wide.

Zen design lesson #6:
'Break' is an important part of any breakthrough.

7. Seijaku (stillness, tranquility)
The principle of *seijaku* deals with the actual content of *datsuzoku*. To the Zen practitioner, it is in states of active calm, tranquility, solitude and quietude that we find the essence of cre-

ative energy. For over two decades, neuroscientists have been studying Buddhist monks in Tibet, because the most experienced practitioners – those with over 10,000 hours of meditation to their name – exhibit abnormally high levels of 'gamma brainwaves'. These brainwaves have been shown in studies of complex problem solving to be the exact signal to immediately precede sudden creative insights – the aforementioned *aha!* moment. It is the quiet mind that stimulates the brain to produce strokes of genius.

Perhaps this why so many high-performing athletes and executives meditate or use neurofeedback training. Ford chairman **William Ford**, former corporate chiefs **Bill George** of **Medtronic** and **Bob Shapiro** of **Monsanto**, **Phil Jackson**, **Tiger Woods**, and Italy's 2006 World Cup champion soccer team, along with executives at **GE**, **3M**, Google, **Bloomberg Media**, and **Salesforce.com** all designate daily time to calm and quiet the mind, to free it from thought. These leaders realize how important is it to be able to do *absolutely nothing* in order to achieve maximum impact. But doing nothing is far from easy. If I asked you to do nothing for the next five minutes, my bet is that you couldn't – you would undoubtedly do *something* during that time, and most likely you would think. What we normally consider the easiest thing in the world to do – nothing – is in reality, often the hardest.

Zen design lesson #7:
Doing *something* isn't always better than doing nothing.

In closing
While there is nothing easy about achieving *shibumi*, if taken together as a cohesive set of design principles, the concepts described herein will guide and inform your efforts. Keep in mind that very often in life, although something looks effortlessly simple, it takes a great deal of effort and refinement to reach such a state. And keep close the wisdom of **Antoine de Saint Exupery**: "Perfection is achieved not when there is nothing left to add, but when there is nothing left to take away." ***R***

Matthew May is the founder of Edit Innovation, a Los Angeles-based creative consultancy. His most recent book is *The Laws of Subtraction: 6 Simple Rules for Winning in an Age of Excess Everything* (McGraw Hill, 2012).

Experiential Knowledge

Conceptual Knowledge

Directional Knowledge

Artistry is difficult to comprehend and achieve because it is an emergent, holistic way of being. Understanding and developing your Personal Knowledge System can get you started on the path.

ARTISTRY: THE TERRITORY, THE MAP AND A COMPASS

By **Hilary Austen**

WHETHER WE WORK IN A HOSPITAL, a bank or a consulting firm, we all face problems that run the gamut from the *simple* to the *complex*. Simple problems are comfortingly clear: we know where we have to go and how to get there. Such problems often come with a set of instructions, so that anyone following them can arrive at the same solution. The steps involved are relatively few; the difficulty level, relatively low. Most managers would agree that fewer and fewer of today's problems qualify as 'simple'.

The complex problems we face nowadays go by many names: 'social messes', 'wicked problems' and 'big hairy problems'; I like to call them 'enigmatic problems'. As the definitions of 'ends' (where to go) and 'means' (how to get there) become more ambiguous and the number of variables increases, the difficulty of solving such problems intensifies dramatically – a difference not just in scale, but in kind.

As we go about solving enigmatic problems, the ends and the means are not only unclear, they are also interdependent: as efforts to solve them proceed, the ends evolve as means are generated. Likewise, as means unfold, new ends become possible which, in turn, may demand new means. All of which invites an observation: that the enigmatic problems we face are comprised of features identical to those routinely found in the arts – including uncertainty, ambiguity, complexity, change, surprise, choice, subtlety, indeterminacy, uniqueness and the aforementioned interdependence between ends and means.

Until now, little has been done to make use of this observation. Executives looking to artists for help to solve real-world problems? At first blush, it seems absurd. Let's face it, in rational circles, artists don't have great reputations as problem solvers. I believe that what we can all learn from is the *approach* that artists take to their work. Artists see the features of enigmatic problems not as obstacles, but as exciting opportunities; rather than fearing ambiguity, they seek it out; and rather than avoiding surprises, they embrace them.

Might this mean that the enigmatic problems that permeate modern organizations can be treated as opportunities for artistry? I believe so, but only if we cross an oft-forbidden boundary and enter a world that has always been open to artists, but seldom to the rest of us: the world of *qualitative thought and experience*, where judgment and imagination take their place alongside quantitative analysis and deductive reasoning.

Qualitative vs. Quantitative Thinking

In both academic and professional circles, two armies have divided into proponents of *quantitative* and *qualitative* thinking. This enduring conflict between *structure* and *openness* surfaces in any number of guises. In business, organizations are pulled between strategies that focus on exploitation of current skills and those that court the exploration of innovation; in self-improvement circles, right-brain and left-brain partisans offer conflicting advice on how to achieve well-being. At the root of this war of paradigms lies a dispute over the very definition of intelligence – over which processes of mind our society chooses to value, educate and reward, and which it chooses to marginalize.

I have spent most of my career working to bridge the divide between these two modes of thinking, and I have come to the conclusion that to perform artfully, committed practitioners in any realm must rely on both quantitative *and* qualitative intelligence. Of the two modes, quantitative thinking – the application of numerical values to enhance understanding – is easier to define. We can all count and are comfortable applying numeric values to such day-to-day activities as shopping, driving and scheduling; we observe speed limits and set meeting times. We measure intelligence quotients to identify smart people and measure businesses by accounting conventions that tabulate gross profit and net earnings. Indeed, we even mark our lives by passing units of time.

In our schools, the Sciences (and sometimes even the Liberal Arts) are taught as perfect expressions of quantitative thinking. We are all exposed to Mathematics, Statistics, Chemistry and Physics, subjects driven by quantitative, single-answer problem solving. These disciplines provide formulas that allow us to repeat our work predictably and reliably. Quantitative thinking allows us to be precise and to share understanding; we use it to define fairness, rationality and effectiveness, and it is this utility factor that has led so many people to equate quantitative thinking with intelligence.

Qualitative thinking is very different. Qualities cannot be objectively measured as temperature can be measured with a thermometer. Qualities are physical and tangible rather than abstract: we perceive and feel them: tones, textures, movements, flavours, interactions, relationships and materials all

have qualities. While we can count the number of people in a room, the number tells us little about the mood – upbeat, angry, intense – of the group's interaction. Also, different people might perceive different qualities, or they may experience the same qualities differently.

Whenever you reason with sensory experience rather than with abstract symbols; whenever you act without hesitation upon what you know, while courting the possibilities of surprise; whenever you use a combination of immediate and remembered experience to predict and then revise immediate action – these are the times when you are exercising qualitative intelligence. The painter sees an interplay between orange and blue and structures the rest of her image around this emerging relationship; the President weighs the effects of public opinion and congressional pressure, then makes a far-reaching decision on Civil Rights or health-care reform. As they work, neither the painter nor the President limits his or her judgment strictly to quantitative intelligence or deductive reasoning.

Although few of us will be presidents or painters, we, too think in qualities every day. Without qualitative thinking and abilities, we could note the speed limit, but couldn't maneuver a car in the ever-changing flow of traffic or appreciate the unfolding stages of a relationship, the beauty of a well-designed machine or the impact of a powerful speech. The connection between qualitative work in the arts and work in other disciplines has a venerable history that stretches from **John Dewey**'s work in the 1930s through

To work *downstream* is to exploit past knowledge ('mastery') and to work *upstream* is to seek new knowledge ('originality'). Artistry requires both.

to the latest research on multiple intelligences, as exemplified by **Howard Gardner** and **Daniel Goleman**. Standing out is a seminal 1983 book called *The Reflective Practitioner*, in which MIT's **Donald Schön** highlights the similarities between fine artists and professionals across practice disciplines: "The artistry of painters, sculptors, musicians, dancers and designers bears a strong family resemblance to the artistry of extraordinary lawyers, physicians, managers and teachers."

Despite the efforts of Schön *et al*, the purposeful development of qualitative abilities rarely occurs outside the arts, and quantitative thinking is still the primary focus of most educational programs. Qualitative thought tends to be overlooked, even shunned in most mainstream schools; its powers, like that of a mysterious magical object, are either feared or left to those who are willing embrace perilous experimentation.

On the surface of things, this makes sense, as qualitative approaches can seem dangerously vague and hard to pin down. Critics deem them 'too subjective' to rely on. Ask musicians how they turn a string of notes into music, how they develop an ear, or how they pluck a string to create one mood or another with a single note, and you'll get very different answers. Ask a quality-sensitive teacher how he judges student involvement or designs learning that motivates, and he'll say that it depends on the student, the subject and the moment. When qualities are used to guide action, what works for one person can seldom be used by another to get the exact same results in another time and place.

Real people doing pragmatic work are beginning to see the value of qualitative capabilities in areas normally reserved for those with quantitative expertise. My own study of practitioners across disciplines indicates that when you scratch the surface, the apparent rupture between quantitative and qualitative thinking transforms into a dynamic interaction *between two sides of the same coin*. The good news is that if you know how to handle this interaction, you can turn it into a force that fuels action and progress.

Handling the Interaction: Our Personal Knowledge System

What can you do with this type of thinking that is so subjective, so hard to pin down? How can you develop it without losing everything that your quantitative expertise has gotten you? And what is the reward in trying? To answer such questions,

I've developed a Personal Knowledge System that supports the kind of artistic pursuit we've been exploring. Understanding how it works to organize and integrate knowledge is the key to achieving artistic practice.

The model's main components are three distinct kinds of knowledge: Directional, Conceptual and Experiential. The links among them, whether working 'upstream' or 'downstream', suggest fundamental differences in how we approach our practice. To work downstream is to exploit past knowledge ('Mastery') and to work upstream is to seek new knowledge ('Originality'). True artistry depends on both.

Of the model's three components, Experiential Knowledge is the messiest; it's the vast territory in which you immerse yourself directly in the medium of your practice and all of its qualities. Conceptual Knowledge is the map of that territory; it's the sum of all the theories, equations and models you use to find your way through the thickets of first-hand experience and pass your knowledge on to others. Directional Knowledge is your compass; it's the body of ideals and motivations and traditions that guide your practice – even your identity. Let's examine each in turn.

EXPERIENTIAL KNOWLEDGE includes know-how, skills, sensitivities, feel, intuition, techniques, methods, expression and awareness. These elements allow you to experience and shape qualities in your medium to produce results. Gaining useful Experiential Knowledge means developing a nuanced awareness of the qualities in your medium, as well as the skills to create and manipulate those qualities.

Qualitative awareness comes as you immerse yourself into qualities themselves: we ingest food, listen to sound, play and build, observe colours, light, and objects, or interact with others and even industries to find out what we can make of them. This is actually a process of learning to see, taste, hear and feel; of discerning and discriminating through participation and observation; of becoming a connoisseur, and making distinctions; and of developing a personal intimacy with the qualities that comprise the activity of your interest. Once achieved, this intimacy establishes a new baseline for what can be perceived.

Such development is not automatic; instead, it must be treated as an active search for awareness. It is achieved when thinking happens in the qualities of the medium itself, when the need for

Directional Knowledge	Conceptual Knowledge	Experiential Knowledge
What ideals about self, action and results are possible?	What concepts are used to organize action?	What qualities can be experienced?
How do these ideals guide the selection, development, and application of conceptual knowledge?	How are concepts used to guide attention and interpret qualities?	What skills can be developed?
How do these ideals influence action?	What concepts have been created to deal with enigmatic features and the tension between structure and openness?	How are awareness and skill linked?
		How can experience be used to create new conceptual knowledge?

translation disappears. Developing awareness alone is not enough; developing skill also takes a lot of work, intention and participation, but of a different kind – the kind that takes practice, practice and more practice.

An artist's unity with his medium means that awareness and skill come together in action that can occur within the blink of an eye. When he achieves this unity of awareness and skill, he no longer needs translation time: fans enjoy seamless performance they can barely comprehend; artists enjoy an incomparable thrill. When work is disconnected from this kind of personal qualitative experience, practice can become rote, laborious and dull. By contrast, when awareness guides skill, working in any medium becomes an irresistible activity full of pleasures and rewards. Also, awareness guides the application of skill. When this happens, the employment of skills can leave the mechanical realm; skill flows in response to awareness of immediate or anticipated qualities. This means skill can be applied automatically and responsively, rather than by referencing a recipe or a past routine.

When we miss or misunderstand qualitative information, our results fall short or diverge from everything we intended. Little else in life is so discouraging. Building your Conceptual Knowledge in a medium – allowing you to sort out, evaluate, organize, prioritize, and sequence what you encounter and produce – can buffer the impact of disorienting or disruptive outcomes.

CONCEPTUAL KNOWLEDGE includes concepts, theories, equations, categories, heuristics, schema, recipes, standards, criteria and models. These elements provide understanding and organization and help practitioners preserve and communicate what they know about their medium. Every discipline has a store of shared Conceptual Knowledge, and every practitioner has a set of personalized variations. It can also come in such narrative forms as stories, anecdotes, parables and sayings. Some Conceptual Knowledge is explicit, and some remains intuitive. Much of the early work in any discipline is spent trying to find and incorporate shared Conceptual Knowledge.

In many disciplines, Conceptual Knowledge includes a lot of powerful quantitative, numeric tools. Connectable to physical and logical laws, these tools enjoy a high level of acceptance in the areas they address. The tools used to make sense of qualitative experience are a bit more varied and contentious. Some are highly detailed, others offer simple guiding advice, like, 'keep your eye on the ball'; some attempt to capture predictable sequences, others predict important relationships; still others identify critical features that signal approaching success and error. All are intended to help you decide what to do in what order, which elements are most important, how you should approach those elements, and how to judge the results of your work when there are multiple alternatives. A few examples include:

· Colour wheels
· Musical notation
· Reverse-engineering strategy templates
· Navigational maps
· Parables
· Biological taxonomies like the Evolutionary Tree
· Systems diagrams
· Organizational charts

Typically, Conceptual Knowledge is used like a recipe to constrain action and reduce error. As such, it can present a trap that is all too easy to fall into. The artistic take on 'recipes' is somewhat different. Working artistically means using pre-existing Conceptual Knowledge to guide masterful action, but also to:

· Recognize the potential in surprises
· Evaluate rather than measure products and performances when quantities don't apply
· Design experiments that might yield better qualities and
· Find overlooked or novel qualities in what is produced.

DIRECTIONAL KNOWLEDGE includes purposes, ideals, motivations, identities, directions, themes, traditions, contexts and missions. These elements provide meaning, motivation, focus and orientation. Conventional wisdom tells us that the road to progress is paved with systematic steps toward measurable goals. A lucrative motivational industry, corporate-compensation programs, and the nation's educational infrastructure are all built on this premise. But true artists have an uncanny ability to elude this approach. Instead, they rely on their desire to connect the immediate qualities they produce in their medium to the ideal, somewhat ill-defined qualities they can imagine.

Like a compass, Directional Knowledge provides a heading without establishing the final destination – it is felt like a magnetic pull. When the passion to pursue work in a medium is composed of self-determined, idealized qualitative ideas about action, identity and purpose, this is the signature of Directional Knowledge. This knowledge can then generate meaning, motivation and orientation.

Progress toward idealized directions is often marked by measurable wins and losses and by demanding experiences. Artists pursuing these ideals often appear obsessed or single-minded. They display a stubborn commitment to acting in their medium even when things aren't going well. Wins and losses are used to mark direction, rather than predict current capability or ultimate potential. Ideals provide the motivation to withstand difficult experiences.

Another feature of Directional Knowledge is that differences in it allow practitioners working in the same medium to create a wide variety of outcomes, even when they share much of the same Conceptual Knowledge. For example, two painters with the same paint, brushes and canvas, having learned the same theory of colour relationships, can use differences in Directional Knowledge to create images as different as **Da Vinci**'s *Mona Lisa* and **Van Gogh**'s *Starry Night*. Using the same economic infor-

mation, two CEOs can point their respective organizations toward different strategic directions, be it 'customer service' or 'product design'. We rarely question Directional Knowledge except in times of disruptive change within a personal practice or a disciplinary practice community.

When the ideals that form your Directional Knowledge guide the models you use, or when those models guide your direct experience, you are working downstream with the forces that drive *mastery*. These forces are essentially conservative; they emphasize control and predictability based on past experience. *Originality*, by contrast, is driven by unpredictable responses to immediate experience. Working upstream – cultivating your first-hand experience such that it informs your Conceptual and Directional Knowledge – means leaving behind some of what you know. Artistry is driven forward by the interplay of these two competing forces.

In closing

In a world plagued by increasingly-intractable enigmatic problems, quantitative thinking alone is not up to the challenge. If artistry is difficult to comprehend and achieve, it is because it is an emergent, holistic way of being. On the one hand, it cannot be simplified or broken down into accessible parts without generating misleading, fragmented and confusing distortions; on the other hand, if not dismantled, novices can't even begin to learn.

Using the Personal Knowledge System model outlined herein is one way out of this difficulty. Using it, students of artistry can better understand what artistic practitioners say about what they know and do, even when what they say seems incomplete or inconsistent. Listen closely: practitioners actually do reveal their knowledge system in what they say and do – although they may often sound like they are speaking in code. Students who can observe and listen with the Personal Knowledge System in mind can make sense of the overwhelming stream of information that artistic practitioners generate in word and deed. **R**

 Hilary Austen is an adjunct professor at the Rotman School of Management and a member of the Dean's Advisory Board. She is the author of *Artistry: A Guide to Pursuing Great Performance in Work and Life* (Rotman-UTP Publishing, 2010).

Engineers have long viewed design as a core activity. Managers would be wise to turn to them for **creative inspiration**.

Possibility Thinking

Lessons from
Breakthrough Engineering

By **Jeanne Liedtka** and **Robert Friedel**

BUSINESS STRATEGISTS TEND to be well-versed in the identification and analysis of constraints. But what of possibilities? If the ability to see new possibilities is fundamental to creating innovative designs – whether of products, cities or business strategies – what do we know about state-of-the-art possibility thinking?

Not much, it seems. Business strategy has historically been seen as a largely analytic endeavor, with relatively little attention paid to the creative aspects of strategy formulation. In this article, we will describe eight ways to illuminate new possibilities taken

from Engineering success stories and discuss what each might look like if applied to business strategy.

1. Challenge Assumptions

Challenging assumptions and defying convention are often the first steps in creative Engineering. To produce something original, an engineer raises questions about the way things are done and entertains doubts about what is assumed to be necessary, natural, or customary.

For example, 'seismic base isolation' is a system of protecting buildings from earthquake damage by using bearings or supports, typically made of layered rubber and steel pads, to separate buildings from the ground on which they sit. The bearings allow a building to move freely on shaking ground. This approach challenges the customary view that we make a building stable by fixing it firmly to the earth. In describing the traditional method of limiting earthquake damage in *The Seismic Design Handbook*, **Ronald Mayes** wrote, "The basic approach has not changed [over the years]: construct a very strong building and attach it securely to the ground. This approach of arm wrestling with nature is neither clever nor subtle." The new technology breaks from this radically by allowing a building to move, but to move without destruction. Putting 'bearings' underneath a building's foundations separates the building itself from a potentially moving earth. One ambitious application has been the work of **Eric Elsesser** and his associates in retrofitting the San Francisco City Hall following the Loma Prieta earthquake of 1989. This building is now separated from the earth by hundreds of steel and rubber isolation bearings, making it the largest base-isolated structure in the world.

In the realm of business strategy, we see much the same process at work when managers challenge mental models and industry assumptions. New possibilities emerge when they refuse to accept existing paradigms and constraints. The potential opportunities revealed when managers look through a different lens can be enormous. Consider the incremental value created at **Raytheon** with the development of the new Vigilant Eagle anti-terrorism device, designed to protect commercial airliners from over-the-shoulder missiles. Conventional wisdom decreed that each plane be outfitted with its own protection device at a cost of approximately one million dollars per plane. With estimates for protecting all U.S. commercial aircraft of $20 billion, creative managers at Raytheon hit upon a new possibility – that of protecting *airports*, rather than individual planes. They estimate that 70 per cent of U.S. air traffic can be protected for less than $2 billion. Challenging existing approaches became the path to a cost-effective solution.

2. Make Connections

Making connections between seemingly unrelated ideas is also often at the heart of creative Engineering. Novelty can result from going outside of a single field or discipline and bringing together diverse concepts, tools, capabilities, and ways of thinking.

'Tissue Engineering' is a new specialty that creates usable human tissues for repairing or replacing damaged ones. Engineers have tackled this problem by relating medical and biological approaches to those of chemical engineers, materials scientists and engineers, and mechanical and electrical engineers. Some of the basic approaches of tissue engineers borrow from Civil Engineering: 'scaffolds,' for example, provide biodegradable structures on which tissue cells can grow. Another key device used by some tissue engineers is the 'bioreactor,' a vessel especially designed for the cultivation of living tissue. Tissue Engineering is now emerging from the laboratory into medical applications and producing experimental products including skin, cartilage, and liver tissues.

Connecting can be equally powerful in the business environment. The use of analogies that connect different fields can provide a window of insight into new possibilities for value creation. While adhering to the mental models of one's own industry is limiting, trying on the mental models of another can surface intriguing new opportunities. The story of **Ethel M. Candies** demonstrates the power of connecting across business boundaries. **John Haugh**, Ethel's new president, faced the daunting challenge of growing the business in a confectionary market suffering from slow growth and consumers who preferred **Godiva** – despite Ethel's superior quality in blind taste tests. Rather than continue to pursue the existing packaged-goods strategy, John combined his own career experiences in retail with close observation of the success of **Starbucks**. If Starbucks could do it with coffee, why couldn't Ethel create a similar experience around chocolate? Thus was born **Ethel's Chocolate Lounge**.

3. Visualize

For an engineer, making something new often means first thinking about how it might look – picturing it in the mind's eye. Engaging the senses beyond what words describe sometimes opens new paths to creativity.

Visual thinking is a key element in many kinds of Engineering, particularly those dealing with large structures. In some projects, however, the visual element is particularly striking and the creative act appears to be tightly bound to thinking about problems pictorially. One recent example is the Gateshead Millennium Bridge, carrying foot traffic across the River Tyne between the cities of Newcastle and Gateshead in northern England. This remarkable structure was envisioned as a 'blinking eye': it opens to allow river traffic not by lifting up, but by pivoting. The movement of its supporting arch and its curved foot surface creates a remarkable sight, enhancing the visual aspect of the engineering both while stationary and while in motion.

Visualizing is perhaps the most challenging concept to transfer from the world of Engineering to the world of business strategy. After all, strategies represent ideas, not concrete objects: they are comprised of numbers and words – how can they be made visual? Yet there is significant value in pushing our thinking along this dimension. Designers, we are told, 'think with their pencils' – allowing the emerging visual images they sketch to deepen their understanding of what they are designing as it unfolds. If strategists think only with their spreadsheets, how much use of imagination can we expect?

Trader Publications, a producer of free classified product guides, has taken the dictum to use visuals to heart. As part of its strategic planning process, managers not only describe competitive publications, they obtain copies of them. These copies are aggregated at corporate, where managers array them in conference rooms for examination. This experience – the visual and visceral experience of handling these publications, according to Trader executives, produces far richer possibility discussions than reading reports about them. In a similar vein, organizations have begun to experiment with creating strategy maps – pictorial guides that use analogies to portray both their and competitors' strategies. The act of creating these maps often triggers profoundly new insights.

4. Collaborate

Many Engineering innovations are the product of cooperative effort and could not be developed any other way. Groups bring together a range of talents and capabilities, applying them to generate results that reflect both individual skills and a collaborative creativity that is more than the sum of the separate endeavors.

A jet airliner is one of the most complicated products designed by modern engineers. It contains literally millions of individually-designed parts, which must work together to meet the highest standards of performance and safety. **The Boeing Company**'s 777 jet is a model of collaborative creativity on an extraordinary scale. The collaboration behind it, however, is interesting not simply for its scope but also for the pioneering communication methods it relied on. This was the first major aircraft designed using extensive computer networking – more than 2,200 work stations linked by eight mainframes – to bring together thousands of engineers working on every phase of the project at the same time. Although many never met in person, the computer system promoted a collaborative process so central to the project that the 777's slogan was 'Working Together.' At the heart of the system was software developed by **IBM** and **Dassault Systèmes**, called CATIA (Computer-Aided Three-dimensional

Interactive Application). Boeing extended this with EPIC (Electronic Pre-assembly In the Computer), allowing engineers in disparate locations to design and test 'virtual' prototypes of crucial components of the airplane.

Interestingly, in Boeing's design of its newest product, the 787, the firm has pushed collaboration beyond groups of engineers to collaboration with customers as well, creating special Web portals that solicit their input on likes and dislikes to incorporate into the design process. These examples of collaboration with suppliers and customers represent just two of many 'white space' possibilities.

At **United Technologies Corporation**, collaboration between in-house technical talent at two separate divisions – jet engine designer **Pratt & Whitney** and cooling specialist **Carrier** – created the breakthrough Purecycle product with virtually no new components needed. Purecycle converts waste heat to electricity – an opportunity that went unrecognized until engineers who thought in terms of power met up with engineers skilled at using heat exchange to produce cold air. Crossing such functional and business unit boundaries can provide rich sources for enhanced value creation.

5. Harmonize

In every area of human effort, creativity is intimately associated with the quest for beauty. This is most obvious in the Fine Arts, but it is no less true in the practical arts like Architecture and Engineering. Here, especially, there is an aesthetic quality that often lies in harmony, in fitting the products of human ingenuity agreeably into their environment.

In Colorado's Glenwood Canyon, a key link in the interstate highway system required the construction of a viaduct to carry the road over a narrow, curving stretch of the Colorado River. The Hanging Lake Viaduct fits aesthetically into this precious natural setting, while providing an efficient and reliable transportation link. Meeting this challenge involved not only designing a structure that would harmonize with its environment, but also minimize harm to the river and its surroundings. The builders used a giant gantry and crane to set the pre-cast concrete box girders into place from above. The number of piers supporting the road was reduced by producing spans as long as 300 feet. Bridge members were designed with straight lines to blend with the striations of the canyon walls.

In business strategy, we have a long history of paying attention to the 'fit' of an organization's strategy, both in terms of its internal consistency and in its appropriateness for its larger environment. Good strategies, we know, are aligned along many dimensions. We have an equally long history, however, of largely ignoring aesthetics – of treating them as trivial adornments to high-end products and services. In fact, it is somewhat difficult to even describe what the 'aesthetic' dimensions of a strategy might be.

What makes a strategy more than merely functional – a thing of beauty? The origin of the word 'aesthetic' lies with the Greek term *aisthetikos*, meaning 'of sense perception.' Thus, we might conjecture that it relates to strategies that appeal to the senses, rather than merely to cognition – new possibilities that have an *emotional* appeal, a 'presence' that commands attention and invites engagement. Yet consider how banal and clichéd so many corporate missions are; no wonder they fail to command attention, much less emotion. Then consider instead the emotional engagement **The Body Shop** evoked when it committed to natural products and lack of animal testing coupled with a recycling ethic. These simple aesthetics created a unique and compelling value proposition for targeted customers who shared their values. Change, psychologists tell us, is primarily driven by *desire* – it is in that sense of the term 'aesthetic' that we can learn from designers how to make business strategies more compelling and new possibilities more evident.

6. Improvise

Outer space exploration is one of the last places we would expect engineers to improvise. Few activities appear to be so thoroughly planned from start to finish: whether executing repairs on a device millions of miles away or devising ways to extend the work of multimillion dollar instruments, the spacecraft engineer may work with the most extreme constraints of all. The Voyager 2 space probe was launched in August 1977, primarily as a backup for the Voyager 1 flight to Jupiter and Saturn. Designed to operate for five years, it ended up carrying out important missions for more than 12 and is still sending data back to earth. Voyager 2 has been constantly re-engineered, repaired, reprogrammed, and reconfigured by earth-bound engineers working with the constraints of a device which receives its communications in a dead language minutes after the commands are sent.

In the business context, limitations to action are often seen as 'stop signs' – signals to give up the quest for an innovative solution. For designers, the response is the opposite: constraints act as trig-

gers to seeing new possibilities. Some of the most successful business strategies were not the result of careful forethought; instead, they were the products of improvisation, created out of necessity when familiar options were unavailable. **IKEA** offers a case in point. Nearly every element of its now famously-harmonized strategy – furniture packed flat in pieces, customer home assembly, and self-service in their warehouses – was a clever response to an unanticipated problem. Customer self-service, for instance, originated with the opening of the Stockholm store, which was so unexpectedly popular (and hence understaffed) that frustrated customers grew tired of waiting for scarce warehouse personnel to bring their purchases to them, and went in search of them themselves. What distinguishes IKEA is not that such problems developed, but that it was able to observe new possibilities inherent in them, and to build these serendipitous discoveries into its strategy.

7. Reformulate

New possibilities can emerge from new formulations of problems rather than new solutions. When people change goals or revise notions of what is important and what isn't, different priorities and approaches may be more appropriate.

Engineers' goals and priorities may shift for a variety of reasons. Changes in fashions, markets, or politics may make approaches that were once considered desirable or necessary seem inappropriate. Or, engineers and society at large may learn new things that lead to a re-evaluation of results and a reorientation of efforts. Few better examples can be found than the re-engineering of South Florida's rivers and wetlands. The Kissimmee River begins near Orlando and flows southward for about 100 miles. Historically, it meandered through a one-to two-mile wide flood plain, covering all but a small portion of the land for most of the growing season. In periods of large storms or hurricanes, waters from the Kissimmee and other rivers would destroy homes and crops over a wide area. To reduce flooding, the **U.S. Army Corps of Engineers** straightened the river in the 1960s, and drained much of the nearby wetlands.

However, even before the project was completed in 1971, it was clear that this effort had resulted in devastation of wildlife habitats and the displacement of many animal and plant species. State and federal agencies decided that engineers' efforts needed to be reoriented toward undoing the damage: recovery of the River became one of the most ambitious restoration projects ever undertaken. Slowly the Corps of Engineers and the **South Florida Water Management District** are returning major portions of the Kissimmee from a canal back into a meandering river, to make the environment once again hospitable to its historic inhabitants.

Re-examining the definition of a problem holds great potential for generating new possibilities in the business realm. One of

The single-minded pursuit of
efficiency and optimization
can lead to 'analysis paralysis'
and leave little room for the
emergence of new possibilities.

our favourite stories is that of **P&G**'s creation of the Swiffer mop. After decades of focusing on the problem of 'producing more effective detergents,' P&G re-oriented its thinking to focus on 'creating a cleaner floor,' as well. This led to the realization that detergent was only part of the solution, and that significant opportunities existed in producing a better mop. A similar shift occurs, at a generic level, whenever business strategists move from focusing on the problem of 'How do we sell more of product X?' to 'What need is the customer trying to satisfy?'

8. Play

To an extent that is often unrecognized, play is a key element of the creative act. Perhaps the best example is the design firm **IDEO**, which stocks each of the firm's offices with an identical 'tech box.' As the firm's Web site describes it, "Each tech box has several drawers holding hundreds of objects, from smart fabrics to elegant mechanisms to clever toys, each of which are tagged and numbered. Designers and engineers can rummage through the compartments, play with the items, and apply materials to their current project." Computer and database linkages allow sharing of tech box play among the firm's offices, and each box has a 'curator' who constantly updates the contents.

The idea of play may appear ill-suited to the business environment, but the single-minded pursuit of efficiency and optimization can lead to 'analysis paralysis' and leave little room for the emergence of new possibilities. To play is to try to do something, not merely to think about it. Play does us the great service of calling attention to the value of the experiment, the willingness to forfeit certainty in the name of learning. Organizations good at finding new possibilities are quick to conduct low-cost experiments rather than detailed market feasibility studies. For example, consumer products companies are increasingly likely to talk their key retailers into just a small amount of shelf space in a few stores to test new ideas, preferring to fail early and on small volume rather than do major roll-outs based on predictions of consumer behaviour that may prove incorrect. This kind of 'serious play' is likely to pay big dividends in opening up new possibilities.

In closing

We suggest that business strategists begin by asking themselves a simple set of questions that draw on the approaches described

here and provide a warm-up for the possibility-thinking muscles of our strategic brains:

1. Take an absolute industry 'truth' and turn it on its head. Ask "what if *anything* were possible?" and look at the new opportunities that appear.
2. Look outside the boundaries of your usual world. Ask, "what if we were operating in an industry quite different than ours – what would we be doing instead?"
3. Put the numbers aside and get some images down on paper. Try using a napkin. What emerges?
4. Find a partner and go forth and co-create. Ask, "what can we do together that neither of us can do alone?"
5. Push yourself beyond the 'workable.' Try to get to 'intriguing.' Ask, "What is really worth doing – what can I get excited about?"
6. Act as if necessity truly was the mother of invention and make surprises work for you instead of against you. How can you turn an unexpected development into an asset?
7. Try on a different definition of the problem. Step away from your product and ask, "what is the problem my customers are really anxious to solve?"
8. Go out and conduct low-cost experiments instead of forming a committee. What can you do *today* to move a new possibility forward?

As we look across the approaches for surfacing new possibilities outlined here, their applicability to business strategy is clear. Engineers have long viewed design as a core activity. As managers – particularly strategists – come to share this view, we would be wise to turn to them for creative inspiration. *R*

Jeanne Liedtka is the United Technologies Corporation Professor of Business Administration at the University of Virginia's Darden School of Business and the former chief learning officer at United Technologies. She is the author of three books, most recently *Solving Problems with Design Thinking: Ten Stories of What Works* (Columbia University Press, 2013). **Robert Friedel** is a professor in the Department of History at the University of Maryland.

A longer version of this article appeared in the *Journal of Business Strategy*'s special issue on design and business, published in May 2009.

Looking for the qualities of 'design thinkers' within your own team and encouraging them is a great way to build innovation capacity.

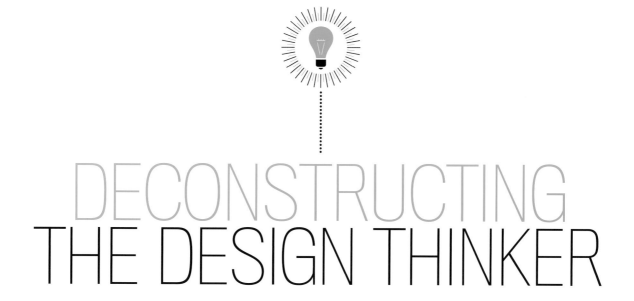

DECONSTRUCTING
THE DESIGN THINKER

by **Sohrab Vossoughi**

THE TERM 'DESIGN THINKING' has lost some of its lustre of late, particularly in business publications. This is the natural result of throwing around a new term with a little too much enthusiasm and not quite enough understanding. This is truly unfortunate, because the qualities of design thinking have never been more important.

The core of design thinking's problem could be that it's so difficult to pin down. While its effects are fairly clear – a combination of deductive, inductive and abductive reasoning that leads to an unusually-pragmatic strain of creativity – thinking of any sort is a human activity, and humans are hard to figure out. Discussions about design thinking tend to focus on companies that employ it and the successes they achieve, rather than the people who actually do it. This poses a problem for the rest of us, because when companies see the value in a design thinking approach, the next step is to try to build that capability through directed hiring, and this is universally frustrating. For one thing, the term itself is probably a misnomer. Design thinkers are just as likely to be business people or engineers as designers, and very few of them went to design school. In fact, the great examples of design thinking in business – **P&G**, **Apple**, **Umpqua Bank**, **Zappos** – are

The complexity and difficulty is
what interests design thinkers –
not recognition,
and certainly not wealth.

led by folks with no design training whatsoever. The fact is, a great design thinker can come from anywhere.

To verify this point and to get a better idea of what traits to look for, I spoke with three people from the vibrant creative economy in Portland, Oregon, who exemplify the innovation-driven success usually associated with design thinking: **Kenton Gregory** is an inventor of life-saving medical technologies, including solutions to battlefield injury problems that have challenged medics for decades; **Naomi Pomeroy** is a chef who has pushed the boundaries of Portland's renowned food scene for a decade, first with **Ripe** – a group of restaurants and supper clubs that redefined the city's culinary direction – and more recently with her *prix fixe* restaurant **Beast**, which often occupies Best Of lists for the entire west coast; and **Michael Czysz** is an award-winning architect who transformed at the height of a promising career into a designer of groundbreaking electric transportation.

Of the three, only Czysz attended design school – two years of Architecture – which he abandoned to pursue projects with more personal interest. Over a series of focused interviews with them, some common traits began to emerge.

1. Design thinkers are internally-motivated by challenge and curiosity.
As technical challenges go, building the world's fastest electric motorcycle is among the most difficult and most expensive a small shop could take on. Yet that's what **Michael Czysz**'s tiny company **Motoczysz** decided to pursue, and it's been an uphill battle ever since. This fascination

with difficult, complex problems showed up in all three interviews. The complexity and difficulty is what interests these people – not recognition, and certainly not wealth. Money, in fact, is mentioned by both Czysz and Gregory as a building block or an obstacle; a means of achieving solutions rather than a goal in itself. Design thinkers are internally motivated by personal curiosity, a desire to effect change and the pleasure of figuring something out. Here's what they told me.

Kenton Gregory: "The world's a great place, full of great problems. I want to really make a big jump: not just a slightly better hypertension drug – a whole a new drug."

"Looking at a problem or a creation from different angles generates an energy that is addicting. You don't do it for the money, you do it because of that high – of creating something and sharing that energy. In fact, resources are usually the biggest obstacle, to putting the team together, building something, or buying the gear you need."

"I tend to like enormously complex, intricate things of beauty. Everywhere you look, there is something you can make more beautiful."

Naomi Pomeroy: "If something isn't extraneously pushing on me, I will set my life up so that it is. Taking on too much work, having too much to do: that's when I find myself most productive and creative."

"You know in the airplane they tell you to put your oxygen mask on before you put your child's mask on? I do that all the time in my life. I can't make you happy if I'm not happy. That's why we keep things fresh and interesting. That's why I'm always trying to create."

Michael Czysz: "I was drawn to the motorcycle by passion. In the second chapter of my life, I wanted a harder task than architecture – a challenge with a need for more accuracy, but also with bigger potential. Greater reward and possibly greater loss."

"We all have open minds as children, but they get closed as we grow older. We don't let ourselves explore. Everybody has had a good idea, but they immediately think, 'Oh, I can't do anything about it,' and they close the door. I think more people could do it – they just don't try."

2. Design thinkers alternate between intuition and analysis.
Perhaps the main reason it's so hard to identify the problem-solving approach of design thinkers is that *there isn't one*; there are two. Creative people can be outgoing, collaborative and intuitive, or they can be introverted, focused and analytical, but design thinkers embrace both. A pattern of oscillation, between periods of playful exploration and periods of detail-oriented deep focus showed up in all three interviews. The result is a powerful hybrid approach – an 'informed intuition' that exposes new solutions and brings them to fruition.

Naomi Pomeroy first welcomed customers to her Portland, Oregon restaurant, Beast in 2007. *Bon Appètit* named her as one of the top 6 of a new generation of female chefs and *Food & Wine* magazine has recognized her as one of the 10 Best New Chefs in America. She has been a finalist for the prestigious James Beard Award and *Marie Claire* named her one of the 18 most powerful women in business in 2010. A 24-seat restaurant where people chat freely with each other at communal tables. Beast serves a six-course prix-fixed menu at two seatings, four nights a week and a four-course brunch on Sundays.

Michael Czysz is the founder and head designer of MotoCzysz. In 2003 he abandoned a successful, 20-year architecture career to build a world-class MotoGP racer. He re-imagined the motorcycle from the ground up, arriving at radical solutions like a 'frameless' carbon-fiber chassis and a longi-tudinally mounted, narrow-angle V4 engine with twin counter-rotating crankshafts. He won both the 2010 Isle of Man TTXGP and the inaugural North American round of the FIM's ePower electric-bike world championship at Laguna Seca.

Kenton Gregory and his 15-member research team recently joined Oregon Health & Science University to establish a new independent research entity. At the Center for Regenerative Medicine, Dr. Gregory and his team will build on their pioneering basic science discoveries and innovative applications, which include novel bandages and wound dressings used by military personnel, civilian first responders and medical professionals to rapidly control severe bleeding, saving the lives of thousands.

Kenton: "To get something done, you really need to have intense focus. You have to shut everything out and use all your resources, especially if you're solving a new problem. That's why I don't mind being by myself. I can spend two or three hours out at my ranch and come back and have figured something out."

"If you're a driven, creative person and you don't 'defocus', you can get myopic. You might create something genius, but it's irrelevant. There's a need for reality testing. I think that's good for all careers – to be able to focus intently and then defocus and look at the big picture, and be doing that constantly – mixing and matching intuition with analysis."

Naomi: "When a painter goes to a canvas, how do they decide what to paint? It's a million different things. Everything is firing in the brain – what's the weather like outside, what's in season now – it all tumbles down from a general mood of the world, a sort of collective consciousness. I try to tap into that when I'm making a menu."

"If I am focused and my head is down, anybody off the street can see it. I just can't help it. I can't hear anything, I can't see anything, I can only do the thing in front of me."

"You can get sparked by an inspiration, but after that it's as much about thinking and talking as it is about listening and learning. You have to have rigor, otherwise it's just messing around."

Michael: "My process for arriving at innovation is *not stressing*. I relax, and take a kind of trip. I allow myself to take it all the way through, and when I get back to the starting point, I've touched all the bases and I'm comfortable that it's a solid idea. I can stop second-guessing. But after that, you have to focus and edit. I think that the deeper your focus, the better the return."

"Sometimes, you just use your intuition and you pray. But your intuition is always better when you have more data and more personal experience."

3. Design thinkers are inherently multidisciplinary.
Kenton Gregory is a doctor who studied Engineering and now develops wound treatment processes and energy production systems in parallel; Naomi Pomeroy is a chef who's never taken a culinary class, but found herself managing 95 cooks and staff by the age of 30; Michael Czysz grew up riding motorcycles, left Architecture school to do interiors, and now designs innovative battery systems without the benefit of formal Engineering study. An innate desire for new knowledge and abilities – even if there's no immediate application for them – forms the core of this multi-disciplinary tendency, and

contributes to the curiosity that design thinkers exhibit. It also pushes them to seek out collaborators they can learn from, and teams with a level of diversity that mirrors their own.

Kenton: "I did bounce around, which gave me a relatively broad background. I wanted to make a contribution, to create something, to add something to the planet. So I did Environmental Engineering and learned how to make things, how to solve problems. Then I went into Medicine, and there are unlimited problems to solve there, too. I'm planning to work on Photovoltaics next. This is a method of generating electrical power by converting solar radiation into direct current electricity using semiconductors that exhibit the 'photovoltaic effect'. I'm usually working on about 20 things at once."

"When I'm at any kind of professional meeting, I try to wander off into other rooms and see something completely different. I may not have any inkling of understanding, but it always challenges my brain."

"The number one thing you need in a team is diversity. When I'm putting one together, I feel like Noah: I want one or two of everything. I expect more than just respect for diversity of gender or religion or politics, I expect respect for diversity of thought. It's difficult for one person to do everything, so I fill in for my weaknesses, which are many, and put together a group of people that are very diverse and that have optimism."

Naomi: "Chefs can fall into a kind of tunnel vision – most aren't 'people persons' and they can get too focused, like a scientist in his Lab. But you have to come outside of your box in order to stay current."

Michael: "You need experience and you need some stick-to-it-iveness, but it's nice to be able to step over and look into other areas that you don't have a lot of experience in, because you'll come at it from a different perspective. That's clearly healthy. In many cases, everybody in an industry comes at it from the same perspective, so they all get the same results. You need somebody from the outside to take a look."

4. Design thinkers are optimistic and tenacious.
If these interviews are any indication, the best design thinkers may actually fail *more* than the rest of us. Completely absent from these discussions was any sense that what they're doing comes easy, or that they possess some unique ability to get things right the first time. The key qualities instead tend to be optimism, tenacity and a willingness to learn from mistakes.

Kenton: "One of the essential ingredients that college students have in abundance is optimism. Maybe they are a little too cocky – 'Yeah, we can solve any problem!' But what I've told my students when they're trying to be creative, is that being brilliant is helpful, but not essential: what's more important is tenacity. The sheer force of will that doesn't let you give up, and keeps you working until three or four in the morning. Together, optimism and tenacity are a powerful force."

Naomi: "Being 30 years old and having 95 employees was daunting, but it was a good opportunity to learn, learn, learn. There's always this sort of golden thing that happens when you take what you've learned from failure – whether it's a single dish that didn't work out right, or on a large scale, like your business failing. But in both cases you have to say, 'So, now what?' There's always a next opportunity there, just around the corner."

5. Design thinkers prefer prototypes to theories.
Design thinkers are a thoughtful bunch: smart, literate and well-read. Yet they will always prefer trying something out to theorizing about it. Of the five common traits that came out in these interviews, this one is the most striking. Whether it's Czysz tinkering with the size of a gear, Pomeroy developing a new recipe through instinct, trial and error, or Gregory helping to cobble together a model of an artery probe with **Legos** and duct tape, the distance between a design thinker's idea and a testable prototype is remarkably short.

Kenton: "Our military friends wanted something like Fix-a-Flat for wounds – a can of foam that you could use to stop the bleeding in someone who's been shot. People have been working on that in pigs, but it kills the pig every time. It stops the bleeding, but it also stops the blood supply. I let my students give it a try, testing out some ideas using foam shaving cream. They all failed, but they kept pushing, and eventually one of them thought, 'Foams don't work, but **Williams-Sonoma** has these pop-up sponges that expand rapidly.' So they chopped up some sponges, we injected them, and it stopped the bleeding instantly. It looks smart now, but we started out with shaving cream and some sponges."

"One of my young protégés, **Andrew Varoski**, is a very smart guy – he went home and got his Lego set that has a little motor on it, and made a model that rotates an artery so we could cross it with UV light. There was some duct tape, of course, and cardboard. That's where that high is, getting stuff together and making it, and then you see it work the first time and you go, 'That is so cool.'"

Naomi: "I experiment every day. Most every time people come in here for dinner, I have never made the thing before. I could be looking at a book for inspiration but I don't read the recipe and copy it and then do it."

"It's all fast, it's experimentation, it's prototyping. You're working towards an end goal and you don't know what the best approach is going to be. Recently I needed to get a lot of yield off some lamb and thought, 'Okay, let's clarify some butter and put the lamb in that.' I had never done that before, or even heard of it. So I guess that's like prototyping. It was so delicious that I thought, "Oh we could do this with pork, or ... with anything!"'"

Michael: "If it's truly a new part, there's really nothing to analyze until you build it, so you've got to build something, and that comes from intuition."

"I'll give an idea to the engineer and they will start modeling while I sit with them. We get a few variations on there, minor ones. We rarely get to fully realize it, put it on the shelf and start a new product – the prototype *is* our finished product. We make the prototype, that's what goes on the bike, and that's what we race with. This is a gamble that only a start-up would take, whereas a more mature company wouldn't. That's why bigger companies move more slowly and potentially innovate less."

Finding Design Thinkers

So how can companies find design thinkers? Clearly, the typical filters of schooling, experience and recommendations aren't a very reliable guide. The traits I have described herein are the product of both education and experience, but there is no single program of study or career track that reliably produces them. None could, after all, because a diverse background is one of the key indicators for design thinking.

So the first thing to look for is an unusual CV. An orderly career progression can produce an excellent employee, but probably not a design thinker. Look for shifts in task and education that seem odd, but make sense on deeper examination. The developer who gains great expertise in traditional Web coding and then sidesteps to pursue a new technology is a good example; so is the engineer whose skill with structural analysis leads her to a side project with an artistic or entrepreneurial bent. In discussions and interviews, it's important to

determine the reasons for career shifts. Design thinkers take side-steps to find interesting challenges, even if it involves a reduction in status or pay.

During phone conversations and interviews, look beyond achievements and learn about *motivations*. Asking about a candidate's favourite or most surprising project can yield tremendous insights. Responses should convey fascination with the process, respect for their team, and an embrace of challenges. Design thinkers constantly seek opportunities to learn, so look for inquisitive candidates, and interviews that 'go away', slipping from question-and-answer into conversations about process, goals and potential projects.

Where you look is just as important. Companies that are frustrated by applicants with conventional approaches may have better luck drawing from unexpected career paths: different from the position being filled, but with related skill sets. Remember, a design thinker isn't just another competent employee, but someone who challenges the way you do business. Dr. Gregory explains, "If you're coming to me, you've already tried the obvious solutions, and they didn't work. So the solution lies outside the box." The same can be true of the obvious candidate.

One of the most productive places to seek out design thinkers is within your own organization. Motivation, skills and tenacity are important, but need the right environment to develop. For every design thinker who is able to express her unique approach and foster innovation, there are dozens who never get the chance.

Looking for these qualities within your own team and encouraging them is an outstanding way to build innovation capacity. It also makes it easier to bring the right people on board. Consciously foster the five traits described herein, and you may find that design thinkers start seeking *you* out. **R**

 Sohrab Vossoughi is the founder and president of Ziba, a leading design consultancy based in Portland, Oregon. Ziba's clients include 3M, Dell, FedEx, Microsoft and Starbucks.

Observation is an underrated skill, and one that is in great demand for those in pursuit of wicked problems.

By **Matthew May**

OBSERVE FIRST, DESIGN SECOND:

TAMING THE TRAPS OF TRADITIONAL THINKING

THE IMPOVERISHED ECONOMY in rural northern Nigeria is based on subsistence farming. The large population inhabiting the many isolated communities survives by growing, consuming and selling fruits and vegetables nourished by the many streams and rivers that flow into Lake Chad. However, the arid heat of the semi-desert geography presents a significant problem: rapid food decay. Perishables last no more than a few days before spoiling.

The solution would seem easy enough: refrigeration. But the problem is far more complex than simply being too poor to afford a refrigerator. For starters, there is no electricity. **Mohammed**

Bah Abba, a Nigerian-born adviser to the **United Nations** Development Program in Jigawa, knew that this problem was even more far-reaching. The women of this predominantly polygamist society are segregated from the men and confined to their homes—a cultural practice called *purdah*. As a result, the young girls of the family are forced to travel long distances to large markets each day to sell the food as soon as it is harvested, leaving little, if any, time for school. Furthermore, much of what is produced is either sold cheap or wasted, resulting in losses to an already meager income, or sold in a partly spoiled state, resulting in health hazards.

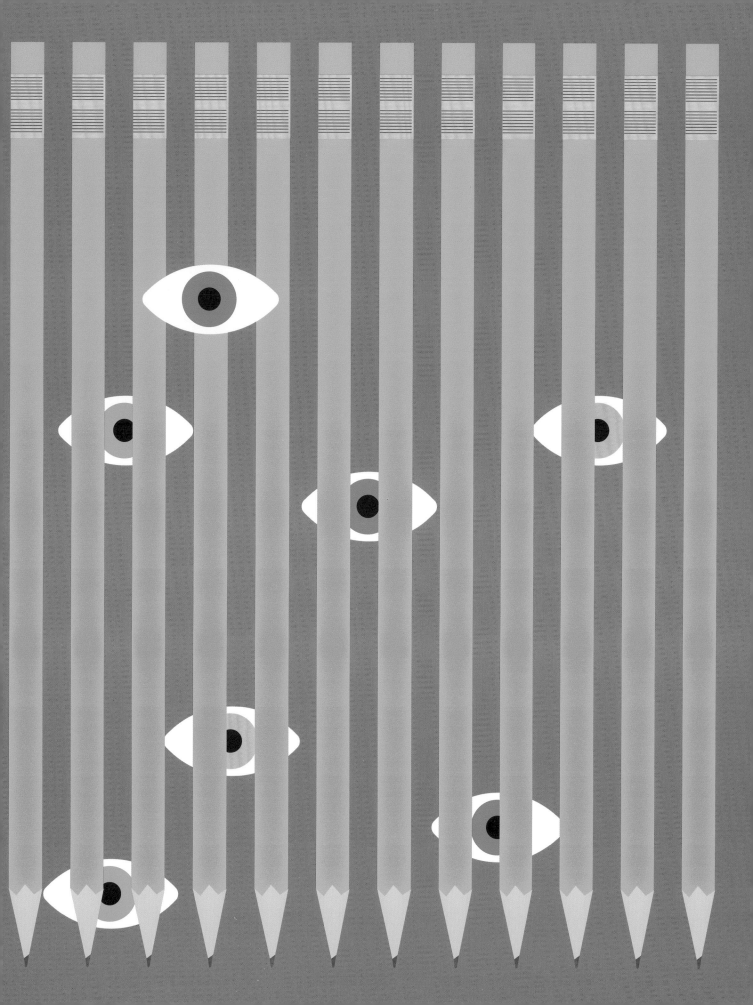

The very health, welfare and education of Abba's people was tied to the ability to keep produce fresh. Although he is neither an inventor nor an entrepreneur, he set out to find a way to address the situation, knowing that whatever he came up with would have to cost nearly nothing to construct and maintain, work without electricity, use readily-available materials and skills, and be acceptable in a conservative Muslim community.

Faced with daunting constraints, Abba thought long and hard. Then he remembered, from his youth, clay pots that had been central to the lives of northern Nigerians. Once used for everything from cooking to coffins, the pots had since been replaced by more modern aluminum and plastic containers. But they hadn't disappeared entirely, and neither had the indigenous skills used to shape them; Abba remembered the basics of traditional claywork that his grandmother had taught him. He also remembered enough of his secondary-school Science to hit upon an idea: cooling by evaporation – nature's way of dropping the temperature a few degrees.

Abba's idea for storing vegetables? Clay pots. Or rather, double clay pots. The solution couldn't be simpler: place one pot inside another; fill the gap with something moist enough to keep both pots damp – like wet river sand; and cover the inner pot with a wet cloth. As the moisture in the gap evaporates from the outer pot toward the dry outside air, the inner pot cools, with the wet sand playing the dual role of insulating the inner pot. The drop in temperature of several degrees chills the contents of the inner pot, killing potentially-harmful microorganisms that flourish only at higher temperatures. The end result: Abba's pot-within-a-pot desert cooler kept contents a dozen degrees cooler than the surrounding air. Instead of lasting for three days, eggplants stayed fresh for nearly a month; peppers and tomatoes stayed ripe for three weeks, and spinach lasted twelve days instead of one.

Today, farmers and traders use these desert coolers to store their produce at home and sell it – fresh – at a good price to the 100,000 customers of the Dutse Market. Now that they're able to sell on demand, their income levels have noticeably risen. The invention has also freed young girls to attend school, because they no longer have to worry about traveling far and wide every day. Furthermore, married women can now contribute to household income by making soft drinks – called *zobo* – and selling them from the coolers. This extra income is often used to buy soap and other essentials.

Abba's solution captured the attention of the world and received numerous awards and accolades. By 2006, well over 100,000 desert coolers had been sold and distributed through-out Nigeria, and an adapted version is now being used to preserve insulin vials for diabetic patients in remote rural areas. This is a prime example of how to solve a wicked problem with an elegant solution. But let's see how fiendishly difficult it can be to apply similar thinking to a far simpler challenge.

Please Be Kind, Rewind
Imagine it's 1991, and you are the manager of the local video store, a branch of a large chain. Back then, VCR machines didn't have the automatic rewind feature on them, and DVDs hadn't yet been invented. Your store has a problem: despite the fact that the rental contract clearly states that all videos must be rewound by the customer, 30 per cent of your customers don't bother rewinding the tape. According to comment cards, this situation is a great source of customer dissatisfaction amongst 'conscientious rewinders'.

You've tried a number of things to solve the problem: incentives, penalties, 'be kind, rewind' reminders – you've even installed a row of rewinding machines in the store. Nothing has improved the situation. You decide to ask your employees to help solve the problem, and give them four non-negotiable conditions:

1. The solution must achieve a level of 100 per cent customer rewind accountability—it's the customer's responsibility, not the store's;
2. There can be no additional burden on the customer;
3. Any solution must be of extremely low, and preferably no, cost—pennies per tape, at most; and
4. The solution must be easy to implement, without disrupting the normal operation of the store.

You tell your employees that they are free to be as innovative as they wish, as long as all conditions are met.

Why not try your own hand at solving this problem? If you're up for it, put this magazine down for 10 minutes and let your mind play with the possibilities. What you're looking for is a simple solution that fits within the limitations imposed by the four conditions and solves the problem with finality. Hint: Enlist the help of someone nearby if you like—sometimes it's easier to brainstorm together. Oh, and don't frustrate yourself trying to invent auto-rewind VCRs and DVDs—not only will you violate the conditions of the challenge, but they aren't necessary to solve the problem.

Jot down all your ideas, select the best one, and then we'll continue.

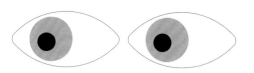

* * *

This problem is based on the true story of **Star Video**, which solved the issue many years ago. I have given this thought exercise to over 50,000 people in seminars and workshops, and the results are always the same, regardless of the makeup of the group. The solutions people come up with are remarkably similar, but the simplest solution is discovered *less than 10 per cent of the time*.

Moreover, the conditions of the challenge – which are similar to the kinds of constraints under which Mohammed Bah Abba labored – are generally ignored. I have observed that it appears to be easier, or at least more common, for people to think 'outside the box' than inside it; and that is not necessarily a good thing.

Following are the top ten solutions people provide, in no particular order:

1. A loyalty program that gives you a free rental if your rewind record is clean for a length of time;
2. A small monetary fine;
3. More rewinders in the store with good signage;
4. Splicing reminders into the tape itself;
5. A video case that doesn't allow the tape to be put back in if it hasn't been rewound, or modifying the cassette itself so that it won't fit back in the case if it hasn't been rewound;
6. Putting the movie on both sides of the tape;
7. Cutting the tape to put the ending at the front;
8. Eliminating the after-hours drop box, monitoring every customer return, and reminding them their tape needs rewinding;
9. Enlisting volunteers to rewind tapes in exchange for free rentals;
10. The all-time favorite: a drop box that rewinds the tape when it is inserted.

Each of these solutions violates one or more of the limitations I imposed, and furthermore, none solves the problem. The reason I like this exercise is that, while it is clearly less complex than the typical business problem today, it nevertheless catches people doing all the things that get in the way of good problem solving in any scenario.

Over and over again I see what I call the 'sins of solutions' being committed, and my bet is that they appeared in some form during your own attempt to solve the problem. The first thing I regularly observe is an almost immediate leap to the solution itself. Unfortunately, leaping to solutions in an instinctive way almost never leads to an elegant solution to a complex problem, because deeper, hidden causes don't get addressed.

The primary reason we tend to jump right into ideating is that most of the problems we face are routine, and don't require much more than a quick work-around. Former **CIA** analyst **Morgan Jones** uses the example below to demonstrate how our predilection for 'leaping' can interfere with our efforts. Read the description below, and then name the individual described here:

A new chief executive, one of the youngest in his nation's history, is being sworn into office on a bleak, cold, cloudy day in January. He was raised as a Catholic. He rose to his new position in part because of his vibrant charisma. He is revered by the people and will play a crucial role in a military crisis that will face his nation. His name will become legendary.

The vast majority of people conclude that it is **John F. Kennedy**, and they arrive at their answer before the third sentence. But given this description, an alternative answer could be **Adolf Hitler**. In rather non-scientific terms, as soon as our brain recognizes a piece of information as being *part of a pre-existing pattern*, we leap, subconsciously jumping ahead to a plausible conclusion, instinctively abbreviating our thinking. The unfortunate result is that very often, we fail to consider a broader range of possibilities.

How much time did you spend thinking about why people don't rewind their videos – i.e. the root cause of the problem? My guess is that you probably spent nearly all of your 10 minutes focusing solely on solutions, devoting little time to *why the problem exists* in the first place. You are not alone: after years of observing people trying to solve this problem, I can assure you that very few ever consider the 'why'. Most settle on a solution first, and then try to manipulate it to fit the conditions. When that doesn't work, the conditions quickly get downplayed or downright ignored. This is natural, because it is easier and requires less mental effort than labouring under limits – but it also prevents tough problems from getting solved.

The Perils of Pattern Recognition

Our habit of leaping to solutions is related to the 'blind spots' in the human brain—an umbrella term for the assumptions, biases, mindsets and reflexive processing that our brains automatically manufacture and utilize. Simply put, your brain is constantly filling in gaps for you.

For example, u cn ndrstntd ths sntnc wth lttl dfficlty. That's because the brain is a pattern-making, pattern-recognizing machine. All day long, unbeknownst to us – and for the most

part uncontrolled by us – our brains record every single experience, sending sensory information in the form of electrical impulses to our cerebral cortex, the 'grey matter' that houses the brain's higher functions. Each new experience is automatically stored as data in our brain. The process is additive and cumulative, and generally goes unedited. Even though the electrical impulses themselves disappear in milliseconds, their passage to the nerve cells triggers a grouping mechanism, filing new information with other like data as it comes in, which in turn creates specific and unique patterns.

Different patterns combine to make memories and perceptions, and those connections are reinforced over time, becoming mental models—mindsets, biases and paradigms. For the most part, these mental models allow us to function much more efficiently by helping us rapidly sift data and sort information into useful knowledge, according to whether it confirms or contradicts the strong patterns already embedded in our minds. There is no sophisticated term for this phenomenon; it's basically guesswork by the brain.

Neuroscientists love to demonstrate just how smart this guesswork is by demonstrating the effect of the 'physiological blind spot of the eye', which is called the *punctum caecum* in medical literature. Here's how it works.

Hold this image up a few inches from your face. Close your right eye and focus your left eye on the X. Now slowly, *really slowly*, move the book away from you. At some point the O will disappear and in its place is not a hole, but a uniform grey background, courtesy of the 'filling in' power of your brain. The O disappears the moment the image falls on a small patch of retina called the *optic disk*, an area with no receptors. This is where the optic nerve pierces the retina as it exits the eyeball and heads back toward your brain. Using what's called a 'surface interpolation' process, your brain fills in the spot with information taken from the immediate area – in this case, the grey background. Such filling-in actions pervade our problem solving, and we cannot get to deeper problem solving until we tame them.

Back to our videotape challenge: the filling-in that your brain did likely resulted in your making an assumption—that the videotape must come back to the store rewound. However, the problem simply required the tape to be rewound; the issue of *when* the tape was to be rewound was never stipulated.

By spending more time thinking about the *cause* of a problem, we are often better able to frame the issue without making unwarranted assumptions. The true root cause of the problem of un-rewound tapes is that one-third of customers are simply lazy and willing to pass their responsibility on to others. Once you understand that, you can see why previous solutions didn't work: nothing at such a low transaction level is going to change a basically lazy person into an accountable one. But you don't need to: the real issue revolves around making it impossible *not* to rewind the tape, and to do so with little or no cost and without placing additional burden on the customer.

Star Video's solution: let the tapes be rented out un-rewound. They simply put a small sticker on the video case, stating that the tape may have to be rewound before watching. The solution placed no additional burden on the customer – one rewind was all that was ever required—and that didn't change. What changed is where and when the rewind occurred. If you got a tape that hadn't been rewound, you rewound it *before* watching. The stickers were very inexpensive, and there was no ongoing burden on the store. Problem solved. If you think about it, the solution is the same one most of us employ when doing laundry: we clean the lint screen *before* our next dryer load, not after the last one.

The 'sins of solutions' I have described are interconnected, and they lead to three related thinking traps. I will describe each in turn.

Not invented here. With the video challenge, many of the top ten solutions are really just a version of what hasn't worked in the past: incentives, penalties, reminders and rewinders. The impulse to do something – anything – leads us to focus on *execution*, and as a result we ignore the facts. This causes tunnel vision that goes something like this: "Hey, if I (we) didn't come up with the solution, it won't work. They probably didn't do it right." We adopt this mindset unknowingly, shutting out another person's or group's idea immediately and without due consideration merely because *they* came up with it. The next time you're in the lobby waiting for the elevator to go up to your office or hotel room, count how many people hit the up button even though they can see that you've already pushed it. By nature, we don't trust other people's solutions.

Satisficing. In 1957, economics Nobel Laureate **Herbert Simon** published a book called *Models of Man*, in which he examined the default decision-making process by which we tend to go with the first option that offers an acceptable payoff. Simon said that

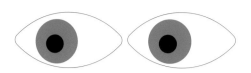

by nature we 'satisfice'—his term, combining *satisfy* and *suffice*. In other words, we have a tendency to settle for 'good enough', opting for whatever seems to expeditiously meet the minimum requirement needed to move us closer to achieving a given goal. We then stop looking for other ways, including the best way, to solve the problem. We rationalize that the optimal solution is too difficult, not worth the effort involved, or simply unnecessary.

Allow me to demonstrate. Take a look at the incorrect Roman-numeral equation below. Imagine that the numbers are movable sticks. Leaving the plus and equals signs where they are, what is the least number of sticks you need to move to turn the equation into a correct one?

$$XI + I = X$$

Most people get to the answer of 'one' almost immediately. They jump in and start moving things around right away, seeing X + I = XI or IX + I = X as good answers, and stop at that point. But these are satisficing answers, and they are only 'good enough'. If you stop and think for a moment about the optimal answer, you realize that the answer ideally would be 'zero'. Is that possible? Yes. Turn the image upside down for a moment or reflect it in a mirror: you don't need to move a single stick. The elegant solution is achievable if you stop for a moment, think about the question a bit more deeply, look at the problem from another perspective, and aim for the ideal. This, though, is the opposite of satisficing.

When we satisfice, we ignore the constraints that carry the paradoxical power to open up new and different ways of looking at things. We mistakenly pose the question "What should we do?" before asking "What is possible?" We want a solution, but we don't have the patience to wait for the optimal one, favoring implementation over incubation. We throw some resources at the problem and move on, or tweak a previous solution and fit it to the current situation. In short, we fail to look more holistically at the challenge, and the result is that we never get to the best solution.

Complicating. In looking at the list of most common video-rewind solutions, notice that many require the addition of technology not in existence, which not only violates the conditions of the challenge, but is completely unrealistic. In the interest of acting and doing, we often inadvertently leave out the most critical facts, which blocks the discovery of a simpler and more robust solution. This is the mirror opposite of the filling-in effect. Closely related to this is the tendency to simply downgrade the requirement of '100 per cent customer rewind', claiming it is impossible. Naturally, we then offer up a reduced objective – getting *more* or *most* people to rewind – and declare victory. But as anyone familiar with football will tell you, the goal is not to reach the 97-yard line.

In closing

The video challenge demonstrates that we face two major obstacles in trying to solve seemingly-intractable problems: *acting* and *adding*. Each of the top ten solutions to the video challenge can be attributed to one or both of these. How can we tame these thinking traps? The answer is surprisingly simple: become a better observer.

Mohammed Bah Abba was not an expert problem-solver, but he was an expert observer. It was his intimate knowledge and deep understanding of a multi-dimensional problem that helped him devise the desert cooler. His insight sprang from being able to *immerse himself in the problem*, observe it up close, and gain an intimate and empathic view of it. This is exactly what the best scientific investigators, detectives, and designers do. As UK urban designer **Ben Hamilton-Baillie** says, "Most of what we accept as 'the proper order of things' is based on assumptions, not observations. If we observed first and designed second, we wouldn't need most of the things we build."

Regardless of the work we do, we must constantly fight the urge to 'fill in the blanks' immediately and instead, observe first and design second. In today's world, this will become increasingly important, for the simple reason that the vast majority of the challenges we face are far more complex than getting someone to rewind a videotape. *R*

Matthew May is the founder of Edit Innovation, a Los Angeles-based creative consultancy. His most recent book is *The Laws of Subtraction: 6 Simple Rules for Winning in an Age of Excess Everything* (McGraw Hill, 2012).

While there are many roads to innovation, there is reason to believe that it often arises from the adaptation of *known solutions* to *new problem domains.*

SUPPORTING INNOVATION THROUGH ANALOGICAL REASONING

by **Arthur Markman, Kristin Wood, Julie Linsey, Jeremy Murphy** and **Jeffrey Laux**

HUMAN BEHAVIOUR CONTAINS A STRIKING MIX of habit and creativity. On the one hand, much of what we do in life is routine: we take the same route to work each day; we sit in the same seats in meetings; and we purchase the same products at the grocery store each week. On the other hand, our daily life is marked by language whereby we produce novel sentences in new contexts, communicating our thoughts with sequences of words that we have never uttered before.

Much of our everyday behaviour – both the habitual and the productive – feels effortless. In contrast, innovation settings often feel effortful and frustrating. Consequently, we are prone to think that innovation requires cognitive processes quite different from those involved in our daily behaviour.

We suggest that the feelings of frustration and effort involved in innovation settings arise from an inability to retrieve relevant knowledge that suggests a solution to the current problem. That is, a critical bottleneck in innovative problem solving is the ability of a problem solver (or team) to identify prior instances or principles that facilitate problem solving. Once we understand people's strengths and weaknesses in their ability to retrieve background knowledge, we can develop tools that improve these abilities.

The key to analogical problem solving is to find known problems that have the same structure as the problem being solved.

Cognitive Science typically takes one of two approaches to studying problem solving: **the problem-space view**, whereby problems arise when people have a goal that they must achieve and a set of steps or operations that are available to solve the problem, but the sequence of steps or the set of relevant operations is not known *a priori*; and **the background-knowledge view**, whereby a central method for solving a new problem is to find a prior problem that bears important similarities to the current problem and then to adapt the solution to the old problem to the new situation. The background knowledge might be an analogous situation or a specific case from a similar domain.

It is often easy to see the role of background knowledge in innovations retrospectively. For example, barbed wire was modeled on briar bushes that were grown in the west to provide livestock barriers, and **George De Mestral** invented Velcro after noticing burrs sticking to the fur of his dog.

The critical issue for promoting innovation is to understand how people come to recognize that the knowledge they have in one domain might be useful to solving a current problem. That is, how can we learn to use analogy proactively?

Analogical Reasoning

People have a remarkable facility to make analogies – to notice similarities between domains that, on the surface, are not alike. Involving parallel sets of relationships between domains, analogies also allow people to extend their knowledge of one domain by virtue of its similarity to another. For example, take the analogy between an inflatable mattress and water weights: an inflatable mattress is used by campers to provide a comfortable surface for sleeping. The mattress is a plastic shell that is inflated with air when it is set up. Water weights are a workout set consisting of inflatable plastic pouches connected to bars. The plastic pouches are empty when packed, but can be filled with water to allow travelers to lift weights on a trip. These devices are not particularly similar either in the way they look, their specific

functions, or the way they operate: an inflatable mattress is large, water weights are small; mattresses are for sleeping on, while weights are for lifting; an inflatable mattress is filled with an air pump, water weights are filled with a faucet.

However, these products are analogous, because *they preserve a common set of relationships*: mattresses are hard to travel with because they are heavy, so an inflatable mattress removes the heavy component and replaces it with a resource (air) that provides the same functionality and is available at the location where the mattress will be set up. Likewise, weights are hard to travel with because they are heavy; water weights replace the heavy components with a resource (water) that provides the same functionality and is available at the location where the weights will be used.

The ability to make such analogical inferences is crucial to problem solving. When solving a new problem, the problem statement is only a partial match to the known solutions; the key to analogical problem solving is to find known problems that have the same structure as the problem being solved. For example, if someone were trying to create a set of weights that could be used during travel, the representation of that problem domain would not contain any information about potential solutions. Solving this problem by analogy requires matching the *problem statement* and the *obstacles to problem solution* (create weights that can be used for travel, because regular weights are heavy) against known problems that have solutions (such as the inflatable mattress). The problem solver can then try to adapt the solution to the new domain.

Adapting solutions is itself not a trivial process. For example, to adapt the inflatable mattress solution to water weights, the weight must be reconceptualized as 'a container that can be deflated'; then, rather than filling the weights with air, they must be filled with something easily available and heavy, and so water is substituted for air. This process of adapting a solution may itself be accomplished by drawing on further analogies.

Retrieving analogous problems is not nearly as easy as recognizing an analogy between two domains that are already being compared. A classic demonstration of this point comes from a study where researchers told people a story about a general who split his army into groups and had them attack a fortress from a variety of directions, because the main road leading to the fortress had been mined. Later, people were asked to solve a radiation problem in which they had to treat a patient with an inoperable tumor with radiation. The problem: radiation sufficient to kill the tumor would also kill the healthy tissue surrounding it. The solution was to split the radiation into weaker rays and converge them on the tumor so that the tumor is the only area of tissue that receives enough radiation to be destroyed.

Despite having seen the story about the general earlier in the experiment, few people in this study recognized the similarities between the general's story and the radiation problem. People tend to retrieve information from the same domain as the current situation rather than information that is analogous to it. When solving a problem about Oncology, they are likely to think of other medical solutions, or perhaps other solutions involving radiation. Military solutions are unlikely to come to mind.

Another study demonstrated that the way that relations are described in the *base* (current state) and *target* (future state) domains affects analogical retrieval. Participants were asked to read short passages and then, a few days later, they were asked to read other passages. The passages presented later told similar stories, but using very different characters. For example, one might have been about alien creatures and a second might be about satellites. Thus, the analogous passages were different in their surface information. Given this setup, people were better able to retrieve the earlier passage they read when the relations were described using *general* language than when they were described using *specific* language. For example, the specific relations might have involved 'the alien creatures eating rocks and the satellites taking photographs', while the more general relational language might refer to 'gathering rocks and collecting photographs'. These more 'domain-general' relations made it easier for people to retrieve stories with relational similarities, despite the difference in story domains. Thus, the study demonstrates that the content of the stories had an important influence on the likelihood of analogical retrieval.

Recently, research has begun to examine analogical retrieval abilities in the context of design. In one set of studies, Mechanical Engineering students with some background in design were given descriptions of products that would be useful in later design projects. For example, they might have read about an inflatable mattress like the one discussed earlier. Later, they were given difficult design problems to solve (e.g., 'design weights that can be used for travel'). Researchers varied the level of abstractness of the description of both the base analogy in memory as well as the abstractness of the description of the

design problem. For example, the air mattress might have been described as being filled with a substance at the location where it would be used (a domain-general description) or as being inflated with air in the home where it would be slept on (a domain-specific description).

The results of this study supported previous work in that the domain-general description was more likely to be used than was the domain-specific description of the analogous solution. Interestingly, people were much better at solving the new problem using the analogous solution when the new problem was described in domain-specific language than when it was described in domain-general language. In addition, people in all conditions including the domain-general problem statements produced numerous additional solutions that were not based on the presented analogous solution.

This study suggests that another factor may be important for improving analogical retrieval: participants solved the problem in phases. In a late phase of the study, designers were given a 'function structure' that described the problem. Function structures are representations drawn by designers to convey the abstract functional relationships of a design. While they do involve some process choices about the design, they are more abstract than most descriptions of a design problem are likely to be. Giving participants a function structure that is consistent with a solution to a problem suggested by an analogy also increased people's likelihood of finding the analogous solution.

The two takeaways from this research are that a) people should re-describe their design problems in a multitude of representations and b) other representations of the design problem are likely candidates for facilitating the innovation.

Tools for Analogical Innovation

Teams are often constructed by making guesses about the relevant expertise required for the task at hand. For example, a team may have an expert in customer research who has done empirical work on customer needs as well as experts in the particular area of expertise required to create the product (e.g., Mechanical Engineering or Software Design). In addition, there might be representatives from management and marketing. A potential problem is that the analogy necessary to create an innovative solution may not exist in the heads of this group. Obviously, it is not possible to foresee the domains for which there will be analogous solutions, and consequently, experts in domains that have potentially-innovative solutions may not be represented on the team.

This suggests that when a team is created, individuals with expertise *outside of the obvious areas* might also be included to provide a perspective on other potential solutions to a problem that might not occur to those within the domains of expertise in which the problem is set. It also suggests that individuals with broader backgrounds, interests and preferences, perhaps

Inflatable Mattress:

Goal: Mattress that can be easily packed
Obstacle: Regular mattress is heavy
Solution: Replace mattress filling with air
             Air-filled mattress supports body
             Mattress can be filled on-site

Water Weights:

Goal: Weights that can be easily packed
Obstacle: Weight sets are heavy
Solution: Replace weights with water-filled bag
             Water is heavy
             Weights can be filled on site

termed as 'design generalists,' may facilitate the exploration of potential solutions that may not be readily apparent to a group composed solely of highly-specialized individuals.

In order for people to retrieve analogous examples from other domains, they must be provided with techniques for formulating problem descriptions that will capture the 'relational essence' of the problem. That is, tools must be provided to create a 'scaffold' for devising a *problem representation* that will support finding analogies.

The first element of this scaffold entails ensuring that team members have a clear understanding and representation of the problem to be solved, or, indeed, multiple understandings and representations. This might seem trivial, but there are two reasons why it is not. First, research on causal reasoning suggests that people often believe that they can give a causal explanation for more things than they are actually capable of explaining. This is called 'the illusion of explanatory depth.' Similarly, people may believe that they have a better understanding of the problem to be solved than they actually do. Thus, as a first step, teams should be encouraged to restate the problem-at-hand as explicitly as possible from multiple perspectives and contexts. This step will root out aspects of the problem that are actually unclear.

Second, many teams are confronted with problem statements that are initially vague. For example, in one study, researchers gave a design team the simple problem of designing 'a spill-proof coffee cup.' Even in real design settings, the problem statement is often not much more specific than that, and as a result, members of a team may not agree about what problem they are really trying to solve. While at the outset it can be useful for team members to consider a variety of problems that they might be solving, as the process progresses, the team must begin to agree on the problem being solved. The group may choose to consider a variety of

different potential problem statements, but it is important that they agree on the set of problems that they are solving.

The problem-statement process begins with each member of the team being given the problem statement as it has been initially formulated. Each team member is then encouraged to provide a detailed description of the problem on their own. These descriptions should be explicit about where the problem lies (particularly when redesigning existing products and services), and what methods are to be brought to bear on solving the problem. Team members must also be explicit about the critical constraints on the problem to be solved. For example, there are often cost or energy constraints on solutions. If those constraints are not made explicit initially, teams may develop innovative solutions that cannot be made practical because they violate fundamental constraints on the problem.

Before settling on a problem statement, the group should also evaluate the degree to which it is focused on existing solutions for this problem (if any). For example, a company that made film-based cameras in the 1990s might have wanted to 'make film less-expensive to produce'. Such an endeavor would likely have focused on the chemicals in film that lead to the expense and on a search for alternatives. An alternative, however, is to focus on whether there are less expensive mechanisms for capturing images; this formulation of the problem might have allowed the group to consider alternatives to image storage beyond film. Once the team agrees on the problem to be solved, the next step is to find similar problems with known solutions; that is, the retrieval of analogous problems.

There are three things that maximize the likelihood of retrieving analogous problems. First, people should be encouraged to focus on the *causal* and *relational* aspects of the problem rather than on its *surface contextual elements*. For

⫿⫿

The group may choose to consider a variety
of different potential problem statements,
but it is important that they agree on the set of
problems that they are solving.

example, a team thinking about 'how to make photographic film less expensive' could begin by thinking about improving image-storage media rather than film itself. By recasting the terms of the problem into 'image storage,' team members can then be reminded of many different methods for storing images (including photocopies and digital scanning).

A second and related tool involves encouraging the use of abstract relational terms to describe the problem. Many of the terms we use to describe problems are verbs and 'gerunds' (nouns derived from verbs). Often in technical situations, we use precise language. For example, when describing film, we may refer to particular chemical reactions brought about by exposure of chemicals to light. In the previous paragraph, however, photographic film was described as 'an image-storage medium.' 'Storage' is a more abstract relation than a description of a chemical reaction. There are many tools that can be used to promote more abstract re-descriptions of problems. For example, online language databases like WordNet can be used to find abstract terms to describe a problem.

Third, there is a tendency for tools that support innovation to present information in written format. However, there is some reason to believe that analogical retrieval is easier when information is presented in other modalities, and as a result, the tools for innovation should encourage discussion during design sessions to make the conditions more conducive to analogy finding.

As indicated earlier, in many cases the relevant domains required for solving a problem may not be familiar to members of the team. In such cases it can be useful to have tools to search broader databases for potential solutions to problems. There are many possible sources for solutions, including the patent databases and the broader Internet. For example, we can examine a concept such as 'carry' in the Library of Generic Concepts devel-

oped by the University of Texas at Austin's **Ken Barker** and **Bruce Porter** and **Boeing**'s **Peter Clark**. In this library, the specific event of 'carrying' is broken into the concepts of 'moving', 'locomoting' and 'holding.' Thus, an innovation team could focus on making any of these steps easier to carry out.

In closing

People have a remarkable facility to notice similarities between domains that, on the surface, are not alike. However, finding a relevant analogous domain to assist in problem solving requires first agreeing on the nature of the problem being solved. Once this is achieved, the 'scaffolding' we describe herein can enable innovation teams to embrace analogy and develop creative solutions to problems. **R**

Arthur Markman is the Annabel Irion Worsham Centennial Professor of Psychology and Marketing in the Department of Psychology at the University of Texas at Austin. **Kristin Wood** is the Cullen Trust Endowed Professor in Engineering and University Distinguished Teaching Professor in the Department of Mechanical Engineering at the University of Texas at Austin. **Julie Linsey** is an assistant professor in the Department of Mechanical Engineering at Texas A&M University. **Jeremy Murphy** is a Mechanical Design Engineer at Schlumberger Ltd. **Jeffrey Laux** is a professor of Psychology at the University of Texas at Austin.

Illustration by **Hennie Haworth**

UNVEILING THE MAGIC OF DESIGN: THE ROLE OF SYNTHESIS

by **Jon Kolko**

The unique skill of design is beginning to unveil itself as that moment of *synthesis* when a designer supplements his own perspective with that of another.

DESIGNERS OFTEN DESCRIBE THEIR PROFESSION as 'a way of organizing complexity' or 'finding clarity from an overwhelming amount of data'. For instance, **Jeff Veen**, founder of leading design consultancy **Adaptive Path**, has noted that "Good designers can create normalcy out of chaos." **Jim Wicks**, vice president and director of **Motorola**'s Consumer Experience Design Group, gives the name 'synthesis' to this ability to create normalcy. As he explains it, design always includes synthesis – in his case, a synthesis of market needs, technology trends and business needs.

Synthesis is defined as "the process or result of building up separate elements, especially ideas, into a connected whole." The term indicates a push towards organization, reduction and clarity. Yet despite the acknowledged importance of this phase of the design process, it continues to appear somehow 'magical' when encountered in professional practice. This is because the act of synthesis is frequently performed privately – either in the head of the designer or on scratch paper, and the *outcome* is all that is observed. The resulting sense of 'magic' is both good and bad: the idea of 'designers-as-magicians' can be intriguing, but for those who value logical and linear thinking, synthesis can appear to be a frustrating part of the innovation process.

In this article I will explore the importance of synthesis to design and will propose that it consists of two key stages: sense-making and framing. A better understanding of these concepts can lead to the emergence of a professional methodology for innovation by design.

> One should not try to escape one's past or one's emotions in an attempt to be objective, because these elements are central to making sense of complicated problems.

The Role of Sensemaking

Cognitive psychologists define sensemaking as 'a motivated, continuous effort to understand connections – among people, places and events – in order to anticipate their trajectories and act effectively'. This process occurs over time, as one or more people try to connect disparate pieces of data. In a large organization, various people may hold different pieces of data that are all critical to the success of a product or project. An individual may go through the sensemaking process by collecting these pieces of data, meeting with all of the players, and bringing the data to a central place where it can be shaped and manipulated.

This definition builds on communication theorist **Brenda Dervin**'s theory of sensemaking, which implies that we learn when we make meaning. Rather than absorbing facts as bits of predigested elements (the way we might learn Spanish by repeating vocabulary words to a tape), we make sense of complexity by *doing* things (the way we might learn Spanish by visiting Spain for an extended period.)

Consider the student who is miserably failing a required Chemistry class. He does not understand the formulas being presented, or even why he should *care* to understand them. The class is boring, always the same: the professor comes in, writes on the chalkboard, and the students take notes. Class after class, nothing sticks out, and the student has trouble remembering anything at all. Then, one day, the professor shifts to an experimental style. As class starts, he pours two liquids together and a giant fireball shoots out of the beaker. The student is intrigued. After overcoming his surprise, he considers other fires he has seen: cigarettes, candles, gas stove burners, campfires. Some of these thoughts are triggered automatically, while others are purposefully recalled through experience cognition, like "that reminds me of when John lit the napkin at that restaurant. I can't believe he was so clumsy; we almost got kicked out!"

Unwittingly, the student has made connections between the experiment and his own life, integrating the class experience into his world of knowledge and making associations between them. Because of this, he is more likely to remember the class and to view it as meaningful. If the professor is further able to hold this student's attention through the presentation of the formulas and can tie this representational information to the visual demonstration, the student will be able to forge powerful connections between a symbolic illustration of a reaction and the experiential and emotional example of it.

This is sensemaking in action – learning in a way that draws from the unique, subjective and rich experiences of an individual. The student is forming associations and connections between some formulaic and objective data, some vivid and sensory experiences in the classroom, and some of the rich, personal knowledge he has gathered through his own past experiences. One should not try to escape one's past, or one's emotions in an attempt to be objective, because these elements are central to making sense of complicated problems.

Karl Weick of the University of Michigan's School of Business has tied sensemaking directly to Organizational Behaviour and particularly to the generation of organizational knowledge. As he describes it, "Sensemaking is an issue of language, talk and communication. Situations, organizations and environments are 'talked into existence'. Sensemaking is about the interplay of action and interpretation rather than the influence of evaluation on choice." From Weick's perspective, sensemaking is a shared and communal activity that produces knowledge appropriate for action, but that is biased heavily based on the individuals involved in doing the sensemaking. That is, each group of people who have the various sensemaking conversations will 'talk into existence' a very different set of situations, organizations and environments.

Design is not entirely subjective, nor is it entirely objective, but it is both at different moments. This explains why two designers will approach the same problem in the same way and follow the same methods and steps, yet end up with two very different solutions. Sensemaking unleashes the unique aspects of the designers themselves – their 'style', or 'design sensibility' – which is the collective and additive whole of their lives.

An understanding of sensemaking is important because it taps deeply into the ability of a designer to make judgments – albeit through a highly-subjective 'frame' – about the design problem she is attempting to solve. An awareness of frames is therefore equally important to achieving synthesis.

The Role of Framing
A frame is an active perspective that both describes and perceptually changes a given situation. Even though frames define what counts as 'data', they also actually shape the data. For example, a house fire will be perceived differently by the homeowner, the fire fighters, and the insurance investigator.

A frame is often simplistically thought of as a point of view, but it is actually quite different: often, a point of view has little objectivity, so it is deemed 'biased' or 'irrelevant'. In this way, a point of view may differ from moment to moment and can be thought of as a short-term perspective. But a frame, shaped over the aggregation of thoughts and experiences, is a larger view of the world and the situations that occur in it. Like a point of view, frames too will change, but over the long term rather than the short term.

We use frames to make sense of situations. Consider the house fire mentioned above. The homeowner, obviously distraught, may react to the event in one of the following ways:

· "I just can't get a break – my life is a series of unfortunate events, and this is just another example of my bad luck";
· "Thank goodness we escaped. It's only stuff – it can all be replaced – the important thing is that we are still alive";
· "My life is basically over: all of my important things were in that house, and I don't know how I'll be able to get my life back together again".

Each of these statements will have been shaped by a lifetime of subjective experiences, and in turn, each of these *frames* will continue to shape further thinking and behaviour. If the home-

owner views his life as 'over' because his things were destroyed, he is approaching the situation from a materialistic standpoint. Through his statement, he indicates that objects and artifacts have a direct connection to his self image, and we can infer with some degree of accuracy how he might react to another situation, as this 'materialistic frame' transfers. In the realm of design, framing can be thought of as the designer's perspective when approaching a problem, both in conceptual and pragmatic terms. The frame itself describes a set of subjective constraints of the problem and is built on the types of experiences referenced during sensemaking.

Take the real-world example of designers who have been tasked with building software for use with a consumer wireless router, which will bring Internet access into a home and distribute it. The client has provided a set of practical constraints: the software must be easy to use and must provide access to all of the functionality provided by the router. The client may even have quantified the constraints in a requirements spreadsheet that says things like, "the user will have the ability to connect to the Internet," or "the user will have the ability to enable port forwarding."

The design team can frame this problem from a conceptual point of view in any number of ways. Consider the following high-level frames:

· **Ease of use**. The user should never encounter confusing things or technical jargon.
· **Power**. The software should afford complete control over the robust feature set of the router, so the user should be able to manage even the most nuanced setting on the router.
· **Pleasure**. The act of using the router software should be pleasing and emotionally fulfilling. The user should always feel a deep and emotional response to the various routing activities.

In fact, each of these frames was suggested by various designers on this project. Not surprisingly, the first one was suggested by a designer with an interest in usability engineering, the second by a more technical designer, and the third by a designer who specialized in visual interface creation. All of these frames add extra constraints to those supplied by the client, yet these extra constraints should not be viewed as a burden: they actually allow designers to move forward with their work, as they funnel the realm of 'all possible choices' into a much smaller and workable set of 'appropriate choices'.

Framing manifests itself at a much more detailed level, too. Consider the following conversation, which occurred later in the router-software design process:

Designer: "When the user clicks on the image of the router, the context menu should animate outwards and to the right, as if the user caused the menu to appear."

Developer: "But if it animates to the right, it will cover whatever content is there. Shouldn't the user be able to see all of the content on the screen?"

Designer: "Maybe, but it's more important that the user feels like he caused the menu to appear – it's important that we show a sense of causality on mouse-click."

Developer: "But it's going to cover things up; that seems completely inefficient."

Because the designer's and developer's frames are different, they result in different practical design considerations: the designer is pushing for a more aesthetically-compelling animation that reinforces causality while the developer is more interested in presenting an uninterrupted array of content. The designer is drawing on a frame of temporal aesthetics; while the developer has framed the problem in a context of utility.

A Professional Methodology Emerges

Taken together, sensemaking and framing can form the beginnings of a behavioral theory of design synthesis. These two theoretical constructs point to a structural framework upon which professional methodologies can be created – explicitly helping designers (both traditional and non-traditional) accomplish their work.

As indicated, sensemaking is a process of making meaning that is highly dependent upon unique perspectives and frames. In the realm of design, this personal process becomes a communal and collaborative process and is used to create one or more working 'design frames'. These frames are dynamic in that they change and adapt based on the circumstances of the project. Ultimately, they serve as the artificial boundaries of perspective, containing the scope of design work and acting as flexible constraints around a given design problem.

As both sensemaking and framing are normally internal mechanisms for understanding reality, design teams have begun to adopt technically rudimentary – but highly effective – methods and tools for externalizing them to create a shared 'canvas' for synthesis. Consider, for example, the following snapshot of dialogue that occurred at **frog design**. The conversation took place between interaction designers who had just completed research for a new project and were beginning the 'concepting' phase of the project. They were tasked with simultaneously understanding a very vague business problem – "create a new competitive product for baby boomers and their parents" – and defining technical requirements for a supporting technology platform decision that was going to be made quickly.

Will: "Let's try to get to a core concept and a set of high level constraints before we break for lunch."

Matt: "Yeah, why don't you take the viewpoint of the older segment."

Will: "OK, I'll be my grandpa..."

Matt: "OK; so, we know we have to use full and high bandwidth video transfer..." (draws two big circles on the whiteboard, each labeled 'mobile phone', and draws another big circle on the whiteboard, labeled 'cloud'. Draws a line from one phone, through the cloud, and back to the other phone, labeled 'video – fast and HD') "...because it's pretty awesome, and it's basically the only known piece to the whole puzzle."

Will, in character: "I don't care about awesome, but I really want to be able to watch Junior at the soccer game..." (grabs the whiteboard marker, and draws three stick figures. He labels one 'grandma', another 'grandpa', and the third 'junior') "...because all I care about is being a part of his life."

Grant, pointing at the figure labeled 'grandpa': "Yeah, but on your end, you don't want to watch on a tiny screen. My grandma can't even figure out how to use her answering machine, I think there must be messages on there from two or three years ago." (scratches out one of the Mobile Phones, and writes "TV").

Matt: "Cool, so in our list of technical issues, I know we're gonna run into some TV platform issues..." (starts a list called 'potential issues' and writes 'TV platform – unknown, Microsoft? Open Source?')

Will, in character: "If it's going to be on my TV, I need an easy way to record Wheel Of Fortune, because it's really pushing it to think I'll miss the four o'clock game shows for little Will's baseball game."

Matt: "OK, so it has auto-DVR, and if you are watching streaming video, it automatically records..." (writes 'auto-DVR = cloud storage; Boxee?')

Will, as an aside: "God forbid he misses *Wheel Of Fortune*, and God help me if I ever get old and watch game shows..."

Grant: "A DVR seems really advanced for old people."

Will, laughing: "What if there was a giant TV on wheels at the game instead of in their living room, and junior could see grandma and grandpa on the jumbotron, just like they can see him?" (draws a TV on wheels)

Grant: "Yeah, I mean, we add a low-fi version [of the software] that works with a webcam on the TV."

Matt: "So we need bidirectional video, streaming?" (writes 'tons of bandwidth. 4G?' in the 'potential issues' list).

In this brief snippet of creative dialogue, three main synthesis techniques and approaches are used:

1. Reframing from a new perspective, to empathize.
Will elects to represent the target audience, saying "OK, I'll be my grandpa". He clearly doesn't intend to become his

grandpa, but instead, actively attempts to view the design space simultaneously as both a designer and as an older, grandfather-like figure. He then participates in the discussion viewing the emerging design concept through at least three unique lenses, switching between them quickly and without much prompting:

· He contributes to the discussion as an older man, with particular wants, needs and desires related to television watching and inter-generational communication;
· He offers colourful commentary of his specific grandfather, describing the idiosyncrasies that make his grandfather unique (the need to watch *Wheel Of Fortune* every night, the prioritization of a game show over a loved one); and
· He offers contributions as a member of the design team, realizing that he can feel free to be provocative at this stage in the process by describing off-the-wall ideas (i.e., the TV on wheels) without fear of being called 'inappropriate'.

2. Creative leaps, based on personal sensemaking. Each team member offers ideas that change the nature of the problem frame:

· Matt has begun to add constraints related to technology capabilities, creating a list of more pragmatic issues and features. His role in this conversation is one that is focused on technical realism. He translates the design and feature ideas into technological barriers, opportunities and issues to warrant further discussion. This knowledge comes from his own personal interest and experience in technology; the knowledge is separate from the design problem that has been provided from the client, and it is up to Matt to bring this information to the problem;
· Will has begun to add constraints and opportunities related to his personal and intimate knowledge of his own grandfather. While his input is biased and highly subjective, he clearly has a vivid mental image of his grandfather's peculiarities and uses these to spark new design ideas;
· Grant offers statements that are practical, building on but simultaneously tempering the 'blue sky' and biased qualities of Will's ideas. Grant clearly speaks from his own experiences with the elderly, as he describes his grandmother's inability to cope with technological complexity. He, too, offers new constraints and opportunities.

3. Externalization, to create shared sensemaking. Through the use of a whiteboard, and through the shared pooling and visualization of the ideas into a single democratic (and 'unowned') diagram, the team goes through a process of shared sensemaking. Grant and Matt have never met Will's grandfather, and neither Grant nor Will would have described the technological requirements that Matt saw from his unique perspective; but all three now have a shared view of the design space, the technological implications of design decisions, and the beginning of a central, high level, very conceptual design system idea.

Thus, the normally personal phenomena of sensemaking and framing are recast in a public light in the design studio. The result:

1. The team builds a shared understanding of the data that has been gathered, and acts on that data through organization, externalization, pruning and interpretation.

2. The team collectively develops a series of artificial constraints, informed by but separate from the design space being studied and their own respective experiences. This is collaborative sensemaking in action.

3. These artificial constraints are applied in the context of the design problem as a flexible 'container', within which the designer can begin to solve a problem. This becomes the normative (accepted) frame.

Perhaps the most exciting thing this design team could do next would be to 'reframe' the situation, actively shifting the normative frame (the grandfather) and simultaneously shifting the design problem into the confines of a new container. For instance, the team might ask Will to play the role of the baseball-playing grandson, or a salesman at a consumer electronics store. Each of these new perspectives would generate richer frames of reference, resulting in richer design outcomes.

In closing
The quest for synthesis is a useful way of thinking about and approaching complicated, multifaceted problems with a repeatable degree of success. In order to get there, the designer must proceed through the stages of sensemaking and framing. Only then will she be able to embrace her own unique experiences, emotions and history while simultaneously embracing someone else's unique experiences, emotions and history.

The elements of synthesis described herein are critical to making sense of complicated problems in any realm, and in many ways they represent the unique skill of design: the ability to temporarily exchange, or at least supplement, one's own perspective with that of another in order to create value. **R**

Jon Kolko is the founding director of the Austin Center for Design and the former associate creative director at frog. He is the author of *Thoughts on Interaction Design* (Morgan Kaufmann, 2009) and *Exposing the Magic of Design: A Practitioner's Guide to the Methods and Theory of Synthesis* (Oxford University Press, 2010). You can visit his personal site at jonkolko.com or follow him on twitter @jkolko.

Every organization has deeply held beliefs about 'how things are done around here.' Leaders can use a five-step game plan to challenge – and overcome – ingrained orthodoxies.

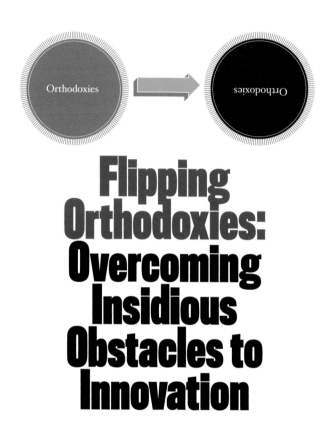

Flipping Orthodoxies: Overcoming Insidious Obstacles to Innovation

by **Bansi Nagji** and **Helen Walters**

IN 1982, JAY DOBLIN AND LARRY KEELEY walked into a meeting with the top executives at **Xerox**, including newly-appointed CEO **David Kearns** and co-founder **C. Peter McColough**. These were serious guys who were pioneering incredible advances in Physics, Optics and Engineering. Xerox was the undisputed king of copiers. Yet Jay had sacrilege in his hands: the **Canon** PC10.

Xerox's leaders were distinctly unimpressed by this chugging machine, which laboriously churned out a series of fairly poor quality copies right there in the boardroom. As Larry tells the story today, their scowls said it all: "We are busy people. Why are you showing us such an inferior product?"

They were right, the copier *was* inferior – and yet, as we know from disruptive innovation theory, the Canon design heralded the end of Xerox's dominance in this market and introduced a self-service revolution.

Without realizing it, Xerox's leaders demonstrated the threat posed by *orthodoxies* – tightly-held beliefs that guide a company's decisions. Xerox believed that copiers would always break down at some point, so the key to success was to build the world's best copier repair force, along with ever more high-tech products. Commitment to this system was woven into Xerox's culture, and a matter of pride for the firm's leadership. Canon, in

contrast, knew that it couldn't compete on these terms, so it flipped the orthodoxy to imagine and develop a totally different kind of service. In so doing, it left Xerox reeling.

Why Orthodoxies Matter, and Where to Find Them

Orthodoxies range from seemingly-innocuous biases or conventions to, at their most extreme, something that approaches religious-like devotion to a specific set of ideals. Oftentimes they are easy to see, but more often they are not explicitly recognized. Unstated assumptions that go unquestioned, they are the 'entrenched wisdom' that employees don't even think to challenge – leading to blind spots that prove to be the insidious, seductive handmaidens of stasis and resistance to change. The end result: people fall into autopilot mode and fail to imagine better ways to tackle challenges and everyday activities.

To be clear, orthodoxies are not all bad. In fact, it's a mistake to assign any kind of judgment to them, because they are neither good nor bad; they just *are* – but it is critical to be conscious of them. As the late **CK Prahalad** and **Gary Hamel** wrote in *Competing for the Future*, "All of us are prisoners, to one degree or another, of our experience." The roots of an organization's orthodoxies can be found in the 'sensible practices' through which the company first found its feet and place in the world. But if executives are not hyper-vigilant, these careful systems can calcify as the industry evolves, providing a reassuring but false sense of security, even as the sands of disruption shift beneath the organization. It's only a matter of time before a competitor spots and exploits an opportunity.

Looking for orthodoxies needs to be a conscious process throughout an organization. Admitting your organization is rife with them is a good first step toward dealing with them, even while some orthodoxies, particularly those related to security or legal issues, may never – for good reason – be overturned. But, as economist **Daniel Kahneman** wrote in the June 2011 edition of *Harvard Business Review*, "Knowing you have biases is not enough to help you overcome them." All orthodoxies need to be subject to regular scrutiny, and leadership needs to ensure that nothing becomes too sacred to be rethought. It is useful to think about orthodoxies in two distinct categories: internal and external.

Internal Orthodoxies. These are often embedded in a company's culture, so finding them is a major challenge. This means that leaders have to be ready to openly question beliefs and practices that at one point may have defined a company's success. Gauging when an orthodoxy has morphed from being helpful, inspirational and useful – and instead become an obstruction – is enormously challenging. Being conscious of internal practices and how the rest of a team approaches its work will help.

A good example of internal orthodoxies in action comes from Detroit. American car companies are known for their fierce internal cultures, which proved to be more of a millstone than a boon as the 21st century rolled around. In 2006, **Alan Mulally** left **Boeing** – his corporate home of 37 years – to join the **Ford Motor Company** as president and CEO. The company was in crisis, hammered by multiple forces, includ-

ing the deeply-ingrained manufacturing processes and systems on which the firm was run, with tightly controlled fiefdoms run by executives accustomed to running their own shows. Within three months of his arrival, Mulally hosted the year's earnings call, announcing that the company had lost $17 billion. As he explained in a later **BBC** interview, "You can run out of money really fast when you lose $17 billion a year."

Mulally – viewed with suspicion as an industry outsider unfamiliar with the mores of the auto industry – had a few ideas of his own. He recognized that tackling the entrenched belief systems and practices of his team was the most important point of order. His tactic was simple: he instituted a weekly, global meeting. At 7:00 a.m. on a Thursday, no matter where in the world the members of his senior team were located, they were on that call. Together, they looked at screens showing the progress of the various current projects, colour-coded by status: red for serious issues; yellow if a project was potentially problematic; and green for projects that were on track.

The only problem? None of Mulally's lieutenants was prepared to admit that they had a problem. The screens were a sea of uniform green; given the $17 billion loss, there was clearly a disconnect somewhere. The internal orthodoxy of 'managers getting work done on their own, often in secret', had morphed from being the way things were done at Ford to hampering the potential survival of the company itself. Mulally abruptly stopped the meeting and asked outright for his lieutenants to come clean, to reflect reality so they could get on with the business of fixing it. Silence prevailed, with eyes pointed at the floor. But the next week, **Mark Fields**, head of Ford's Americas division, showed a chart concerning the Canadian launch of the Ford Edge. The chart, featuring everything from technical readiness to the business plan to proposed schedules, had transformed into a sea of red.

Everyone on the call fell silent. "Now we'll see what our new leader is going to do," Mulally realized the managers were silently thinking. And so he clapped. He clapped his hands, congratulated Fields on the visibility he'd afforded the team, and asked him what they could all do to help. This one moment, he says, had a galvanizing effect. Within minutes, various department heads were volunteering solutions and manpower. The following week, the 320 charts considered in the meeting had turned into what he describes as "a rainbow of honesty."

Ford executives had given up their long-held orthodoxy of tightly managing information in order to show what was really happening. The exercise also helped them to overcome two more orthodoxies: that asking for help is a sign of weakness, and that only good news gets discussed in public. And while Ford's turnaround can clearly be attributed to more than this one culture-changing shift in thinking, in April 2011, the company posted its best first-quarter profit since 1998.

External Orthodoxies. Industries and markets can be just as beholden to the 'way things are done' as companies are. That's why outsiders so often seem to be able to come along and upend

COMMON INTERNAL ORTHODOXIES

Not Invented Here
Characteristic: Constant need to reinvent the wheel
Conquerer: **Netflix** famously overcame an ongoing issue with its recommendation engine by challenging anyone from the public to solve the problem. It worked.

That's The Way We Do Things Around Here
Characteristic: Resistance to change
Conquerer: **Ford**. When **Alan Mulally** became CEO, he knew one of his major challenges was to change the entrenched systems by which his managers worked.

We Work from 9 to 5
Characteristic: Static, inflexible structure
Conquerer: **Best Buy**. With its "Results-Only Work Environment," it became the poster child for an organization that allows its employees to dictate their own hours.

Quantity over Quality
Characteristic: Strict rules for sales/support staff to expedite business
Conquerer: **Zappos** takes customer service very seriously, training the loyalty team to take the time to make sure a customer's needs are met – no matter how much time it takes.

COMMON EXTERNAL ORTHODOXIES

Airlines
Orthodoxy: Charge business travelers the highest fares
Conquerers: **Southwest**; **RyanAir**. Southwest flipped numerous orthodoxies, including the system by which the rest of the industry operated. Its no-frills approach has been mimicked both within the U.S. and globally.

Rental Cars
Orthodoxy: Focus on business travelers
Conquerers: **Zipcar**; **BMW DriveNow**. Many rental car companies focused on business travel and are located at airports. Zipcar had a different idea, focusing on urban centers and betting on consumers who might need to rent a car for a day (or even an hour or two). In April 2011, BMW and **Sixt** launched DriveNow, a car-sharing pilot scheme in Munich, Germany.

Government
Orthodoxy: Baffle with bureaucracy
Conquerers: **Gov 2.0** initiatives; **Arab Spring**. While it's still too early to estimate the true impact of social media on the various countries that experienced political upheaval in 2011, it's plain to see that these tools are being applied in ever more innovative ways, preventing business-as-usual and forcing office holders to face up to long-held orthodoxies.

or disrupt an entire industry, simply by having a fresh way of looking at things. And that's why Harvard Professor **Clayton Christensen**'s theories of disruptive innovation retain such resonance, years after they were first published.

External orthodoxies were already rife within the American airline industry by the time **Southwest Airlines** started flying its planes in June 1971. Founder **Herb Kelleher** was determined to take on the incumbent airlines – the likes of **Braniff**, **Trans-Texas** and **Continental**. It's not like the competitors didn't see Southwest coming. In fact, Southwest faced 31 separate judicial proceedings from established players looking to shut down the young upstart in its first five years of operation. Yet that neither deterred Kelleher nor stopped Southwest from establishing itself as a major player. It did so by refusing to play along with the accepted industry orthodoxies, insisting on doing things its own way.

Back then, the airlines all ran very similar kinds of businesses: they flew passengers in multiple types of planes via major hubs,

then on to their desired airport. The airline was king, and customers flew according to its rules. Kelleher wanted to do things differently. He refused to stock his fleet with multiple aircraft, instead buying only one type of plane (the Boeing 737) to cut down on maintenance problems and make sure he had access to the right plane parts wherever he needed them. He refused to design a 'hub and spoke' geography of routes, instead developing a system whereby not only did all planes fly directly 'from point to point', but customers bought one-way flights each time. And he utterly rejected the dismissive attitude shown by other airlines towards their customers, putting Southwest passengers at the center of a unique type of service, where the emphasis was on fun.

The unorthodox system sparked a revolution in the airline industry, but at the time, people thought Kelleher was nuts. "It wasn't just the other airlines that were contemptuous of what we were doing. The New York financial community was, as well," recalled Kelleher in a 2002 interview. "After maybe nine or 10 years, [an analyst] with **Credit Suisse First Boston** got up at an

Asking "why not?" isn't simply the prerogative of whiny children: it's a useful exercise to ensure you're not slipping into bad habits.

investor seminar and said, "For 10 years we've been telling Herb Kelleher how to run Southwest Airlines, and for 10 years he's been telling us to bug off. Since they're the most profitable airline in America, how about if we all bug off?'"

Many of Southwest's flips of the entrenched airline industry are still firmly in place. Multiple competitors have tried to mimic the company's success, with rivals such as **JetBlue** (started by Southwest veterans) and **RyanAir** in Europe trying similar tactics. Still others, such as **United**'s **TED**, tried and failed. The company currently flies 548 Boeing 737 aircraft among 72 cities, and 2010 marked its 38th consecutive year of profitability.

How to Flip Orthodoxies
Overcoming orthodoxies rarely happens in isolation or as a one-off exercise. They are generally far too pervasive and deeply rooted to overturn simply by decree or exhortation. Rather, you have to design initiatives in such a way that you can identify, discuss and challenge key orthodoxies.

Following is a five-step game plan to make sure you don't let orthodoxies block your innovation agenda, or allow your organization to be blindsided by a competitor imagining a different reality.

1. Be Ruthless About Finding Them
Leaders need to be extremely open-minded when it comes to confronting truths that might make them feel uncomfortable. Even naming orthodoxies can be an illuminating process, not least to note who agrees with whom, but also to see which suggestions spark the most energetic response. Oftentimes, rigorous deconstruction of iconic stories from within your organization or industry – particularly the failures – might yield surprising results. Younger and newer employees will likely experience your orthodoxies most acutely – so ask them to help. Meanwhile, identifying orthodoxies can help to frame an innovation project and can prove to be a useful diagnostic tool that can smooth the often bumpy path of the process. Consciously pushing back against orthodoxies can help leaders set a truly groundbreaking agenda. The exercise can also prove useful later in a project's evolution, when those involved begin to back away from trying something new or scary. By devising a list of identified, common orthodoxies that need to be overcome upfront, you can remind everyone involved in a project that they've made a commitment – and they need to stick to it.

2. Ask 'Why Not?' on a Regular Basis
One way to challenge preconceived ideas is to keep a simple mantra in mind at all times. Asking "why not?" isn't simply the prerogative of whiny children, it's a useful exercise to ensure you're not slipping into bad habits or missing important opportunities. An alternative way of thinking about this is to turn every response into a version of "yes, and…" In her recent book, *Bossypants*, comedienne **Tina Fey** described how this mantra has been key to her own success. "Whatever the problem, be part of the solution. Don't just sit around raising questions and pointing out obstacles. We've all worked with that person. That person is a drag," she writes. Asking why something might not be feasible, viable or possible may well elicit some reasonable answers, but the exercise will allow leaders to think differently about received wisdom and 'the way things are done round here', which can be the most stifling orthodoxy of all.

3. Widen Your Field of Vision
These days, it's no longer enough just to consider the potential orthodoxies of existing industries or organizations. Look in unfamiliar settings to see where orthodoxies have been flipped – and to get ideas that you might try in your own field. The 'bottom of the pyramid', for instance, is an excellent place to look for inspiration. This environment is teeming with fast-moving ideas, born of necessity, that are flipping the orthodoxies of western economies to create new business models. **General Electric** CEO **Jeff Immelt** has embarked on an aggressive course of implementing the practice of 'reverse innovation' – taking ideas from emerging markets to figure out how to 'trickle up' their inherent ideas to the developed world. Meanwhile, concepts such as mobile phone-based banking don't just serve a new customer in a new way; they challenge the way those of us based in mature economies do things, too.

4. Be a Credible Heretic
To challenge orthodoxies effectively, it's important to understand the potential ramifications of change. **Jeff Semenchuk**, former head of global innovation at **Pfizer Consumer Healthcare** and founder of **Citigroup**'s Global Growth Ventures (currently a senior adviser to **Monitor Group**), puts it this way: "You have to be a credible heretic. You have to acknowledge the orthodoxy and the good reason it existed in the first

place, and then you have to be willing – in an open, positive, sometimes playful way – to challenge that." Another point to bear in mind: orthodoxies can only be effectively flipped from the top of an organization. That's why **Virgin** CEO **Richard Branson** specifically designed his role to allow him to challenge his industry's orthodoxies. "My senior management team, led by CEO **Stephen Murphy**, keeps everything moving along," he says. "My role allows me to dive in and out of situations, ensuring we keep challenging orthodoxies in every sector we're competing in." Of course, Virgin has had some notable failures – in markets from weddings to soft drinks – but Branson keeps pushing and testing. He embodies the spirit of heresy that has seen him build a business based on brands that challenge orthodoxies.

5. Recognize Those Who Dare

Recognizing those who dare to flip orthodoxies can send a powerful, positive signal to the rest of your organization. In recent years, one form of incentive – prizes – has become prevalent as a tool to spark innovation. By opening up a challenge to a wider group than might participate internally, organizations are often able to challenge the industry orthodoxies that plague the incumbents. The Ansari X Prize, for instance, offered $10 million to the first private sector group to fly a reusable spacecraft into space twice in two weeks, and was won in 2004 by a group led by the legendary engineer, **Burt Rutan**. Since then, over $100 million has reportedly been invested in an aerospace industry that had barely existed before.

In closing

Leaders everywhere need to dare to imagine a different future that encompasses more than just business as usual. If the process of overturning orthodoxies is not deliberately adopted by the senior leadership of a company, old patterns are certain to re-emerge.

None of this is easy. There is a fine line between a winning formula and hardwired assumptions that constrain a business. But through careful assessment and conscious choices, you can discern between self-imposed limitations and the true cornerstones of your enterprise. **R**

Bansi Nagji is President of Monitor Group and leader of the firm's innovation practice.
Helen Walters is the Ideas Editor at TED. She is the former editor of innovation and design at *BusinessWeek*.

Embracing Openness:

Designing for the Loss of Control

A new mantra has emerged that leaders will ignore at their peril: we must embrace and design for the loss of control.

by **Tim Leberecht**

OPENNESS HAS BECOME A MEGA-TREND for innovation and the topic *du jour* for organizations of all kinds. Granted, it has been on the agenda ever since **Henry Chesbrough**'s seminal *Open Innovation* came out in 2003, and since then, others have elaborated on the concept from different perspectives. However, little has been said about what this 'new openness' means for the realm of design. In this article I will reframe *openness* from a design perspective.

My interest in this topic was piqued by a particularly powerful phrase coined by **salesforce.com**'s Chief Scientist **JP Rangaswami**, who stated in a recent presentation that we now need to "design for the loss of control." His point – made at last year's Enterprise 2.0 conference in Boston – was IT-specific, arguing that the combination of pervasive digital infrastructure, software-as-a-service, cloud computing, social software and smart phones have enabled employee- and customer-driven solutions to a degree that renders top-down IT systems obsolete. However, this new paradigm has implications far beyond IT.

For one thing, employees – who are facing an increasingly hybridized work/life proposition – are eager to do what they are passionate about, and they will increasingly find the digital spaces and tools that allow them to do this most effectively, without having to ask anyone for permission. Companies have to come to terms with the fact that the traditional model of managerial resource allocation and coordination (mainly coerced through extrinsic motivation in the form of payments, promotions, demotions, etc.) has become outdated and no longer reflects the social fabric of today's workforce.

Customers, too, are seeking relationships with brands that go beyond the merely transactional. Empowered through ubiquitous access to information and radical transparency, through an abundance of choices on the Web, as well as the ability to contribute and tap into social networks (and thus social capital) in real-time and on-the-go, they expect organizations to offer engagement and collaboration models that match the more distributed and multi-layered mechanisms of value creation through social media.

What can leaders do besides bemoan this loss of control and passively observe while the new centrifugal forces of the social, real-time Web disrupt their traditional business and engagement models? As it turns out, plenty.

The Power of Pull

In *The Power of Pull*, **John Hagel**, **John Seely Brown** and **Lang Davison** argue that in our 'pull economy', *influence* is replacing *authority* as the new currency, and the best way to gain influence is to give up control. In doing so, firms position themselves to develop what Hagel *et al* call "levers of access, attraction and achievement" that provide the creation spaces and tools for employees and customers alike to design their own destiny, create their own meaning, and thus convert their own skills and passions into productivity and loyalty.

Indeed, a deliberately-designed loss of control may grant companies the only remaining and arguably the most critical competitive advantage: access. As long as an organization enables and facilitates knowledge flows, ideas, passions, skills and experiences, it will have access to them. In fact, if it fully leverages the 'powers of pull', these assets will actually gravitate towards it.

What the loss of control does is, it enables the creation of more weak ties in a company's network (inside and outside of the

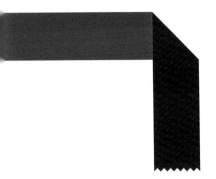

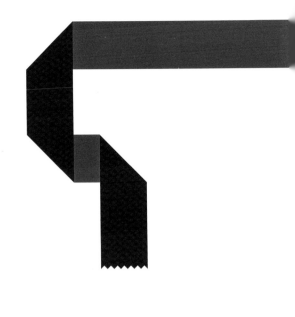

A deliberately-designed loss of control may grant companies the most critical competitive advantage: access.

organization), and as social network research has shown, weak ties are more conducive to transporting foreign ideas, knowledge and skills, because they move faster from one node to the other as the network becomes more accessible and nimble on its fringes. The further you get away from the core of your network, the less control you (may want to) have.

You could argue that designers have been designing creation spaces, feedback mechanisms, and other participatory experiences for some time now. They certainly have, but perhaps without fully recognizing or deliberately orchestrating the amount of *loss of control* that their designs represented. The time is ripe to understand these efforts as part of a broader shift and to consolidate them into a series of formats that, going forward, can serve as blueprints for *designing for the loss of control* across different organizational functions and disciplines.

Frequently, these solutions will involve de-institutionalizing decision-making by removing the intermediary. In many cases, this may imply an act of democratization, but it is also important not to see this as a zero-sum game. Control is not just shifting from one hand to many; rather, it is dissolving and defragmenting and turning into something far more valuable: social capital that resides in the public domain and is no longer controlled by anyone.

The Tools of Openness
The tools that propel this new mode of collaboration and value creation are emergent and informal, and they typically involve a significant amount of tacit ('unwritten') knowledge. Following are ten tools that can be used to embrace and create value from the loss of control.

1. Crowdsourcing. Also called 'open ideation', crowdsourcing is based on the assumption that the best ideas for new products,

services, and business models may come from outside of your organization or from people inside your organization who are typically (by function or hierarchy) excluded from the ideation process. Like all open innovation efforts, crowdsourcing redistributes control from an elite group of thinkers and doers to a broader group of self-selected participants. By broadening the funnel, companies can harness the accumulated or aggregated knowledge of these voices.

Crowdsourcing is usually focused on ideas and insights but can also cover a wider array of collaborations with external parties throughout all stages of the innovation cycle. Among the companies who use this tool: **Dell**, **Starbucks**, **P&G** and **Nike**. Nike partners with **Creative Commons** and **Best Buy** for GreenXchange, a platform that promotes "the creation and adoption of technologies that have the potential to solve important global or industry-wide sustainability challenges." Likewise, **TED** – the non-profit devoted to "Ideas Worth Spreading"– has expanded its reach through 'TEDx', independently-organized TED events, without compromising the exclusivity of its brand. In other examples, **Victors & Spoils** brought crowdsourcing to the world of advertising, and **IDEO** recently launched a crowdsourcing platform, OpenIDEO, inviting the public to join in on creative challenges that tackle social issues through design. All of these companies not only make ideas accessible to more or less open publics (to some extent, giving up control over IP) but also commit to making the follow-up on these ideas (at least partially) transparent, giving up some control over agenda-setting and strategic planning.

2. Open Design Research. frogMob, developed by **frog**, is a tool for crowd-sourced design research, based on the idea that "everyone can be a researcher for a day, just by paying a little more attention to the world around them." frogMob uses guerilla photography and stories to take a quick pulse on global trends, behaviours and artefacts. Launched internally at first – tapping into frog's eight global studios – it has since expanded to a broader public. Through frogMob, designers are able to mobilize not only their internal network around a specific assignment, but also external contributors on an *ad hoc* basis, in a short amount of time – sort of like a Flash Mob. frogMob allows for rapid design research for clients who ask for a 'trend scrape' that identifies patterns and offers unexpected inspiration. The key is to tap into existing knowledge flows in a nimble way that doesn't require too much commitment from the participants and eliminates bureaucratic hurdles.

3. Open Strategy. Crowdsourcing can also take the form of a combination of online and offline collaboration, as demonstrated by **NPR** [National Public Radio] and its Think-In on the future of digital media. Supported and facilitated by frog, NPR hosted an open strategy session, bringing together 60 thought leaders at the intersection of media and technology to explore new approaches to content creation, distribution and funding for NPR and its member stations. The Think-In harnessed the collective expertise and creativity of an exceptional group of entrepreneurs, executives and innovators, and it developed concepts that NPR incorporated into its organizational roadmap. The event was augmented through live-commentary and streaming via various social media channels. This 'social augmentation' made the workshop accessible to a broader audience, which – like the on-site participants – felt so genuinely passionate about NPR that they committed some serious time to this collective brainstorming. Such passion for brands could also be put to work through a more radical version of a Think-In: a 'brand hijack' that convenes customers and other interested parties to explore new directions for a brand – yet with the twist that the brand itself would not participate (but may have the option to co-opt the results of the session afterwards).

4. Open-Source Humanitarian Software. In the software space, open-source projects have long been an established form of open innovation. Random Hacks of Kindness (RHoK), founded by teams from **Google, Microsoft, Yahoo!, NASA** and the **World Bank**, uses open-source methods to 'hack for humanity', describing itself as "a community of developers, geeks and tech savvy do-gooders around the world, working to develop software solutions that respond to the challenges facing humanity." The group runs Hackathons, inviting the best and brightest hackers from around the world to volunteer their time to tackle disaster relief issues through software applications. The Hackathons are designed as so-called 'codejams' – fast-paced competitions that give the participants a set amount of time to solve the challenges they are given. At the end of a two-day hacking marathon, a panel reviews the submissions and the winners walk away with prizes, as well as the right to call themselves 'RHoKstars' ever after.

5. Open-Source Social Networks. Defense contractor **Lockheed Martin** built its own networking site called Eureka Streams and released it, open-source, for the public to use. As indicated on a recent *Fast Company* blog post, "The company's management recognized that an internal social networking tool could have all sorts of procedural benefits for a large and geographically-disjointed organization. Essentially it lets 'knowledge workers' inside the company find and talk with other experts who may have valid input to particular projects, but who would otherwise have zero oversight or input."

Dow Chemical has also set up its own social network, in this case to help managers identify the talent they need to execute projects across different business units and functions. Dow has even extended the network to include former employees – a smart move, because closed networks are of diminishing value. A recent *McKinsey Quarterly* report argues that, "In the longer term, networked organizations will focus on the orchestration of tasks rather than the 'ownership' of workers" and advises executives to "make the network the organization."

6. Open Branding. In the spirit of transparency, design firm **Continuum** has been revealing parts of its creative process to the public. One of their recent challenges was to create a brand identity for the **Design Museum Boston**, a nomadic institution that exhibits mainly in the virtual space. For six weeks, Continuum partnered with design blog **Core77** on a blog series that revealed the firm's process and progress as it took on the challenge. Readers were invited to comment, and may or may not have influenced the creative work. Making a creative project transparent – even somewhat haphazardly – is an interesting experiment that is worth trying. The more radical experiment, of course, would be to completely turn creative control over to the 'smart crowd' and have the creative team steered by a disperse group of 'remote creative directors'– which moves beyond just input comprised of insights and ideas.

Even-more radical models are imaginable. For example, sharing a company's entire communications with the public, which some corporate Twitter accounts can be seen as a precursor to. This would be radical transparency personified, and an experiment with unpredictable outcomes: would the benefit of enabling reciprocal, collaborative relationships outweigh the risk of reputational landmines and IP violations? In the end, is it IP as proprietary 'knowledge stocks', that serves as a company's greatest asset, or is it rather the ability to attract talent and grant access to knowledge and skills? Because transparency is a prerequisite for authenticity, another possible benefit could emerge: the more transparent and vulnerable a brand is, the more authentic it will appear.

7. Open Social-Capital Enablers. Small, ad hoc start-ups are popping up that leverage the principles of self-organization – which **Clay Shirky** so aptly described in *Here Comes Everybody* – to rethink 'capital' and reinvent human resources allocation in order to tackle global issues. Originated from the Sandbox network, an exclusive network of young innovators and entrepreneurs under 30, this movement calls itself "Emergent Transformation." **Max Marmer**, one of its masterminds, writes on its group blog: "Lately we have been observing an accelerated movement of ventures that are revolutionizing how we take initiative on a global scale. They can be mostly found in the areas of education, innovation, collaboration, networks, entrepreneurship and human development – the spaces that will likely dominate the future of value creation in our society. These ventures are leveling the global resource play, unleashing unused and undeveloped human capital and leading to a socioeconomic transformation."

For example, **Supercool School** is an online school platform that strives to give people worldwide access to education by building a new global infrastructure of live online schools. And **Assetmap** is an online platform that helps individuals discover and leverage resources directly from the community around them, using the methodology of Asset Based Community Development (ABCD). According to Marmer, "One huge differentiator that sets these projects apart is their emphasis on 'human potential' or 'social capital' rather than economic capital. The hope is that by creating a clearly-defined space for these organizations to work in, there will be more opportunity to share social capital, enabling the achievement of complimentary aspects of mutually-shared visions."

8. Open Conferences. The antidote to the conventional conference format, 'un-conferences' radically disrupt the delineation between curator and attendee, speaker and audience. Facilitated face-to-face, these participant-driven conferences are centered on a specific theme or purpose, but the attendees are the experts. Many organizations and groups have begun to use un-conferences to capture and externalize the full breadth of expertise assembled at conferences. Some conferences prefer to incorporate only some un-conference formats into their program – such as participant-driven sessions that are developed on site in real time.

9. Open Conversations. Modernista did it; so did Skittles and ad shop **Crispin Porter + Bogusky**. All of them use their corporate Web sites as social hubs that curate what is being said about their brand rather than staging what their brand has to say. These efforts are attempts to at least co-opt the conversation on the social Web before brand-specific aggregators could benefit from being parasites of the brand's social universe.

In other words, what if a brand faced unexpected competition from a third-party site that provided a much more comprehensive and easier-to-access curation of Skittles conversations than the brand itself? Or if **McDonalds** suddenly saw itself confronted with a site aggregating blogs, videos, news and tweets, all *about* but not *by* McDonalds? Think of this as the logical extension of the company profiles that already exist on **LinkedIn** and **Glassdoor.com**, which aggregate individual member data into a fairly transparent view of companies, including employee information, salary information and recent news. Indeed, third-party 'brand curators' might realize that brands live in the social commons, and that whoever builds the right aggregation mechanism and establishes the most popular channels to reach a mass audience will 'own' the branded conversation on the Web. Take a look at how **Get Satisfaction**'s "community-empowered customer support" plays this. You could also spin the idea of a 'social homepage' a bit further and not only curate the social Web conversation about your brand but actually give away your whole homepage to third parties and to public service announcements, stories or art. The take-away: Giving up control = gaining social currency.

10. Open HR. Of all the critical business functions, HR might be the one with the greatest potential for innovation. With dynamic, quickly-accessible expertise replacing static piles of proprietary knowledge, and companies moving from organization-centric to network-centric *modi operandi*, HR can become an enabler of assets by fostering a culture of openness and participation that includes new tools and methodologies that radically alter the relationship between employee and firm.

A recent study by **Birkman International** that surveyed nearly 20,000 HR professionals found that 83 per cent of respondents see great potential in social media-based HR solutions, particularly when it comes to improving communication, learning and knowledge sharing. At frog, we have launched frogForward, an open-ended, conversational and social performance management app that allows our employees to provide 360-degree feedback any time throughout the year (not just during review cycles). Goal-setting is entered as a stream, and the feedback – peer, managerial and employee feedback – can be shared openly or privately. This new approach reflects the changing realities of work performance, from a task-driven control and coordination approach with quantifiable goals to a holistic view that is more situation-and context-aware, gives the employee significantly more control of the process, and considers intangibles such as tacit knowledge, social intelligence and relationship-building. frogForward shares this approach with **Rypple** [founded by Rotman MBA '00 **Daniel DeBow**] an ad-hoc social network that provides simple, direct, anonymous and ongoing customer and employee feedback.

Stepping back, we can see that all of these initiatives – whether they apply to brand, CRM, product development, R&D, customer service or HR – exhibit some shared characteristics:

- Easy access
- Open platforms that harness the creativity and expertise from people outside of the organization or untapped sources inside
- Open-ended formats that can evolve as the problem statement changes
- Ample room for participation and emergent self-organization
- Easy mechanisms for tinkering and hacking (e.g. through open-source formats)
- Small formats that can be easily shared

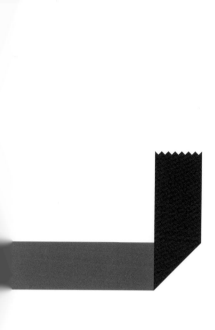

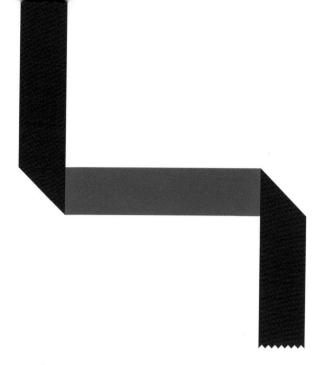

- Strong incentives (ideally intrinsic motivation or social currency)
- Real-time visibility (through shareable content)
- Tie-ins to dormant or active social networks and
- Distributed decision-making.

Designing for Variance

The most urgent manifestation of a loss of control is, of course, a crisis. At a time when terrorism, financial downturns and natural disasters are a regular occurrence, designing for crisis has become a default skill, forcing managers and designers alike to make contingency planning an integral part of the experiences they create. Often, this means developing 'exit scenarios' that are flexible enough to provide a structure for emergent solutions in response to emergencies – in other words, an easy way out. And *in*, because exits are entry points, as well. If you design ways *out* of the system, they might as well serve as ways *into* the system.

This insight provokes a different notion of openness – understanding it as a system where *exit* and *entry* are identical. In this line of thinking, an ecosystem on the social Web could be seen as a system in permanent 'crisis': always in flux, its composition and value are constantly threatened by a multitude of forces, from both the inside and the outside.

What if we understood 'designing for the loss of control' as 'designing for structures that are in a permanent crisis'? Crises are essentially disruptions that shock a system; they are deviations from routines, and the very variance that the advocates of planning and programs (the 'Push' model) so despise – at their own peril, because they fail to realize that variance is the mother of all meaning; it is variance that challenges the status quo, pulls people and their passions towards you, and propels innovation. In the end, *designing for the loss of control* means *designing for variance*.

One system in permanent crisis that contains a high level of variance is **WikiLeaks**. The most remarkable thing about this site appears to be the dichotomy between the uncompromised transparency it aims at and the radical secrecy it requires to do

so. The same organization that depends on the loss of control for its content very much depends on a highly-controlled environment to protect itself and keep operating effectively. Ironically, secrecy is also a fundamental prerequisite for the appeal of WikiLeaks' "there are no secrets" claim. Simply put: there is no light without darkness. And there is no WikiLeaks without secrets.

Applied to systems and solutions design, this means that *total openness* is the antidote to openness: when everything is open, nothing is open. In order to design openness, one of the first decisions designers have to make is therefore to determine *what needs to remain closed*. This is a strategic task – making negative choices for positive effects. You need to build enough variance into a system to make it 'flow' and yet retain *some* control over the underlying parameters – access, boundaries, authorship, participants, agenda, process, conversation, collaboration, documentation, etc. Only if you maintain the fundamental ability to at least manage (and modify) the conditions for openness, will you be able to create it. To design for the loss of control, you must control the parameters that enable it.

In closing

From this point forward, designing for the loss of control will quickly rise to the top of the list of management challenges. In the new open environment, commitment is fickle, reputation volatile, and loyalty scarce. Rather than bemoan this fact, smart leaders will embrace the new openness and realize that, as **Charlene Li** has pointed out, they never really *were* in control: what they are actually being forced to give up is their *need* for control. **R**

As Chief Marketing Officer of NBBJ, **Tim Leberecht** helps spark and nurture new thinking (and great architecture and design) for companies around the world. Previously, he was the Chief Marketing Officer at the design and innovation firm, frog. He writes the iPlot blog, and his thoughts on business and society have appeared in outlets such as CNET, *Fast Company*, *Forbes* and *Fortune*. He is the founder and producer of the Reinvent Business hackathon and serves on the World Economic Forum's Global Agenda Council on Values.

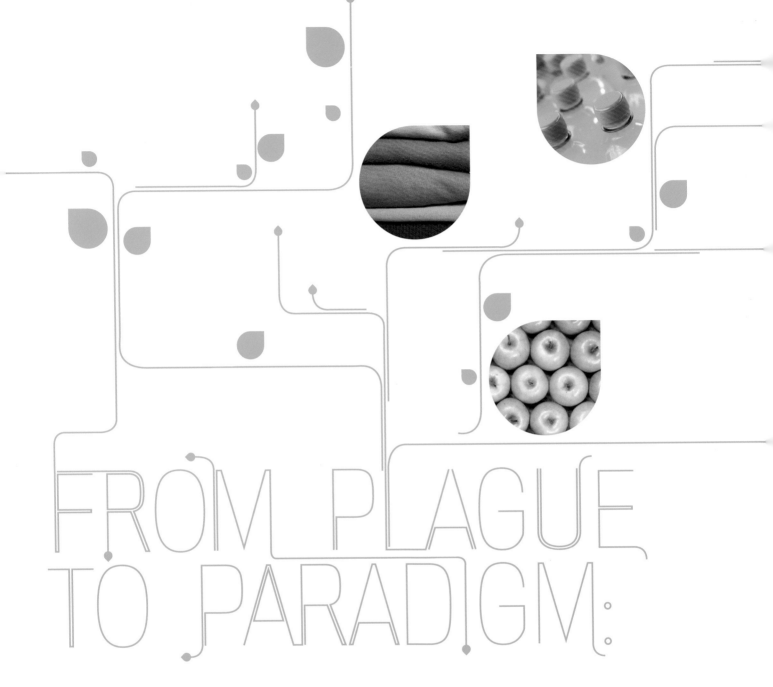

FROM PLAGUE TO PARADIGM:

DESIGNING SUSTAINABLE RETAIL ENVIRONMENTS

by **Steve Bishop** and **Dana Cho**

Considering a shopper's context is the key to understanding their motivations and making green products and services relevant to them.

NOT THAT LONG AGO, the word 'consumption' was used to describe an infectious disease. Today, it's a powerful economic force that drives our economy. 'Green' used to be a colour, but it too has taken on new meaning, representing an increasing demand for a lifestyle that does not compromise our environment. While these two forces have traditionally been at odds, more and more consumers and retailers are showing that they can be aligned for the benefit of all.

We recently set out to explore the opportunities for environmental sustainability that exist at the very heart of any consumer society: the retail space. What we found was an unexpected disconnect between the retailers and consumers that are pursuing sustainability. Frustrated retailers claim, "I want to sell green products, but my customers aren't asking for them." Others have tried, failed, and concluded that it doesn't work. On the flip side, anxious shoppers are saying, "I want to buy green, but there are too few options available."

Evidence supports both claims: 87 per cent of people say they are seriously concerned about the environment, yet studies indicate that sustainability does not often factor in their purchasing decisions. With such strong intentions coming from both sides, why does this disconnect exist?

What is missing from the equation is a focus on context. As a consumer, I may understand the effects of chemical cleaners on our water supply and resolve never to buy them again; but when I'm at the store with both kids, 30 minutes before dinnertime, and I

need clean clothes before my in-laws arrive tomorrow, my impact on the water supply is the last thing on my mind. Surveys like the one referenced above provide valuable information on people's opinions, but when those same people are placed in the context of their actual purchasing decisions, new motivations surface.

If a brand is the relationship between a business and its customers, the retail space is its most visceral conversation. By better understanding what shoppers desire from green offerings and what matters in the context of their shopping experience – i.e. time and convenience – products and services can connect with people in a more relevant way.

Some retailers have begun to address these issues. **Wal-Mart**, for instance, has made great strides by building a green dimension into its supply chain, and as a result, more green products are making it onto its shelves. Other retailers like **REI** have taken a lead-by-example approach, either by making their retail space itself green, or by educating shoppers as to what's available.

Such examples indicate valuable *supply-side* accomplishments. The bulk of the untapped opportunities, however, lie in making sustainability desirable, on the *demand-side* – i.e. in the realm of consumers. Following are four latent opportunities for retailers and some provocative ideas they can inspire.

1. Consider 'Shopping Modes'
Not all shopping is equal. When people shop, they do so in one of five different 'modes' (see **Figure One**). Needs and desires

Mission Mode: These shoppers are looking for something specific, and basically want to 'get in, and get out.' Anything that distracts from their mission is ignored. Time is valued above all else. Offering new information is met with impatience and shut down.

Restock Mode: For these shoppers, the level of emotional involvement is incredibly low. Shopping is about replenishing the basics: it's a commodity experience. Shoppers are on autopilot and resort to habits rather than new ways of engaging.

Background Mode: These shoppers use shopping to accomplish something more important. Shopping with friends is 'background' to conversation – the more valuable outcome. Purchases are incidental, yet these shoppers are open to new ideas. On-site coffee and food offerings enable this mode to flourish.

Celebration Mode: Shopping is an event for these shoppers, who are out to treat themselves and feel they deserve it. For them, shopping is an opportunity for enrichment and exploration. This mode brings an openness to new ideas, and even new stores. Temporary store events and limited quantity items attract this mode.

Beyond-the-Store Mode: Shopping is the physical activity, but the mind is elsewhere. The imagination is already making the leap to the occasion of use. Shopping for a specific event like a vacation or a formal party are examples. An immersive experience like the fitting room makes space for this mode.

A 'local' sticker on an avocado may inform that it is local, but is that enough to make someone want to buy it?

change with each mode, and the mode a shopper assumes depends entirely on context. By considering shopping modes, retailers can begin to explore latent and overlooked possibilities for sustainability. For example, the 'Mission Mode' – whereby shoppers want to get in and get out quickly – may not seem like a promising mode to start with; but once we recognize that time is valued above all else by this shopper, we can look at how sustainability might address that. For instance, could we eliminate the need to spend time and fuel driving to the store? Could green alternatives be placed in more convenient locations?

For 'Background Shoppers', retailers may push the benefits of sustainability rather than removing the barriers to it. What if shelves included cut-out sections featuring a green experience? Imagine a 'morning shower' cutout that features organic soaps, a water-saving showerhead, and non-chlorine bleached cotton towels. Background shoppers open to new ideas might try one or all of them. Supporting shopping modes puts people back in the centre of the equation. It gets beyond survey results and into solutions that help people take action.

Questions for further exploration:

1. What modes do my customers exhibit and how might sustainability support them?

2. How might we enable new modes that would inspire new positive behaviours?
3. Which mode is the most receptive to a green conversation? How do we speak to that mode, and what do we say?

2. Design Moments

When asked to describe memorable experiences, people rarely describe a specific thing, or even a space: instead, they talk about complex, full-bodied moments that take into account things, time, people, and actions. During research for one of our retail projects, a woman described a moment during lunch with her daughter at a hotel: she talked about the time of day, the way the light was shining, the conversation, the music, and the service they received – all contributing equally to a perfect, nuanced moment.

Ritz-Carlton gets moments. At their hotel in Half Moon Bay, California, a bagpiper plays when the fog rolls in, turning cold weather into a memorable moment. Such moments inspire, and inspiration is important. Many retailers feel they need to educate shoppers about their green efforts in order to connect with them. True, there are new dimensions to green that need to be communicated, but without inspiration, those educational messages can get lost.

1.Shopper Recommendations: What if shoppers could recommend green products to each other right at the shelf? Handwritten messages at the moment of selection could provide both confidence in shopper's decisions and feedback for retailers.

2. Third-Party Picks: What if retailers worked with third-party green certification labels to create a 'top picks' shelf? Highlighting Fair Trade one month and USDA Organic the next would raise awareness of both the products and ways to evaluate choices.

3. Aisle Arrangements: What if aisles were organized by:
- Environmental Impact: Making green products easy to reach would make it easier for time-crunched shoppers to make more sustainable choices and more likely for supportive social interactions with like-minded shoppers.
- Location of the Source: Tying the actual distance a product has traveled to its placement in the store would give shoppers a more tangible idea of the benefits of local products.
- Day-to-day Tasks: Mapping green products to a journey in the day-to-day lives of people would increase understanding of the context of their use.

4. Editing Space: What if there was a dedicated area for 'editing' your cart? In the same way online retailers make recommendations based on purchases, checkout could be a place to recommend green products and allow shoppers to swap their items for green alternatives. Shoppers might also put back what they don't truly need.

5. Impact Receipt: What if consumers could receive feedback on the environmental impact of purchase in printed on the back of their receipt? Figures might be compared with their last trip, the store average, or people in their zip code. Feedback inspires goals and competition Can we create a goal of impact that customers can strive for?

6. Showoff: What if you could broadcast your impact score? Bowling alleys often display high scores for their lanes. Imagine putting high positive impact scores above checkout aisles to celebrate green champions.

7. Green Lane: What if green champions were given access to an instant checkout lane? Rather than offer incentives to people with '16 items or less, offer them to shoppers with a proven record of buying green, bringing their own bags, or riding a bike to the store.

Other ideas:
- **Back Story Access:** What if you could dig deeper and find the sustainability back-story for every product on the shelf? Instead of cluttering the aisle with volumes of data, shoppers could access the green story as desired.
- **Green Zone:** What if prime shelf space were reserved for products with low carbon footprint? Suppliers would make their bids for prime placement by creating greener products.
- **Fitting Room:** What if you could 'try on' all sustainable products in-store? Testing helps shoppers answer the first question they often have about green products: 'Is it as good?'
- **Lose the Aisle:** What if retailers presented only one of each product, which shoppers would scan and pick up at the door? The need for shopping carts, maintenance, and replacement would be negated and packaging could be minimized.
- **Experience Moments:** What if 'green' was presented as an experience rather than hard-to-understand instructions or specs? A 'how to wake up to a green world' experience might feature coffee, exercise and other activities supported through sustainable products.

8. Microclimates: What if store environments were controlled by a dynamic biosphere rather than a conventional HVAC system? Temperatures controlled by plants, airflow and sunlight connect the shoppers to natural systems that support them.

9. Parking Privileges: What if priority parking were offered to carpoolers or shoppers who were green in other ways? There's nothing better than rewarding green action with time-saving perks.

10. Village Model: What if the produce section were a community garden or greenhouse? Providing fresh produce and composting waste celebrates local and provides shoppers with a sense of pride and ownership.

11. Staple Delivery: What if weekly staples were mailed to your door? Fitting regular items like eggs, laundry detergent, and toothpaste into a regular delivery stream might reduce trips to the store and make visits more engaging.

Other ideas:
- **Status Flag:** What if the storefront projected its green status? Displaying figures on energy generated, CO_2 saved, and local produce sold would communicate values people could connect with before they even enter the store.
- **Learning Events:** What if the store hosted workshops and events just outside of its doors? A composting workshop, for example, might inspire shoppers to buy more produce and adopt a healthier diet.
- **Store vs. Depot:** What if the store was also a materials depot? Stores could double as central collection centers for recycled items.

A 'local' sticker on an avocado may inform that it is local, but is that enough to make someone want to buy it? How might stores enable moments that inspire shoppers on the importance of buying local?

What if aisles reflected the number of miles the items traveled? Local avocados might be placed closer to cash registers, while those imported from Mexico are placed across the store. What if an outdoor environment celebrated local and seasonal foods? Great effort goes into fabricating unnatural and uniform experiences in the store; an entirely different section inspired by natural systems may in turn inspire shoppers and reconnect with the seasons and better understand the value of local.

Creating possibilities for 'moments' allows shoppers to learn for themselves. Sustainability is a concept that is still new to the retail space: engaging people on this topic will take moments of understanding for shoppers and retailers alike.

Questions for further exploration:

1. How might we make small aisle sections dramatically stand out from the rest of the store, creating the possibility for 'moments'?
2. How might that section inspire more sustainable lifestyle decisions?
3. What kind of sensory experiences might reconnect shoppers with the natural world?

3. Enable Community

Shopping is a social activity, even when we shop alone. In a connected world, opinions and last-minute requests are just a call or text message away. Having been marketed to constantly, today's savvy shoppers seek trusted advice: opinions from friends, or even strangers, are often what matters most in decision-making.

By making space to explore possibilities and seek relevance, retailers can help shoppers aspire to new positive behaviours.

To build trust, many retailers pursue transparency. By telling their stories and making data about sustainability available in the store, the hope is that shoppers will be better able to make informed decisions that match their values. The intent is good, but these efforts can often overwhelm, even cripple decision-making. Say I'm buying a pair of jeans and deciding between one brand made from organic cotton and another made in the U.S. Literature on each product documents two compelling, yet complex stories. How do I know what is most relevant and decide which is the more sustainable choice? It's no wonder that a passer-by with an opinion can be more persuasive than all the information in the store.

Elephant Pharmacy builds trust and community by going beyond data and offering workshops where shoppers can learn from experts and, more importantly, each other. Community provides safety in numbers, disrupts old habits and inspires bold new behaviors. Why not enlist the community to enable transparency and greener decision-making?

Questions for further exploration:

1. How might we enable people to find out more and share with others?
2. What benefit does community offer local suppliers over chains?
3. How might we connect expert shoppers to novices?

4. Help 'Make it Mine'

Shoppers are not always 'at' the store: with a specific occasion in mind, they may physically be there, but mentally they are at the occasion itself. Assuming a 'Beyond-the-Store' mode, shoppers frequently add a healthy dose of imagination and envision how their lives might be different with the potential purchase.

Fitting rooms are one of the best expressions of this opportunity area. Yes, they help shoppers better evaluate fit, but more importantly, they provide an opportunity to imagine stepping into the office or having brunch on the weekend in new clothes. Fitting rooms help personalize the product and better understand how it fits into our lives. **IKEA** brings the fitting room to the showroom floor, illustrating how different products fit in mom and dad's office or in junior's room. Providing 'fitting-room abilities' for sustainability would go a along way in bridging the disconnect with shoppers. It is often difficult to imagine what a more sustainable lifestyle would be like. By making space for shoppers to explore possibilities and seek relevance, retailers can help can shoppers aspire to new positive behaviours.

Questions for further exploration:

1. What if we merchandised sustainability the way IKEA merchandises furniture?
2. What does a sustainable lifestyle look like, and how do we express it?
3. How might we help shoppers imagine living more sustainably?

In closing

We have presented a new perspective on the retail space – one that puts people first and engages them in new ways. Building a relationship with shoppers based on values such as sustainability has impact beyond the storefront. Values go home with them: they are there when they read about climate change, and they're there when they decide where to go shopping.

Down the road, when a brand becomes known for the values it has defined for itself, the relationship evolves to fill an important role as a trusted advisor. When dealing with complex issues like sustainability, we need as many trusted advisors as we can find. **R**

Steve Bishop is the Design and Sustainability Lead at IDEO. **Dana Cho** is a Partner at IDEO. Both are based in Palo Alto, California.

Drawing credits: Emi Fujita and Dana Cho

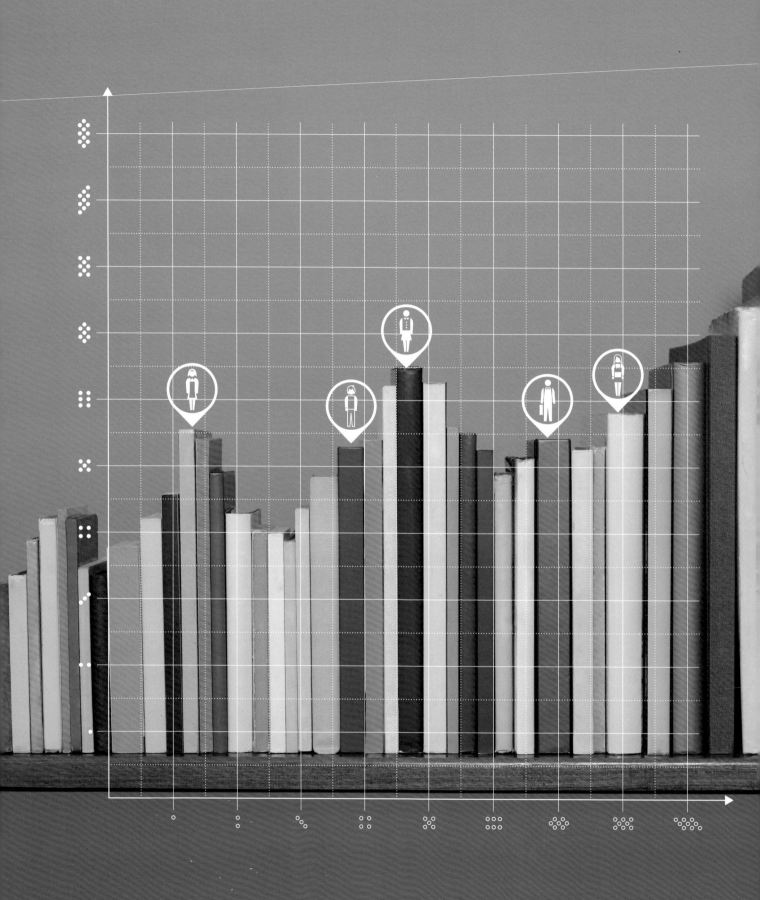

Hybrid Insights: Where the Quantitative Meets the Qualitative

· · · · ·

Taking a human-centred approach to market segmentation can help organizations identify new opportunities for growth.

by **Johannes Seemann**

WHEN ROSARIA WALKED THROUGH the doors of **IDEO**'s Palo Alto studio on her lunch break, she was juggling several 'smart' devices. A 20-something paralegal with multiple family commitments, she depended on these devices to manage a slew of daily commitments as efficiently as she could. When we met her, Rosario was also running a small event-planning business on the side and scheduling appointments for her sister, her husband and other family members. While she used her work computer just for work, she used emerging technology to stay connected throughout the day and was always on the look-out for the next device that could help her stay on top of business and family commitments.

Human-centred design aims
to solve the needs of real people –
not manufactured personas.

Was socially-connected, hyper-efficient Rosaria an 'outlier' – was she unique among early adopters of new mobile technology? Or was she representative of a larger population?

Rosaria was one of 10 in-person interviews my team and I conducted to learn more about emerging mobile device behaviour. Having led with this 'qualitative research', we then turned to quantitative methods to strengthen and refine our initial insights. Linking qualitative and quantitative research would help us determine whether there really was a significant cluster of female early adopters out there, alongside all the classic male 'tech geeks'.

Sure enough, we found that conventional tech wisdom had overlooked a significant early-adopter set: our quantitative findings showed that Rosaria was a statistically-representative member of a segment of 14 per cent of the population that shared the same preferences and allocated the same importance to 20-plus value drivers of mobile devices. One of five real-life customer segments we identified, this group of 'efficiency seekers' skewed heavily towards women and had the highest usage of the first round of iPads.

Based on these insights, some of the design concepts we developed for early adopters of technology pivoted away from *male tech geeks* and towards *female efficiency seekers*. Throughout our iterative design cycle, stories like Rosaria's provided tangible ground for our human-centered designers to create products that met real needs. We knew that Rosaria was representative of both a larger population dataset and the needs-based clusters we had derived, and this gave us the opportunity to scale and the data we needed to attain confidence in an emerging market for several design concepts.

While quantitative methods have their merits, they often lack the design insight and texture that inspires new ways forward. Meanwhile, qualitative research provides invaluable inspiration for human-centered designers, but the insights unveiled can be fragile if they are not backed by hard numbers that represent a larger population. Integrating quantitative research methods with a qualitatively-driven design cycle is a powerful new approach that we have dubbed 'hybrid insights'.

By seamlessly integrating people's real-life stories with hard market numbers, the hybrid insights approach helps strategists leverage the *why* as well as the *what* when making important decisions. We have found this to be a robust and powerful tool for design and innovation.

An Integrated Approach

At IDEO, one of our goals is to assist organizations in identifying new ways to serve and support people by uncovering latent needs, behaviours and desires. Our obligation is to find and launch effective, elegant solutions that meet the needs of real people, and the people with that need have to be a large enough segment for a viable business.

Often, innovators are given traditional market segmentation data to ground them in a new challenge. This data typically reads something like this: "Meet Joe, a blue-collar worker, who is an average user of average computer brands. The segment is 65 per cent male." Which can lead to the cheeky question: "What's the remaining 35 per cent of Joe?"

As a company that believes in maintaining a human-centric perspective, we often wondered: "Why do researchers try to make *people* out of *data*? And why do companies rely on these 'segmentations' to design new products and services for their customers?" In short, *why do people disconnect the human stories from the data in the first place?*

In our ongoing work in this area, three design principles have emerged for achieving hybrid insights.

1. Embed Stories Into Your Data

Human-centered design aims to solve the needs of real people – not manufactured personas. Starting with qualitative research into people's existing needs and behaviour allows strategists to create innovative solutions that are desirable, feasible, and viable for all involved. By placing a real person like Rosaria into a larger data set, the data can 'breathe' with a heart and soul that inspires strategists and helps them connect with the deeper meaning behind the statistics.

Qualitative research often produces surprising and inspiring individual stories, and while these individual portraits are invaluable for designers, more rigor is sometimes needed to generate insights that speak to all parties in the innovation process. The hybrid insights approach serves both concept designers and business strategists by embedding individual stories into larger data sets. By placing an individual's needs in the context of a peer set or market, designers can create human-centered solutions that scale.

Whereas most standardized research approaches emphasize analytics and testing in an abstract way, embedding stories into data can help strategists put faces to the numbers. Further, the continued ability to drill down in the data and reference real stories within a large quantitative dataset allows for new insights to emerge throughout the design process.

2. Cross-validate Insights

In 2009, the American newspaper industry was in crisis. **Craigslist, Google**, and other digital competitors were eclipsing traditional advertising revenue and circulation declines were the grim reality for city papers. Many venerable publications were shutting their doors or severely cutting back staff. Media pundits talked seriously about the collapse of community journalism and the death of the local news industry.

Enter media titan **Gannett Co. Inc.** The company – which shifted the newspaper paradigm in 1982 with the full-colour national daily *USA Today* – was not about to go gently into that dark night. Instead, Gannett intended to shift the newspaper paradigm again and remain at the industry's forefront in the 21st century. But how?

This was the big question IDEO designers and Gannett executives set out to answer using hybrid insights. We were on a tight deadline: in six months, Gannett aimed to launch a new experiment in the San Francisco market. The goal was to create a new local newspaper, unencumbered by existing media structures, which could lead to new learnings about emerging consumer needs.

The team began by conducting a scan of the market landscape that encompassed startups and novel media solutions. We also conducted human-centered field research and in-person interviews with local merchants, community leaders, and San Franciscans of all stripes. Soon, we arrived at two important *qualitative* insights:

- First, most San Franciscans engage with their neighborhood community more through local commerce than through traditional means of civic engagement;
- Second, local readers were attracted to a particular style of content: they appreciated subjectivity (vs. strict objectivity), found narrative writing a refreshing alternative to Twitter-esque communiqués, and appreciated highly-designed premium content.

THE HYBRID INSIGHTS CONTINUUM FOR INNOVATION

The hybrid insights journey for a design and innovation project has four stages: Inspire, Explore, Prioritize, Evaluate.

Inspire: Human-centred field research, observation, interviews, and other qualitative tools identify latent or emerging consumer needs, qualitatively-derived behavioural types, and initial design insights.

Explore: This stage builds on the discovered needs, derived insights and established behavioural types. The team develops concept provocations, a representative set of needs and a behavioural context. These are meant to confirm and scale the behavioural types into clusters / segments. These clusters are validated using the feedback from concept provocations. Quantitative research is seamlessly integrated at this point.

Prioritize: Feedback sessions, coupled with short analytic exercises, highlight the most desirable value proposition and boost confidence to pursue rapid prototyping and further design iterations with a reduced but validated set of features.

Evaluate: Strategists use this stage to identify and confirm the positioning of the product or service. Who do the designs appeal to most? What marketing messages resonate most?

While these four stages are emerging as best practices for hybrid insights, the approach is flexible and every project is different. The key is this: by seamlessly integrating people's stories with population-representative numbers, this approach provides insights that are rich enough to inform design and robust enough to support decision-making.

Based upon these key qualitative insights, we entered an additional round of research where we built concept provocations off our insights and learnings. We then set out to validate our qualitative findings through rigorous quantitative research using a much larger dataset. To achieve this, we designed two detailed customer segmentation studies – one for merchants and one for locals – and asked participants to prioritize between sets of statements that defined their needs, behaviours and attitudes.

Through a mix of qualitative and quantitative approaches to segmenting the market, we found that some 'niche' insights scaled up to a larger dataset. For example, we discovered new insights about local merchants that translated to a bigger segment; and we learned quickly that some small businesses were not interested in growing larger and becoming big businesses. At least one important cluster of iconic merchants in qualitative research told us: "Don't send me more customers! Just send me more of the *right* customers!"

The 'right' customers, as these niche business owners perceived them, were individuals that they perceived as being part of the same small, carefully curated niche community they themselves belonged to. Armed with these qualitative insights, quantitative research then allowed us to understand another cluster of merchants, who were even less interested in a monthly subscription service that would contribute to popularizing their business.

The merchants in this segment were mostly concerned with what other respected merchants thought about their business, validating their work through peers rather than profits or number of customers. These findings helped us consider new ways to create true value for local merchants and neighborhood communities in general. We were also able to prototype based on these insights during an iterative design process.

Within six months, Gannett launched a new local San Francisco online magazine called **The Bold Italic**. The magazine, which exposes San Francisco's cultural core rather than simply its civic image, encourages so-called 'Bold Locals' to engage in new ways. The stories published strive to unearth rare tidbits about the city, outline offbeat urban adventures, and inform citizens about local products and services.

The takeaway here: discovery of seemingly 'extreme' behaviours and latent needs can fuel good design, but cross-validation of insights is critical to identifying the right value proposition and positioning a product within a relevant target market.

3. Do What You Can to Help People Imagine

As **Henry Ford** once said, "If I'd asked people what they wanted, they would have asked for a faster horse." Disruptive design and innovation – in cars, healthcare, or any other industry – requires bravery of the imagination. While designers are experts at imagining and coming up with prototypes and experiments, when *disruptive* concepts are tested in the abstract, people often default to what they already know: research shows that something radically-different almost always scores lower with people than something familiar. How can we tell if something is not scoring well because it is a bad idea, or if it is really just too innovative?

The key to helping people imagine how a new concept can add value in their lives is to use design as a tool to put the new concept *into a context that they can relate to*. By helping people relate to the behaviours enabled by the new concept, they are able to see its value.

In an area such as birth control education, the impact of good concept testing evaluation – via experience-based studies, highly-visual survey design, and iterative prototyping – can be life-altering. For example, the United States has a significant problem with unplanned pregnancy, especially among unmarried 18- to 29-year-olds: seven in ten pregnancies in this demographic are unplanned, a statistic that applies to women of all ethnicities and socioeconomic levels.

To address this gap in effective birth control education, the **National Campaign to Prevent Teen and Unplanned Pregnancy** set out to build a birth-control support network for women ages 18 to 24 and asked us for help. Working with them, we began with qualitative human-centered design research, gathering

Keeping the soul in data is
the great strength of the hybrid
insights approach.

stories from women about their experiences and conducting observations in health clinics and hospitals.

We are used to hearing organizations talk about birth control in a fairly typical way that is medical, clinical, and politically correct. If you pick up a birth-control pamphlet and a dental pamphlet in a doctor's office, the information will often be conveyed in the same factual, logical tone. Perhaps that tone is effective when it comes to the need for regular flossing – but unplanned pregnancy rates indicate that a clinical tone has proven to be largely uncompelling when it comes to emotional topics like sex, birth control and family planning methods.

Our initial hunch was that birth control education needed to be less clinical and more 'sex-positive' to truly connect with the target demographic – a major departure from the traditional textbook-toned birth-control brochures. To cross-validate this insight, we hosted discussions with a number of stakeholders in the birth control web, including young women and men, health care providers, and clinic workers. We also interviewed people to find out what they knew about birth control, plus how they preferred to talk about birth control adherence.

We quickly discovered that learning about birth control in the classroom was analogous to learning how to drive a car in the classroom, six years before being thrown the car keys and told, "Have at it!" We also found that people wanted to be able to talk about birth control and adherence to it as part of normal life, and that they wanted reliable information available online.

We solicited feedback from a larger panel of prospective consumers to prioritize design concepts and prototypes. By placing our concepts as closely as possible into an actual behavioural context, we allowed people to experience, rather than just hear about, the value of what we were proposing. This research led to additional insights and refinements, including the introduction of SMS text reminders and a free birth control method finder.

As we prototyped our way forward with a small group to find out what tone and wording was most well-received for SMS text reminders, we soon discovered that women were forwarding their favourite text reminders to other people, establishing a network effect. The tone they preferred was a witty, 'big-sisterly' informational tone, and this insight led to additional refinements

in messaging. Evaluation of these hybrid research findings led to the design of **Bedsider**, a digital community that offers comprehensive education about existing birth control methods and acts as a vehicle for behavioural change.

After extensive pilot testing of experiences and the construction of indicators to evaluate progress, Bedsider launched nationally in November 2011 with the help of an **Ad Council** campaign that drives sexually-active women ages 18-24 to Bedsider.org. The multi-platform public service announcement effort includes television, radio, print, digital, and non-traditional advertising, as well as an integrated social campaign. Although Bedsider's carefully crafted sex-positive brand is somewhat uncommon for the U.S. healthcare industry, rigorous hybrid insights research cross-validate this approach for the target demographic.

In closing
Researcher **Brené Brown** once said, "Maybe stories are just data with a soul." Keeping the soul in data is the great strength of the hybrid insights approach. Today's groundbreaking innovations are fueled by human-centered design insights coupled with analytic confidence within relevant target markets.

A combination of the best of both qualitative and quantitative market research methods, hybrid insights leads with qualitative research and subsequently integrates quantitative methods in a seamless way. By allowing people to then toggle between the two methods during rapid prototyping and research synthesis with the whole team, hybrid insights points to the future of smart insight generation. **R**

Johannes Seemann is a business designer at IDEO focused on bridging qualitative and quantitative methods through hybrid insights.

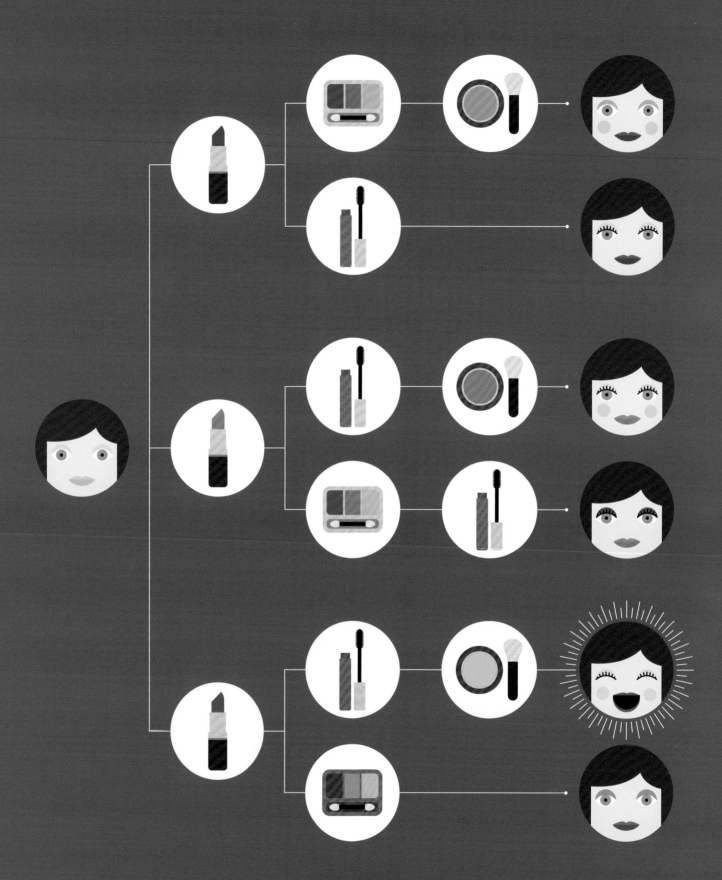

Collaborative Service

How Doing Less Can Satisfy Customers More

Service providers who recognize our growing desire to navigate our own experiences are on their way to greater customer satisfaction.

By **Heather Emerson** and **Ashlea Powell**

FEW PEOPLE WILL BE SURPRISED TO HEAR that the number-one reason for customer complaints these days is poor service: long wait times, impersonal delivery, inconvenient hours and locations – the list goes on. Perhaps this is because everything from marketing slogans ("have it your way," "affordable luxury") to new technologies ("always-on," "on demand") has led people to believe that the customer is always right, no matter what.

The same technologies that have led us to expect instant gratification from service providers have also enabled businesses to develop innovative, efficient models for accommodating customers' intensified demands. Emerging web-based healthcare provider **Hello Health** is a prime example. By some accounts, the platform has become *the* new business model for primary care, one that helps physicians get paid for *everything* they do (whether they practice inside or outside of the insurance

Collaborative service lets consumers
decide when and how to participate
in a service – a stark contrast to the passive
role they play in full-service scenarios.

system) while enabling better, more affordable care for patients. Basically, Hello Health consolidates the administrative tasks associated with running a doctor's office – scheduling, billing, maintaining medical records, etc. – and eases the service burden by giving patients more control over their experience. After an initial visit, patients can opt to consult their doctors via e-mail, instant messaging or video chat, often after hours, instead of trekking across town for long waits and brief face-to-face encounters. Hello Health also provides secure online access to lab results, personal medical records, prescription renewals and other services.

The Hello Health model hinges largely on the idea that *patients* and *providers* are more likely to fix what is broken in the health care system than government or institutional reform. It also reinforces the growing consensus among medical professionals that the most effective way to encourage and sustain behaviour change (and create new market opportunities) is to ask – and enable – patients to take responsibility for their own health. In doing so, patient expectations are shifting: the 'fix me' mentality of the past is evolving into a 'help me' one.

Sound familiar? It should. Many industries are seeing a similar shift in consumer mindsets from 'do it *for* me' to 'do it *with* me'. Whether we attribute this trend to the rise of our do-it-yourself (DIY) culture, frugality in a tough economy, the commoditization of service, the proliferation of mobile devices or myriad other factors, the takeaway for organizations is that collaborative service gives you a means of satisfying customers and boosting your profitability. It's a win-win, and companies that fail to recognize peoples' growing desire to navigate their own experiences may stand to lose.

Let's take a closer look at how this works and how a few industry leaders have used the model to identify market opportunities, reinvent a category, extend consumer touch points, and evolve along with customer needs.

A New Model for the Service Economy
At its height, the 'service' in service economy truly meant 'to serve', as typified by the **Ritz-Carlton** hotel chain's motto, "We are Ladies and Gentlemen serving Ladies and Gentlemen."

Although that sentiment still exists in certain circles, consumers today tend to think of full service as an occasional, even unnecessary, luxury. Rather than get waited upon, people increasingly want to seize control of their experiences. Today's customers know more, expect more and pay more attention, and they're coming to see service providers as gatekeepers or partners rather than assistants or servants. Innovative companies are learning when to get out of the way and how to help people to help themselves.

Collaborative service borrows the best elements of DIY (tools and freedom) and full service (personalized, rapid results) models and alleviates their pitfalls. Whereas DIY is typified by compromise and trade-offs, collaborative service lets consumers decide *when* and *how* to participate in a service – a stark contrast to the passive role they have played as recipients in full-service scenarios. Instead, customers become active collaborators with providers, sharing ownership of the service and its outcome, which helps to ensure that the experience meets their needs. In other words, companies supply the tools and environments and then customers imagine and create the experiences they want.

Collaborative service is made possible by distributing service delivery across multiple channels: people, space and tools. This frees the service provider from an unachievable standard set by the highly-staffed luxury category. It also breaks away from the legacy of a service standard, and allows businesses to create distinctive offerings that reflect their capabilities, customer and category. Not only can people serve themselves better and faster than you can, doing so makes them feel empowered, which results in more meaningful and fulfilling outcomes.

Although no two instances of collaborative service look exactly alike, they all share a few fundamental elements: invitations to participate; tools and rules of engagement; and ongoing dialogue. Let's consider each of these in the context of high-end cosmetics retailer **Sephora**, whose collaborative service experience reinvented the modern beauty counter. Sephora was the first chain to respond to today's highly engaged, educated consumer by liberating high-end beauty products from behind the counter and from brand-specific experts.

Invitations can come in many forms and range from subtle to overt. Sephora customers receive two initial invitations: first, the

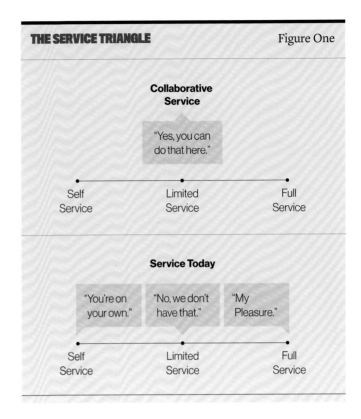

Collaborative Service

"Yes, you can do that here."

Self Service   Limited Service   Full Service

Service Today

"You're on your own."   "No, we don't have that."   "My Pleasure."

Self Service   Limited Service   Full Service

store layout puts the retail clerk (aka 'Beauty Expert') and the shopper on equal ground. Unlike traditional department-store counters, Sephora offers customers the same access to products as staff; nothing is hidden behind a counter, out of reach or off-limits. Additionally, Beauty Experts roam the retail floor, fielding questions and requests on demand across lines of beauty products. Second, upon entering the store, shoppers are offered a basket. This simple gesture invites them to assemble their own beauty regimens, including mixing and matching brands. Together, these invitations put the customer in control of their service experience.

Tools for engagement further enable customers to take an active role in the experience. Sephora sets up cosmetic stations at the end of each aisle so that customers can try samples of any product it carries. Each station is equipped with a mirror, cotton pads and swaps, tissues and make-up remover. These tools invite customers to test out new looks in a no-pressure way and take pressure off staff by allowing customers to help themselves, with the option of asking for assistance if and when they want it. As in any productive partnership, both parties – the provider and customer – need well-defined roles and responsibilities. Although we call these the **rules of engagement**, it's important that they do not feel like *rules* but rather 'nudges' towards collaboration that *suggest* how the customer should use the tools for engagement. In Sephora's case, inviting customers to sample products in an unsupervised way requires a certain level of trust and benefits from a few simple guidelines: good behaviour is encouraged by putting clearly-marked open samples on display in front of each product for sale (which are still sealed in the box). Meanwhile, supplies at the cosmetic stations promote hygienic practices, and conveniently placed trash bins cues customers to clean up after themselves.

Sephora's **ongoing dialogue** with customers helps shift the whole interaction from a *transaction* to a *relationship*. Such an approach helps a service provider get to know its customers and respond to their evolving needs over time. Of course, it's important that the dialogue feels genuine and beneficial to the customer, as opposed to seeming like a marketing tool for the service provider. For instance, customers should see evidence that their feedback is inspiring meaningful, timely service ges-

tures. Sephora's Beauty Insider program offers member customers deluxe samples, points for future freebies and purchases, and makes product recommendations based on prior purchases. A recent extension of this program, a mobile app called *Beauty to Go*, enables customers to access their purchase histories and account information from their phone. Sephora also offers tutorials and product demos, a gift registry and a connection to beauty advice on **Facebook**.

This collaborative service model has helped Sephora gain significant market share: since the retailer's 1998 arrival in North America, parent company **LVMH** has opened more than 350 stores. According to the company, it continues to increase its lead over competitors across all regions in which it operates and recently broke into a promising new market, Latin America.

Seeing Things Through the Customer's Lens
Established businesses can use a collaborative approach in three ways: to reinvent touch points that are standard in their industry; to extend their service offering into new touch points; and to evolve with customers' needs. Meanwhile, new businesses can use this approach to reinvent entire categories.

One particularly successful example is **Panera Bread**, a pioneer of 'fast-casual' restaurants. Since its founding in 1981, the chain has grown from a modest bakery in St. Louis to the largest company in its category, with 1,400 locations in Canada and the U.S., a workforce of 50,000, and a reported $3 billion in sales. Panera's collaborative service model allows diners to select high-quality foods served with its artisanal baked goods, and then

Control

When people feel in control they become 'expert' users, confident in their ability to achieve successful outcomes. This leads to repeat engagement and long-term loyalty.

Ownership

When people feel a sense of ownership – that it is their responsibility to take control of a situation – they engage more deeply with a service or brand, establishing an emotional connection that makes them want to incorporate the experience into their lives.

Enrichment

People often seek experiences that go beyond transactions and help them learn and grow. When a customer feels 'enriched' by gaining new knowledge or a skill, they are more likely to share their experience with others – and advocate for your service or brand.

Value

People are often willing to trade luxury for value. Collaborative or do-it-yourself experiences are often viewed as empowering moments rather than compromises.

choose whether they want a fast-paced or leisurely meal by providing 'to-go' and 'dine-in' preferences. It offers free Wi-Fi and encourages customers to socialize on the premises, whether holding business meetings or convening book clubs. Under this collaborative service model – which falls somewhere between fast food's informal self-service and more formal full-table service – companies such as Panera ask customers to share the responsibility for creating better experiences and outcomes.

"We obsess about ways we can improve the customer experience," CEO **Bill Moreton** told trade magazine *QSR* in May. "We look at every decision first through the customer lens, then through the operator lens, and finally, through the cost lens." Panera isn't the only enterprise benefitting from adopting a collaborative service approach: the nascent 'fast casual' is the fastest-growing dining segment, with sales up 30 per cent since 2006 and patronage rivaling that of full-service casual restaurants, according to a recent *Mintel Report*.

Another way to grow through collaboration is to extend into new service touch points. **Pizza Hut**'s Pizza Tracker online experience offers service where service previously didn't exist: the website gives customers a window into every step of their order, from dough through delivery, tracking not only the process, but also the people responsible for their dinner. Pizza Tracker is voyeuristically entertaining, but it also reinforces customers' need for control by keeping them informed about their order's progress and expected delivery time.

Often in the food service realm, touch points are the same from one service provider to the next, and they are neither differ-

entiating for companies nor delightful for consumers. Until recently, airline food and beverage service in coach class was a perfect example. In the classic model, flight attendants push pre-loaded carts down the aisle and generally determine who gets served what, when, and in which order. **Virgin America** reinvented this model by introducing an in-flight ordering system that gives passengers control. From the TV screen on the seatback in front of them, travellers can order snacks and drinks whenever they want them. Selections include popular brands such as **Toblerone** chocolate and **Patron** tequila; anything that isn't complimentary can be paid for with a credit-card swipe. Virgin's in-flight ordering system turns a standard touch point into a signature service moment.

For a classic case study in category reinvention, look to **IKEA**. The Swedish retailer transformed the typical eight- to 10-week service-intensive furniture purchase experience into a collaborative one from start to finish, by offering do-it-yourselfers instant gratification. In doing so, it successfully differentiated itself from competitors' worldwide, creating unique touch points that customers have grown to love, associate with the brand, and return for, again and again. IKEA's service approach has become core to its brand experience, making the store a destination for far more than furniture shopping: some customers make the trip just to have lunch in the family-friendly self-service cafeteria; others to simply get inspired by the model living spaces before embarking on interior-design projects. IKEA's new slogan – "The life-improvement store" – captures the degree to which its service signature has transcended the furniture business. The retailer continues to evolve with its customers' needs worldwide – and that has translated into healthy growth: sales increased 7.7 per cent to $29.3 billion by the end of 2010. IKEAHackers.net, a user-run website that tracks the many ways in which people have customized the company's furniture, not only enriches customers' experience of the brand by providing a constant stream of fresh ideas, but also helps IKEA understand how to better serve customers in diverse markets, continue to develop its product offerings, and grow the brand.

We're seeing examples of category reinvention through collaborative service in many other industries. Florida-based **Portable On Demand Storage** (PODS) seized the opportunity in the residential moving space by bridging the market gap

Ask yourself:
which service touch points
might my customer prefer
to deliver herself?

between the do-it-yourself rental truck model and the full-service movers route. By understanding that most people want to do their own careful packing and then supporting them in the logistics of moving and storage, PODS created a new category in a saturated, largely undifferentiated market. By rethinking service roles, PODS has replaced the 'pain points' of both full-service and self-service moves – e.g., coordinating the logistics of tight time windows on each end of a move, the pressure to rush loading and unloading, the redundant storage pit-stop and factoring in a third party's scheduling availability in an already-complex personal matrix – with a collaborative approach that creates a logistic-free alternative to movers or a rental truck with the added benefit of flexibility, a sense of security, and a stress-free experience for customers. In 2010, PODS sold its first franchise in the UK and continued its expansion into Canada. To date, its network has handled more than 250,000 long-distance relocations and surpassed one million deliveries.

Identifying Your Opportunities

The collaborations we have described create a win-win situation for businesses and customers: companies can reallocate resources, provide more personalized and meaningful service, and engender consumer trust and loyalty; while consumers can obtain better and often more affordable service that is closely aligned with their needs.

To find the collaborative service model that is right for your business, we suggest starting with the following three-part exercise in self-reflection.

Step 1: To effectively refocus or reallocate your resources, you'll need to consider the primary service you provide. Ask yourself, Which service touch points might my customer prefer to deliver himself? Which touch points can I deliver on that my customer cannot? What could we do better if we worked together?

Step 2: To build trust and loyalty, take a good hard look at your relationship with your customers. Ask yourself, Are there holes in my customers' ability to trust me? If so, what are they? How might I better align my interests with those of my customers? Remember: *Engaged* customers are *loyal* customers.

Step 3: To offer truly personal and meaningful service, you need to *understand* your customers. Think about their 'journey' with your service and try to identify the emotional moments. Ask yourself, How might we better support or be present during deeply meaningful touch points? And conversely, how might we better support the customer – perhaps by getting out of her way – during purely transactional touch points?

In closing

Far too often, companies get caught up in chasing the traditional model of service for their industry, even though it may be unrealistic or inappropriate for customers. Rather than get caught in a vicious cycle of 'new and improved' services, we recommend that companies collaborate directly with customers to increase their satisfaction.

As demonstrated by companies like Hello Health, Sephora, Panera and IKEA, a collaborative approach to service can not only break the vicious cycle of incremental service improvements, it can also transform a brand's service offering from a 'cost of doing business' to a 'signature brand touch point'. Because collaborative service expands the service model from a *single* standard of good to *many* – each appropriate to a specific customer need – service can now become a point of differentiation across industries.

For the first time ever, companies can innovate service models that are unique to their clientele and evolve as they do. Collaborative service represents an opportunity to break loose of tired models of service, discover what's meaningful to your customers, and use your imagination to design category-changing service gestures that not only better serve people, but also make a strong statement about your brand. ***R***

Ashlea Powell is a design lead at Palo Alto-based design firm IDEO, where she focuses on storytelling and designing brand and service experiences for clients as diverse as the Department of Education and GS Home Shopping, a Korean home shopping network. **Heather Emerson** is also a design lead at IDEO, focusing on translating customer needs into the design of brand and service experiences for clients including The Mayo Clinic, The U.S. Department of Energy and Chase Bank.

Business   Design

BUSINESS DESIGN: BECOMING A BILATERAL THINKER

by **Heather Fraser**

The emerging discipline of Business Design requires a particular combination of mindsets, methods and thinking skills that exercise the whole brain.

AS WE TEACH AND PRACTICE IT AT Rotman DesignWorks, 'Business Design' is a methods-based approach to innovation that helps teams get to bigger breakthroughs faster and define strategies for competitive advantage. In our work over the last six years with hundreds of students and executives around the world, my colleagues and I have seen some clear patterns emerge regarding the particular attributes required to excel in this emerging discipline.

What we are finding is that it takes a combination of the right mindset (*being*) and a rigorous methodology (*doing*) that unlocks a person's *thinking*, and that one must consider all three of these factors to fully realize the potential of Business Design as a platform for enterprise success. Let's examine each in turn.

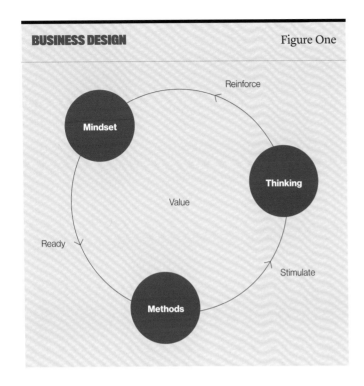

Reinforce

Mindset

Thinking

Value

Ready

Stimulate

Methods

3. Intrinsic Motivation. While extrinsic motivation such as raises, promotions and recognition is a natural part of the human psyche, intrinsic motivation has been identified as an important fuel for creativity. Individuals motivated intrinsically by purpose or passion have a genuine interest, excitement and engagement in their work. Whether it be the challenge of a 'wicked problem' or the pursuit of a purposeful ambition, these individuals become very involved in the development process of design. This is often evidenced in organizations like hospitals and schools, but is equally intrinsic in for-profit enterprises of all types that have a clear mission to create true value (economic and human) for stakeholders.

4. Mindfulness. Consciousness of one's thoughts, feelings and surroundings is critical to both maximizing inspiration and adaptability. In the design process, everything is relevant and can be a source of inspiration. Greater mindfulness of both the self and the world around you will serve to create an expanded repertoire of reference points and stimulation in solving complex problems. Mindfulness also positions you to capitalize on serendipity – an integral part of seizing design opportunities.

5. Adjustment. Adjustment captures the general tendency to be emotionally stable, calm, even-tempered and functional in the face of ups and downs. Given the nature of the design process (collaborating with others, participating in a 'mash up' of ideas, and soliciting feedback as part of the development process), those who have a high adjustment profile are able to face challenging situations without becoming upset. This also manifests itself in *comfort with ambiguity*, enabling people to find joy in the journey of tackling wicked problems.

6. Optimism. Just as adjustment can be critical in dealing with the present, optimism can help drive people forward toward creative and productive resolutions. Optimism also fuels resiliency and perseverance. The design process is a dynamic one, filled with many twists and turns in the quest to iterate through to a breakthrough solution. A hopeful view of the future will fortify one's ability to see a project through to successful completion.

Taking a personal stance on the above dimensions is the first step towards being 'ready' to design.

Being: Design as a Mindset
A design mind is characterized by a collection of mindsets that determine one's 'design-readiness' and define **emotional agility**. These can come from the 'self', and can also be shaped by the enterprise environment or culture. Importantly, it is one's personal choice to cultivate self-awareness and decide how to harness, manage or develop these dimensions in working with others. Some of the important mindsets observed in great designers of include:

1. Openness. This entails being open to new ideas, new people and new ways of doing things. Elements of openness include an active imagination, sensitivity, attentiveness to inner feelings, preference for variety, intellectual curiosity, and an ability to suspend judgment. People who are very open are willing to consider novel ideas and unconventional values. Without an open mind, one cannot fully realize the potential of the design approach to innovation.

2. Empathy. Human-centric design stems from a genuine sense of caring about people and being able to understand and appreciate their feelings, thoughts and needs. In designing something, we create value with and for other people. Whether understanding vital stakeholders or valuing team member emotions and perspectives, the ability to listen empathically and incorporate diverse perspectives into the design process lies at the heart of effective design.

Doing: Bringing Methods to the Madness
Business Design combines thinking and doing through a rigorous methodology and thrives on **tactical agility**. Methods, frameworks and tools are learnable, skill-based 'exercises' that help to shape behaviour, shift mindsets, enhance thinking capacities, and ultimately boost both individual and team performance. There is no pre-set process or 'formula' for *doing*, but rather a

repertoire of tools that help to harness the wisdom and ingenuity of teams. Most of the 'ways of doing' that can be used throughout the design process, including the design of business strategies and models, fall into one of the following 'buckets':

1. Multi-Disciplinary Collaboration. Designers find value and inspiration in diverse perspectives and skills. Not only does this enable them to harness the wisdom of the team across functions and disciplines, it will accelerate progress by tapping into the team's intuition and creative energy and establish a broad base of ownership that will give the outcomes traction. Important mindsets for collaboration include openness, empathy, and adjustment. Intrinsic motivation and optimism will also help you get past the rough patches in the collaboration process.

2. Understanding and Need-Finding. This is all about seeking to understand people's motivations on a deeper level, both inside and outside the enterprise, leading to the discovery of unmet needs and new opportunities to create greater value. There are many examples where companies have leveraged user insights not considered by the competition. For example, **Nike**'s deep understanding of the runner's need to push her personal athletic performance to a higher level has driven an ongoing stream of innovation in products, services, events and community development. To get to this kind of understanding, one must draw from many of the mindsets noted earlier, including empathy, openness, mindfulness and intrinsic motivation.

3. Iterative Prototyping and Experimentation. Prototyping entails building out ideas in order to make the abstract and the conceptual concrete, as a tool for thinking, communicating and advancing development. This is valuable in the broadest sense: creating physical prototypes or 'experiences' during the development process, enables a team to explore multiple strategies and business models to deliver value. Even 'in-market prototyping' serves as an important experiment to test out new ideas, leading to important learning and quick wins. For example, **Four Seasons Hotels and Resorts** tried many different hospitality formats and business models on their path to number-one hotel status in the world, and **Procter & Gamble** has gained new insights into consumer needs by experimenting in pop-up concept stores. All of the dimensions of a design mindset are critical here, with the most essential being empathy, intrinsic motivation, adjustment (for when your great ideas get trashed by consumers!) and optimism, especially when you have a breakthrough concept but are challenged in making it viable from a business standpoint.

4. Systems Mapping. In the discipline of Business Design, everything is part of a system comprised of stakeholders, solutions, and business strategies and activities. The more

BILATERAL THINKERS   Figure Two

Creative   Analytical
Abductive   Deductive
Generative   Synthesis
Random   Critical
Factual   Intuitive
Feeling   Thinking

one can map the connections between them, the more one will see that business is like a rain forest, with a myriad of connections and interdependencies. In order to spot those connections, you can employ a number of systems-mapping methods – from mapping 'the mess' (the core challenge to be solved) to mapping stakeholders (who matters and how they relate to one another) to solutions (how the parts work together) to the business system itself (flow of value, strategies and activities). For example, the mapping of health care challenges captures the complexity of the system and helps identify the leverage points where the most value can be created. In mapping **Apple**'s business system, one sees that its true competitive advantage lies in its unique and seamlessly-integrated business model. In creating new models, as in the development of new solutions, openness, adjustment and optimism are key mindsets.

5. Storytelling. Like systems mapping, this technique can be powerful at any time during the design process. Customer stories are an immensely valuable source of 'unfiltered insights' that can often reveal unmet needs. Creating your own stories around 'personas' can be valuable in bringing your consumers or other stakeholders to life. Expressing your envisioned idea and creating a story around your strategy and business evolution will also inspire and motivate others. The mindsets of empathy, mindfulness, intrinsic motivation and optimism will all contribute to a compelling story.

6. Co-creation. Co-creation is a vital 'feedback loop' for the development team in the prototyping and experimentation process. It is about welcoming input and feedback from others, particularly users, but also from those outside the development team – enterprise partners, decision-makers and outside partners (in both the solution development and strategic business design phases). Inviting others into the development process helps to create more robust and relevant solutions, fortify your concepts and increase your chances of breakthrough success. For example, **Google Labs** allows developers to gather critical user feedback on beta applications from key testers. Empathy, adjustment and optimism are important in successfully harnessing the power of co-creation in the design process.

A masterful Business Designer considers the uniqueness of the challenge at hand and designs the process, frameworks and tools to most effectively and efficiently yield results. That means being able to see the bigger picture of the challenge ahead, having a clear 'plan for doing' in mind to keep the team productive and progressing, and having a good grasp of how frameworks and tools can help draw the most out of the team and shape solutions during the development process. Ultimately, however, the purpose of the entire process is to draw the best *thinking* out of the group.

Thinking: Developing a Well-Rounded Mental Capacity

The value of Business Design methodologies lies in their ability to stimulate breakthrough thinking in a structured and productive manner, thereby fostering ***intellectual agility***. Through the practice of these methodologies, all forms of intelligence can be more fully developed and make the brain more 'whole' on an individual level and more synergistic on a team or enterprise level. Following are six thinking skills that serve as important 'boosters' in the value creation process.

1. Emotional Intelligence. Building on the empathy mindset, this entails more than just an attitude toward others and appreciation for their thoughts and feelings; it's about knowing how to fully *leverage* the power of emotions throughout the entire design process. It is a thinking skill focused on identifying, assessing, and controlling the emotions of one's self, of others, and of groups. A masterful Business Designer applies emotional intelligence to every step of development and execution, to one's self (in terms of awareness and management of one's own emotions), the team (in understanding and managing the dynamics of productive teams), and the market place at large (in terms of 'social intelligence' – the awareness of and consideration of contextual human dynamics).

2. Systems Thinking. In Business Design, it is important to recognize virtually everything as part of a broader 'ecosystem' of human systems, solution systems and business systems. Enhanced through the process of mapping (noted earlier), a competent Business Designer has the capacity to think holistically and integratively, and understand how people, solutions components and activities relate to and influence one another within a broader context.

3. Visualization. This form of thinking involves envisioning and communicating at every step of the design process. This includes the ability to 'see' the end result as a concrete and complete picture: to 'see' the complete solution played out in its most robust form, to 'see' the way the business will work with all of the necessary partners and enterprise systems' and even to 'see' success in the market and the potential paradigm shift that a breakthrough can trigger. The methodologies described in the *doing* section help stimulate this type of thinking through persona development, rapid prototyping, business model design and storytelling. All of these bring ideas to life and lead to a more natural inclination to envision new possibilities. This kind of 'destination thinking' can also help bring teams into alignment ("I know what we're heading for") and pull people forward ("This is a dream worth pursuing"). Many paradigm-shifting innovations trace back to a combination of visualization and abductive reasoning; for example, **Medtronic** founder **Earl Bakken**'s inspiration from *Frankenstein* that electricity could extend and improve the life of mankind. Again, without the right mindset, new possibilities will never materialize into new realities.

> Creating new solutions may draw
> upon a number of 'existing elements'
> reconfigured in a new way.

4. Abductive Reasoning. Tapping into one's imagination and believing that the seemingly impossible is actually quite possible requires a form of logic called 'abductive reasoning'. New-to-the-world ideas are difficult, if not impossible, to prove. The ability to believe in possibilities requires a combination of thinking skills, one of which is the ability to process many points of reference and make an intelligent 'leap of logic' in making the case that there's a great chance that an original idea *could* prove to be successful. There are a number of examples in game-changing successes in which the organization didn't constrain itself to existing solution sets or models, but instead pursued *what could be*. From a business perspective, they may have moved vertically or horizontally, exited old categories and created/entered new businesses. For example, **FedEx**, **eBay**, **Google**, **Southwest**, **Tata** and **Grameen Bank** are all examples of new-to-the-world ideas that made a breakthrough impact on culture and enterprise value creation. Not only did these initiatives require a keen sense of imagination and abductive reasoning, they took a healthy design mindset to persevere and see the innovations through to success.

5. Synthesis. Throughout the design process, taking many disparate bits and pieces and transforming them into a new thought or solution is critical to new value creation. In my advertising and design experience, we used to differentiate between those who 'transmitted' (i.e., just passed on 'information') and those who 'transformed' (and identified the 'insight' that could catalyze the creative process). This is an essential notion in Business Design – the identification of an unmet (and often unarticulated) need. It is also essential in creating new solutions which may draw upon a number of existing elements reconfigured in a new way or the design of new strategic models inspired by many different existing models in the pursuit to create an entirely new configuration.

6. Intuition. This entails more than just using 'gut feel' to guide development. Rather, it is a very important and developable thinking skill that involves gathering, articulating and evaluating one's own intuition and that of others. By recognizing the value of intuition, being able to effectively 'deconstruct' it and extract valuable 'data', one can capitalize on the wealth of wisdom within a team. Leveraging intuition also requires elements of the design mindset, most notably openness, empathy and mindfulness.

In closing

Ultimately, the practice of Business Design entails much more than 'design thinking'. Different types of thinking are activated throughout the process on both an individual and a group basis. As described herein, Business Design calls for bilateral thinking and adaptive doing, enabling a constant toggling between a variety of ways of thinking and doing. Such agility is essential for innovation and becomes even more powerful if you are able to rewire your brain to be bilateral throughout the process. *R*

Heather Fraser is the co-founder of Rotman DesignWorks™ and Adjunct Professor of Business Design at the Rotman School of Management. She is the author of *Design Works: How to Tackle Your Toughest Innovation Challenges Through Business Design* (Rotman-UTP Publishing, 2012) and recently opened a business design consultancy, VUKA Innovation.

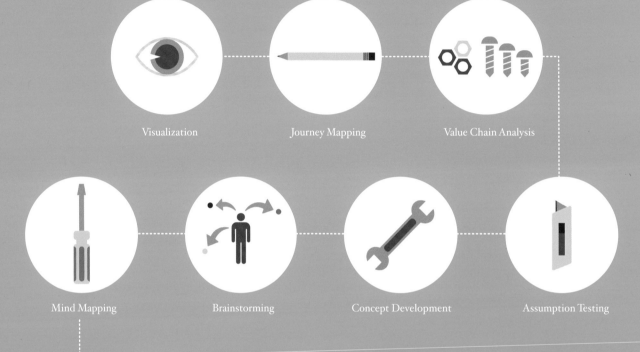

Visualization   Journey Mapping   Value Chain Analysis

Mind Mapping   Brainstorming   Concept Development   Assumption Testing

Rapid Prototyping   Customer Co-Creation   Learning Launch

While many business people appreciate the power of design, a formal process for its practice has been elusive; until now.

by **Jeanne Liedtka** and **Tim Ogilvie**

Designing for Growth:
A Tool Kit for Managers

WHEN DESIGNER HUGH DUBBERLY asked **Tim Brennan** of **Apple**'s Creative Services group to define design for his book, *How Do You Design?*, Brennan drew the following picture:

Design, this drawing asserts, is simply magic – a mysterious

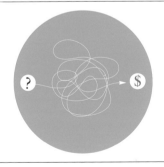

no-man's land where only the brave dare tread. Such a definition mocks the idea that a formal process could possibly exist for navigating its many hairpin turns.

Our advice: don't be put off by Brennan's view of design. Design has many different meanings, and the approach we will describe here is more akin to Dorothy's ruby slippers than to a magic wand: you've already got the power; you just need to figure out how to use it. Can the average manager be transformed

into the next **Jonathan Ive**? No more than your local golf pro can turn you into **Tiger Woods**. But can you improve your game? Without a doubt.

If Managers Thought Like Designers

What would be different if managers thought more like designers? We have three words for you: empathy, invention and iteration.

Design always begins with *empathy* – establishing a deep understanding of those for whom you are designing. Managers who thought like designers would consistently put themselves in their customers' shoes. We all know we're supposed to be 'customer-centered', but what we're talking about is deeper and more personal than that: true empathy entails knowing your customers as real people with real problems, rather than as targets for sales or as a set of demographic statistics around age or income level. It involves developing an understanding of both their emotional and their 'rational' needs and wants.

In addition, managers who thought like designers would view themselves as *creators*. For all our talk about the 'art and science' of management, we have mostly paid attention to the science part. Taking design seriously means acknowledging the difference between what scientists do and what designers do: whereas scientists investigate today to discover explanations for what already is, designers invent tomorrow to create something that isn't. Powerful futures are rarely discovered primarily through analytics. They are, as **Walt Disney** once said, "Created first in the mind and next in the activity."

Finally, design insists that we prepare ourselves to iterate our way to a solution, so managers who thought like designers would view themselves as *learners*. Most managers are taught a linear problem-solving methodology: define the problem, identify various solutions, analyze each, and choose the best one. Designers aren't nearly so impatient – or optimistic; they understand that successful invention takes experimentation and that empathy is hard won. The task, first and foremost, is always one of learning.

A Tool Kit for Designing for Growth

Remember that initial drawing of the design process? Our version looks quite different:

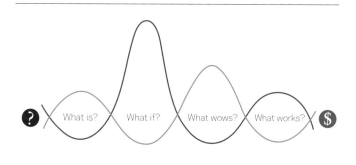

We start and end in the same place as Brennan did, but we've untangled the hairball into a manageable process. Despite fancy vocabulary like 'ideation' and 'co-creation', the design process actually deals with four very basic questions, which correspond to the four stages of design:

1. What is?
2. What if?
3. What wows?
4. What works?

What is explores current reality; *What if* envisions a new future; *What wows* makes some choices; and *What works* takes us into the marketplace. The widening and narrowing of the bands around each question represent 'divergent' and 'convergent' thinking: in the early parts of the process, we are progressively expanding our field of vision, looking as broadly around us as possible in order to not be trapped by our usual problem framing. That's divergent thinking. After we have generated a new set of concepts, we begin to reverse the process by converging – progressively narrowing down our options to the most promising ones.

There are ten essential tools that a design thinker uses to address these four questions. Before we begin, we want to call your attention to one very special design tool: **visualization** (Tool#1). This 'meta tool' is so fundamental to the way designers work that it shows up in virtually every stage of the process. Visualization is an approach for identifying, organizing and communicating in ways that access 'right brain' thinking while decreasing our dependency on 'left brain' media such as numbers. It consciously inserts visual imagery into our processes and focuses on bringing an idea to life, eventually creating stories that go to the heart of how designers cultivate empathy in every phase of their work.

USING IMPROVISATION TO ENHANCE BRAINSTORMING SESSIONS

By Elizabeth Gerber

When groups want to generate new ideas, brainstorming is often their first course of action. When this technique is effective, participants draw on each others' pre-existing knowledge to create new combinations of ideas not previously considered. But brainstorming can fail in at least as many ways as it can succeed. Over the past eight years I have worked closely with designers who take brainstorming very seriously and together, we have added a new technique to the brainstorming mix: improvisation.

Like brainstorming, improvisation is a creative collaboration between people with a common goal of developing engaging ideas within a prescribed amount of time. To date, I have taught improvisation techniques to approximately 60 practitioners, 170 undergraduate and graduate students and 80 faculty members at Stanford and Northwestern Universities.

Early on, participants are exposed to the rules of effective brainstorming developed by **BBDO** founding partner **Alex Osborn**. While 'Osborn's Rules' for effective brainstorming remain pertinent, my experience indicates that they can be optimized by importing techniques from the world of improvisation. Let's look at each rule in turn, and how improvisation can enhance it.

1. Identify a Leader. Rarely do groups explicitly commit to a structure and set of processes to enhance the session's effectiveness. One strategy that can help is to identify a leader to oversee group dynamics. In improvisational theatre, participants select a coach who takes a step back and offers advice. For example, if one individual is not being heard by his fellow 'players', the coach may publicly advise him to speak up. Active coaching can also benefit brainstorming sessions. During one session, a leader noticed that a colleague was drawing interesting ideas on his notepad; she asked him to share his ideas and upon doing so, he received praise from the rest of the team. From that point on, he positively informed the output of the brainstorm.

2. Withhold Judgment. A variety of improvisation activities can help a group transition to the non-judgmental frame of mind required for brainstorming. One such activity, called Malapropism, involves individuals walking around a room, pointing to familiar objects and calling them by another name out loud. For example, a one might point to a lamp and call it a 'garage'. The goal of the activity is to misname as many objects in the room as possible. As participants move through the room, they hear others misnaming objects, thereby normalizing 'failure' and breaking free

Now let's take a look at how the process unfolds across the four questions, and how each tool fits within them.

Question 1: What Is?

All successful innovation begins with an accurate assessment of the current reality. When we think of something new, we usually think about the future – so why start with the present? For lots of reasons. First, we need to pay close attention to what is going on *today* to identify the real problem or opportunity that we want to tackle. People often throw away all kinds of opportunities for growth before they even get started by framing the problem too narrowly. For years, product developers at **Procter & Gamble** focused on improving the detergents that were used to clean floors. One day they realized (with the help of design thinking) that what their customers *really* wanted was cleaner floors, and that this could be achieved through means other than better detergents – such as *a better mop*. This insight produced a runaway best-seller, the Swiffer, a growth initiative that revolved around a product invented in the middle ages. Fruitful searches always go back to the basics: what is the job to be done?

A funny thing happens when we pay close attention to what customers are up to: we often find that the clues to a new future lie in dissatisfaction with the present. Ultimately, growth is always about solving peoples' problems – even if they don't yet know what they are. If you pay close enough attention to their life and its frustrations, you might see what they don't, and that's why the most promising place to start any growth initiative is to find out what customers don't like about today.

Design offers a number of tools to help with this stage, such as **journey mapping** (Tool #2), to help assess an idea's potential for value creation. This tool teaches us how to 'follow customers home' and develop a deep understanding of their lives and the problems they struggle with, so that we can bring our capabilities to bear on the ones in our sweet spot. It is also important to assess the potential for value capture, so we need to do a deep dive on the value chain in which this new idea is likely to be implemented: Who are the powerful players? What are their incentives? Will they be able to help us? Accurate information on your organization's own capabilities and resources (and those of key competitors) is essential. You'll also want to recognize early on the capabilities you are missing and locate the right partner to provide them. All of this involves a **value chain analysis** (Tool #3).

When will you know that you've explored enough? This is always a judgment call. Gathering high-quality information usually requires field research, which is expensive and time consuming. Keep in mind that the primary objective in this exploration stage is not to build a 'business case' for any particular idea; that comes later. The purpose here is to prepare to generate ideas – not evaluate them. Designers have come up with a number of tools for looking for patterns in and making sense of the wealth of data amassed in this exploratory stage. One approach is **mind mapping** (Tool #4), which helps organize the information you've collected and enables you to draw insights from it about the qualities of the innovation needed. You will then use these criteria to generate ideas in the next stage.

Question 2: What If?

Having synthesized the data and identified emerging patterns, ideas begin to pop into our heads and we start to consider new from the mindsets that constrain us to see the world as we are accustomed to seeing it.

3. Build on the Ideas of Others. Brainstormers can practice this skill by playing a popular improvisation activity called Yes, Let's. This involves picking an imaginary activity in which the group will participate, such as planning a party or going on a trip. Participants generate ideas and offer them to each other, beginning each offer with the phrase, "Let's...", and the group responds with, "Yes, let's." The first player makes a suggestion such as, "Let's travel to Paris" and then gestures in a way that supports her suggestion. Withholding any criticism that might spontaneously arise in a group member's mind, the group responds, "Yes, let's!" A second player adds a suggestion: "...And let's climb the Eiffel Tower," and gestures accordingly. The group responds, "Yes, let's." A third person adds, "...And let's return home and teach our friends how to speak French," and so on, until the energy of the group begins to falter.

In my class, designers often modified this activity to be product-focused. One group decided to design a product and a company to support their product. The first designer began by saying "Let's design enterprise software that is easy to use." Withholding criticism, the group members smiled and said, "Yes, let's." A second designer made a second suggestion building on the first, offering, "And let's make software that people look forward to using every day at work." The group responded in agreement saying, "Yes, let's." The exercise continued until a company and product had been defined. These designers reported generating an idea that – while it seemed crazy at first – actually led to a discussion of a viable idea.

4. Generate a Large Quantity of Ideas. Brainstormers can practice being prolific idea generators using a modified improvisation activity called New Choice. For this activity, two people stand side by side, and a third player stands to the side. The two players begin to have a conversation about building a new product. When the player to the side doesn't like what has been said, she asks the player who last spoke to offer a new choice. If she is still not pleased with that response, she asks the player to offer another new choice. The goal is not to critique, but to have the players generate ideas as quickly as possible. For example, one player might say "Let's create a product for the elderly." The other might say, "Yes, let's build a safer walking cane." The third player coaches the second player to come up with a new choice by saying "New choice." The second player responds, "Yes, let's build a wheelchair for

possibilities, trends and uncertainties. Even without trying, we are beginning to develop hypotheses about what a desirable future might look like. It's time to move from the data-based exploratory question *what is?* to the more creativity-focused question, *what if?*

Designers call this stage *ideation*. To generate truly creative ideas, it is crucial to start with possibilities. Often, in our attempts to be practical, we start with constraints, which can be deadly to breakthrough thinking. If we start by accepting all the things that *don't* allow us to do something better, our designs for tomorrow will inevitably look a lot like today's. The only hope is to ignore some key constraints in order to identify a new set of possibilities. Then the real creativity kicks in – figuring out how to get those constraints out of our way. It takes a lot of momentum to do this, and that can be created in a good possibilities discussion that energizes the hard work of overcoming constraints. In many of the innovations we've been involved with, the creativity that really matters lives in *how* the new future was accomplished, not *what it looked like*.

During this stage, we look at how customers currently frame their problems and the mental models and constraints that we impose on them. We will use this information to formulate hypotheses about new possibilities using a familiar tool, **brainstorming** (Tool #5) – although we will apply it with more structure than the free-form approach that is often used. A disciplined approach to brainstorming is crucial to overcome its inherent pitfalls. A key reason that brainstorming is often unfulfilling is the lack of a formal process to convert the output into something valuable. The design thinking tool we introduce here, **concept development** (Tool #6), will take the output of the brainstorming process, organize it into coherent clusters, and architect the most compelling clusters into a robust concept. We

THE TEN TOOLS   Figure One

1. Visualization: Using imagery to envision possible future conditions.

2. Journey Mapping: Assessing the existing experience through the customer's eyes.

3. Value Chain Analysis: Assessing the current value chain that supports the customer's journey.

4. Mind Mapping: Generating insights from exploration activities and using those to create design criteria.

5. Brainstorming: Generating new alternatives to the existing business model.

6. Concept Development: Assembling innovative elements into a coherent alternative solution that can be explored and evaluated.

7. Assumption Testing: Isolating and testing the key assumptions that will drive success or failure of a concept.

8. Rapid Prototyping: Expressing a new concept in a tangible form for exploration, testing and refinement.

9. Customer Co-Creation: Engaging customers to participate in creating the solution that best meets their needs.

10. Learning Launch: Creating an affordable experiment that lets customers experience the new solution over an extended period of time, so you can test key assumptions with market data.

USING IMPROVISATION TO ENHANCE BRAINSTORMING (cont'd)

snowy weather." The third player coaches the second player for a new choice again by saying "New choice." The second player says, "Yes, let's build a new limb for the elderly." The coach requests new choices until s/he is satisfied with the new direction.

5. Free-wheel. This simply means generating ideas free of constraints, and can be practiced by playing a modified version of an improv activity called Presents. During this activity, participants pair up and pass a familiar object back and forth. When the object is received in hand, the player names the object and then describes an alternative use for it. The goal is to pass the object back and forth as quickly as possible while generating as many alternative uses as possible, until the original use of the object becomes just one of many 'possible uses'. For example, one pair of players passed a small trash can back and forth, developing multiple uses for it including "a stool" and "a door stop." The students realized that to gener-

ate more alternate uses, they had to relinquish their preconceptions of what a trash can could be. As they continued the activity, the trash can became more imaginative things, including a cup for giants and a boat for a mouse.

In the end, brainstorming will always be an unreliable process, but it remains one that shows great promise for idea generation. As indicated, theatrical improvisation offers a new set of tools to support the group dynamic that enhances brainstorming effectiveness.

Elizabeth Gerber is a professor at the Segal Design Institute at Northwestern University. With student designer Molly Lafferty, Elizabeth's lab created Betterbrainstorms.com, a collection of improv inspired games for brainstormers. She previously spent five years developing programs and teaching at Stanford University's Hasso Plattner Institute of Design ('the d.School'). She is also the faculty founder of Design for America, an award-winning educational initiative building creative confidence in students through design for local and social impact.

moved from data to insights in the first phase; in this phase, we'll move from insights to ideas to concepts.

Having developed some hypotheses (in the form of concepts) about new possibilities, we'll begin to think systematically about prioritizing the concepts we have come up with and figuring out what 'wows'.

Question 3: What Wows?

If all has gone well in the preceding stages, you probably have far too many concepts to move forward with all at once. One firm we worked with recently generated more than 300, which they narrowed down to 23. Of these, only five eventually made it to marketplace testing. Clearly, you will need to make some choices. What you are looking for is ideas that hit the 'sweet spot' – where the chance of a significant upside in customer value meets attractive profit potential. This is what we call the 'wow zone'.

This necessitates starting with some kind of evaluation of the only data you've got – data about today. Again, keep in mind that you are not 'proving' the value of an idea; you're just ready to do some thought experiments to begin to assess what the business case might look like. Because it is often difficult to assess the long-term potential of a new concept, you will want to tread carefully so that you don't unintentionally favour the incremental concepts and dismiss the more radical ones.

The good news is that you have an approach at your disposal that has been little used in business, but is far more useful in assessing early-stage innovations than much-maligned but still commonly used metrics like return on investment (ROI): the good old scientific method. The scientific method uses both creative and analytic thinking – that's what makes it such a useful tool when we want to be imaginative in the search for possibilities and rigorous in figuring out which ones to pursue. Unlike brainstorming, it doesn't ask us to leave our analytical minds at the door. It invites both the left and the right brain into the process, and it is custom-made to deal with situations involving a lot of unknowns. It accomplishes all of the above by treating our new concept as a hypothesis and then testing it: it starts with the hypotheses generated by the *what if?* question; then it takes these new possibilities (which are really educated guesses about something we think is likely to be a good idea) and tests them by asking, "What would need to be true for this concept to be a good one?"

In other words, you surface and test the assumptions underlying your hypothesis. The hypotheses that 'pass' this first set of tests are good candidates for turning into real experiments to be conducted in the marketplace. As a result, **assumption testing** (Tool #7) is one of the most potent tools in the designer's – and the manager's – toolbox. Remember, the goal here is not uncovering 'truth'. All design is essentially hypothesis driven, which, in the design world, is shorthand for saying that the solutions generated are the outcome of an *iterative* rather than a *linear* process.

Having tested your assumptions as carefully as you can, it is time to move to the real thing: experimentation in the market-

place. In order to do this, you take the concepts that have successfully passed through the screening process and translate them into something actionable: a prototype. **Rapid prototyping** (Tool #8) seems like a challenging task, but all we are talking about here is taking the concepts generated in the *what if?* stage and turning them into something concrete enough to spur conversations with important stakeholders. The intent is to create visual (and sometimes experiential) manifestations of concepts in order to facilitate meaningful conversation and feedback.

Question 4: What Works?

Finally, you are ready to launch and learn. First, we suggest that you try out a low-fidelity prototype on some customers and see how it goes. If it succeeds, build a higher-reliability 3D prototype of the idea and see if any customers are willing to part with their money for it. A particularly powerful approach to determining what works involves inviting the customer into the conversation in an active, hands-on way. The tool you can use here is **customer co-creation** (Tool #9). There is no more effective way to reduce the risks of any growth initiative than to engage customers in designing it.

Prototype in hand, you are ready to move into piloting. To accomplish this, we offer a tool called a **learning launch** (Tool #10), which moves your developing concept into the field. As you design the pilot, you will want to be explicit about the search for disconfirming data – information that disproves your hypotheses. This is the most valuable information you can uncover – and it is also the easiest to miss. To enhance your ability to detect it, you must lay out in advance what disconfirming data might look like.

As you proceed, keep in mind some of the principles of this learning-in-action stage: work in fast feedback cycles; minimize the cost of conducting your experiments; fail early to succeed sooner; and test for key trade-offs and assumptions early. Most important, play with the prototypes in the field instead of defending them in endless meetings.

In closing

An unavoidable but healthy tension will always exist between *creating the new* and *preserving the best of the present*, between innovating new models and maintaining healthy existing ones. As a manager, you need to learn how to manage this tension, not adopt a wholly new set of techniques and abandon all of the old. The process we have described can get you started on the path. **R**

Jeanne Liedtka is the United Technologies Corporation Professor of Business Administration at the University of Virginia's Darden School of Business and the former chief learning officer at United Technologies. She is the author of three books, most recently *Solving Problems with Design Thinking: Ten Stories of What Works* (Columbia University Press, 2013). **Tim Ogilvie** is CEO of Peer Insight, an innovation strategy consultancy and a visiting lecturer at the Darden School. They are the co-authors of *Designing for Growth: A Toolkit for Managers* (Columbia University Press, 2011), from which this is excerpted.

Article
Chronology

All of the articles presented in this collection originally appeared in *Rotman* Magazine.

Back issues can be purchased at rotman.utoronto.ca/rotanmag

To subscribe to Rotman Magazine:
rotman.utoronto.ca/rotmanmag

For more information on Rotman-UTP Publishing:
utppublishing.com